Universal Grammar and Iconicity

Within linguistics, the formal and functional approaches each offer insight into what language might be and how it operates, but so far, there have been hardly any systematic attempts to integrate them into a single theory. This book explores the relationship between Universal Grammar – the theory that we have an innate mechanism for generating sentences – and iconicity – the resemblance between form and meaning in language. It offers a new theory of their interactions, the "UG–iconicity interface" (UG-I), which shows that not only do Universal Grammar and iconicity coexist, but in fact they collaborate in intricate and predictable ways. The theory explains various recalcitrant cross-linguistic facts surrounding serial verb constructions, coordination, semantically and categorically obscure "linkers," the multiple grammatical aspects of the external argument, and noncanonical arguments. This ground-breaking work is essential reading for researchers and postgraduate students in linguistics, as well as scholars in psychology and cognitive science.

Yafei Li is Professor of Language Sciences at University of Wisconsin-Madison and affiliated part-time with Nanjing University, China. Notable publications include *X°: A Theory of Morphology–Syntax Interface* (2005) and *The Syntax of Chinese* (co-authored, 2009).

T0382492

Universal Grammar and Iconicity

Yafei Li

University of Wisconsin-Madison

CAMBRIDGE
UNIVERSITY PRESS

Shaftesbury Road, Cambridge CB2 8EA, United Kingdom

One Liberty Plaza, 20th Floor, New York, NY 10006, USA

477 Williamstown Road, Port Melbourne, VIC 3207, Australia

314–321, 3rd Floor, Plot 3, Splendor Forum, Jasola District Centre, New Delhi – 110025, India

103 Penang Road, #05–06/07, Visioncrest Commercial, Singapore 238467

Cambridge University Press is part of Cambridge University Press & Assessment, a department of the University of Cambridge.

We share the University's mission to contribute to society through the pursuit of education, learning and research at the highest international levels of excellence.

www.cambridge.org
Information on this title: www.cambridge.org/9781108794626

DOI: 10.1017/9781108885935

First published 2022
First paperback edition 2024

A catalogue record for this publication is available from the British Library

Library of Congress Cataloging-in-Publication data
Names: Li, Yafei, author.
Title: Universal grammar and iconicity / Yafei Li.
Description: Cambridge, United Kingdom ; New York, NY: Cambridge University Press, 2021. | Includes bibliographical references and index.
Identifiers: LCCN 2021024781 (print) | LCCN 2021024782 (ebook) | ISBN 9781108840439 (hardback) | ISBN 9781108885935 (ebook)
Subjects: LCSH: Grammar, Comparative and general. | Iconicity (Linguistics) | BISAC: LANGUAGE ARTS &DISCIPLINES / General | LANGUAGE ARTS& DISCIPLINES / General
Classification: LCC P153 .L5 2021 (print) | LCC P153 (ebook) | DDC 415–dc23
LC record available at https://lccn.loc.gov/2021024781
LC ebook record available at https://lccn.loc.gov/2021024782

ISBN   978-1-108-84043-9   Hardback
ISBN   978-1-108-79462-6   Paperback

To those in my life
who have made me be who I am and inspired me to do
what I have done

Contents

Figures

Preface

Four things happened during the writing of this book, all unexpected in one way or another.

First, whereas this is the longest work I have ever written in my academic career, it also turned out to be among the easiest if I put aside the inevitable commitment of time needed to convert the thoughts into words. Part of the reason is that some contents were already written out in the form of papers, a few published and the rest not. What somewhat surprised me was that the ideas in these papers, taking shape separately over a span of thirty years on totally different subject matters, could all fall into place under a single central theme so snugly, reminding me of a long-ago experience of putting together a 3-D jigsaw puzzle of the Eiffel Tower – I did have to figure out where to put which piece, but once that was worked out, all the pieces simply fit. As with the puzzle, I surely had the initial general belief that these apparently unconnected ideas could be assembled together – otherwise the book project would not have been attempted. Still, it would give me a happy surprise each time one more smooth and technically detailed integration not only proved available between thoughts/analyses years and topics apart, but also lent itself readily to more facts and new analyses not imagined while initially planning the book.

Out of professional habit, I sought to explain why this happened and came up with two possible answers. (A) Our current understanding of the human language faculty and our control of the linguistic data are still rudimentary enough to evoke uncertainty, which in turn creates room for more than one seemingly plausible "theory" regarding the design of language and its components. (B) The core analyses in these separately written papers, as well as the particular formulation of the UG–iconicity interface, are overall on the right track. The rational side of me says that both (A) and (B) are partly at work; emotionally, I would like to think of (B) as playing a significant role. Regardless, it has been a totally enjoyable experience that a wide range of linguistic facts, from Chinese verbal compounds to cross-linguistic coordination to applicatives to word order typology, to list but a few, can be unified in a theory consisting merely of two highly general principles (the FICH and the USM), a couple of functional voids ($Void_F$ 1, 2) plus the basic operations of UG.

The surprises described above were rewards any researcher would be glad to encounter.

Second, of the nine months spent on the first complete draft of this book, over half of the period coincided with Covid-19 where I live. I take it that not many authors could claim this "privilege," which has been, let's put it mildly, inconveniencing for everyone. But there is a classic Chinese saying which keeps people optimistic when things look gloomy: *huo xi fu suo yi* 'disaster PARTICLE blessing SUO lean.on'. Ignore *xi* and understand *suo* as a marker when the object DP undergoes A$'$-movement, and the sentence translates into this: Oh disasters, good fortunes accompany them! Pre-coronavirus, the summer months would always have me travel abroad, visiting relatives, giving lectures and attending linguistic conferences. I was mentally prepared not to be able to finish the book on time because a summer itinerary so packed that every half-day slot would be filled for a prolonged stretch of time was not rare. With this hideous virus, however, I have been literally staying in the house for weeks in a row during the past months, even resisting the urge to visit my two-year-old granddaughter in California. So I had no excuse but to concentrate on the book and ended up wrapping things up a few weeks earlier. This pandemic is bad, sad things have been happening because of it, and I personally felt and feel the worries about my family and my relatives first in China and later in the USA. But as the American author Wayne Dyer once said, "You can't discover light, by analyzing the dark." Writing a book that integrates many ideas throughout my whole academic career and being able to finish it on time is the light I have had the good fortune to discover.

The other two happenings carry a heavy emotional weight. Two people passed away during my book-writing time who had life-shaping influences on me: my father LI Ming, and my mentor and friend Wayne O'Neil. On the way to the first day of my elementary boarding school, my father said to me some words to this effect: Your teachers and classmates may have an opinion about a student, and it could be popular, but you should always form your own based on your observations and best judgment. He said it and I forgot it. Only in my mid-50s – exactly half a century later – did I suddenly realize that I had been practicing these words throughout my life and my career. The only deviation I made was the target. My father was talking about people while I applied it to ideas, as reflected everywhere in this book. I met Wayne in China, wrote a term paper on Chinese locative-inversion for his course, and he brought me to MIT without me requesting or doing anything. Looking back, working with the type of linguistics that MIT started and pursuing a career in American higher education is the best choice of life and work for someone with my strengths and weaknesses, a choice which Wayne enabled and which I thank him for, eternally. In brief, Wayne presented me with the opportunity, and my father planted in me the principle through which to pursue that opportunity. I could not be grateful enough.

Acknowledgments

Sincere thanks go to Helen Barton, the linguistics editor of Cambridge University Press, for her support of and confidence in a book project that ventures to construct a UG–iconicity interface. Isabel Collins, also of Cambridge University Press, gave me valuable advice and critical assistance which eased the last stage of preparing the draft. Two anonymous reviewers of my fifty-plus page, single-spaced book proposal are immensely appreciated both for their open-mindedness on a topic which can and did trigger compartmentalized responses, and for their insistence that I spell out certain theoretical and meta-theoretical contents in the proposal. These clarifications ended up benefiting the explications in the book. The final version of the book becomes so much more readable both in content and in wording because of the clearance reader of my first draft. A huge thank-you for the six full pages of suggestions, questions and support. I am also very grateful to Drs. Rebecca Shields and Zhe Chen for being there with initial grammaticality judgments on the English and Chinese data before I turned to more informants, sometimes with their help. The most frequently consulted source for my Chinese data is my wife Qing Xie, who is also the person that I could brag about the book to from time to time. While she almost certainly does not yet understand or care about this, my granddaughter Aria Li-Ciccolo must be on my thank-you list. Many times, it was her happy smiles, progressing baby talk and totally adorable actions that added heart-warming hues to the monotonous color of formal expressions and step-by-step reasoning.

Abbreviations

$3^{rd}F$	third-factor principle
$a(P)$	"light adjective"
A(P)	adjective (phrase)
Adv(P)	adverb (phrase)
Appl(P)	applicative (phrase)
$Appl_H$	high applicative
$Appl_L$	low applicative
APT	Auxiliary Plane Theorem
Arg_E	external argument
&(P)	conjunction (phrase), or as a feature in "[&]"
C(P)	complementizer (phrase)
CApp	complement approach
CCS	categorial complement space
c_n	n^{th} conjunct from left
CSC	Coordinate Structure Constraint
cu	computational unit
CUDH	Computational Unit Disparity Hypothesis
D(P)	determiner (phrase)
Del_C	total count of deletions required to yield superficial conjunct C
$Depth_X$	number of different phrases traversed with respect to X (see specific contexts)
DM	Distributed Morphology
e	event
ECM	exceptional case marking
EM	External Merge
Ep	epistemic (adverb class)
Ev	evaluative (adverb class)
φ-feature	any of [person, number, gender]
F(P)	functional head (phrase)
FCA	first-conjunct agreement
FEO	fact-event object
F_{HL}	human language faculty

FICH	Functional Iconicity Complementation Hypothesis
Focus(P)	focus head (phrase)
Fr	frequency (adverb class)
G/B	Goal or Benefactive
GE	genetic endowment
IM	Internal Merge
L(P)	lexical head (phrase)
LCA	Linear Correspondence Axiom, or last-conjunct agreement (in Serbo-Croatian)
LF	Logical Form (conceptual–intentional)
Ln	linker (in den Dikken's sense)
LPM	Lexical Phonology and Morphology
Ma	manner (adverb class)
MC	Mandarin Chinese
$\mathbb{N}$	smallest node dominating all conjuncts
N(P)	noun (phrase), or category feature with "±" values
NCA	noncanonical argument
NCC	non-constituent conjunct
Neg	negative (as a category label)
NPI	negative polarity item
O(bj)	object
O_i	operator indexed with i
P(P)	pre/postposition (phrase)
P_{AUX}	auxiliary plane
PCC	predicate cleft construction
P_D	default plane
PF	Phonological Form (sensorimotor)
PIC	Phase Impenetrability Condition
Poss	possessor
PR	possessor raising
pro	phonologically empty pronoun
PRO	phonologically empty pronoun as the subject of infinitive clauses
QP	quantifier phrase
QR	quantifier raising
$\sqrt{}$ or r	root (of a lexical item)
R	relator
$R_\&$	'and/or' relation
R_C	lexico-semantic relation
RC	relative clause
R_L	linear relation
R_M	semantic relation of generalized modification

RNR	right-node-raising
R_S	structural relation
R_T	relation of temporal precedence
S	entropy (in Boltzmann's equation only), or clause (only as node label)
S(ubj)	subject
Sa	speech act (adverb class)
SC	Serbo-Croatian, or small clause (only as node label)
sh	shell
SMH	Structural Mapping Hypothesis
So	subject-oriented (adverb class)
Spec	specifier (in X′-theory)
SVC	serial verb construction
SVP	Serial Verb Parameter
t	trace
T(P)	tense (phrase)
θ-	thematic
TopP	topic phrase
T_S	thermodynamic system
TSC	Temporal Sequence Condition
UG	Universal Grammar
UG-I	Universal Grammar-iconicity interface
USM	Uniform Structure Mapping Principle
v(P)	"light" verb (phrase) responsible for introducing the agent argument
V(P)	verb (phrase), or categorial feature with "±" values
VM	verb modifier (in Hungarian)
Void$_F$	functional void (of Universal Grammar)
W	number of microstates in a thermodynamic system with the same macrostate
wh	generic reference to the type of words like *what, which, where, why, how*
X, Y, Z …	generic categorial labels (when used in structure)
XSM	exo-skeletal model

In language examples

1, 2, 3	person
ACC	accusative case
AFF	affix
AGR	agreement

APPL	applicative morpheme
ASP	aspect
AUX	auxiliary
BEI	*bei* (glossing the morpheme without analysis)
C	complementizer
CAUS	causative morpheme
CL	classifier
COM	comitative
DAT	dative case
DE	*de* (glossing the morpheme without analysis)
DECL	declarative
DET	determiner
ERG	ergative case
F(EM)	feminine gender
FOC	focus
FUT	future tense
FV	final vowel (in Bantu)
GEI	*gei* (glossing the morpheme without analysis)
GEN	genitive case
HAB	habitual
IMPERF	imperfect aspect
INDEF	indefinite
IO	indirect object agreement
L	linker
LE	*le* (glossing the morpheme without analysis)
LOC	locative
M(ASC)	masculine gender
N(EUT)	neuter gender
NEG	negation
NML	nominalizer
NOM	nominative case
O(BJ)	object agreement/case
OBV	obviative
P	generic/semantically unspecified preposition
PASS	passive
PAST	past tense
PERF	perfect/perfective aspect (difference being irrelevant to this book)
PL	plural number
POSS	possessive
PRES	present tense
PRT	particle

REAL	realis
REM	remote (with PAST)
S	singular number
SUBJ	subject agreement
SUBORD	subordinate marker
SUF	suffix
T	tense

1   An Interface Theory of Universal Grammar and Iconicity

This work investigates the relation between Universal Grammar (UG) and iconicity.

By definition, Universal Grammar is (a theory of) the innate and dedicated mechanism for generating language expressions up to the sentence level. While many technical details remain unsettled, unknown amounts of linguistic facts are yet to be discovered, and the gap is still huge between such a model of language and the neurology of the brain, a decent amount of in-depth and fairly accurate understanding has accumulated in the past few decades regarding how languages in general construct sentences – they all appear to exhibit these two traits:[1]

1. a. combinatorial operations creating hierarchical and recursive structures;
     b. locality constraints.

(1a) is recognized among linguistic researchers, at least at some level of description, whether its implementation takes the form of phrase structure rules plus feature-percolation, X'-theory assisted by movement, or Merge and Copy (Gazdar et al. 1985, Chomsky 1981, 1995 and Nunes 2001; see Chomsky 2012, 2013, 2015 and Berwick and Chomsky 2016 for highlighting the role of Merge, and Müller 2013 for comparing different generative theories). (1b) includes islands, minimality and binding domains, regardless of whether some such constraints can be further unified (e.g. Chomsky's 2000, 2001a probe-goal, extended in Pesetsky and Torrego 2007 and Wurmbrand 2011). In this book, a mixed model and terminology of syntax from the principles-and-parameters tradition and its more recent Minimalist Program variant will be adopted – depending on how useful a specific technical tool proves to be in accounting for relevant facts – provided that the analysis and outcome are consistent and incur no self-contradiction throughout the chapters.

Iconicity, "a resemblance between properties of linguistic form ... and meaning" (Perniss and Vigliocco 2014: 1), plays a key role in the functionalist approach to language. The notion is usually traced to the seminal work on signs by Peirce (1867/1931), whose identification of "diagrammatic" iconicity, with signs representing "the relation ... of the parts of one thing by analogous relations in their own parts" (Peirce 1902/1932: 157), is most pertinent to linguistics. Subsequent works relating iconicity to language include Haiman (1980, 1983, 1985, 2008), Bolinger (1982), Tai (1985), Dik (1989), Givón (1990), Croft (1990, 1995, 2003), Newmeyer (1992, 1998), Y. Li (1993), Kaiser (1999), Fischer (2006), Fortescue (2014), among many others; see Haspelmath (2003) for a critique. Furthermore, much work has been done to dissect and/or identify different types of iconicity in linguistic behaviors. Haiman (1980, 1985), for instance, decomposes diagrammatic iconicity into two elements: isomorphism and motivation.

As expected, iconicity has received continual attention in a wide range of linguistic and related areas of research: sign languages (Perniss et al. 2010, Meir et al. 2013, Oomen 2017), morphology (Aissen 2003, Fortescue 2014), syntax (Gärtner 2003, Huang and Su 2005, Y. Li and Ting 2013), grammatical-ization (Fischer 2006), word-order origin (Christensen et al. 2016), vocabulary (Dingemanse et al. 2015, Winter et al. 2017), corpus linguistics (Diessel 2008), language acquisition (Perry et al. 2015) and cognitive semiotics (Ahlner and Zlatev 2010), to name just a few representatives.

The two sets of literature (and the comparable efforts thereunder) on UG and iconicity, respectively, are immense. With rare exceptions to be examined in the course of this book, however, there is remarkably little attempt to look at these two significant aspects of language put together. It is the goal of this book to demonstrate that UG and iconicity not only coexist but in fact collaborate in intricate and predictable ways, and that a theory of their interactions, call it the theory of the UG–iconicity interface – UG-I hereafter – should and can be formulated.

1.1   The Central Question: When and How of UG-I

The overall design of the theory of UG-I, to be motivated by the various facts in the ensuing chapters, consists of two hypotheses, one to capture *when* UG and iconicity will start to interact and the other to regulate *how* this interaction is carried out.

The when-question is answered by the Functional Iconicity Complementation Hypothesis (FICH):

2.   Solicit help from iconicity where UG is not programmed to perform.

Given our current understanding of how language operates, an obvious scen-ario where the FICH is put to work is "above" the sentence level. As an example, two consecutive sentences tend to be interpreted as expressing a temporally iconic relation between the two reported situations. This is where certain Gricean conversational implicatures are in full display, including their contextual breakdowns. Such an application of the FICH will not be the concern of this work (with a small exception in the beginning text of Chapter 4) because it reveals little on how iconicity interacts with UG. As far as we know, UG is limited to the generation of linguistic entities up to the sentence and not beyond.[2] Iconicity operating above sentences targets the end-products of UG and therefore rarely incurs any bi-directional interactions between the two mechanisms.

Which brings us to what this book focuses on: identifying the functional voids of UG within the domain of sentence-generation and figuring out exactly how iconicity aids UG in creating, say, a simple clause. To borrow the metaphor in Y. Li and Ting (2013), UG may be compared with a chunk of Swiss cheese (Figure 1.1). While the entire cubic space occupied by the chunk represents the complete capacity of the human language faculty for sentence-generation, the solid (and quantitatively dominant) portion of the chunk corresponds to UG. The holes in the chunk are where UG is inherently unable to act.

If the process of constructing a clause happens to involve one such hole, other cognitive mechanisms such as iconicity are called in to help UG assemble all the involved components into the clause, as is postulated in (2). In sum, the FICH treats UG as the primary apparatus for sentence-generation and activates iconicity only when UG is not up to the job.

One naturally wonders about the validity and/or plausibility of a functionally handicapped UG. An argument will be put forward later in this chapter on the basis of comparing biolinguistics, another appellation for UG for scholars in this framework, with biology. For now, I simply make two points. First,

Figure 1.1 Swiss cheese
Author's own photograph

whether the FICH is tenable and in case it is, how many functional gaps exist in UG, where they are located and exactly in what manner iconicity lends a hand, are all questions to which ultimate answers can be sought only on empirical grounds. Three chapters of this book take up the task and explore where UG can be shown to give up and iconicity to take over in the middle of building a simple clause. Second, the idea of UG having functional gaps is logically separate from the Minimalist view (Chomsky 1995) that whatever functions UG *does* have are optimized, especially when we, presumably, are talking about a biological system (see 1.2.3 below).

It indeed matters to the tenability of the FICH, though, to explicitly identify exactly what UG is and does – lack of a clear definition of the applicational domain of UG can easily void claims about UG's functional voids. To this end, I will assume with the general UG framework that the human language, via the mechanisms in (1), implements at least two layers of mapping: (i) from conceptual entities and relations to linguistic structure and (ii) from linguistic structure to linear order. Mapping (i) is characteristically accomplished by way of lexical items that encode the outcome of our conceptual partitioning of the world. Following the tradition, the study of the relation between lexical items and concepts is called *lexical semantics*, and semantics for short since this work is largely not concerned with how the meaning of a clause is compositionally computed from its components, presumably at logical form (LF). See Jackendoff (1990, 2002) for a theory of lexical semantics and its relations with the other components of language. Given our understanding of UG, it is lexical items that are used for constructing various linguistic constituents in accordance with algorithms in (1).[3]

Mappings (i–ii) are summarized in (3) below, where a conceptual relation is taken to be the meaning of the corresponding lexical item. As such, (lexico-) semantic relations are simply lexically encoded conceptual relations. Thus, the two will be used interchangeably depending on the context (and where no confusions arise). Now let R_C be a conceptual/semantic relation, R_S be a structural relation and R_L be a linear relation. It is expected of UG to participate in two mappings:

3.   a. Map R_C to R_S (characteristically with lexicalization being an intermediate step)
     b. Map R_S to R_L

As an example, the R_C 'participant of an event that undergoes change', aka theme, once lexicalized into the argument structure of a verb, will map to the R_S 'the complement of V' (regulated by the θ-criterion; see Larson (2014) for a recent implementation). The X'-theory initially proposed in Chomsky (1970) – as well as its more recent Minimalist variant (Chomsky 1995, 2001a, b) – guarantees this mapping in (3a) to be algorithmic. Different proposals exist on the R_S-to-R_L mapping in (3b), a particularly notable one being Kayne's (1994) antisymmetric theory of phrase structure. An alternative will be presented in Chapter 4 which I argue to be both empirically and theoretically more desirable. Until then, any analysis having to do with word order will adopt the conventional linearity parameterization usually found in the UG framework.

Building on the mapping model in (3), I postulate (4) as the answer to the *how*-question for UG-I; that is, once iconicity is called in for help under the FICH, in exactly what manner will UG and iconicity interact for clause-generation?

4. The Uniform Structure Mapping Principle (USM)
   Implement a deterministic R_C-to-R_S mapping.

The USM is meant to operate in the same domain as the standard theory of UG in (1), namely up to the sentence level. Evidence will be presented case by case that UG can fail to implement a certain instance of the R_C-to-R_S mapping in (3a) so that a functional void of UG is encountered, which in turn effectively disrupts further mapping in (3b) due to the unavailability of R_S in the first place. When this happens, non-UG mechanisms like iconicity will be mobilized, under USM's regulation, to assist UG in representing the conceptual relation at issue with a fully predictable structural relation, resulting in possibly non-trivial but regulated interactions between UG and iconicity.

I conceptualize that the USM acts as a meta-rule that both UG operations in (1) and general cognitive facilities such as iconicity must comply with so as to generate clauses in a deterministic manner. To wit, one doesn't just call in iconicity and set it loose. Rather, iconicity is allowed to take part only in the same manner as UG, both banned from unpredictable acts while converting a given semantic relation to a structural relation – in fact, something like the USM is conceptually necessary so that the encoding of what we mean with language is not a totally random choice. I argue that it is this collaboration of the FICH and the USM that our brain depends on to carry out any UG–iconicity interactions.

I take it to be conceptually straightforward that the FICH is not part of UG but a natural strategy in problem-solving: If one can't finish a job with the default tool (e.g. UG), then one looks elsewhere (e.g. iconicity) for help. The USM indeed has the flavor of UG due to its clause-level deterministic nature, but I admit that it is not *a priori* clear whether this "rule" is a proper part of UG (in the sense, for instance, that the USM came into existence from the same genetic mutation(s) bringing about UG in (1)) or is a more general principle operating beyond language (at least in certain circumstances). As a more radical alternative, it may even be that UG only encodes the USM and the most basic recursion-capable Merge, with everything else attributed to

UG-external factors (for the latter portion of this option, see Berwick and Chomsky 2016; see Progovac 2016 for a critical review; also see section 1.2 of this chapter and Chapter 5 for related discussions).

Fortunately, finding the answer to this higher-level question is separate from assessing the explanatory capacity of the USM. Therefore, my focus will be on demonstrating that the USM provides better solutions to a few types of facts that have remained recalcitrant to the theory of UG adopted by most of us working in this framework today. Both to put aside the nature of the USM that otherwise does not affect any part of this book, and to minimize possible confusions, I will continue using UG to name the system in (1) like many other scholars do, but will call the sum of UG and the USM (and possibly other similar linguistically indispensable mechanisms beyond the scope of this work) the human language faculty F_{HL}. In this sense, Baker's (1988) Uniformity of Theta-Assignment Hypothesis, to the extent that it captures an inherent bond between θ-relations and syntax (but see Y. Li 2005 for a different view), may be viewed as a specific reflection of the USM. See the starting text of Chapter 4 for related thoughts.

1.2   Putting UG-I in More Perspectives

The essence of the UG-I theory presented above, namely the FICH, was initially articulated in two early works (Y. Li 1991, 1993) on the serial verb constructions. As UG-I amounts to the first attempt at explicitly formulating such an interface, it is of utter importance to make sure that it is empirically founded, technically detailed and, quoting Karl Popper's expression, logically falsifiable. To accomplish this goal, the protocol in (5) will be rigorously followed throughout the subsequent chapters:

5. a. Identify functional voids $Void_F$ of UG with fact-based argumentations.
   b. Articulate precise ways in which a form of iconicity interacts with UG to functionally fill up $Void_F$ while yielding an otherwise UG-compliant outcome.

Just like the FICH, the strategies described in (5) were employed, though not so explicitly stated, in the same initial works. (5a) establishes the empirical base for the FICH and helps reveal that UG inherently lacks the capacity to deal with or make sense of certain significant language facts and that there is no fix via plausible theory-internal revisions. Critically, this is also when the effects of iconicity are observed. The "UG-compliant outcome" requirement in (5b) is taken to be the only plausible expectation of the UG-I model. The whole point of soliciting help from iconicity is to generate R_S in (3a), and R_S is by definition within the jurisdiction of UG in the sense that it must satisfy all of UG's principles. In other words, iconicity may help complete a syntactic structure S where UG is incapable, but S must be such that UG can still interpret it. For the purpose of sentence-generation, creating something not interpretable by UG principles is no help to UG at all.

To further solidify the foundation of UG-I, the rest of this section will look at it from a few different angles.

1.2.1 Related Works

Compared with the huge quantities of works exclusively studying either UG or iconicity, there has been much less non-casual effort to examine the two side by side. Occasionally, iconicity-based analyses of certain linguistic phenomena are refuted in defense of UG or other perspectives (e.g. Baker 1989, Carstens 2002, Newmeyer 2004, Haspelmath 2008). There appear to be more functionalist criticisms of UG which, as Anderson (1999) points out, are rarely at an explicit and detailed enough level for in-depth assessment (see Darnell et al. 1999 for related works). The same general situation also characterizes the rare occasions when one side tries, not as successfully as one would hope in my opinion, to see the values of the other (e.g. Newmeyer 1992, Croft 1999). Lastly, Aissen 2003 explores how languages make use of "the tension" between iconicity and the principle of economy, an approach conceptually closer to the FICH than most other published works in the sense that an explicit and falsifiable way for iconicity to interact with the rest of the language system is articulated on the basis of factual details.

To my knowledge, the most systematic examination of the iconicity–UG relationship in the existing literature is Newmeyer (1992), further elaborated on in Newmeyer (1998). In particular, he dissects the functionalist claim that "linguistic structure ... has an iconic motivation" into three sub-claims:

Iconic principles govern speakers' choices of structurally available options in discourse; structural options that reflect discourse-iconic principles become grammaticalized; and grammatical structure is an iconic reflection of conceptual structure. (Newmeyer 1992: 789)

Each of these sub-claims was then positioned with respect to UG:

The first claim is irrelevant to generative grammar, since the set of structural options for any language need to be characterized independently. The second claim, if correct, poses no challenge to generative grammar, because the autonomy of grammar is compatible with system-external triggers for system-internal changes. And the third claim has literally been built into standard versions of generative grammar, as is revealed by an examination of the properties of the levels of D-structure, S-structure, and logical form. (Newmeyer 1992: 789–790)

For easier reference later on, these three claims are summarized in (6):

6. a. Iconicity affecting the finished products of UG;
    b. Grammaticalization of iconicity-motivated options into UG;
    c. Some UG principle(s) being inherently iconic.

We already echoed his assessment of (6a): It is outside UG how its products are used under iconicity for discourse purposes. This is the first scenario for the FICH which we set aside early on in this chapter.

Newmeyer considers (6b) to pose no challenge to the theory of UG. The matter is not as simple, though, as it all depends on what one considers to be a challenge and how much the nature of grammaticalization is understood. We postpone the second question till section 1.2.2 and focus on the first one for now. In the most general sense, it is surely not conceptually challenging – at least to a researcher willing to entertain such possibilities – to connect what looks like a product of UG to a "system-external trigger" such as an iconic motivation. The devil is in the details, however. Take, for example, the serial verb constructions, which are documented from a fairly wide range of languages and language families. The linear order of the verbs in such a construction has long been claimed in functionalist works to be iconic to the temporal sequence in which the denoted events take place (e.g. Tai 1985). There are also efforts to derive this fact from (revisions of) UG or some other independently postulated principles. As will be shown in Chapter 2, the latter approach has never succeeded and in fact is often amiss by a wide margin, thereby posing a serious challenge to the attempt at letting UG internalize what appears to be iconicity at work. More cases of the same nature are presented in Chapter 3. In addition, the relation between UG and grammaticalization, taken to mean a set of grammatical behaviors captured by a rule, may not be as straightforward as Newmeyer's "system-external triggers" and "system-internal changes" appear to suggest. Related cases will be brought up as we proceed.

So with respect to (6b), challenges not only exist but may well be non-trivial. And such a challenge is at least partially due to the lack of a theory of UG-I. Without the latter's guidance, a suspected connection between UG and iconicity may take any expedient form and one can easily be at a loss on where to look for proof or disproof. Reducing uncertainty in this largely uncharted area of linguistics is precisely the motivation for a theory of UG-I, with the FICH defining the general condition for the two mechanisms to intermingle, while the algorithm in (5) offers instructions on exactly how to argue for it.

In a sense, (6c) is another case of grammaticalizing iconicity by having the latter directly built into the core of UG. Newmeyer makes the intriguing suggestion that "D-structure and LF developed in order for predicate-argument relations and quantifier-scope relations to be expressed iconically"

(p. 788).[4] Chapter 4 of this book will look into part of the clausal structure, typically regarded as a central element of UG, where iconicity seems to be the ultimate solution. Again, the UG-I theory will play a critical role in this investigation. For sure, some specific proposals on how UG internalizes (certain forms of) iconicity may prove to be wrong/misled in the long run – as might any specific idea in the literature of UG (e.g. the notion of government in the 1980s; see Chapter 5), but even failed attempts are to be favored over casual acknowledgments of iconicity without concrete content.

The UG-I theory presented in this book may also be viewed in the context of Chomsky's (2007) "third-factor principles":

Development of language in the individual must involve three factors: 1) genetic endowment . . . ; 2) external data . . . ; 3) principles not specific to [the faculty of language]. (p. 4)

Though separately motivated and almost certainly with familiar interface elements in mind (e.g. sensorimotor), Chomsky's model for language development echoes the FICH, with UG being genetic endowment and iconicity belonging to a "third-factor" principle. At the same time, it must be noted that Chomsky's tripartite division, as conceptually clean as it can be, appears to be blurred by Newmeyer's view that some form of iconicity is built into UG, namely (6b–c). The ultimate question is where the boundaries of the language-specific genetic endowment lie. See different perspectives in Hauser et al. (2002) vs. Pinker and Jackendoff (2005), Jackendoff and Pinker (2005); also see Berwick and Chomsky (2016) and the critiques by Progovac (2016). While inclined to side generally with those colleagues whose views are the opposite of those of Chomsky, I take it to be self-evident that the final solution can be found only by understanding all relevant facts. Consequently, this book will concentrate on what can be done at the moment: to assess what linguistic facts in sentence-generation can be proven to depend on the FICH, the USM and the algorithm in (5) for adequate explanations.

That more attention should be paid at the current stage of linguistics to formulating a concrete model of UG-I is also substantiated by what I consider to be a thought-provoking contrast in the literature.

On one hand, the generative enterprise has recognized from the very start the general roles of factors external to UG in overall linguistic behavior. Newmeyer (1992, 1998) takes multiple quotes from Chomsky's original writings as proof that the UG approach to language never denies the possibility of external factors helping shape the grammar of human language. Section 4.1.1 of Newmeyer (1992), for instance, starts with "[e]very generative model ever proposed has posited a systematic relationship between form and meaning" (with the same content repeated in Newmeyer 2017, subsection 7.3.3), as evidenced by Chomsky's own words:

Nevertheless, we do find many important correlations, quite naturally, between syntactic structure and meaning ... These correlations could form part of the subject matter for a more general theory of language concerned with syntax and semantics and their points of connection. (1957: 108)

Newmeyer's interpretation of these words on the relevance of external factors – in this case the structure-meaning correlations – is confirmed by the afore-quoted and more recent "third-factor" remark from Chomsky, whose primary concern is "[h]ow little can be attributed to UG while still accounting for the variety of I-languages attained, relying on third-factor principles?" (1957: 5).

On the other hand, there are few published works in the principles-and-parameters tradition that take more than casual notice of iconicity. And with rare exceptions (Y. Li 1993, Gärtner 2003, Y. Li and Ting 2013), such works, including Newmeyer's own, present a continual effort to dismiss iconicity despite lack of success (see Chapter 2 for detailed discussions).[5]

The mismatch between the positive general talk and the opposite specific practice regarding iconicity is a good indicator, in my opinion, that if we as a field are sincere about admitting external factors collaborating with UG to produce language in its entirety, then it is our responsibility to start developing effective protocols for discovering exactly how UG and iconicity interact. After all, the ultimate goal of linguistics is to understand what exactly language is, including how each part operates, how they interact with one another, and how they came into existence in the first place. Well-established sub-areas of linguistics, such as phonology and syntax, embody fruitful investigations of language components per se; the various interface studies explore the laws behind their interactions. If sentence-generation, the designated territory of UG, can be proven to rely conditionally on a general cognitive capacity like iconicity to complete certain tasks, be it directly coded in UG or called into action by the FICH, an explicit theory is the only means for us to gain better insights into this part of UG in particular and the F_{HL} in general.

1.2.2   On Grammaticalization

In addition to explaining a miscellaneous pool of cross-linguistic facts that UG alone is incapable of handling, the theory of UG-I, and in particular the USM, also offers a window to see into the nature of grammaticalization, a term so commonly used when what is suspected to be iconicity at work acts as an inherent part of a language's grammar. Newmeyer's (1998) discussions on iconicity, for instance, appeal to the term many times. But in this context, grammaticalization is purely descriptive, reporting nothing more than the fact that a form of iconicity appears obligatory. As will be seen in later chapters, the USM forces specific interactions between iconicity and UG under certain circumstances in rigorous and fully predictable ways. As such, what underlies the so-called grammaticalization of iconicity is merely the result of the USM imposing a deterministic and thereby fully "rule-like" structural mapping.

Logically, there are two possible scenarios for iconicity to participate in sentence-generation under the USM:

7.   a. Directly encoding iconicity into a default operation of UG;
     b. Incurring not-so-straightforward iconicity–UG interactions which create the collective effect of turning iconicity into a single "grammatical rule."

This book is primarily concerned with (7b), where the interactions between UG and iconicity are more intricate and thus more readily subject to controversy. It follows that any findings in this part of grammar will also reveal less-understood operations of F_{HL} and, as a welcome by-product, improve our understanding of the nature of, and specific details in, what has been lumped descriptively under the term grammaticalization. In contrast, the challenge posed by (7a) to the field of linguistics is usually of a different kind. Seldom do researchers disagree on the existence of a rule/principle R when there is enough data to support it, but different theoretical backgrounds may divide drastically in recognizing R's relation with or nature in iconicity. This topic will be picked up in Chapter 4, where specific cases of (6a) are elaborated on in detail. Worth keeping in mind for now are (a) that there is evidence, to be provided as we proceed, that these two scenarios often coexist in what is perceived as a single grammatical phenomenon and (b) that the USM, though separately motivated, may be viewed as the most general case of (6a) in terms of isomorphism in certain functionalist works (e.g. Bolinger 1977, Haiman 1985), as will be examined with concrete cases in later discussions.

The two scenarios in (7) correspond to Newmeyer's (6b–c). In fact, the recognition of (7a) was partially inspired by (6c). At the same time, there are also fundamental differences between the UG-I theory proposed in this book and Newmeyer's works on iconicity.

First, there is a split from the very beginning (Y. Li 1991, 1993 vs. Newmeyer 1992) on how to approach the UG–iconicity relationship. In examining either iconicity alone or the overall relationship between the functionalist and formalist models of language, Newmeyer's primary focus is on the "big picture" so that, in each case, he managed to include as many types of iconicity or other core functionalist concepts as possible. To reach the ultimate understanding of the subject matter, however, progress is needed both in width and in depth. This book, as well as the original works leading to it, aims at depth by pursuing the tried-and-true route of divide-and-conquer. If one can demonstrate – hopefully "beyond reasonable doubt" – that at least one form of iconicity in one particular linguistic construction must join forces with UG to produce an actual sentence in a predictable manner, a convincing statement will be made and a viable road paved on investigating the collaboration of the two cognitive mechanisms.

Second, Newmeyer's works (1992, 1998, 2004) repeatedly deny iconicity's role in the linear order among serial verbs for wrong reasons. More generally, even though Newmeyer formulated an insightful description of the UG–iconicity relationship in (6), it is not hard to detect a desire in his related writings to minimize the role of iconicity in the part of grammar that UG is typically held responsible for. We share this caution when dealing with UG-I but contend that (a) the degree of involvement on the part of iconicity can only be determined empirically, and (b) in this process, the first thing one should minimize is any theoretical biases, whether one happens to work with the theory of UG or to be in favor of functionalist explanations for linguistic facts. We will provide abundant argumentation, both factual and theoretical, in Chapter 2 of this book that at least some of Newmeyer's rejections of iconicity in sentence-generation result from erring in relation to (b).

Third, a direct outcome of the depth-oriented approach is that detailed argumentation allows the formulation of a concrete theory of UG-I, spelled out with the FICH and the USM and aided by the algorithm in (5). Collectively, such a theory can provide multiple linguistic phenomena with a uniform account whose content is specific enough for further assessment and thus further improvement. Compare this prospect, to be solidified and expanded in the following chapters, with, for instance, Newmeyer's (1992) brief suggestion that D-structure and LF are UG's way to iconically represent the argument–predicate and quantifier–scope relations. For all its ingenuity and plausibility, we do not see how one can assess the idea either empirically or theoretically; nor does it help reveal any inner workings of UG that are not known at the moment. This is perhaps why no subsequent research seems to have been triggered by the suggestion either – it is just not clear how to proceed from this point.

1.2.3   A Biological Perspective

As the entire work reported here surrounds the FICH, it is worthwhile to note that the hypothesis might evoke two meta-theoretical concerns: that UG is functionally imperfect and that two mechanisms at work, UG and iconicity, might create functional redundancy, e.g. both being responsible for linearizing lexical items. Significantly, neither concern is a real one if UG and the F_{HL} are taken to be biologically rooted.

Evolution is known to result in functionally imperfect, sometimes horribly flawed, biological systems. The dual function of the pharynx for ingestion and respiration, for instance, lends us humans the danger of choking, with the only means to prevent food from going into the windpipe being the epiglottis. The large brain vs. the disproportionally narrow birth canal is another case of poor design which forces human infants to be effectively born premature and thus drastically increases the cost of survival in many ways. Especially enlightening is the human body's inability to synthesize Vitamin C. Since the compound plays a vital role in keeping the body healthy, being unable to synthesize it amounts to the human body having a potentially deadly functional void (in comparison, for instance, with the goat in this respect), "mended" only by another subsystem of the body: direct intake of Vitamin-C-rich food via digestion. Such design flaws of biological systems result from evolution having no foresight. If UG is biologically rooted, being functionally imperfect should not come as a surprise. It is also worth keeping in mind that for a biological system *S* to lack a certain function and thus to be imperfect in terms of survivability is completely separate from some of *S*'s functions being optimized. In other words, there exists no logical clash between the FICH and the Minimalist view of language.

Trying to remove redundancy has been a driving force in progress in the theory of UG (Chomsky and Lasnik 1993: 515). As Thomas (1993) and Y. Li (1997) demonstrated with cases in biology, however, redundancy falls into different kinds, some of which exist only because of our limited capacity to perceive the world at a certain stage of understanding. In Chapter 2, LeDoux's (1996) groundbreaking study of fear will be recounted. What is perceived as fear is found to result from two separate neural "routes," presumably developed at different stages of evolution, thus creating what looks like redundancy. However, the two routes each make a unique contribution to the ultimate emotion of fear and actually serve distinguishable purposes. This scenario, which I will refer to as *complementary redundancy*, will be shown to also characterize how UG and iconicity collectively yield the linear order of certain syntactic constructions. That is, the two mechanisms are redundant only in the sense that both perform the linearizing function in sentence-generation, but each is responsible for a part of a clause that the other is not. Also see Chapter 5 on related discussions.

1.2.4   A UG-Heavy Approach

A book on the UG–iconicity relationship might be expected to give comparable attention to each side, as did Newmeyer's (1998) *Language form and language function*. Such a division of contents does not characterize this work and in fact cannot do so due to the considerations below:

A. In order to establish the FICH, highly detailed and specific analyses must be provided *within* the UG theory so as to prove that certain up-to-clause-level phenomena are indeed beyond UG's capacity – to merely show that certain linguistic facts can be accounted for via iconicity carries no persuasive force for researchers of the UG framework. In fact, this is a major technical reason why the two schools of thought have not made much progress in benefiting each other. Furthermore, decades of concentrated exploration along the lines of UG have revealed a system of multiple principles interacting with one another behind what might appear to be straightforward linguistic facts. An analogy – keep in mind that analogies are meant not for their accuracy but for illustrating the essence of an idea – is the ripening of fruit, a process so simple in the eyes of humans that a single word, *ripen*, can describe it but so complicated that one needs serious systemic knowledge in biology and chemistry to adequately explicate it. Similarly, a justification of the FICH would depend on taking intricate interactions of underlying factors into consideration. In sum, the central theme of this book determines that its content rests on UG-heavy analyses.

B. Since the FICH is relevant only up to sentence-construction, we are concerned only with the functionally most pertinent "diagrammatic" iconicity (for "represent[ing] the relations . . . of the parts of one thing by analogous relations in their own parts," as Peirce (1902/1932) put it). In the literature, diagrammatic iconicity is found to participate in syntax in several ways. As an example, summarizing the previous works on the topic, Newmeyer (1992: 761–764) listed five types: iconicity of distance, independence, order, complexity and categorization. Of these, only a subset will be investigated, via concrete examples, for their interactions with UG. Chapters 2 and 3 focus on three cases of lexical item linearization (= word order iconicity) and Chapter 4, the structural representation of arguments in different portions of a clause (= iconicity of independence). The logic behind this partial coverage of iconicity is already stated in section 1.2.2 and further echoed in A above: A depth-oriented divide-and-conquer strategy makes it easier to penetrate the surface of the phenomenon and obtain a more specific understanding of how iconicity interacts with UG in sentence-generation. Once this direction of inquiry proves viable, one will be better equipped to investigate other forms of iconicity.

C. Published works on iconicity also compel a question which, to my knowledge, has rarely drawn due attention: When a linguistic phenomenon looks like manifesting iconicity, how does one prove iconicity to indeed be at work? Judging from the literature, the lack of an explicit protocol to answer this question has caused confusion for functionalist and formalist grammarians alike, albeit often from the opposite sides of the problem. As an example, Tai's (1985: 50) Temporal Sequence Condition claims word order to be "determined by the temporal order of the states which [relevant syntactic constituents] represent in the conceptual world." Newmeyer (2004: 19) counters that "there are sentences in which the reverse temporal order reading is the normal one." And both authors found support from Chinese. Chapter 2 of this book presents evidence that both authors are amiss because each one overlooks some necessary condition(s) for linear iconicity to replace UG in sentence-generation. The same problem also takes another angle to see: "the statistical nature of [linguistic iconicity] would be a sufficient reason for generativists to ignore it" (van Langendonck 2010: 3). Judging from the current status of iconicity in the linguistics literature, "statistical" is essentially a euphemistic way to say that there exists little certainty and/or predictability regarding the role of iconicity in our grammatical theories.

A major motivation for postulating the FICH and the USM is to tackle this problem of uncertainty and, to some extent, subjectivity surrounding the study of iconicity. We show that iconicity can work deterministically rather than "statistically" under specific conditions in a linguistic theory endorsing the FICH. The constructions not meeting these conditions may look iconic but are actually the outcome of UG within the grammar of a particular language. In brief, part of defending the UG–iconicity integration is to identify and dismiss various iconicity look-alikes which are often a major reason for confusion and which significantly weaken the empirical motivation for exploring iconicity as part of the overall mechanism for language. To accomplish this goal, however, the analyses provided in this book must again be UG-heavy as most of the conditions for a proper use of iconicity can only be precisely identified and stated with the help of the UG apparatuses.

1.2.5   Further Clarifying the UG-I Interface

First of all, the nature of the FICH deserves elaboration. Recall that the FICH is meant to capture when UG interacts with iconicity in order to generate syntactic structures up to the sentence level. Conceptually, there are two scenarios where UG is unable to finish generating a clause S: S fails a particular principle of UG (e.g. movement encountering an island) or UG is not programmed to complete S (i.e. encountering a functional void). The first scenario goes against "the law" and thus trashes the illegitimate structure. The second one, however, is not ruled bad by any such law and so is not halted, provided that other cognitive means, like iconicity, can help UG get over the hurdle. This is the essence of the FICH (and thus the reference to "UG-compliant outcome" in (5b)).

One way to describe the role of the FICH in language is to make use of Chomsky's (2007) terms of "genetic endowment" and "third-factor principles" (see 1.2.1 above). Presumably, any interaction between the genetic endowment GE and some (natural class of) third-factor principle(s) $3^{rd}F$ may call for an interface theory to capture it. Familiar interfaces of this kind include phonetic form (PF; sensorimotor) and logical form (LF; conceptual–intentional), each with elaborate theories describing when and how UG interacts with the corresponding 3^{rd}F. This work argues for a new interface, between UG and the general cognitive function of iconicity, another 3^{rd}F. As stated at the beginning of this chapter, the FICH defines when this newly identified interface is activated in sentence-generation while the USM regulates the how of the interface.

The very nature of iconicity to directly connect form and meaning determines that many things it does in language have to do with PF (via form) and ultimately LF (via meaning). Nevertheless, the behavior of iconicity in sentence-construction cannot be simply subsumed under any existing interface theories. This is so because the critical task that UG enlists iconicity to help out with is to *assemble certain syntactic structures*. This task is by definition outside the domains of PF and LF. It is the kind that UG, or Chomsky's GE, ought to accomplish but occasionally becomes incapable of due to its inherent functional voids. This book focuses on formulating a theoretical model of the UG–iconicity interface, leaving it for future investigation how interfaces interface in a systematic manner. But see in Chapter 4 how a theory of PF linearization may bear on our UG–iconicity interface.

Now we proceed to exploring how the FICH and the USM assist UG in producing certain linguistic facts which have been resistant to a coherent account by the latter alone.

2   The Serial Verb Constructions

This chapter explores the nature of the word order in serial verb constructions (SVCs).

The term serial verb construction is attributed to Stewart's (1963) work on Akan, a Kwa language. Since then, SVCs have been documented in a geographically wide range of languages of different families (multiple subgroups of the Niger-Congo family, Papuan and Austronesian, East and Southeast Asian, Mesoamerican, and various creoles). As is expected of any descriptive linguistic term applied so expansively, the denotation of SVC varies from author to author. For the moment, we simply understand an SVC to have more than one verb in a mono-clausal structure without any lexical assistance such as a conjunctive. The term will be substantially refined later on.

A frequently mentioned characteristic of SVCs is the iconic order of their verbs. If an SVC contains two verbs V1 and V2, then V1 precedes V2 when the event expressed by V1 happens before the one expressed by V2 (see Muysken 1988). As an example, of the fifteen SVC languages reported and analyzed in Aikhenvald and Dixon's (2006) volume, nine are explicitly mentioned to exhibit this iconic word order. The generalization also holds for the rest of the languages although word order is not within the authors' concerns.[1] The same observation about SVCs is made in Tai (1985) on Chinese, in Croft (1991) on Yao and in Haspelmath's (2016) and Aikhenvald's (2006) surveys of the construction. This phenomenon, assuming its ultimate relevance to iconicity, belongs to what Newmeyer (1992) classifies as "iconicity of order" and, in a more general way, to Greenberg's (1963: 103) language universal (which for Greenberg is meant to refer to a strong and cross-linguistic tendency) that "the order of elements in language parallels that in physical experience or the order of knowledge." To avoid confusion from various overlapping but non-identical definitions, we use *linear iconicity* to refer to any word order that can be eventually proven to iconically express a conceptual relation, R_C in (3) of Chapter 1.

To defend the need for the FICH and the USM to explain the linearly iconic order of the verbs in SVCs, the current chapter is divided into six sections.

Section 2.1 establishes the iconic word order between the verbs in SVCs as a fact beyond doubt by dispelling various misconceptions about the SVC-pertinent data found in the literature. Purported "counterexamples" are shown to arise from misunderstood facts and/or a failure to properly identify the conditions under which iconicity takes part in sentence-generation.

In section 2.2, detailed proof is given that UG as well as the Gricean conversational maxim on the order of presentation are inherently unable to derive the word order of the verbs in SVCs. Specific proposals in the literature that try to reduce the word order of SVCs to any of these general principles are shown to be fundamentally flawed, and this incapacity cannot be fixed with technical tinkering.

Section 2.3 highlights a grammatical property of SVCs which has not received attention in the literature: While the word order remains constant, as established in section 2.1, the structural relation between the verbs varies both inter- and intra-linguistically. This fact further challenges the effort to subsume SVCs under UG since the latter does not have the mechanism to guarantee that different and purely structural relations – head–complement, head–adjunct, head–head – all converge on the same linear order despite the various parametric disparities among languages.[2]

More grammatical traits of SVCs are presented in section 2.4 to help demarcate the boundaries of the relevant facts under investigation, which eventually will lead to the functional void of UG that triggers the activation of linear iconicity for SVCs. It will be argued that the characteristic word order of the phenomenon is always accompanied by the same set of other grammatical facts so that a single explanation is needed to cover all of them.

Such an explanation is given in section 2.5 on the basis of three theoretical claims: the UG-I model in Chapter 1 that specifies the when and how of the UG–iconicity interaction, the Serial Verb Parameter (SVP), a conceptually and technically inevitable element within the theory of UG so as to separate SVC and non-SVC languages, and the existence of a functional void in UG exposed by one of the parameter settings. The general line of logic is that once the SVP is set so that a language allows for SVCs, a functional void is encountered which, given the FICH, activates linear iconicity to help syntactically assemble an SVC clause. In this process, the USM plays a key role in forcing a UG-compliant structure which both supports an iconic word order between the verbs and possesses the whole set of accompanying grammatical traits in sections 2.3–4.

Lastly, section 2.6 compares the collaboration of UG and linear iconicity with the two-route neurological mechanisms behind the human emotion of fear (LeDoux 1996). With this comparison, we not only highlight the strong parallels between the two cases of human cognition but also address one aspect of the meta-theoretical issue of redundancy.

Overall, this chapter demonstrates that an accurate integration of UG and linear iconicity, implemented with the FICH and the USM, is the only coherent mechanism to explain all the relevant facts of SVCs.

2.1   Linear Iconicity in the SVC: Facts and Non-Facts

Linear iconicity is one of those claimed linguistic phenomena that evoke radically different opinions.[3] Some researchers take it for granted, focusing on using it to measure and explain various word-order-related facts (Haiman 1985, Tai 1985, Landsberg 1995, and many articles in Aikhenvald and Dixon 2006, for instance). Practitioners of this approach may find it unnecessary to validate the existence of linear iconicity and view such an effort as telling "nothing that they do not think they know and have been saying all the time."[4] As we will see in the course of this book, this view is overly simplistic. In fact, for linear iconicity to be given the status of a warranted linguistic mechanism in sentence-generation, rigorous proof is needed that goes beyond simply presenting a set of cross-linguistic sentences or, for those objecting to it, offering a few superficial counterexamples.

In the principles-and-parameters model of syntax, while SVCs themselves have received continual attention (Jansen et al. 1978, Muysken 1988, Baker 1989, 2001, Hale 1991, Larson 1991, Lefebvre 1991b, Y. Li 1991, 1993, Law and Veenstra 1992, Déchaine 1993, Veenstra 1996, Collins 1997, Nishiyama 1998, Baker and Stewart 2002, Carstens 2002, Tomioka 2003, Newmeyer 2004, Hiraiwa and Bodomo 2008, Aboh 2009; also see Couvee and Pfau 2018 on SVCs in sign languages), works on linear iconicity are few and far between and contain very diverse views. Baker (1989) and Carstens (2002) each try to derive part of the claimed iconicity-supporting facts from the particular version of UG at the time, Y. Li (1991, 1993) treats linear iconicity as an axiomatic principle and explores the way it operates in the UG context, and Newmeyer (2004) simply denies its existence. A few researchers casually attribute the SVC word order to pragmatics (Collins 1997: 467, Nishiyama 1998) or tentatively to linear iconicity (Hiraiwa and Bodomo 2008). But overall the issue is avoided entirely, there being no terminology within the principles-and-parameters model of syntax to even talk about it. In this section, we will establish linear iconicity as a true phenomenon that affects word order in a way different from the well-studied linearization algorithm of UG.

2.1.1   The Basic Pattern

The examples below illustrate the characteristic word order between the verbs in SVC:

1. Sranan (Jansen et al. 1978)
   Mi e   teki a   nefi koti a   brede.
   I   ASP take the knife cut the bread
   'I cut the bread with the knife.'

2. Taba (Bowden 2001)
   n-babas welik n-mot do.
   3s-bite pig   3s-die REAL
   'It bit the pig to death.'

3. Nupe (Baker and Stewart 2002)
   Musa du   etsi kun.
   Musa cook yam   sell
   'Musa cooked the yam and sold it.'

4. Dagaare (Hiraiwa and Bodomo 2008)
   ò   dà   sɛ   lá   nenè ɔɔ.
   3s PAST roast FOC meat eat
   'He roasted meat and ate it.'

5. Chinese (Y. Li 1993)
   Taotao zhui-lei-le   Youyou le.
   Taotao chase-tired-ASP Youyou PRT
   'Taotao chased Youyou and made her tired.'

6. Ịjọ (Williamson 1965)
   Áràú zu-ye ákì buru teri-mí.
   she   basket take yam   cover-PAST
   'She covered yams with a basket.'

7. Miskito (Hale 1991)
   Witin ai pruk-an   kauhw-ri.
   he   me strike-OBV.3 fall-PAST.1
   'He hit me and made me fall down.'

8. Korean (Song 2005)
   Chelswu-ka   chayksang-ul twutulki-e pwusi-ess-ta.
   Chelswu-NOM   desk-ACC   hit-AFF   break-PAST-DECL
   'Chelswu broke the desk by hitting it.'

These examples differ in many ways. With respect to geographic and familial distributions, (3, 4, 6) are from different groups (Nupoid, Gur and Ijoid) of the Niger-Congo family while the rest are from Sino-Tibetan, Austronesian, Altaic, Misumalpan, plus a creole. In terms of word order, (1) through (5) are from head-initial languages and (6) through (8) from head-final languages. In grammatical form, the SVC may be either a compound (Chinese and Korean) or a series of verb phrases. Finally, (1) and (6) have an instrumental relation between the two verbs, (2, 5, 7, 8) a causal (aka resultative) relation, and (3) and (4) simply a temporally consecutive relation. Despite these intermingled differences, what remains constant is that the linear sequence of the two verbal constituents in each sentence matches the temporal sequence in which the corresponding sub-events take place in the human conception of the world.[5] For instance, one needs to grab the knife before cutting the bread with it, hitting as the cause precedes the dog's consequential running away, etc. To facilitate discussion, we follow the convention by calling the first verb of the SVC V1 and the second verb V2.

The arguments in the UG literature against the existence of linear iconicity in SVCs may be divided into two types: (i) to show that part of the claimed iconic word order is derivable from UG, and (ii) to argue that the rest of what is purported to be iconicity in action does not hold due to counterexamples. As it turns out, both (i) and (ii) are based on misunderstanding the relevant facts and/ or on flawed logic. This section focuses on type (i) in order to have a cleaner factual basis, returning to type (ii) in section 2.2.

2.1.2   Newmeyer on the Causative Construction

Consider the Yimas examples from Foley (1991) and Foley and Olson (1985):

9. a. na-Na-tmi-kwalca-t.
        3sA-1sO-say-rise-PERF
        'She woke me up.' (by verbal action)
    b. na-bu-wul-cay-prakiak.
        3sO-3ss-afraid-try.to.make-come-REM.PAST'
        'They tried to make him afraid as he came.'

Newmeyer (2004: 18) notes that while "the verb of causation precedes the verb representing the causee" in (9a), "we also find totally non-iconic orders" in (9b), with his latter observation referring to *wul* 'afraid' preceding *cay* 'try to make'. He concludes therefore that "the order of constituents in an SVC is not necessarily iconic" (ibid.).[6]

What is missed in this reasoning is an observation by Y. Li (1993): Causative constructions follow a completely different linearization pattern from the SVC because their word order is, and should be, regulated by UG (p. 499). Compare Chinese in (10), which has typically head-initial verbal projections, with the head-final Korean in (11):

10. a. zhege   xiaohua dou-xiao-le   tamen.
        this   joke   cheer-smile-ASP them
        'This joke cheered them up and made them laugh.'
    b. ta   you-hua-le   zhege fang'an.
        s/he   optim-ize-ASP   this   plan
        'S/He optimized this plan.'
    c. neige xiaoxi rang tamen xiao-le   haoji   tian.
        that news   make them smile-ASP several day
        'That news made them smile for several days.'

11. a. Chelswu-ka   Swuni-lul   ttayli-e ewuk-i-ess-ta.   (Song 2005)
       Chelswu-NOM Swuni-ACC hit-AFF   die-caus-PAST-DECL
       'Chelswu hit Swuni and caused her to die.'

    b. Chelswu-ka   Swuni-lul   chayk-ul   ilk-key   ha-ess-ta.
       Chelswu-NOM Swuni-ACC book-ACC read-AFF make-PAST-DECL
       'Chelswu made Swuni read the book.'

(10a) and (11a) illustrate the observation that resultative compounds linearize in compliance with linear iconicity. Morphological causativization in Chinese is shown in (10b) in which the causativizing affix, -*hua* '-ize', follows the root, presumably because the language, like many others, is head-final in derivational morphology (Di Sciullo and Williams 1987; also see Kayne's (1994) attempt to account for this general tendency). The same head-final causativization also applies to the Korean example (11a) where V2, meaning *kill*, is actually composed of the root *ewuk* 'die' and the suffix -*i* 'cause'. Remarkably, morphological causativization does NOT respect linear iconicity, with the 'cause' morpheme following, rather than preceding, the 'effect' morpheme. Moving to syntactic causatives in (10c) and (11b), notice that the matrix causative verb precedes the effect-denoting embedded clause in the head-initial Chinese but follows it in the head-final Korean. In sum, whether in morphology or in syntax, causativization ignores iconicity.

Y. Li (1993) notes that this difference between causativization and the resultative SVC is expected. There is a thematic relation between the causative morpheme and the root (or embedded verb). When one verb (or its syntactic projection) is the thematic object of another, their semantic relation is one that UG is capable of dealing with, so it is only natural that the syntactic representation of this relation complies with other verb–object structures in the language. On the other hand, there is no thematic relation between the verbs in a resultative construction in the sense that *hit*, for instance, semantically selects *die*, or any situation-denoting predicate for that matter, as its internal argument of effect. In other words, *a necessary condition for linear iconicity in SVCs is that there is no thematic relation between the verbs in a clause.* We return to Y. Li's (1993) theory in detail later.

Back to the Yimas examples in (9), it is clear now that the "non-iconic order" in the morphological causative (9b) should not be taken to dismiss linear iconicity.[7] In fact, as the Chinese and Korean sentences demonstrate, (9b) is predictably outside linear iconicity's jurisdiction. As for (9a), the translation of the sentence clearly indicates that the subject's verbal action (*saying*) causes the object's getting up (*rising*). Note that verbs like *say* take "irrealis" clausal objects; i.e. the entire sentence with *say* as the matrix verb has a truth value which doesn't rely on its CP complement. But *rise* in (9a) does not have such an irrealis reading, with the object actually getting up from bed. It follows that *say-rise* is indeed an SVC for lack of any thematic relation between them. And as Newmeyer noted already, the example complies with linear iconicity.

2.1.3 Baker on the Purposive SVC

As part of his general theme that the word order in the SVC is not a phenomenon independent of UG, Baker (1989) offers an objection to linear iconicity on the basis of (12) from Ijo. Simply to facilitate discussion, this SVC will be called purposive for now.

12. duma tun-ni a-piri   (Baker 1989: 525, quoted from Williamson 1965)
     song sing-∅ her-give
     'sing a song for her'

According to Baker (1989: 526),

the singing action and the pleasing/benefiting action happen simultaneously. One might say that the singing leads to "her" being pleased, but one could just as well say that the will to please "her" leads the subject to sing. Thus, a function approach might expect a variability in word order . . . . In fact, the order of "sing" and "give" is fixed.

This quoted objection can be decomposed into two parts: (i) the actions represented by the two verbs *sing* and *give* happen simultaneously and thus their word order cannot be determined by linear iconicity; (ii) even if there were any temporal order between the two actions, there would still exist two plausible interpretations that should produce opposite linear orders between the verbs under linear iconicity, and not the only one shown in (12). As it turns out, both objections result from failing to understand the real semantics of the purposive SVC.

Part (i) is based on Baker's assumption that singing a song and pleasing the beneficiary with it happen at the same time. Not true. In our perceived world, one has to take the action of producing a musical note, e.g. doing something with one's vocal tract, before the note can be heard and produce any effect on the listener. The temporal sequence here is cognitively unequivocal. The confusion is also partially due to V1 being *sing*, which allows each musical note to be appreciated before the song is complete. But many verbs for V1 require the completion of the object O before O can be "given" out. With no native speakers of Ijo available, we use a Chinese purposive SVC sentence to illustrate the point, pending proof in section 2.4 that (13) is indeed an SVC:

13. ta zuo-le   yidun fan   gei wo.
     3s cook-ASP a   meal give me
     'S/He cooked a meal for me.'

The sentence can only mean that s/he completed some identifiable event of cooking and gave me at least each dish *in totality*. Logically, then, completing a meal/dish needs to precede giving it as a whole to the recipient. And the word order in (13) directly reflects this real-world sequence.

Regarding part (ii) of Baker's objection, the temporal sequence of events in a purposive SVC is perhaps the most misunderstood, with the flawed reasoning that since a purpose precedes the action to accomplish it, the action of "giving" in (12–13) ought to be linearized before, and not after, the action of cooking/ singing. It follows that this type of SVC may be viewed as evidence against linear iconicity. What this logic does not distinguish is the event of forming a purpose, call it e_f, and the event that realizes the content of the purpose, call it e_c. *Give her/me* with the intended meaning of benefiting her or me in (12–13) stands for e_c, not e_f – you can't benefit anyone with a mere thought. While e_f indeed happens prior to cooking/singing (= e_{act}), e_c is the event that e_{act} is meant to help accomplish and thus is necessarily later than e_{act} if it happens at all. In other words, the natural temporal sequence is e_f before e_{act} before e_c, and there is *no* verb in (12–13) that describes e_f.

Back to Baker's reasoning under (12), even if *a-piri* 'her-give' indicates the subject's desire to benefit "her" as Baker puts it, the VP describes *not* the event of forming this intention but that of its content to be hopefully realized in the future. So either one of the suggested semantic relations between the verbs should produce the word order in (12) under linear iconicity: If singing led to her being pleased, *tun-ni* 'sing' should come first; if *a-piri* 'her-give' corresponds to what the subject hoped to happen with the help of his singing, its realization (if ever) is again later than the subject finishing each note (or the entire song). Instead of a problem with linear iconicity as Baker believes, (12) conforms to it completely. The same analysis applies to (13).

2.1.4   *Another "Problem" with Linear Iconicity from the Purposive SVC*

Examples like (12) and (13) also bring up a complication that adds to the overall confusion about iconicity. The examples below are from Newmeyer (2004: 2):

14. a. Zhangsan gei   wo mai yifu.   (Chinese)
         ZS   give/for me buy clothes
         'ZS bought clothes for me.'
     b. Mi wroko gi   en.   (Sranan)
         I   worked give him
         'I worked for him.'

What is translated as *give* occurs as V1 in Chinese but as V2 in Sranan, apparently leaving linear iconicity useless for explaining the word order of the purposive SVC. In fact, the problem appears to exist even within Chinese: The linear location of *give* in (13) patterns with Sranan and is opposite of (14a). If the location of *give* is not even consistent inside a single language, how could one not doubt the relevance of linear iconicity?

The key to a solution is that *gei* in (14a) is not the same as its homophonous counterpart in (13), as explicitly noted in Chapter 1 of Huang et al. (2009). The difference is most clearly seen when *gei* pairs with a path-of-motion verb such as *song* 'send' and *chuan* 'pass, transfer':

15. a. Ta gei wo chuan-le ge xiaoxi.
       3s GEI me pass-ASP a message
       'S/He passed a message to/for me.'

    b. Ta chuan-le ge xiaoxi gei wo.
       3s send-ASP a message GEI me
       'S/He passed a message to me.'

    c. Zhege xiaoxi gei ni.
       this message GEI you
       'This message is given to you.'

When *gei* and its object precede the matrix verb *chuan* 'pass', as in (15a), it is ambiguous between the goal reading and the beneficiary reading; but when *gei* is postverbal in (15b), only the goal reading is available. This contrast follows if the postverbal *gei* is still the regular verb and thus retains its lexical meaning of giving which necessarily entails a goal argument. On the other hand, the preverbal *gei* must have undergone some change from the base form and acquired semantic ambiguity. For one thing, while suffixing an aspectual marker such as the perfective *-le* to the postverbal *gei* in (15b) may sound somewhat redundantly unnatural, doing so to the preverbal *gei* in (15a) is downright impossible. For another, examples with *gei* as the sole verb of a clause never produce the beneficiary reading. (15c), for instance, can only mean the message sent to you but not on your behalf.

Given the current literature, we may think of two possible analyses of the preverbal *gei*. One is to treat it as a preposition resulting from grammatical-ization of the verbal *gei*. It is common knowledge in the field of Chinese linguistics that most prepositions in Modern Chinese have verbal origins (Chao 1968, Li and Thompson 1981). Treating this *gei* as a preposition opens up the possibility of the same prepositional form introducing either a goal or a beneficiary argument, as is found in some Bantu languages. The analysis is also compatible with this ambiguous *gei*'s rejection of aspect markers and with its use as the sole predicate, both characteristic of Chinese prepositions (cf. Huang et al. 2009, Ch. 1). If it is a preposition, however, (15a) and Newmeyer's (14a) are simply examples of a PP modifying the verb *chuan* 'pass' or *mai* 'buy' and are no longer part of an SVC. Not being an SVC exempts these examples from linear iconicity, a significant point to be elaborated on later. In comparison, *gei* in (15b) is still a verb and thus acts as V2 while complying with linear iconicity as expected of an SVC.

The second possibility, less likely in my view (see Chapter 4), is for this particular preverbal *gei* to have morphed into a lexical element resembling the Bantu applicative morpheme which typically introduces a goal or a benefactive. As Y. Li (2005) has argued, the Bantu applicative is best analyzed as the matrix verb taking a VP complement headed by the verbal root. In such an analysis, the relation between *gei* and *chuan* 'pass' in (15a) is no longer one for the SVC but rather one patterning with the causative verb discussed in 2.1.1 above. Because Chinese is head-initial for verbal constructions, the "applicative" use of *gei* naturally precedes its VP complement. In brief, there is more than one plausible analysis of *gei* in (14a) and (15a) that captures the extra semantic property of ambiguity and snugly accommodates other facts in and outside Chinese. What matters for now is that these analyses unanimously exempt the preverbal *gei* from linear iconicity and instead subject it to the linearization pattern of UG.

What remains to be explained is why the cross-linguistic purposive examples in (14b), (13) and (12), which all have V2 glossed as *give*, are often reported with the beneficiary reading if, as shown through (15), the postverbal *gei* 'give' is necessarily a "goal" verb and not one to introduce a beneficiary argument. The answer is found by looking into the details of these examples. It is worth emphasizing, though, that even if the beneficiary reading of *give* is indeed an option in the SVC of some languages, it is still consistent with linear iconicity because, after all, benefiting "her" in (12), for instance, is the hoped-for result of singing a song and its actual realization can only happen after the song is heard.

Back to the Chinese examples in (13) and (15b), the inconsistency in the meaning of *give* seems confusingly random until the semantics of V1 is taken into consideration. In (13), V1 falls into the class of "creation verbs" which describe events that bring the object into existence. In our world, if X creates Y (through cooking for instance) and gives Y to Z, then Z is not only the goal of the transfer but also understood to be the beneficiary of the whole *cook-give* event. In other words, *give* in both (13) and (15b) introduces only the goal argument in itself. The beneficiary reading is neither the direct product of the syntax of these sentences nor derived from the lexical meaning of *give*; instead it results from our knowledge of the world.

There is enough evidence for this pragmatic account of the "beneficiary *give*." First note that the Ijo example (12) also contains the creation verb *sing*. The particular song heard by *her*, referred to by the object of *give*, is literally "created" by singing out each note. Secondly, we correctly predict that in Chinese, *give* as V2 generally acquires the beneficiary reading as long as V1 can be interpreted as bringing the object into existence in some broad sense: *gei ni* 'give you' may follow *xie shu* 'write book', *yan xi* 'play opera', *gai fang* 'build house' or *tou qian* 'steal money' with the 'for you' reading. And thirdly, the analysis is most clearly supported by comparing the two examples below:

16. a. ta xie-le   yiben shu   gei ni.
        3s write-ASP a   book give you
        'S/he wrote a book for you.'

    b. ta xie-le   yifeng xin   gei ni.
        3s write-ASP a   letter give you
        can mean: 'S/he sent a letter to you.'
        can't mean: 'S/he sent a letter for you.'

At first sight, the semantic discrepancy of *gei* is problematic for our theory because V1 is the creation verb *xie* 'write' in both cases. But in the real world, writing a book with the purpose of giving it to someone is a (hugely) benefactive act, whereas writing a letter for the same purpose doesn't have that extra flavor as the whole point of a letter is to reach its recipient. In other words, the so-called beneficiary reading associated with *give* as V2 is truly the result of our knowledge of the world and not a purely syntactic or lexical phenomenon.

This leaves us with (14b), the Sranan example in which V1 is unergative and not a creation verb. We cannot give a committed analysis for lack of access to Sranan speakers. But Jansen et al. (1978) reported that PP adjuncts are postverbal in this language (see 2.4 later). It is likely, then, that *gi en*, glossed as 'give him', is used as a PP, much resembling one of the possibilities for the preverbal *gei wo* 'give me' in the Chinese example (15a), with the beneficiary reading. We leave this to further investigation, merely noting at the moment that a direct word-by-word translation of (14b) to Chinese in the same word order is downright unacceptable, as is expected because *work* is not a verb of creation.

2.1.5 Carstens' Objections to Linear Iconicity

In addition to quoting Baker's (now demonstrably erroneous) argument from the purposive SVC, Carstens (2002) offers two more reasons to reject linear iconicity, the first of which questions whether every SVC indeed involves two (sub)events. If an SVC encodes only one event, "[t]he fixed order of the verb pairs in these examples is thus not predicted" by linear iconicity (p. 35):

17. a. aya bara-ki aki   duma tun. (Ijo, quoted from Williamson 1965)
        new way   take song   sing
        'sing a song in a new way'

    b. mo fi   ogbon   ge   igi. (Yoruba, quoted from Stahlke 1970)
        I   use cleverness cut tree
        'I cut down the tree with cleverness.'

Since Carstens doesn't elaborate on her reasoning, it is not entirely clear why these examples don't describe scenarios of double events. I suspect that for Carstens, the instrumental verbs *take* and *use* no longer describe events when their objects do not refer to concrete entity-type instruments. But this is simply untrue. Though finding it non-idiomatic, English speakers can certainly understand *They took a new way to sing the song*, in which *take* is marked with past tense and therefore must be syntactically treated as event-denoting. Furthermore, if English can *use caution*, why can't Yoruba *use cleverness*? After all, a light verb is still a verb and gets treated grammatically as expressing an event.

Carstens' second objection to linear iconicity comes from an Ijo example:

18. eri beni duo   you-mi   (p. 36, quoted from Williamson 1965)
    he   water go.through paddle-PAST
    'He paddled through the water.'

She observes that "[t]he action of paddling must begin before the action of passing through ... the water ... Yet according to Williamson, the verb *duo* is always V1, never V2" (p. 36). But in addition to providing this example, Williamson (1965) also remarks that "[s]entences containing *duo* as the only verb are rather unusual ... It is possible that *duo* is in the process of losing its verbal status and becoming a particle" (p. 49). An interpretation of this remark may be this: In modern Ijo, *duo* is no longer a verb, which is why it normally doesn't serve as the predicate by itself. The "rather unusual" exceptions either result from coercing *duo* into a verb by appealing to its historical status or perhaps are simply idiomatic leftovers from the past. In other words, the productive use of *duo* in the so-called SVC context is actually postpositional. This is enough to place (18) outside the phenomenon of SVCs, as we already mentioned above with the preverbal *gei* in Chinese (15a) and will elaborate on in section 2.4 below.

Interestingly, Carstens' intuition about paddling preceding river-crossing, though not seen in Ijo, is instantiated in Chinese. In (19), the verb *guo* 'cross' indeed occurs after the verb *hua* 'paddle'. And matching this iconicity-compliant word order is the productive use of *guo* as a verb, illustrated in (20).

19. ta   hua   chuan   guo   he.
    3s   paddle   boat   cross   river
    'S/He paddled the/a boat and crossed the river.'

20. a. guo   zhetiao jie
       cross this   street
       'cross this street'

    b. guo   yizuo da   shan
       cross a   big mountain
       'climb over a big mountain'

    c. guo   anjian
       cross security.check
       'go through the security check'

In other words, (19) displays linear iconicity precisely because path of motion is described with a verb in Chinese, in contrast to the postposition in Ijo.

Lastly, we note that even Carstens' own structural analysis of Ijo favors treating *duo* as P and not as V. For Carstens, V1 is the matrix verb and V2, an embedded non-finite verb. If *duo* in (18) were the matrix verb as she claims, then the past-tense affix would skip the matrix verb but attach to the embedded non-finite verb, a claim which demands substantial justification both in Ijo and cross-linguistically. If *duo* heads a PP left-adjoined to VP, however, *you* 'paddle' is the only verb in (18) and naturally carries the tense morpheme.

In conclusion, the explicit arguments in the UG literature against linear iconicity in SVCs, be they based on the causative constructions (2.1.2), the purposive SVC (2.1.3–4), or the path-of-motion verbs (2.1.5), all fall apart under closer scrutiny and turn into facts either in support of it or in compliance with it. In fact, no real counterexamples are known once the relevant facts are examined without a theoretical predisposition. On this basis, we will proceed to construct the proof that what appears to be an iconic word order observed with SVCs is not a derivative of other linguistic theories such as UG.

2.2   Un-deriving the Derivational Efforts on Linear Iconicity

As noted earlier, the other form of objection to linear iconicity in the UG literature is by deriving (part of) it from some general mechanism. Methodologically, such efforts are certainly legitimate. In fact, an empirical field typically makes progress by trying to account for the maximal number of facts with the least number of theoretical apparatuses, in accordance with Occam's razor (Sober 2015). The real question is whether linear iconicity is indeed reducible to something else. In this section, we provide proof that it cannot be and that this inability is not due to particular formulations or implementations of UG but for fundamental reasons.

2.2.1   Baker's Multiple-Headed VP

The key in Baker's (1989) theory of SVCs is to add this parameter to UG:

21. a. VPs {can/cannot} count as the projection of more than one distinct head.
    b. The verbs in an SVC always share an object.
    c. The head–complement relation requires linear adjacency; the subject–predicate relation does not.

For the instrumental SVC in a head-initial language, as exemplified with the Sranan example in (1) and repeated in (22a), the double-headed alternative structures in (22b and c) need to be considered:

22. a. Mi e   teki a   nefi koti a   brede. (= example (1))
         I   ASP take the knife cut   the bread
         'I cut the bread with the knife.'

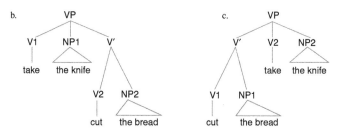

(21a) allows such double-headed structures as a parameterized option to separate SVC and non-SVC languages. In (22b-c) alike, the VP contains two heads V1 and V2 which take NP1 and NP2, respectively, as their direct objects. Since each object occurs next to the corresponding head, (21c) is satisfied. Assuming that NP1 in (22b) is also the instrumental object of V2 under object-sharing (cf. (21b)),[8] it must be placed to the left of the immediate projection of V2 because an argument not being the sister of V2 is essentially in the subject–predicate relation with V2, and the subject precedes the predicate in SVO languages. In a word, (22b) is well formed once UG is enriched with (21). In contrast, (22c) is ruled out because NP2, being the shared object, must hold the subject–predicate relation with V' in order to be interpreted as the instrumental argument of V1. But placing NP2 after V1 fails to comply with the subject–predicate order. Critically for Baker, UG thus revised only generates the word order that matches what is thought to reflect linear iconicity and prohibits the word order that is counter-iconic.

The conclusion holds equally for the SVC in a head-final language like Ijo:

23. a. Áràú zu-ye ákì buru teri-mí.   (= (6) above)
         she   basket take yam cover-PAST
         'She covered yams with a basket.'

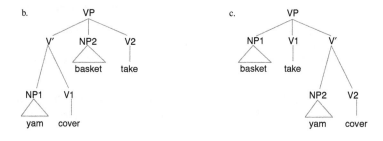

(23b) yields the nonexistent (and counter-iconic) string, whereas (23c) represents the good example in (6/23a). In both cases, the verb *cover* is assumed to
have a patient argument and an instrument argument, the latter as the shared
object also receiving a patient θ-role from *take*. In (23b), the linear relation
between NP2 – the shared object – and the V′ projection of V1 doesn't conform
to the subject–predicate order. In (23c), NP1 serves as the shared object. It
occurs to the left of V′ under the subject–predicate relation which does not
require adjacency between the two constituents (see (21c)).

   In sum, the only word order permitted by (21) for the instrumental SVC is
also the one that appears to be linearly iconic, whether it is in the head-initial
Sranan (and most Niger-Congo languages) or the head-final Ijo. What looks
like linear iconicity now becomes a derivative of UG. The same outcome is
produced when (21) is applied to the resultative SVC such as (2), under the
plausible assumption that the object of V1 *bite* is also the internal argument of
V2 *die*, a cross-linguistically unaccusative verb. The reader is referred to the
original paper for details.

   Baker's addition to UG, namely (21), does not explain why a VP enjoys the
parametric option of being doubly headed while other lexical phrases do not
(given the fact that no "serial adjective constructions" are reported, for
instance[9]). This question aside, it suffers from the more fundamental problem
of being unable to account for one popular type of SVC, the consecutive, shown
with (3–4). Two more examples are given below, with (24a) from the head-
initial Yoruba and (24b) from the head-final Ijo. Baker's own analysis of these
examples is given in (25).

24. a. Bóló sè   ẹran tà.   (Lord 1974, quoted by Baker 1989: 529)
        Bola cook meat sell
        'Bola cooked some meat and sold it.'
    b. Áràú ingo déri   pịtẹ-mí. (Williamson 1965, quoted by Baker 1989: 525)
        she   trap weave set-PAST
        'She wove a trap and set it.'

25. a.   b.

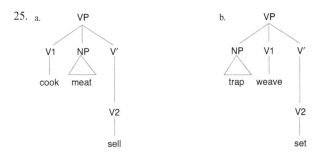

The shared NP object is well formed with respect to V1. In both (25a and b), this NP occurs to the left of the V′ projection of V2, as required by SVO and SOV alike. The subject–predicate relation between the two doesn't need adjacency according to (21c), correctly allowing (25b) as well. Again, the word order in both cases complies with iconicity, regardless of the head-initial or head-final choice in a given language. So far so good.

What Baker has overlooked is that his analysis also allows *Bóló tà ẹran sè 'Bolo sell meat cook', which reverses the two verbs in (24a). The structure would be (26):

26.

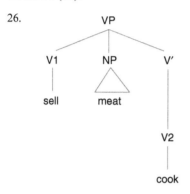

Structurally identical to (25a), (26) should be equally well formed, meaning that *sell meat cook* is predicted to be just as acceptable. In fact, since phrase structure does not in itself encode temporal sequence among its constituents, there is no UG-internal reason why (26) cannot be both grammatically good because of (21) and semantically subject to the same interpretation as (25a). The same prediction extends to a head-final language like Ijo. Judging from the SVC patterns documented in the literature (e.g. Sebba 1987, Aikhenvald 2006), this prediction is wrong because the consecutive SVC is not known to swap its two verbs while keeping the same interpretation. Data from Chinese directly confirms the point:

27. a. ta   mai-le   xie   shu   kan.
         3s   buy-ASP   some   book   read
         'S/He bought some books and read them.'
     b. *ta   kan-le   xie   shu   mai.
         3s   read-ASP   some   book   buy

The problem posed by the consecutive SVC for Baker is theoretically significant because it reveals UG's intrinsic limit as well as the nature of the iconic word order in the SVC. Both verbs in this construction, say *sell* and *cook* in (24a), are used as simple transitive verbs with identical thematic properties.

Provided that neither is a thematic argument of the other (see 2.4 below), simply swapping them will not result in any structural or grammatical disparity, leaving UG incapable of imposing a particular word order between them. For the same reason, Baker's theory cannot account for the word order of the resultative SVC when both V1 and V2 are (used as) simple transitive verbs, as can be observed cross-linguistically. Two such examples are given below, one from Sranan (Sebba 1987: 62) and one from Classical Chinese (SIMA Qian, *Shi Ji*, 90 BC):

28. a. Kofi naki Amba kiri.
      Kofi hit   Amba kill
      'Kofi struck Amba dead.'
   b. ... an beng,   jin ya   sha wozhe.
      bank collapse all crush kill lying.down.person
      ' ... the bank collapsed, crushing to death all those sleeping underneath it.'

From a purely syntactic perspective, *hit/crush* and *kill* are interchangeable without altering any part of the phrase structure that houses them, leaving syntax incapable of enforcing a particular linear order between the verbs.

The same logic also explains why Baker's definitions in (21) achieve partial success with the word order in the instrumental SVC and the type of resultative SVC in (2) where V2 is unaccusative. First, in each of these examples, the two verbs either have different numbers of θ-roles (i.e. *bite* and *die* in (2)) or are presumed to (with *take* having two θ-roles and *cut* having three, of which one is instrument; see (22–23)). Secondly, these two verbs are taken to necessarily share an object. Since the object is located inside the VP, structurally sharing it with two verbs, each with a different number of θ-roles, provides a way to affect the VP-internal structure and thereby make the structural relation of the two verbs asymmetrical.

Consider the Sranan instrumental SVC in (22), for instance. Once the patient argument of *take* and the instrument argument of *cut* are represented as a single shared NP1 object, it becomes possible under (21) to tinker with the internal organization of VP so that each verb has a different set of sisters – with *take* having NP1 and V′ as sisters and *cut* having just NP2. The immediate consequence of this structural disparity is that swapping the two verbs will inevitably alter the VP-internal structure (the reader may want to switch *take* and *cut* in (22) to verify this). As long as UG is formulated or revised in such a way that only one particular structure of VP is legitimate and all the rest not, the structural relation between *take* and *cut* can be asymmetrically set. Such an asymmetry in turn becomes the basis for the two verbs to be linearized in a particular order because in UG, linearization is a function of structural asymmetry (see Kayne 1994 for an explicit articulation of this idea, to which we return in Chapter 4).

However, when the two verbs have identical argument structures as in the duo-transitive consecutive and resultative SVCs, swapping them creates no structural change, as we noted above by comparing (25a) with (26). And with no distinction in structure, it is impossible for UG to tell the two alternatives apart. Importantly, this conclusion holds independently of Baker's particular implementation in (21). Even if each verb in the consecutive SVC projects to a full clause and object-sharing is created by coindexing the overt NP object in one CP with a *pro* object in the other CP,[10] the entire structure will still remain the same from the viewpoint of syntax, no matter which verb is in which clause, precisely because they have identical argument structures and therefore are thematically and structurally indis-tinguishable by UG. See 2.2.2 below for a concrete case.

This understanding of why UG inherently fails to impose a particular linear order on duo-transitive SVCs not only pinpoints UG's limitation in handling the iconic word order, but *it also removes object-sharing from UG's available toolbox for explaining the entire linear iconicity phenomenon*, contra Baker's assumption in (21b). After all, duo-transitive SVCs are the clearest cases of object-sharing, with the single NP understood as the thematic object of both verbs by any standard, and they are precisely the SVCs whose iconic word order is unable to be guaranteed by UG. Still, we believe that Baker is right in noting the correlation between the word order of the SVC and object-sharing, as shown and explained in the later parts of this chapter.

2.2.2   Carstens' Antisymmetric Structure for the SVC

Drawing on Kayne's (1994) theory of antisymmetric phrase structure, Carstens (2002) proposes a uniform account of word order in the SVC. The structure in (29) is assigned to the instrumental SVC for both head-initial and head-final languages:

29.   (Carstens 2002: 5)

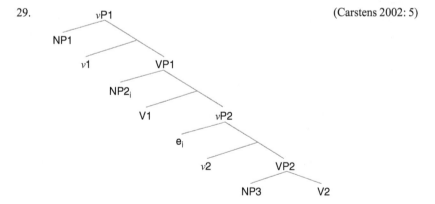

For the Ijo example (6), let V1 be the instrumental verb *take*, V2 be *cover* and NP2, NP3 be their own patient/theme objects respectively. Here *e* stands for the phonetically empty instrumental argument of *cover* that is coreferential with NP2 through some standard UG operation such as local binding. (29) directly generates *basket take yam cover*. Raise both V1 and V2 to the corresponding *v*1 and *v*2 positions, respectively, and the typical head-initial *take basket cover yam* is derived (cf. (24a)). For Carstens, the simple parameter of V *in situ* vs. raised to the local *v* resolves Muysken's (1988) puzzle that the linear order of the verbs in an SVC remains constant in head-final and head-initial languages alike.

But this theory faces the same problem that Baker's does: Why isn't the opposite word order possible for duo-transitive SVCs (e.g. *cook meal sell* in (24a))? (30) illustrates why Carstens' theory fails the task:

30.

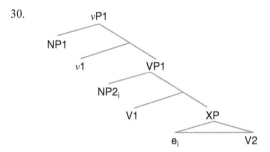

Whether XP is best labeled as *v*P2 or VP2 is inconsequential for this discussion, as is the precise nature of *e*, provided that it stands for the single object of V2 locally bound by NP2. What matters is that *cook* and *sell* have identical argument structures, rendering UG unable to distinguish them in such a way that *cook* must occur under V1 and *sell* under V2. Put differently, Carstens' theory cannot explain the iconic word order in the case of an SVC composed of verbs of identical argument structures. In this respect, a Kaynean tree does no better – or worse – than Baker's double-headed VP.

2.2.3   Other Efforts to Derive the Iconic Word Order of the SVCs

Practically all recent UG-based analyses of the SVC share a common trait: a uniform structural setup for all instances of SVC[11] in which some projection of V2 is placed in the complement position of V1. See Baker (1989), Collins (1997), Carstens (2002) and Aboh (2009) for a few representatives of this idea, hereafter referred to as the complement approach (CApp) for ease of reference. The meta-theoretical advantage of a uniform CApp is straightforward; but in nature, whether CApp is valid or not is not a meta-theoretical question but an empirical one. As CApp is at the core of most efforts to accommodate linear iconicity in the theory of UG, it deserves a closer evaluation in its own right. This task is postponed to 2.3. It will be shown then that there exists no inter-linguistic or even intra-linguistic uniform structure for the SVC.

Newmeyer also hints at an entirely different approach in which linear iconicity is suggested to be replaced by one of Grice's conversational maxims. On Tai's (1985) iconicity-based account of certain Chinese verbal sequences, Newmeyer (1998: 121, note 7) makes this remark:

> Tai does not analyze [his SVC examples] as a grammaticalization of a Gricean implica-ture. Rather, he appeals to an independent 'Principle of temporal sequencing' ... For reasons that I do not understand, functionalists virtually never appeal to Gricean maxims, but tend to propose instead discourse-based principles of lesser generality.

The specific Gricean implicature Newmeyer has in mind in this case is "be orderly" (1998: 139), a component of the general Maxim of Manner that orders the sequence of expressions to most clearly describe the subject matter.

But there are at least two reasons for not turning to Grice for help with the word order of SVCs à la Newmeyer's suggestion. First, as already noted in Chapter 1, when a tendency or option – something "statistical" in van Langendonck's terms – becomes obligatory in certain linguistic contexts, calling it grammaticalization merely renames the fact without offering any insight into the matter. What is needed is a more specific account for why and how the transition happens. We return to this in section 2.5, spelling out for now the second reason why "be orderly" is no explanation for the word order of SVCs.

Simply put, even if this implicature were the factor at work for SVCs, Newmeyer seems to have got its role backward. His reasoning assigns more generality to Grice's conversational maxims than linear iconicity. In reality, most of these maxims are essentially collections of separate communicational guidelines of which at least some may have deeper roots. "Be orderly," which Newmeyer proposes to replace linear iconicity, is one of the four components of the Maxim of Manner (the rest are "be brief, avoid obscurity, avoid ambigu-ity"). However, why is it that aligning the sequence of expressions with the order in which the content of each expression takes place is orderly[12] whereas reversing that match is not? Provided that we humans follow a consistent direction of description, it would be equally orderly and unambiguous to report the event chain either from the beginning or from the end – in essence, this is just a choice between first-in-first-out or first-in-last-out in data-retrieval, which, in terms of the cost of computational resources, are completely equal. Minimally, the fact that conversation takes the iconicity-compliant sequence to be orderly argues against Newmeyer's assumption that iconicity is of "lesser generality" than "be orderly" and thus ought to be replaced by the latter. In fact, it would seem much more plausible for some form of iconicity to be underneath "be orderly."

2.3 De-unifying a Uniform Treatment of the SVCs

We start by recapitulating the clarification that by "a uniform treatment" of the SVCs is meant CApp, namely, to place a projection of V2 in the complement position of V1 in all SVC types and cross-linguistically. With rare exceptions, work in the UG framework on the SVC assumes such a configuration, often with little or no independent proof for it. This practice deserves scrutiny for two closely related reasons.

First, the exact structural relation between V1 and V2 should and can be determined only from linguistic facts, there being no *a priori* ground for assigning them an automatic head–complement structure.[13] As a matter of fact, if one pays attention to the data scattered in the literature, including those treated with CApp, clear evidence can be found that such a uniform take on the SVC is on the wrong track. The real picture seems best described by an old Chinese saying "If no change can be made to the shoe, then one must try to adjust his foot to fit in." Here, the iconic linear order of V1 and V2 is the constant, i.e. the shoe; the structural relation R linking V1 and V2 forms the foot, with R tailored by a particular language L in such a way that R makes use of the grammar of L so as to fit into the iconically arranged V1 and V2. In this sense, the only thing necessarily uniform about SVCs is the word order, contra the (tacit) common assumption in the UG literature. Four pieces of cross-linguistic evidence will be given for this conclusion.

Second, the data in this section and the conclusions drawn from them also serve as an extension to the previous section 2.2, adding to the proof that UG is unable to derive all the facts about SVCs. In the UG model of language, linearity is a function of structure, namely the R_S-to-R_L mapping in (3b) of Chapter 1. At least for head-initial languages, the uniform head–complement setup between V1 and V2 renders R_S constant, thereby providing the possibility to generate a uniform R_L. It is for this reason that works on SVCs in the UG framework can often afford to totally ignore the word order of the phenomenon – with the projection of V2 being the complement of V1 in a head-initial language such as Yoruba or Nupe, V1 precedes V2 by default. On the other hand, if the R_S of a given SVC is not an inter-linguistic or even intra-linguistic constant (and being so independently of the specific semantic relation between V1 and V2, as will be shown below), then UG has no means to guarantee the varying R_S to always result in the V1-V2 sequence, making it inevitable to look elsewhere for a solution.

2.3.1   Take It to Vary

Jansen et al. (1978) reported a disparity in native speakers' judgments on Sranan *wh*-movement:

31. a. San   Kofi teki koti a   brede?
       what   Kofi take cut the   bread
       'What did Kofi cut the bread with?'
    b. (*)San   Kofi teki a   nefi   koti?
         what   Kofi take the   knife   cut
         'What did Kofi cut with the knife?'

As these authors noted, the contrast in (31) suggests that V1, *teki* 'take', is the matrix verb and thus allows its complement to be freely extracted. As V2, *koti* 'cut' may be treated either as a structural complement of the matrix verb (also see Lefebvre 1991b) or as an adjunct, resulting in the typical island effect and explaining why some speakers find (31b) unacceptable. This analysis is corroborated by (32):

32. Mi e   koti a   brede nanga a   nefi.
    I ASP cut the bread with the knife
    'I cut the bread with the knife.'

The instrumental PP occurs after the verb and its object, indicating that adverbial adjuncts adjoin to the right of V', conforming to the adjunct analysis for (31b). In sum, a particular word order of the SVC is not equal to a single structure, even within the same language.

The mismatch between word order and structure is confirmed by Chinese. As Y. Li 1991 noted, to the extent that the examples below represent the instrumental SVC (Chao 1968), the extraction pattern is the opposite of that in Sranan, with *t* marking the pre-movement position:

33. a. Taotao   na/yong zheba   dao   qie nakuair   dangao.
       Taotao   take/use this   knife cut that.piece   cake.
       'Taotao cut that piece of cake with this knife.'
    b. nakuair   dangao, Taotao na/yong   zheba dao   qie   t.
       that.piece cake   Taotao take/use   this knife cut
       'That piece of cake, Taotao cut with this knife.'
    c. *zheba dao,   Taotao na/yong t qie nakuair   dangao.
       this   knife   Taotao take/use cut that.piece   cake.
       Intended reading: 'This knife, Taotao cut that piece of cake with.'
    d. na/yong   zheba   dao,   Taotao t qie nakuair   dangao.
       take/use   this   knife   Taotao   cut that.piece cake
       'With this knife, Taotao cut that piece of cake.'

34. a. Taotao cong Nanjing mai-le   guihua   jiang.
         Taotao from Nanjing buy-ASP   osmanthus.flower jam
         'Taotao bought osmanthus flower jam from Nanjing.'
     b. Cong Nanjing, Taotao *t* mai-le   guihua   jiang.
         from Nanjing   Taotao   buy-ASP   osmanthus.flower jam
         'From Nanjing, Taotao bought osmanthus flower jam.'
     c. *Nanjing, Taotao   cong *t* mai-le   guihua   jiang.
         Nanjing   Taotao   from   buy-ASP   osmanthus.flower jam
         Intended reading: 'Nanjing, Taotao bought osmanthus flower jam from.'

The ungrammatical status of (33c) follows from the known fact that Chinese
places most adverbials to the left of the matrix verb (Chao 1968, Li and
Thompson 1981, Y. Li 1990c, A. Li 1990). Opposite to Sranan in this respect,
V2 *qie* 'cut' is the matrix verb and V1 *na* 'take' or *yong* 'use' heads an adjunct
phrase, resulting in the island effect. (33d) indicates that *na/yong* and the DP
after it form an extractable constituent excluding *qie* 'cut' and its object,
indirectly confirming the adjunct analysis of (33c). Note that if *na/yong*, as
V1, were the matrix verb taking VP2 (headed by *qie*) as a complement, as is
found in typical UG-based analyses of SVCs, V1 and the NP immediately after
it would not form an exclusive constituent, contradicting the movability test in
(33d). Furthermore, (33) patterns well with (34) where the preposition *cong*
'from' occurs in the linear position comparable to *take/use*: The entire PP
adjunct can be moved (34b) but the object in this adjunct cannot (34c).

The unacceptability of (33c) also contrasts with the superficially similar
causative construction. In colloquial Chinese, the (b)-examples in (35–36)
are all acceptable, contrasting with the hopelessly bad (33c):

35. a. ni   jingran rang/jiao nizijide   fumu   zhaoji!
         you   even   let/make your.own parents   worry
         'You even let your own parents worry!'
     b. nizijide   fumu   ni   jingran rang/?jiao zhaoji!
         your.own parents   you   even   let/make   worry
         Literally: 'Your own parents, you even let worry!'

36. a. bugai   rang/jiao zhexie zhongxuesheng zuo daxue   de ti.
         shouldn't let/make these   middle.schooler do   college DE problem
         'One shouldn't let these middle school students do college-level problems.'
     b. zhexie zhongxuesheng bugai   rang/jiao zuo daxue   de ti
         these   middle.schooler shouldn't let/make   do   college DE problem
         Literally: 'These middle school students, one shouldn't let do college-level
         problems.'

As the matrix verb, *rang* and *jiao* allow the DP after them, be it the matrix
object (Alsina 1992) or the exceptional case-marked subject, to be extracted,
thus corroborating the conclusion that *take that knife* in (33c) is a preverbal
adjunct and not the matrix verb as in Sranan.

Prosody is known to affect sentence acceptability in Modern Chinese (Feng 2000). Overall, if an example containing some monosyllabic word sounds bad, substituting a disyllabic synonym might fix it. For reasons not yet understood, some Chinese verbs carrying the causal meaning prohibit the DP after them from topicalization and relativization, such as *bi* 'force' and *shi* 'make', but their disyllabic counterparts with the same roots (*bi-po* 'force-force' and *zhishi* 'lead.to-cause') are more forgiving:

37. a. nide shiwu   zhishi nage fang'an buneng shishi.
       your mistake make that plan   cannot materialize
       'Your mistake made that plan unable to materialize.'
    b. ?nage fang'an, nide shiwu   zhishi buneng shishi.
       that plan   your mistake make   cannot materialize
       'That plan, your mistake made unable to materialize.'
    c. (?)nide shiwu   zhishi buneng shishi   de fang'an
         your mistake make   cannot materialize DE plan
       'the plan that your mistake made unable to materialize'

38. a. gongsi   bipo   zhege   jingli   dangzhong daoqian.
       company force   this   manager in.public   apologize
       'The company forced this manager to apologize in public.'
    b. zhege   jingli,   gongsi   bipo   dangzhong daoqian.
       this   manager company force   in.public   apologize
       'This manager, the company forced to apologize in public.'
    c. gongsi   bipo dangzhong daoqian   de nage jingli
       company force in.public   apologize DE that manager
       'the manager who the company forced to apologize in public'

But the disyllabic forms of *na* and *yong* still reject such movements, confirming the conclusion that VP1 is an adjunct to some projection of V2:

39. a. *zheba   dao,   Taotao shiyong/shouna   qie   mianbao.
        this   knife   Taotao use/hand.hold   cut   bread
       Intended reading: 'This knife, Taotao used for cutting bread.'
    b. *Taotao   shiyong/shouna qie   mianbao de naba dao
       Taotao   use/hand.hold cut   bread   DE that knife
       Intended reading: 'the knife that Taotao used for cutting bread'

More support for treating V1 in a Chinese instrumental SVC as heading an adjunct comes from anaphors and epithets that obey Binding Conditions A and C, respectively. The coindexed DPs are italicized to help the reader:

40. a. *wo dasuan rang *Xue Pan*ᵢ xiahu   *zhege wangbadan*ᵢ de
        I   intend let   XP   intimidate this son.of.a.bitch DE
       chouren.
       personal.enemy
       *'I'm planning to let XPᵢ intimidate this SOBᵢ's enemies.'

b. wo dasuan rang *Xue Pan* he *Jia Lian*$_i$ xiahu   *gezi*$_i$ de
   I intend let XP   and JL   intimidate each.self DE
   chouren.
   personal.enemy
   'I'm planning to let XP and JL$_i$ intimidate each one's own$_i$ enemies.'

41. a. (?)wo dasuan na/yong *Xue Pan*$_i$ xiahu   *zhege wangbadan*$_i$
       I   intend take/use XP   intimidate this   son.of.a.bitch
       de   chouren.
       DE   personal.enemy
       'I'm planning to make use of XP$_i$ to intimate this SOB$_i$'s enemies.'
    b. *wo dasuan na/yong *Xue Plan* he   *Jian Lian*$_i$ xiahu   *gezi*$_i$
       I   intend take/use XP   and JL   intimidate each.self
       de   chouren.
       DE   personal.enemies
       Intended: 'I'm planning to make use of XP and JL$_i$ to intimate each one's own$_i$
       personal enemy.'

As a coindexed r-expression, the epithet *zhege wangbadan* 'this SOB'
cannot be bound by the DP after the matrix causative verb *rang* 'let' in
(40a) because it is c-commanded by the DP. But it is easier for this
epithet to take the DP after *na/yong* 'take/use' as antecedent in (41a),
suggesting that VP1 in the instrumental SVC is an adjunct to some
projection of V2 *xia* 'intimidate' so that the object of V1, *XP* in (41a),
does not command the epithet, as dictated by Binding Condition
C. Similarly, the anaphor *gezi* 'each self' is properly bound in the
causative (40b) but not in the instrumental (41b). Again, V1 *na/yong*
must not be the matrix verb – or the object of V1 would be a qualified
c-commander and thereby invert the grammaticality judgments of the
pair in (41).

Next consider a complication with the instrumental SVC in Chinese.
Huang (1982) associates the presence of aspectual markers with finite
clauses. Whether this is generally correct or not, it is still plausible that
when more than one verb is present, the aspectually marked one heads the
main predicate, which would explain (42):

42. zheba dao, Taotao na-zhe *t* qie nakuair   dangao.
    this knife Taotao take-ASP cut that.piece cake
    'This knife, Taotao took *t* to cut that piece of cake.'

The imperfective *-zhe* turns *na* 'take, hold' into the main verb, which in turn
enables the topicalization of its own object *zheba dao* 'this knife'. This result
contrasts with the unacceptable (33c) that differs from (42) only in not having
-zhe suffixed to *na*. It seems, then, that Chinese processes SVCs as follows:

Given the mono-clausal nature of these constructions, V2 is the main verb and V1 heads a left-adjoined adjunct (= (33)), the setup that complies with the language-specific grammar of Chinese. The structure is reanalyzed only when V1 is overtly marked as the main verb, as in (42). Regardless of technical details, though, (33c) and (42) further confirm the conclusion so far: There does not exist a single syntactic structure for all SVCs, even for the same semantic type (e.g. instrumental) in the same language.

The structural variations of V1 in Chinese receive further support from the long and short passives in the language. Feng (1995) was the first to prove that the long passive, with the semantic subject S_{sem} of the passivized verb present, actually results from moving an empty operator comparable to *tough*-movement in English, which explains why, among other things, the semantic object of an embedded clause can be "long-distance passivized" to become the syntactic subject of the entire passive sentence. Subsequently, Ting (1995) presented evidence that the short passive, without S_{sem}, is formed with the same NP-movement as in English passives and thus is a strictly local operation. See Chen and Li (2021) for a recent rendition of these two passive forms.

Combining the long and short passives with the instrumental SVC gives an interesting pattern:

43. a. nakuai   dangao bei (Taotao) na   zheba dao   qie-guo.
       that.piece cake   BEI Taotao   take this   knife cut-ASP
       'This piece of cake was cut on (by Taotao).'
    b. nakuai   dangao bei *(Taotao) na-zhe   zheba dao   qie-guo.
       that.piece cake   BEI Taotao   take-ASP this   knife cut-ASP
       Literally: 'This piece of cake had *(Taotao/someone) use this knife to cut.'

Bei is the passivizing morpheme in Mandarin Chinese. In (43a), V1 is bare and thus heads the left-adjoined VP1. Since V2 is the main verb, both long and short passives are possible, as indicated by the optional presence of S_{sem} *Taotao*. V1 is suffixed with the aspectual *-zhe* in (43b) and, given the analysis earlier, is the main verb. The fact that long passivization (with *Taotao* present) remains acceptable indicates that VP2 is, or at least can be, positioned in the complement position of V1. This is sufficient to avoid any island effect for operator movement (recall Sranan (31b)). As already mentioned, long-distance passivization is independently permitted in this context. When *Taotao* is not around, however, (43b) is a short passive with NP-movement. It no longer matters whether VP2 is treated as a postverbal complement or not, V1 is the main verb and the only candidate affected by "normal" passivization, resulting in complete unacceptability.

To summarize the cross-linguistic facts on the instrumental SVC, Sranan has V1 serve as the matrix verb while VP2 is taken as either a complement or an adjunct; on the other hand, in Chinese, V2 is the matrix verb by default with VP1 being an adjunct, though a structural reanalysis takes place when forced by the aspect marker on V1. Interestingly, such variations make sense because, whereas Sranan is a strictly head-initial language where both adjuncts and complements occur postverbally, Chinese adjuncts generally occur to the left of the modified head (cf. Huang et al. 2009). In other words, iconicity is responsible for linearizing the two verbal projections, but the actual structural relation between them is left to the parametric settings of UG in the given language.

This conclusion has implications. First, it reveals that iconicity as a linearization algorithm in human languages is blind to the structural hierarchy characteristic of UG. While UG organizes all constituents into hierarchical structures through such notions as head, complement, adjunct, etc., linear iconicity only operates on the temporal relation between the events being described. This point, as will be shown later in the chapter, is the key in understanding the various traits of the SVC. Secondly, the cross-linguistic facts from Sranan and Chinese argue against any attempt at a structurally uniform theory of the SVC. As desirable as such efforts may appear by some meta-theoretical standard, the actual data indicate otherwise. In fact, if there were any universal design for the structure of the SVC, it would be a mystery why Sranan did not have *cut the bread take the knife*, which would maximally synchronize it with Chinese by placing the instrumental VP consistently in an adjunct position in both languages!

2.3.2 An Unwitting Argument against the Uniform Analysis of the SVCs

Even some explicit efforts toward a uniform structural analysis of SVCs end up providing arguments against or weakening it once we look into them. We have already recounted in section 2.2.2 Carstens' (2002) theory which assigns a uniform CApp structure to head-initial and head-final languages alike. As a matter of fact, her theory can truly derive the word order of the instrumental SVC, a plus not mentioned in her work. The discussion at this point is in reference to Carstens' structure introduced in (29) above, represented below in the bracket format and with Greek letters marking each argument position "__":

44. $[_{vP1}\ \_\_\ v\ [_{VP1}\ \_\_\ V1\ [_{vP2}\ \_\_\ v\ [_{VP2}\ \_\_\ V2\ \_\_]]]]$
       $\ \ \ \ \ \alpha \ \ \ \ \ \ \ \ \ \beta \ \ \ \ \ \ \ \ \gamma \ \ \ \ \ \ \ \delta \ \ \ \ \ \epsilon$

With two vP–VP suites as projections of V1 and V2 respectively, each suite provides three argument positions: the Spec of vP, the Spec of VP and the complement of V. If *take* is V1, its own two DP arguments are placed in the two Spec positions α and β in the vP1-VP1 suite, leaving the complement position to host vP2 in which V2 is *cut*. Under the object-sharing hypothesis which she (as well as Baker and several other authors, but see Aboh 2009 for a different view) adopts, *cut* has three arguments, agent, instrument and theme, which fill all the three argument positions in this suite, namely γ, δ, ε. Now let us swap the two verbs and make *cut* = V1 and *take* = V2. Then all the three argument positions inside the higher vP1-VP1 suite would be occupied by the three arguments of *cut* so that there would be no structural spot to accommodate the lower vP2-VP2 suite containing *take*. Hence, *take* … *cut* … is the only legitimate string in the strictly head-initial structure for the instrumental SVCs of Yoruba and Ijo.

Next consider the Chinese consecutive SVC using the ditransitive *gei* 'give' as V1:[14]

45. wo   ganggang   gei-le   Jia Lian yikuair yuebing   chi.
    I   a.moment.ago give-ASP JL   a.piece moon.cake   eat
    'I just gave JL a piece of moon cake to eat.'

That both internal arguments of *gei* 'give' are shared with *chi* 'eat' is in itself an interesting fact to investigate later. More pertinent to the current concern is that V1 has three DP arguments of its own: *wo* 'I', *JL* and *yikuair yuebing* 'a piece of moon cake', thereby leaving no argument position for the vP–VP suite of V2 *eat*. What helps Carstens to prohibit the wrongly ordered SVC *cut* … *take* is to place vP2 in the complement position of V1. But now the same logic dictates two options. Either (45) is wrongly ruled out (because the complement position of *give* is already filled by *a piece of cake* and thus unable to house the *eat*-headed vP2 at all), or this vP2 must be placed in some structural position *other than* the complement of V1. In other words, Carstens' uniform CApp structure of SVCs either fails to extend to Chinese or must depart from its initial goal and allow a different configuration between V1 and V2 from the uniform structure.

In this context, we would also like to point out another weakness in Carstens' attempt at a uniform account of cross-linguistic SVCs. As support for the same underlying structure in both the head-initial Yoruba and the head-final Ijo, Carstens demonstrated that O1, the object of V1, c-commands everything inside vP2 in both languages (see her sections 3.5 and 3.6). The specific arguments include O1 binding O2 and O1 controlling or raised from the Spec of vP2. Although the data from Yoruba establish the point rather convincingly, thereby placing Yoruba in line with one dialect of Sranan in treating (at least some cases of) V1 as the matrix verb and V2 as heading V1's complement, the empirical evidence from Ijo is not as robust as it is believed to be. Consider the only two Ijo examples (her (55) and (56a)) provided by Carstens as clear evidence:

46. a. Ari *keni tobou keni tobou* aki-ni   *wo* yengli piri-mi.
       I   one   child one   child take-PRT his mother give-PAST
       'I gave each child$_i$ to his$_i$ mother.'
    b. Ari wo fun-bi   aki geeboogeeboo piri-mi.
       I   his book-the take author.author give- PAST
       *'I gave his$_i$ book to each author$_i$.'

(46a) has the pronoun *wo* 'his' interpreted as a bound variable, which is taken to signal c-command of *wo* by the quantifier *keni tobou keni tobou* 'each child'. No such coreference is possible in (46b) because *geeboogeeboo* 'each author' as the object of V2 doesn't c-command the pronoun inside the object of V1.

It should be noted first that (46b) is not really informative where Carstens' analysis is concerned. If V1 *aki* 'take' is the matrix verb c-commanding V2 *piri* 'give', as Carstens assumes the structure to be, then raising *each author* (i.e. the object of V2) across *his* inside the object of V1 would not help rescue the sentence as that would result in weak crossover. But suppose that V1 heads VP1 (or *v*P1) which in turn left-adjoins to some projection of V2 (note that left adjunction is permitted by Kayne's antisymmetric syntax adopted by Carstens). Then *his* is inside VP1 and raising *each author* across it still results in weak crossover. Perhaps aware of this fact, Carstens considers it only "partial success" (p. 16) to obtain no more than (46b) for testing her uniform structure. Strictly speaking, though, it is not partial success but simply irrelevant data.

The theoretical force of (46a) hinges on there being S-structure c-command from the quantifier to the bound variable, but this widely accepted assumption deserves more careful scrutiny, a point independently made by Progovac (1998) on which I will elaborate in Chapter 3. In fact, cross-linguistic evidence can be found that S-structure c-command does *not* seem to be required for the bound-variable reading of a pronoun. Consider the English examples in (47) and the Chinese ones in (48–51):[15]

47. a. Every candidate$_i$ bragged about his$_i$ accomplishments.
    b. From every candidate$_i$, we heard about his$_i$ accomplishments.

48. (?)meige xin xuesheng$_i$ dou jiandao-le tade$_i$ laoshi.
       every new student   all meet-asp 3s.POSS teacher
       'Every new student met his/her teacher.'

49. a. (?)wo ba meige xin xuesheng$_i$ dou jieshao-gei-le   tade$_i$ laoshi.
           I BA every new student   all introduce-to-ASP 3s.POSS teacher
       'I introduced every new student to his/her teacher.'

    b. (?)ba meige xin   xuesheng$_i$ wo dou jieshao-gei-le   tade$_i$ laoshi.
       BA every new   student   I   all introduce-to-ASP 3s.POSS teacher
       'Everything new student, I introduced to his/her teacher.'

50. a. (?)women cong meiwei houxuanren$_i$ nali   dou tingdao-le ta$_i$ dui
      we   from every   candidate   there   all hear-ASP   3s   to
      gongzhong   de xunuo.
      the.public DE promise
      'We heard from every candidate his/her promises to the public.'

    b. (?)cong meiwei houxuanren$_i$ nali,   women dou   tingdao-le ta$_i$
       from   every   candidate   there   we   all   hear-ASP   3s
      dui   gongzhong de   xunuo
      to   the.public DE   promise
      'From every candidate, we heard his/her promises to the public.'

51. a. (?)wo na/yong meiwei yishujia$_i$ de shengping   shuoming-le
      I   take/use every   artist   DE life.trajectory illustrate-ASP
      tade$_i$ chuangzuo linggan.
      3s.POSS creativity   inspiration
      'I, using every artist's trajectory of life, explicated his/her inspiration for creativity.'

    b. (?)na/yong meiwei yishujia$_i$ de shengping,   wo shuoming-le
      take/use every   artist   DE life.trajectory I   illustrate-ASP
      tade$_i$ chuangzuo   linggan.
      3s.POSS creativity   inspiration
      'Using every artist's trajectory of life, I explicated his inspiration for creativity.'

(47b) is easily accepted by native speakers of English, even though the QP *every candidate* is the object of *from* and thus does not c-command the coindexed third-person pronoun. Chinese generally disfavors pronoun binding, even when it's simply the subject binding into the object in (48). Given this fact, having a QP introduced by *ba* 'hold' or *cong* 'from' does not prevent this QP from coindexing with a postverbal pronoun, shown in (49a) and (50a). The examples in (49b) and (50b) have [*ba* QP] and [*from* QP] moved to the clause-initial position, making sure that each cluster is indeed a phrasal constituent properly containing the QP.[16] Still, no detectable deterioration results between each (a-b) pair. In all these examples, QP is too deeply embedded to c-command the pronoun. The last pair, (51a–b), uses the familiar instrumental verb *na/yong* 'take/use' to introduce a QP. Pragmatics, plus the fact that Chinese pronouns must be animate, prevents constructing straightforward tests, resulting in embedding the QP even more deeply inside the object NP of *na/yong* 'take/use'. The intended readings are still available, further weakening the connection between QP-bound pronouns and straightforward c-command.

All the examples in (47–51) can be accounted for with the plausible assumption that a QP may first undergo a local raising at LF so as to be at the edge of the PP or

VP that immediately contains it. From there, utilizing the distinction between a segment and full node (cf. Chomsky 1986), QP may indeed c-command the pronoun inside the object of the matrix verb (cf. note 87 of Chapter 4). But this solution, or any solution compliant with (47–51) for that matter, effectively refutes Carstens' conclusion from (46a): As long as QP does not need to c-command the pronoun prior to quantifier raising at LF, QP-bound pronouns do not serve as an argument for the structure in (29). Whatever is the reason for the examples in (47–51) also endorses an adjunct analysis of VP1 in (46a–b). Specifically, since both verbs in an instrumental SVC share the same external argument, and since there is evidence that the external argument is thematically related with v rather than V (Marantz 1984, Larson 1988, Hale and Keyser 1993, Chomsky 1995, Kratzer 1996, Chen and Li 2021), the plausible hypothesis is that subject-sharing SVCs have only one vP, namely that of the matrix verb (see section 2.5 below for a detailed discussion of this idea). It follows that the adjunct VP, headed by *take* in (46a), has no vP of its own. In effect, then, such a VP is structurally identical to the PPs in (47b, 50a–b) and is expected to exhibit the same behavior with respect to variable binding, as is paralleled in the Chinese instrumental SVC in (51). Also worth noting is that treating VP1 as an adjunct happens to echo the preverbal PP adjunct we suggested for the path-of-motion example (18). In both cases, it is the (second) verb that is likely to head the matrix predicate. Note again that this verb also carries the tense suffix in the head-final Ijo.

Overall, there may be language-specific evidence for a particular type of SVC to have V1 taking some projection of V2 as complement, but efforts to generalize it are not well grounded, some with misanalyzed data and others even amounting to arguing in the opposite direction.

2.3.3   Cleft or No Cleft? That Is the Question

Hiraiwa and Bodomo (2008) (H&B) study the predicate cleft construction (PCC) in the SVCs of Dagaare, of the Gur family, in comparison with related languages. (52) shows the basic Dagaare facts (H&B (26–27)):

52. a. o   da   sɛ   la   nɛne   ɔɔ.
       3s PAST roast FOC meat   eat
       'He roasted meat and eat it.'

    b. (nɛne) seɛo   la   ka o   sɛ   (nɛne) ɔɔ.
       meat   roast.NML FOC C   3s roast meat   eat
       'It is roasting that he did and ate meat.' or
       'It is roasting meat that he did and ate.'

    c. (nɛne) ɔɔo   la   ka o   sɛ   (nɛne) ɔɔ.
       meat   eat.NML   FOC C   3s roast meat   eat
       'It is eating that he roasted and did to meat.' or
       'It is eating meat that he roasted and did.'

d. (nɛnɛ) se-ɔɔo   la ka o da sɛ   (nɛnɛ) ɔɔ.
   meat   roast-eat.NML FOC C 3s PAST roast   meat   eat
   'It is roasting and eating that he did to meat.' or
   'It is roasting and eating meat that he did.'

In essence, either V1 or V2 or both can be cleft in the SVC, each with the option of pied-piping the shared object *meat*. Because the PCC may cross a long distance and is sensitive to islands (p. 804), H&B conclude that the construction is derived from the focus-movement of a predicative phrase which we refer to as VP to avoid irrelevant details. The pied-piped object occurs left of the fronted V due to the latter also getting nominalized, with Dagaare nominal phrases being head-final. The object appears optionally pied-piped because one can choose to pronounce the NP in either the original copy of VP or the moved one.

Of significance to the current work is that the cleft pattern varies among the related languages in what appears to be a rather intricate manner, shown in the following chart (H&B (40)), with "*" meaning "not allowed":

53. Cross-linguistic variations of PCCs and SVCs

	Buli	Yoruba	Edo	Nupe	Fɔngbe	Dagaare
V1	Ok	Ok	Ok	Ok	Ok	Ok
O+V1	Ok	Ok	*	*	*	Ok
V2	*	*	Ok	*	Ok	Ok
O+V2	*	*	*	*	*	Ok
V1+V2	Ok	Ok	*	(*)	*	Ok

A further note is added about the simultaneous fronting of V1 and V2 in (53): Nupe is given an optional "*" for this case. H&B refer to Kandybowicz (2006) as saying that "only the initial verb of a serial verb construction can be clefted" (p. 811) in the language and then add in their note 8 that according to personal communication with the same author, V1+V2 "is rather marked" and limited to "certain resultative SVCs." As resultatives may act differently from other SVCs in other languages too (to which we return in 2.5), we take Nupe to simply have "*" for V1+V2.

With all six languages allowing V1 fronting, the obvious analysis is that V1 at least always has the option of serving as the matrix verb (as is indeed how H&B analyzed Dagaare). No explanation is given in their paper for why the other languages in (53) behave differently, but it is reasonable to suspect that the multiple variations are at least partially due to these languages not sharing the same syntactic structure for their SVCs. The rest of this section explores one such analysis by bringing in more data from Kwa languages.

First of all, primarily due to the facts in (52), H&B argue that Dagaare SVCs have the multi-dominance parallel structure in (54), their (68–69):

54.

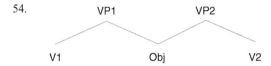

If the shared object is dominated by both VP1 and VP2, either VP can be focus-moved with its own verb and the shared object. We take this to be a possible solution to (52b, c), but will explore an alternative analysis for two intertwined reasons: (i) the multi-dominance structure will be a much better fit for coordination, to be extensively argued for in Chapter 3 of this book, and (ii) data from languages related to Dagaare call for a structural distinction between coordination and SVCs. For now, we assume (i) but look into (ii) in detail.

The two sets of Gungbe examples below are provided by Aboh (2009):

55. a. Sɛsinu na   kun   moto ce   sɔ   ado!
       Senisou FUT drive   car my   hit   wall
       'Sesinou will drive my car and hit the wall!'
    b. Ete   wɛ   Sɛsinu na   kun sɔ   ado?
       what   FOC Sesinou FUT   drive hit wall
       Literally: 'What will Sesinou drive and hit the wall?'
    c. Ete   wɛ   Sɛsinu na   kun moto ce   sɔ?
       what   FOC Sesinou FUT   drive car my   hit
       Literally: 'What will Sesinou drive my car and hit?'

56. a. Sɛsinu da   lɛsi bɔ Suru du nusɔnu.
       Sesinou cook rice and Suru eat soup
       'Sesinou cooked rice and Suru ate soup.'
    b. *Ete wɛ   Sɛsinu da   bɔ   Suru du nusɔnu?
       what FOC Sesinou cook and Suru eat soup
       *'What did Sesinou cook and Suru ate soup?'
    c. *Ete wɛ   Sɛsinu da   lɛsi bɔ Suru du?
       what FOC Sesinou cook rice and Suru eat
       *'What did Sesinou cook rice and Suru eat?'

The SVC in (55) permits the object of either V1 or V2 to do *wh*-movement, in contrast to the coordination structure in (56), where no movement out of either conjunct is grammatical. Also keep in mind that the Gungbe SVC in (55) is consistent with Fɔngbe and Edo SVCs in (53). In all these languages, movement out of either VP1 or VP2 is equally good whether the moved element is V or the *wh*-object.

Viewing this generalization in the context of Chinese and Sranan in 2.3.1, let us hypothesize that some SVC languages resemble Chinese and Sranan in allowing the structural relation between V1 and V2 to vary provided that any variation complies with the given language-specific grammar so that either V1 or V2 could (conditionally) serve as the main verb. Given this language-internal structural adjustment, it follows from UG that either VP can become transparent to movement and thus is subject in itself to predicate cleft, the operation that presumably targets the main predicate of a clause.

The chart in (53) also reveals another split among the languages, observed as a correlation by H&B (p. 812): "those languages that allow pied-piping [of the object] also allow predicate clefting of entire serial verbs," meaning the V1+V2 option. According to this correlation, the six languages in (53) divide into two groups. One group, consisting of Buli, Yoruba and Dagaare, allows both object pied-piping and V1+V2 fronting. A verb plus its DP object is VP. Assuming Niger-Congo SVCs to be syntactic in nature, placing V1+V2 at the beginning of the clause is most plausibly treated as fronting an inclusive VP containing both verbs. In sum, this group sports VP-movement, as H&B proposed. The second group has Edo, Nupe and Fɔngbe and represents the other end of the correlation, rejecting object pied-piping as well as V1+V2 fronting. Since there is no evidence that phrasal movement is involved here, these languages are plausibly taken to put focus on V only, via head-movement of V (Koopman 1984, Y. Li 1990a). In sum, the Niger-Congo languages that support predicate cleft all implement the focus-fronting of V but parameterize in whether to allow VP-fronting.

Together, these two parameters classify the Niger-Congo languages under investigation into four types:

57.

Structural adjustment	+	+	−	−
VP cleft (and V cleft)	+	−	+	−
	Dagaare	Edo Fɔngbe Gungbe	Buli Yoruba	Nupe

Those that permit either V1 or V2 to be treated as the main verb have "+" for structural adjustment and thereby sanction movement out of VP1 or VP2 alike. This group includes Dagaare, Edo, Fɔngbe and Gungbe. The group is further divided in accordance with VP and V cleft or V cleft only. Dagaare allows both operations for predicate focus, resulting in all the possibilities in (53), (O+)V1, (O +)V2 and (O+)V1+V2, with the last option due to the matrix VP containing the other VP. On the other hand, the languages in the second column of (57) choose to front V only. Since either VP can be the main predicate, either V1 or V2 can move up. It is also predicted that the object of either VP can move out, giving rise to the Gungbe examples in (56). Assuming as H&B do that predicate-fronting aims at a single position, it is also anticipated, correctly, that the clause-initial head position for V-fronting can be filled by V1 or V2 but not by both simultaneously.

The rest of the languages, namely Buli, Yoruba and Nupe, must have V1 as the main verb, meaning only VP1 is qualified for entertaining the types of movement in predicate cleft. Buli and Yoruba pick VP-fronting so as to have O+V1 in (53). Nupe moves V only and thus ends up being the most restricted.

In sum, the apparently messy variations in (53) might be attributed to two parametric factors in the Niger-Congo family: focus-fronting VP or V and limiting the main verb to V1 or not. Critically, the second factor provides another support for the central theme of this section: SVCs do *not* necessarily share identical syntactic structures despite the constant iconic order between the verbs. In fact, it is precisely such structural disparities that lend us ways to explain why the SVCs are similar and dissimilar among different languages.

2.3.4   A Compound Support

Structural variations within the confines of linear iconicity are not only observed among syntactic SVCs, they are also found inside serial verb compounds. This section develops what is initially investigated in Y. Li (1993), starting with the following contrast:

58. Jia da-si-le   Yi. (Chinese)
     X   beat-die-ASP Y
     'X beat Y and as a result Y died.'

59. a. *X-ga   Y-o   naguri-shinu-ta.   (Japanese)
         X-NOM   Y-ACC   hit-die-PAST
         Intended reading: Comparable to (58).
     b. X-ga   Y-o   naguri-korosu-ta.
         X-NOM   Y-ACC   hit-kill-PAST
         'X hit Y and as a result killed Y.'

While Chinese allows V2 to be unaccusative (i.e. *si* 'die'), Japanese must use the transitive counterpart (*korosu* 'kill') instead. Furthermore, resultative compounds exhibit semantic ambiguities in Chinese, as reported and analyzed in Y. Li (1990c), that are not found in Japanese. Korean patterns exactly like the latter (cf. (11a)).

This contrast between the two languages correlates with the different locations of the morphological head. Chinese verbal compounds such as *da-si* 'beat-die' are head-initial whereas the Japanese (and Korean) counterparts are head-final. Abstracting away from technical details, Y. Li's (1993) account of (58–59) makes use of the idea that the head of a compound W determines certain key properties of W (Di Sciullo and Williams 1987), including its basic thematic traits. Specifically, the agent argument of W must be inherited from that of W's head. In Chinese, it is V1 *da* 'hit' that heads the compound. As long as the subject *Jia* is interpreted as the hitter, the object *Yi* may receive the single θ-role of V2 *si* 'die'. In Japanese, the compound is headed by V2. To guarantee the subject of the sentence, *X-ga*, to be also the thematic subject of this verb, the latter must be in the causative transitive form so as to yield the intended reading that X caused Y to die by hitting Y, which in effect forces the use of the transitive verb *korosu* 'kill'. See Li's original work for details.

Remarkably, Japanese and Korean do not have the option of reversing the linear order of the two verbal morphemes in the compound so as to have *die-hit*, a mirror image of *hit-die* in Chinese. This is especially intriguing because for conjunctive verbal compounds where the two morphemes hold an 'and/or' relation, linear reversion is indeed observed:

60. Chinese
    lai-wang 'come-go', *mai-mai* 'buy-sell' → 'business',[17] *jin-chu* 'enter-go.out', ...

61. Japanese (from Y. Li 1993: 489)
    yuki-ki 'go-come', *uri-kai* 'sell-buy', *de-iri* 'go.out-go.in', ...

If UG were the deciding factor for the linear order of the verbal morphemes in the resultative compound, one would wonder why Japanese maintains the same morpheme order as Chinese only in resultative compounds, especially when this must be accomplished at the cost of an extra requirement on the thematic property of V2. Note that under UG, *die-hit* would be well formed in the head-final structure of Japanese and Korean, with *hit* being the head and determining the thematic subject of the compound as it does in Chinese in the initial position. The mystery disappears if the linear order inside a resultative compound is decided by linear iconicity, with cause perceived before effect. Meanwhile, the examples in (60–61) encode relations that have no intrinsic temporal order, leaving it to other factors in a language to determine the linearization of the morphemes.

In conclusion, the linear order of a resultative compound W must obey iconicity cross-linguistically, but the morphological structure of W varies according to the grammar of the given language. In the head-initial Chinese, V1 is the head and V2 is given leeway in its argument structure and how its θ-roles are associated with the arguments of W. Japanese is a rigidly head-final language, making V2 the morphological head. This "weight shift" in word structure places a strict limitation on the thematic options of V2. Just like SVCs in syntax, UG displays parametric variations at the structural level as long as iconicity determines the linear order of the verbal morphemes.

2.3.5   In Sum ...

The proof that linear iconicity in the SVC is both a fact and independent of UG consists of three parts:

(A) What have been regarded as counterexamples to linear iconicity in the UG literature are based on misunderstanding the relevant facts and hurried conclusions (section 2.1).

(B) The few efforts to derive (part of) linear iconicity from some formulation of UG or other general rules have not succeeded, primarily for the fundamental reason that UG is incapable of distinguishing V1 and V2 when both of them are simple transitive verbs. This is no surprise because the core UG operations are based on asymmetry while two verbs with identical argument structures are "symmetric" with respect to one another (section 2.2).

(C) There is cross-linguistic evidence that even the same type of SVC exhibits different syntactic and/or morphological behaviors from language to language. These differences are seen to comply with language-specific grammars while the iconic word order is the only constant element (section 2.3).

Note that the structural disparity in SVCs does not exclude the possibility that in some cases, V1 takes a projection of V2 as its complement. For instance, V1 in a language may have acquired the status of a light verb with VP2 being one of its complements (see Aboh 2009 for argumentation of this kind in a subset of Kwa languages). But whether this is a shared design for all SVC instances is an empirical matter to be resolved only through willingness to let the theory of SVCs be driven by facts and not by any *a priori* belief about what the human language faculty ought to be.

2.4   Linear Iconicity and Its Company

Establishing linear iconicity as a linguistic fact is the first as well as a critical step toward understanding the phenomenon. At least for SVCs, however, merely recognizing the role of iconicity is far from being sufficient for understanding how this role is played out. Specifically, there is an additional cluster of grammatical traits T associated with SVCs and thus with linear iconicity. While most of T are mentioned in the literature (e.g. Aikhenvald 2006), no attempt is known to cover them with a uniform analysis. But until and unless an explanation is formulated for the co-occurrence of T, our understanding of how linear iconicity interacts with the rest of the human language faculty is at best superficial, not to mention that some of T apparently have circumvented due attention and therefore are underneath various misled criticisms of iconicity. These traits of SVCs are listed below:

62. a. mono-clausal
     b. verbs only

c. no θ-relation between verbs
d. no lexical linkers to connect verbs
e. argument-sharing
f. linearly iconic between verbs
g. varying structural relations between verbs.

Of these, (62f–g) are already established in the foregoing sections. The mono-clausal nature of SVCs in (62a) is evidenced by these examples from Aikhenvald (2006, with (63b–c) quoted from Van Leynseele 1975):

63. a. Nhuta   nu-thaketa-ka   di-ka-pidana. (Tariana)
       1s+take 1s-cross+caus-SUBORD   3s-see-PAST
       'He saw that I took it across.'
    b. cua nji   akɔ   n-ni.   (Anyi-Sanvi)
       dog NEG+catch+HAB   chicken NEG+eat+HAB
       'The dog never catch and eat a chicken.'
    c. cua ci   akɔ   oŋgu   i.
       dog catch+HAB   chicken 3s+NEG+kill+HAB   it
       'The dog catches a chicken and does not kill it.'

There is only one embedded object clause in (63a), marked by the subordinate marker -ka, which contains the SVC *nhuta nu-thaketa* 'take cross'. (As a side note, the head-final VP structure in the Tariana example, like its Japanese and Korean counterparts in 2.3.4 above, correlates with V2 not being an unaccusative verbal root meaning 'cross' but instead a causativized transitive.) (63b) is another SVC. Though negation is "spread" on both verbs, the sentence does not yield a doubly negated interpretation, indicating the standard UG structure of one Neg per clause. In comparison, (63c) is a case of coordination, shown by the second verb *kill* having its own object *i* 'it (to which we return in the section on argument-sharing), and clausal negation operates only on the verb it is physically associated with.

The consecutive SVC in Chinese provides a different type of argument for the mono-clausal nature of the construction:

64. a. ta   mai-le   yijia   zhishengji kai.
       3s   buy-ASP   a   helicopter drive
       'S/He bought a helicopter to fly with.'
    b. yijia zhishengji (*kai) shi   ta-de   bisheng   mengxiang.
       a   helicopter drive be   3s-DE   life-long   dream
       'A helicopter (to fly with) is his/her life-long dream.'

In (64a), V2 (= *kai* 'drive') shares the object *yijia zhishengji* 'a helicopter' with V1 *mai* 'buy' at least on the surface, leaving V2 with a gap in its standard postverbal object position. A comparison of (64a–b) proves this gap to rely on the "serial verb" context to occur, effectively eliminating the possibility that

(64a) has a postnominal clause of some sort structurally comparable to the non-finite clause in the English translation. In fact, there is no independently justifiable analysis of an object-gapped V2 in (64a) in Chinese grammar other than treating it as part of an SVC with the characteristic property of object-sharing listed in (62e). But as shown above, SVCs are mono-clausal in languages where direct proof is available.

The mono-clausal nature of SVCs turns out to be at the core of all other traits in (62). But let us elucidate (62b, c, d, e) first.

2.4.1 A Serial Verb Construction Must Involve ... Only Verbs

The title of this subsection may seem tautological, but overlooking it is the reason for some instances of confusion which in turn interfere with the recognition of linear iconicity in SVCs. Consider Tai's (1985: 50) iconic Temporal Sequence Condition (TSC), quoted in (65):

65.   The relative word order between two syntactic units is determined by the temporal order of the states which they represent in the conceptual world.

The TSC can be easily countered with these Sranan examples:

66. a. Mi e   teki a   nefi   koti   a   brede. (Same as (1))
       I   ASP take the knife cut   the bread
       'I cut the bread with the knife.'
    b. Mi e   koti a   brede nanga a   nefi. (Same as (32))
       I   ASP cut   the bread with   the knife
       'I cut the bread with the knife.'

(66a) is an SVC, with the instrumental VP *take the knife* occurring prior to *cut the bread*, in full compliance with linear iconicity given that holding a knife in hand necessarily precedes cutting bread with it. But "in our conceptual world," the instrumental PP in (66b) expresses the same scenario/state of using the knife in hand in some action, though it is post-*cut* and thus contra linear iconicity.

The TSC is primarily based on Chinese, but even Chinese is well known to be problematic for it:

67. a. najia feiji   zai jichang jiangluo-le.
       that airplane LOC airport land-ASP
       'That airplane landed at the airport.'
    b. najia feiji   jiangluo-zai jichang le.
       that airplane land-LOC   airport LE
       Same as (67a).

Putting aside the use of the string-final morpheme(s) *le* which is unrelated to the point at hand, these two sentences can describe exactly the same event even though the locative morpheme *zai* may occur on either side of the verb *jiangluo* 'land'. According to the TSC, (67b) is expected because landing necessarily precedes the airplane being physically located in the airport. It follows that (67a) is counter-iconic since the sentence certainly does not express the impossible scenario of the airplane being in the airport already before its landing (barring a horrible crash).

In both Sranan and Chinese, the culprit is for the TSC to be categorially indiscriminative. Merely linking concepts iconically to linear order while completely bypassing the structure- and category-sensitive part of grammar, namely mapping R_C to R_L by skipping R_S as defined in (3) of Chapter 1, may look simple and general but it is obviously not how language actually operates. Specifically, linear iconicity, when at work in the SVC, appears to hold only between verbs. This conclusion is upfront in Sranan and fully consistent with the grammar of Modern Chinese, where PPs and adjunct phrases headed by morphemes of the verbal origin but with bleached/altered semantic content must occur preverbally (recall the benefactive–goal ambiguity of the preverbal use of *gei* which in itself means 'give', discussed in 2.1.4 on the purposive SVC). An example will be given shortly. As a result, no matter what category the postverbal *zai* has in (67b), it is entirely plausible to treat the one before *land* as a preposition. As in the case of Sranan, a PP is exempt from linear iconicity.

The conclusion that the mono-clausal expression of multiple conceptual states – to use Tai's terminology for the moment – exhibits linear iconicity only when all individually expressed states are lexically realized with verbs, can be further substantiated with cross-linguistic facts. Consider Korean first, with all the examples from Song (2005):

68. a. Chelswu-ka   Swuni-lul   ttayli-e ewuk-i-ess-ta. (same as (11a))
        Chelswu-NOM Swuni-ACC   hit-SUF kill-PAST-DECL
        'Chelswu hit Swuni and killed her.'
    b. Chelswu-ka   thakca-lul   kkaykkusha-key ttak-ass-ta.
        Chelswu-NOM table-ACC   clean-SUF   wipe-PAST-DECL
        'Chelswu wiped the table clean.'
    c. Chelswu-ka   mok-i   swi-key   oychi-ess-ta.
        Chelswu-NOM throat-NOM hoarse-SUF shout-PAST-DECL
        'Chelswu shouted his throat hoarse.'

(68a) is an instance of the resultative SVC, with the two verbs aligned iconically. (68b–c) illustrate another construction with the resultative interpretation, which consists of an adjective preceding the verb it modifies, contra iconicity but expected from Korean having a head-final VP. The same logic applies to the resultative in German, which displays the opposite order to its counterpart in English (with (a–b) from Kratzer 2004 and (c) from Y. Li 1993):

69. a. Sie   haben ihn   tot   geschossen
       they have   him   dead   shot
       'They shot him dead.'
    b. Sie   habe   ihn   er-schossen
       they have   him   dead-shot
       'They shot him dead.'
    c. Er   will   das   Eisen   flashschlagen.
       he   wants the   iron   flat.pound
       'He wants to pound the iron flat.'

The adjectives expressing the result occur before the verbs *shot* and *pound*.
Being non-verbal, they respect the head-final order of the German VP and
contrast with the head-initial VP structure seen from the English translations.
Still another case is the Ijo *duo* 'across' examined in 2.1.5. Williamson (1965)
was quoted as noting that this morpheme no longer acts like a normal verb,
which we took to mean that it is likely to have become a postposition heading
a PP. As such, its preverbal location is expected of a head-final language such as
Ijo and no longer bears on linear iconicity. In contrast, *guo* 'cross' in Chinese is
a verb and linearizes iconically. See (18–20) earlier.

To complete the proof for the all-verbs requirement of linear iconicity in
SVCs, the opposite side of the situation deserves equal emphasis: What is
consistent with linear iconicity is not necessarily evidence for it once categorial
sensitivity is proven to matter. Consider Chinese again:

70. najia feiji   cong jichang   qifei-le.
    that   airplane   from airport   take.off-ASP
    'That airplane took off from the airport.'

For Tai's TSC, (70) is an empirical support for iconicity since *cong jichang*
'from airport' is the starting point of the takeoff event and thus ought to be said
earlier than the verb *qifei* 'take off'. But in Modern Chinese, *cong* can only be
used as a preposition (whose verbal origin in Classical Chinese meant 'follow')
and, as we already know, PPs must be preverbal in the language. Put differently,
from the airport precedes *take.off* not because of linear iconicity but because of
the grammar of Modern Chinese. For exactly the same reason, the
resultative *pound the metal flat* in English appears iconic, with pounding
necessarily preceding the metal's becoming flat in our perception of the
world. But this word order results from the English VP being head-initial
plus the fact that resultative small clauses, typically an AP or PP in European
languages, are placed, for independent reasons, in the complement positions
(Rizzi 1990, Levin and Rappaport-Hovav 1995). If the language had a head-
final VP like German, we would have *flat pound* instead, just as in (69c).

In conclusion, at least in the case of SVCs, a critical factor to keep in mind
while studying linear iconicity is its categorial sensitivity. What appears

supportive of iconicity may not be so, and what looks like a counterexample may be an entirely irrelevant fact. Failure to pinpoint the precise conditions under which iconicity truly participates in clause-construction is a major reason behind the "statistical" impression that the current literature generates (van Langendonck 2010). And it is at the very center of this book to argue that at the level of sentence-generation, the use of iconicity is fully predictable when investigated with the FICH.

2.4.2   Neither Verb Is the Thematic Argument of the Other

The data from Yimas, Chinese and Korean in (9)–(11), section 2.1.2, demonstrate clearly that linear iconicity happens when neither V1 nor V2 takes the other as a thematic argument. In particular, when the causal relation is expressed in the SVC, the two verbs (such as *hit* and *kill* in Korean) display iconicity; but when a lexicalized causative verb (e.g. *make* in English) is used, its linear relation with the other verb obeys the standard head–complement pattern initially inspired by Greenberg (1963) and well understood in the UG framework. It has also become clear that the word order of the SVC is not reducible to simply hypothesizing V1 to be a light verb or assigning a θ-role to VP2, as often proposed/implied in the literature (e.g. Lefebvre 1991b, Aboh 2009 and much literature in between). For sure, under either of these hypotheses, V1 will necessarily occur before V2 in a head-initial language; and for researchers opting for Kayne's (1994) antisymmetric syntax, all languages would be head-initial anyway (see 2.2.2 above). It is possible that some SVC language may indeed treat its counterpart of *take* as a light verb or a θ-assigner to VP2. But such a scenario cannot be universal, or the object of V2 would always be extractable in Sranan (31b) and the instrumental SVC in Chinese would be syntactically indistinguishable from the analytic causatives in terms of binding and DP-extraction in (33–40). The overall situation here is no different from the verbs-only factor above: Some parts of UG may produce a structure that happens to look iconic or even like an SVC, but that is no replacement for an adequate account of the consistently iconic order of all the SVCs that accommodate multiple structural relations between the verbs cross-linguistically.

Bearing on the lack of a thematic connection between the verbs in an SVC is Carrier and Randall's (1992) observation that is sometimes viewed as suggesting s-selection in the resultative construction, namely only a negative mental state can be paired with the verb *drive* in the resultative below:

71. X drives Y crazy/to the brink of lunacy/*happy/*to the brink of ecstasy.

In the UG tradition, s-selection is easily linked to the selector assigning a θ-role to the selected. Along this line of logic, (71) might appear as evidence for a thematic relation between *drive* and the subsequent result phrase, and the reasoning may be extended to the SVCs of which one type is the resultative (see (11a) from Korean, (28) from Sranan and (53b) from Japanese). If V2 is thematically selected by V1, however, linear iconicity is no longer correlated with a missing thematic relation among the SVC verbs.

The issue at hand is how to determine the nature of s-selection. To be more specific, what is the boundary that separates s-selection from idiomaticity? While many idioms in English are built on the verb–object relation (e.g. *kill the cockroach* vs. *kill the bottle* in Marantz 1984 and Kratzer 1996), others are found with the adjunct-head relation too. To take leftover food with you from a restaurant, you may request a *doggy bag* but not a *canine bag* or a *puppy bag*. There is certainly a semantic relation between the two lexical morphemes – in fact there is a semantic relation between any two lexical constituents that yield a legitimate interpretation – but that relation is not through thematic assignment and does not prevent *doggy bag* from being idiomatic. One way to think of (71), then, is whether an idiom is word-specific or type-specific. The former requires the exact wording whereas the latter has at least part of it built on types. In this view, (71) simply exemplifies *drive* requiring expressions of certain negative mental states to form an idiom. It is in the same spirit, I think, that Goldberg and Jackendoff (2004) treat English resultatives as a family of syntactic constructions listed in the lexicon. What matters for now is that the rigid or semi-rigid choice for lexical words in examples like (65) can, or even should, be treated as idiomatic and not as automatic evidence for manifesting a thematic relation inside a resultative construction.

That V1 and V2 in an SVC are not thematically linked is substantiated by the Chinese consecutive SVC. In this language, one can *buy fruit eat* 'buy and eat fruits' but not *eat fruit buy*. On the surface, this asymmetry in terms of what verbs qualify for V1 may be taken to mean that only a subset of verbs such as *buy* have the potential to accept an extra VP complement, a point also made in Aboh (2009) on Niger-Congo SVCs. But at least in Chinese, what happens is no more than our knowledge of the world at work:

72. a. xuan   ji-jian   yangpin mai
       choose   a.few-piece   sample   buy
       'choose a few samples to buy'
    b. mai   ji-jian   yangpin xuan
       buy   a.few-piece   sample   choose
       'buy a few samples to choose from'

73. a. kan   yixie mutou shao
       chop some   wood   burn
    'chop some wood and burn it (in the stove)'

   b. ?shao yixie mutou kan
       burn   some   wood   chop
    'burn some wood (so that it is easier) to chop'

Inside a complex event of shopping, a normal sequence of sub-events is to choose a few samples and then buy them, but there is also a somewhat less common but real possibility that one buys a few samples first so as to give each a try and then decide which one to use (or to buy more of). Hence (72a–b) are both acceptable even though (72b) feels more "marked". Similarly, (73a) describes the natural series of sub-events where one gets wood ready (through chopping) before burning it for warmth. No obvious intrinsic connection exists in our world when the sequence of these two sub-events is reversed. But if we imagine a scenario in which burning the wood could somehow facilitate chopping it, (73b) acquires an interpretation. In other words, the marginal status of (73b) is not a matter of grammaticality but reflects the degree to which it can be allotted a plausible reading. In fact, if *kan* 'chop' is replaced with *ke* 'carve', (73a–b) will stay acceptable with a reversed judgment – it is easier to imagine burning a piece of wood to make it easier for carving than seeing why one would want to carve the wood and then burn it. More generally, what connects V1 and V2 in these examples is readily accounted for via how we perceive the universe operates and how naturally a sequence of events are cognitively connected. Phrasing the phenomenon with a thematic relation between V1 and V2 not only is unnecessary, but in fact would require ad hoc assumptions about a verb's semantic and syntactic connectivity and effectively deprive the notion of θ-roles of any falsifiable denotation. At the meta-theoretical level, enriching the syntactic model this way would also run counter to the general effort of the past twenty-plus years to minimize the theory of "genetic endowment" by attributing as much as possible to independently needed general cognitive facilities.

2.4.3   No Relational Words Around

It is in the definition of SVCs that no relational words are used to, in one way or another, specify a semantic relation between the verbs. The underlying mechanism for this fact will be discussed as part of our analysis of SVCs and linear iconicity in section 2.5. What is at issue for now is a confusion in the SVC literature.

Objecting to Tai's iconic TSC (see (65)), Newmeyer (2004: 19) offers (74) from Chinese, the same language that motivated Tai's theory, and notes that "there are sentences in which the reverse temporal order reading is the normal one ... if the first conjunct contains the particle *qian* 'before'." We add the English examples in (75) to echo Newmeyer. The spelling and glossing of (74) are adjusted:

74. wo chu   men qian,   yiding   guanhao menchuang.
    I   go.out door before certainly shut   door.window
    'I will close the door and the windows before I go out.'

75. a. (In order) to cut cakes, Pam picked up the knife.
    b. Chris left, having offended several people at the party.

(74–75) are indeed problems for Tai because, as already noted, the TSC lacks any grammatical conditions under which linear iconicity takes place. As it makes the very general reference to "the temporal order of the states ... in the conceptual world" with no mention of syntactic interference, iconicity is bound to over-generate: If closing the door and the windows happens before going out as (74) describes, the two verbs should indeed be linearized in the opposite order to (74) under the TSC. The English examples in (75) present the same problem.

Whereas Newmeyer is right in pinning down a problem with the TSC, he is amiss at the same time by using examples like (74) to deny linear iconicity. At issue is the presence of an overt lexical item in each of these examples that explicitly expresses a semantic relation between the two verbs: *qian* 'before' for temporal precedence; the aspectual and/or non-finite tense markers in (75) for expressing the temporal relations between the verbs. Pending an incorporation of such relational morphemes into an analysis of the SVC, it is clear that their presence highlights the widely recognized need for defining SVCs and the iconic word order with their necessary absence. Put intuitively, a necessary condition for linear iconicity is when the semantic relation between the verbs is not lexically spelled out.

2.4.4 Argument-Sharing

Baker (1989) tried to derive the word order of the SVC from object-sharing and, as proven in 2.2.1, failed for principled reasons. Nevertheless, object-sharing is indeed correlated directly with the iconic word order. The evidence is based on examining the SVC against Gricean implicatures.

The Gricean "being orderly" (see 2.2.3) is known to be contextually reversible:

76. a. ta   zaoshang dique   mai-le   baozhi,   kan-le   baozhi. (Chinese)
       3s morning   indeed buy-ASP newspaper read-ASP newspaper
       'S/He did buy a newspaper and read the newspaper in the morning.'

b. buguo ta   shi   xian   kan   hou   mai   de.
   but   3s   be   first read then buy   DE
   'But s/he actually read it first and then bought it.'

If (76a) is uttered alone, it is understood as buying before reading, in accordance with the Gricean maxim of being orderly in communication and, more pertinently, with linear iconicity. When (76a) and (76b) are given together, however, the default sequence of the buying-before-reading events is reversed so that reading happened before buying. It should be noted that at the semantic level, *mai* 'buy' and *kan* 'read' can share the object and, in this actual case, must do so due to the extra context provided by (76b). This is significant because simple semantic object-sharing through contextually aided coreference does not necessarily comply with linear iconicity. The type of object-sharing relevant for the SVC must be implemented at the syntactic level, to which we turn next.

The two verbs in (76) can also form a consecutive SVC, shown in (77a), where, at least superficially, there is but one NP referring to the newspaper:

77. a. ta   zaoshang dique   mai-le   baozhi   kan.
       3s   morning   indeed buy-ASP   newspaper read
       'She did buy and then read a newspaper this morning.'

    b. #buguo ta   shi   xian   kan   hou   mai   de. (Same as (76b))
       but   3s   be   first read then buy   DE
       'But s/he actually read it first and then bought it.'

The two sentences can still be said together, though (77b) is no longer able to reverse the buying-before-reading interpretation of (77a). Instead, (77a–b) collectively can describe only one scenario: There is one buying event but two separate reading events. For instance, the person first read the newspaper in order to decide whether it was worth purchasing or not, and then read (or would read) it again – perhaps more carefully or with a focus on a particular article in the newspaper – after buying it. This contrasts with (76), where it is perfectly plausible to have only one instance of newspaper-reading (and one instance of purchasing of course) whether the temporal sequence between them is iconic or reversed. In sum, linear iconicity is not breakable if and only if the two verbs involved share an object grammatically as in the SVC. Contextually determined semantic coreference is not sufficient to guarantee a particular word order. See Baker (1989) and Collins (1997) for arguments that even the instrumental SVC has a shared object.

Using data mostly from Kwa (Niger-Congo) languages, Aboh (2009) argues against the claim of object-sharing in the SVC, rejecting in particular Baker's (1989) theory of SVCs (see our 2.2.1) and the more popular object-control structure as adopted by Carstens (2002; our 2.2.2). Aboh's major arguments are examined below. Unless specified otherwise, all examples are from his work.

The Gungbe SVC-coordination comparison in (55–56) earlier is taken by Aboh to "weaken" object-sharing because the sentences in (55) are "bona fide SVCs" in which "V1 and V2 appear to take different internal arguments (and therefore violate [the object-sharing hypothesis])" (2009: 7). The reasoning here is obscure, especially when compared with the analysis of the instrumental SVC later in the same paper:

78. a. Sɛtu ze   kpo lɔ   xo Kɔjo. (Gungbe, Aboh 2009 (36a))
    Setu take stick DET hit Kojo
    'Setu hit Kojo with the stick.'

   b. ... [$_{vP}$ the stick [$_{v'}$ v$_{appl}$ [$_{VP}$ hit Kojo]]]   (adapted from Aboh's (37a))

where v$_{appl}$ stands for an applicative head "introduce[ing] the instrument in its specifier," namely *the stick* (Aboh 2009: 16). But if *xo* 'hit', a simple transitive verb otherwise, can acquire an instrumental argument (*kpo lɔ* 'stick the') this way, there is no reason why the same phonologically empty applicative cannot happen to *sɔ* 'hit' in (55a), another simple transitive verb, effectively providing the latter with the instrumental *moto ce* 'car my'. To put it intuitively, if one can hit Kojo with a stick, one should be able to hit the wall with my car. For sure, using an applicative to bring in the instrument argument jars technically with Baker's double-headed VP. But it has already been shown that that theory does not work anyway (see 2.2.1). What matters is that the very structure in (78b) essentially refutes the reasoning that there is no object-sharing because V2 in (55) is a "bona fide" transitive verb with its own internal argument. On the contrary, it is a logical derivative that V1 in (55) may "share" *my car* with an applicative-enriched V2.

The Fɔngbe example below is considered problematic for object-sharing because with the stranded preposition *na* 'with', "V2 *sɛn* 'cut' cannot be a triadic verb that jointly θ-marks the object of V1 *jivi ɔ* 'the knife'. Accordingly, V1 and V2 do not share the same object in a Fɔngbe [instrumental SVC]" (Aboh 2009: 7).

79. Kɔku sɔ   jivi ɔ   sɛn wɔxuxu ɔ   na.
    Koku take knife DET cut bread   DET with
    'Koku cut the bread with the knife.'

Just as with the previous argument, (79) indeed poses a non-trivial problem with Baker's particular implementation of object-sharing. But an extra instrument-introducing *with* is no different from a hidden applicative head for the current purpose. In fact, both mechanisms enforce a form of object-sharing because the instrument argument thus brought into the clause must be coreferential with the theme argument of V1. I return to more details in section 2.5.

Whereas the previous two arguments reject object-sharing by questioning the number of internal arguments of V2, Aboh also argues that V1 does not contribute any internal argument, which, if true, removes the very ground of object-sharing. To this end, V1 is shown to be a "functional verb [which] does not select for an internal argument" (2009: 26).

The empirical core of this claim is that in SVCs, V1 has different behavior both thematically and semantically. One such case is that in (some) Kwa languages, ditransitive verbs such as the counterpart to *give* do not occur as V1 in consecutive SVCs, which is interpreted to indicate "a thematic restriction on elements that realize [the V1] position" (p. 26). Aboh argues that this is not predicted by the object-control structure to implement object-sharing (i.e. with the overt object of V1 controlling some *pro* argument of V2 so as to "share" the object). If this structure fails to work, then object-sharing built on it is negatively affected.

Our response is four-fold. First, whether there is object-sharing or not is an empirical question, separate from how exactly the claimed phenomenon is technically handled (via control, for instance). Even if the latter is proven wrong, the like of which happens *a lot* in all aspects of syntax, it does not follow logically that the empirical question is settled. As an example, having different definitions for minimality (Rizzi 1990, Chomsky 1995, Y. Li, Shields and Lin 2012) does not refute the existence of minimality. Second, ditransitive verbs are indeed allowed as V1 in Chinese consecutive SVCs, as example (45) shows, proving minimally that Aboh's conclusion, even if valid for Kwa, cannot be extended to other SVC languages in terms of object-sharing. Third, it was pointed out in section 2.3.2 that Carstens' structural representation of SVCs, the type Aboh argues against, can indeed rule out *give* as V1. Lastly, for a ditransitive verb to be banned from the V1 position in Kwa does not by itself exclude the possibility that a non-ditransitive V1 shares its object. Put together, these considerations indicate that the rejection of ditransitive verbs from the V1 position is a language-particular phenomenon which (i) has no clear bearing on object-sharing and (ii) is more likely explained by looking into the differences in the grammars of the languages under comparison. See a specific analysis below.

Another abnormal behavior of V1 is seen in (80) (Aboh's (63–64), which I assume to be from Gungbe) where a lexical verb used as V1 no longer retains its original meaning:

80. a. Asiba   bɛ   lɛsi   du.
       Asiba   collect rice   eat
       'Asiba collected rice and ate it → Asiba ate a lot of rice.'
    b. Asiba   bɛ   xo   dɔ.
       Asiba   collect word   say
       'Asiba said a lot of nonsense.'

c. Asiba,   din   nu   de   du   to   adokɔn.
   Asiba   search   thing   INDEF   eat   at   kitchen
   'Asiba, get yourself something to eat in the kitchen.'
   *'Asiba, look for something in the kitchen and eat it.'

For Aboh, these examples "indicate that V1 *bɛ* does not assign an internal
θ-role to the object to its right" (2009: 26).

To start with, I take it for granted that a certain verb frequently used in
a certain structural context (cf. Goldberg and Jackendoff's (2004) lexicon-
stored syntactic constructions) may be subject to semantic deviation or bleach-
ing and eventually be used as a functional head. How widely spread this is,
however, can be determined only on a case-by-case and, obviously, language-
by-language basis. The counterpart of (80c) in Chinese, for instance, can be
shown to retain the base meanings of both verbs. Given the scenario where
someone sits at the table while the speaker points at the food in front of them, *na*
'take, grab' and *zhao* 'search, look for' make a sharp contrast:

81. a. ni ziji na   dongxi chi.
       2s self take   thing   eat
       'You grab food and eat. → Help yourself.'

    b. (#)ni ziji zhao   dongxi   chi.
       3s   self look.for   thing   eat
       'You look for food and eat.'

The "generic action" verb *na* in (81a), as V1, is always appropriate in the
setting, but *zhao* 'look for, search' in (81b) relies for its felicitousness on how
many different kinds of food are on the table. If there is only bread and a bowl
of soup around, for instance, (81b) is extremely odd since no effort is needed to
look for (i.e. to make a choice of) anything.

Trying to generalize the few examples in (80) to all verbs used as V1 is not
only empirically inappropriate, it also ends up hurting Aboh's own line of logic.
For one thing, if V1 "does not assign an internal θ-role to the object to its right"
anyway, whether a lexical verb can be used as V1 or not is totally severed from
its original argument structure. Then what prevents a ditransitive verb such as
give, or any verb for that matter, from occurring as V1, especially when the
semantics of such verbs is otherwise contextually felicitous, as Aboh noted
himself ("[in terms of interpretation,] these examples are perfectly grammatical
in English" (p. 26))? For another, a truly functionalized V1 is technically no
longer V1 in its intended sense any longer, just as a modal verb in a typical
Romance language results in a "bi-clausal" structure while the corresponding
modal in English can only be part of a mono-clause. So assuming Aboh's

account of the Gungbe (80) to be correct, we must conclude that it says nothing about true SVCs where V1 is a bona fide lexical verb.

On the other hand, an explanation for the semantic deviations of V1 can be provided that critically relies on V1 sharing its object with V2. Since Marantz (1984), it has been known that the object of V may influence the meaning of V (cf. *kill the rat* and *kill the evening*). Kratzer (1996) presents a formal semantic account of this fact. The phenomenon is called idiomatic for the good reason that the semantic shifting is word-specific and language-specific. In Chinese, for instance, *sha laoshu* 'kill rat' is good as expected but **sha bangwan* 'kill evening' is unimaginable. In brief, a language must decide, mostly arbitrarily, that a particular object is allowed to alter the meaning of a given verb. Back to SVCs, let V2 pick the object – via object-sharing – for V1. Once the object is settled, it may end up forcing a semantic shift in V1. In this sense, what happens to *bε* 'collect' in Gungbe consecutive SVCs is no different from what happens to *kill* in Marantz' object-induced English idioms.

Also note that this account of V1's semantic deviation is compatible with V1 being either the matrix verb or heading an adjunct. For one thing, such a semantic deviation does not automatically rule out V1 from being a lexical verb in an SVC. After all, *kill* remains a verb even in *kill the evening*. For another, suppose V1 to have lost its lexical nature. If V1 was initially a main verb, it is now turned into a light verb or functional verb taking a VP complement (cf. modals being either V or T in European languages). Alternatively, the adjunct use of V1 might make it available for a categorial change to P (recall the earlier discussion of *cong* (V: 'follow' → P: 'from') in Chinese). What matters is that any carefully proven categorial change or lexical-to-functional change to a verb removes the latter from the SVC and hands it to the jurisdiction of UG. Consequently, it becomes irrelevant to the topic of object-sharing of SVCs.

As it happens, SVCs also share the subject, with the exception of resultatives in some languages (see the Chinese compound in (5) and the Miskito SVC in (7)). Subject-sharing will participate in explaining the cluster of traits of SVCs in (62), and its absence in some resultative SVCs will be addressed as well. In itself, however, subject-sharing is not correlated with the iconic word order of the SVC, as our discussion of Gricean implicature proves with the help of (76).

2.4.5   Summing Up the SVC Traits

The SVC has a constant iconic linear order between its verbs (2.1) but varying structural arrangements matching the grammars of particular languages (2.3). This fact is totally un-UG-like because, as made clear in Chapter 1, UG takes linearization to be a function of (asymmetric) structural relations. If everything were up to UG to decide, what is made maximally constant should be the structural representation, typically via lexicalization (e.g. the causative verb always serving as the matrix verb), from which to compute the word order that varies parametrically with languages and with the specific semantic relations encoded. In other words, what we see with SVCs is in effect opposite to how UG operates.

Furthermore, this oddity happens when the targets of linearization are restricted to verbs only (2.4.1) without a thematic relation in between (2.4.2) or the help of a relational word (2.4.3), and all within a mono-clausal context (2.4). In addition, though object-sharing is necessarily correlated with the obligatory iconic word order (2.4.4), it cannot be the source for the latter because its clearest manifestation, in the consecutive SVC, also happens to be where UG is unable to distinguish V1 and V2 and thus has no way to structure them in a way helpful for linearization (2.2.1–2) (also see the discussion on (72–72)). It follows, then, that object-sharing is more likely to be on the effect side of the correlation with the word order of the SVC, if they are causally connected at all.

Assuming our current understanding of UG is sufficiently accurate where pertinent to the SVC, what we have learned so far collectively points at this conclusion:

82. UG is unable to structurally position two verbal projections in a consistent manner in the absence of thematic or extra lexical specification of their relation.

(82) describes the context where linear iconicity is called into action. The next step is to figure out the real culprit for (82) and how the traits in (62) are derivable from it.

2.5   Analyzing the SVC with the FICH and the USM

To facilitate the upcoming analysis, we recapitulate the general model of the UG–iconicity interface (UG-I). When a functional void of UG stops the derivational process of a clause, iconicity is activated, as stated in the FICH. The subsequent interaction must obey the USM, which demands that every conceptual/semantic relation R_C be deterministically mapped to a structural relation R_S.

2.5.1   The Serial Verb Parameter

Because the SVC as a phenomenon happens only in a fraction of languages, there must exist a variable of some kind in the overall human language faculty that enables the option. We will follow the terminology in the UG tradition by suggesting a parameter. A convenient candidate is to let a language choose between housing one or more verbs inside a clause. Technical subtleties aside, this is exactly what Baker (1989) did (2.1.1). There are two considerations, however, that would favor looking beyond this.

First, the SVC is more than just having multiple verbs in a clause; it also encodes a cross-linguistically tiny and consistent set of semantic relations between the verbs: resultative, instrumental, purposive and consecutive. A parallel relation, such as that of AND, is not part of the phenomenon even though it may also be manifested as a series of verbs in an SVC language (see (76a) from Chinese; also cf. (56) from Gungbe). As seen, the linear order may be iconically interpreted in such a case, but there is no object-sharing and the Gricean implicature may be contextually nullified. The semantic traits of the SVC are a key part of the phenomenon not captured by merely setting the parameter as a choice between one verb per clause and more. The second consideration is how to link linear iconicity to the SVC-related traits in (62). Baker's (1989) model of the double-headed VP has proven inadequate for this purpose, and neither can Carstens' (2002) structure with two suites of vP–VP or the multi-dominance analysis by Hiraiwa and Bodomo (2008) accommodate any of these traits. An alternative theory of whatever brings about the SVCs in a language is needed.

Our Serial Verb Parameter (SVP) is defined as follows:

83. a. A language *may* or *may not* overtly express the components of a composite event in a single clause.
     b. With $1 \leq i < n$, a composite event E consists of sub-events $e_1 \ldots e_n$ such that
         i.   each e_i is intrinsically earlier than e_{i+1} in time, and
         ii. each E has no more than one external argument.

A language choosing a positive value for (83a) will allow a simple clause to contain the overt expressions of the sub-events of a given composite event, thereby giving rise to the SVC with all the accompanying traits.[18] A negative value means no innards of a composite event are overtly manifested, leaving E to be encoded by a single verb which might be further assisted by other grammatical means such as a PP to explicitly introduce, say, an instrument argument. If the sub-events must be expressed overtly in an SVP-negative language, other UG means such as embedded clauses or coordination will be utilized. It must be made clear upfront, however, that each such grammatical means to (help) express the sub-events may carry its own semantic flavor so that languages with a negative SVP setting often provide at best "near-synonymous" translations for SVCs.[19] (83a) also determines that SVCs are inherently mono-clausal. Using a clause for each sub-event equals the negative setting and thus no SVC to begin with.

In the definition, (83b-ii) is derivable from the current model of UG. Since the early 1990s, a series of independently motivated works (Bowers 1993, Hale and Keyser 1993, Chomsky 1995, Kratzer 1996, Marantz 1997, Borer 2005,

Chen and Li 2016, 2021, among others) have accumulated evidence and motivations from different languages that the agent argument is brought into syntax with a head H separate from the lexical verb and that it is part of UG to have one H per clause. Furthermore, there is a consensus that it is lexical verbs that define sets of events (see Higginbotham 1985 for an early rendition of Davidsonian semantics in the UG framework; also see Ernst 2002 on the semantics of various verbal projections). Thus, whether the composite event E is expressed with a single lexical verb or more than one, it is up to the structure of the hosting clause to provide no more than one agent argument. In terms of theory-formulation, then, (83b-ii) does not need a separate statement. We include it in (83) only to highlight a factor of UG theory for subsequent analyses.

According to (83), the sub-events inside an SVC-relevant composite event are linked by a simple asymmetric temporal relation; call it R_T. When R_T is interpreted in an actual SVC example, it acquires the particular instrumental, resultative, purposive or consecutive "flavor" from the specific lexical properties of the verbs involved and the structural context in which they are used. If V2 can support an instrumental argument and the object of V1 meets the semantic requirement, the SVC is said to be instrumental (e.g. examples (1, 6)). If no instrumental argument is involved, the two verbs will end up sharing their patient/theme objects, yielding either the so-called consecutive SVC (3, 4), resultative SVC (2, 5, 7, 8) or purposive SVC (12, 13, 16), depending on such factors as whether in the SVC context, the lexical meaning of V2 expresses a necessary change of state on the part of its (now shared) object and whether V1 is a verb of creation, etc.

Specifically, *buy newspapers read* in (77a) is consecutive because reading a newspaper does not change its state, but *hit someone kill* in (28) has the "causal" reading since *kill* as V2 necessarily describes a change of state on the part of the shared object *someone*. Intuitively, when a composite event E describes hitting and then killing X, E stands for an internally causal event in human conceptualization. An interesting contrast is with *chop wood burn* in (73a). One may burn something, say a diamond, for hours without affecting it at all. This means that *burn* as V2 is a verb of action and not one of telic events, thereby giving (73a) the consecutive rather than resultative flavor. The purpose reading is the most "demanding" on the verbs, with V1 a creation verb and V2 expressing change of possession such as *give* or *send*. See subsection 2.1.4 for details. In brief, there really is only one semantic relation in all SVCs, i.e. 'earlier-than'. The perceived semantic variations are but products of context and lexical choice.

The SVP in (83) also correctly excludes parallel relations from the current concern. The 'and' relation, for instance, is not intrinsically temporally asymmetric and thus is not part of the SVC but instead covered by other parts of the human language faculty. At the bottom of it, this is why a parallel relation between two verbal projections is susceptible both to the Gricean implicature and to its contextual reversal. We return to this topic in Chapter 3.

2.5.2   *Verbs Only, No Relational Words and the Iconic Word Order*

The ultimate question is how to express the asymmetric temporal relation R_T in the overall territory of UG once a language picks the positive value of the SVP. Since R_T is a conceptual relation, namely an instance of R_C in (3a) of Chapter 1, and is a critical portion of the composite event E to be expressed by a linguistic construction (i.e. an SVC), it is subject to the R_C-to-R_S mapping (see (3a) of Chapter 1) under the USM. In "normal" cases, an R_C is to be lexicalized and becomes the semantics of a lexical item. From what we know about language, this lexicalization manifests R_C in two ways: (i) associating the semantic content of R_C with a particular phonological form (e.g. *make* and *let* both encode a causal relation but differ in the degree of the causer's exertion and active involvement) and (ii) molding the parties in R_C into the θ-role(s) of the lexical item resulting from (i). In the case of a composite event E with the positive value of the SVP selected, no lexicalization apparently happens to R_T, so the expression of R_T must be carried out with other means available to the human language faculty F_{HL}, of which the major apparatuses are from UG.

For this task, two intertwined issues need resolving. The first is what category or categories should be used to express the sub-events of E connected by R_T. We contend that the logic goes as follows: The essence of R_T is a relation of time between events; the temporal frame in which events happen is grammaticalized as tense; the lexical category in UG that both denotes events and is grammatically associated with tense is V. Consequently, V becomes the only category for UG to use in its expression of the R_T-connected sub-events. *This is why the SVC requires verbs only* (i.e. (62b)) – no other category, not even the stage-level adjective which can indeed denote situations (Rothstein 1999, Husband 2010, Wellwood 2016, among others), is grammatically capable of interacting directly with time/tense and is thus permitted in the SVC.[20]

If sub-events are expressed with verbs, then for R_T to semantically connect two verbs V1 and V2 means that R_T takes in two sets of sub-events and calculates the Cartesian product to yield a set of ordered pairs of sub-events:

84. $\{<e_1, e_2>|e_1 \text{ earlier-than } e_2\}$

where e_1 is a member of the sub-event set defined by V1 and e_2, by V2. It is (84) that forms the set of composite events, denoted by the entire VP containing both V1 and V2. Keeping this mind, we will talk about the SVP both in precise set-theoretic terms when needed, namely that R_T connects two sets of sub-events to form a set of composite events, and in a more intuitive way where no confusion arises, namely that two sub-events are linked by R_T to form a composite event.

Just as UG provides very limited means to materialize the sub-events under the positive SVP setting, it appears to be a fact that, aside from semantically symmetrical conjunctives such as *and* and *or* which I will argue to embody mere grammatical features (see Chapter 3), UG never lexicalizes asymmetric semantic relations between sets of events. Stowell (1981) defended the idea that a necessary condition for a thematic argument X in natural language is that X is itself thematically saturated. In effect, this would mean that each θ-role is semantically interpreted as defining a set of first-order entities such as e and t. Furthermore, it is certainly reasonable to think of θ-roles as the result of lexicalizing conceptual properties or relations into linguistic predicates. Back to R_T, then, lexicalizing it would yield a morpheme/word with two θ-roles whose syntactic behavior goes by Stowell's observation. In English, this word is *before*, of which an example will be considered shortly. What matters for now is that this is *not* what R_T is expected to be for the purpose of expressing the composite event E because in the actual linguistic expression of E, R_T needs to link two sets of sub-events (i.e. what lexical verbs denote), not two thematically saturated first-order propositions. In sum, if R_T were lexically expressed, it would become something else – in effect an obligatory semantic type-shift – which would be unable to link two verbal projections. If its intended meaning in the SVP stays intact, there is simply no lexical expression for it.

What the previous paragraph boils down to is that UG is unable to provide a legitimate lexicalization for R_T in the composite event E. Take this to be the first functional void of UG, whether it has a deeper logic behind it à la Stowell (i.e. with thematic relations built only on first-order semantic entities) or is just coincidentally not programmed into UG. (85) gives the logically most general formulation of this void:

85. $\text{Void}_F 1$
     UG cannot lexicalize an R_C that connects two sets of non-first-order entities.

The SVC trait of *no lexical relational word between verbs* is a restatement of $\text{Void}_F 1$. It is no less important to note that R_T cannot be expressed in the form of a modification relation between V1 and V2 either. For the sake of discussion, let R_T be combined with V2 first – recall that this is actually not possible since V2 is thematically unsaturated and thus is not even a legitimate linguistic argument. But let us ignore that and pretend a legitimate merge so that R_T-V2 functions like a modifying PP (cf. *before dawn*). Still, while R_T-V2 indeed needs another party because R_T is a relation, no intersection can be formed between this combo C and V1 which C is meant to modify:

86. a. $[\![V1]\!] = \lambda e_s.\mathbf{V1}(e)$
    b. $[\![R_T\text{-}V2]\!] = \lambda P_{<s,\ \triangleright}.\mathbf{R_T}(P, V2)$

The two sets are about different types of semantic objects, making their intersection an empty set, which in turn means that there is no modifictional relation between V1 and R_T-V2, contra the initial intention.[21]

Not only is there no UG-legitimate expression of R_T, but there is *no thematic connection* between V1 and V2 either. Given the SVP, no sub-event is a semantic part of another sub-event, directly ruling out the possibility that, say, V2 heads a phrase serving as the thematic object of V1.[22] Furthermore, neither V1 nor V2 can directly modify the other either. Given Davidsonian semantics on adverbial modifiers, the relation is consummated with set-theoretically intersecting two event sets. But the intersection formed with V1 and V2 is necessarily empty, with V1 denoting events of cooking and V2 events of eating, for instance (see the Yoruba example (24a)). So no relation of modification exists between V1 and V2 in the formal sense of the word.

In conclusion, given the SVP and UG, R_T is not expressible in UG due to $Void_F1$ in (85) and the semantic nature of linguistic modification. Nor is any sub-event-denoting verb thematically connected with another verb since they each, by definition, denote sub-events of a different kind. Despite the perfectly legitimate *E* as a conceptual entity, its linguistic expression is a perfect impasse.

If UG were the only toolbox to build sentences with, the impasse at hand would end the derivation before it even starts, thereby never generating SVCs in human languages. Now suppose the FICH to capture how F_{HL} actually operates: Solicit help from iconicity when UG admits incompetence, specifically in the form of $Void_F1$ in this case. The task is to express R_T, and R_T is temporal precedence. The iconic solution is to align the two verbs with the temporal sequence of the corresponding events. Because this is the only way to have R_T overtly manifested, it holds in all SVC languages.

The list below summarizes what has been achieved up till this point in accounting for the property-cluster of the SVCs:

87. a. No relational word used:
       = $Void_F1$, likely resulting from UG requiring θ-saturated arguments.
    b. Verbs only:
       Due to the positive setting of the SVP plus UG's handling of time-tense.
    c. No thematic relation between verbs:
       Derived from the SVP and UG's basic semantic operations.
    d. Constant iconic word order:
       $Void_F1$ activating linear iconicity under the FICH.
    e. Mono-clausal structure:
       In the nature of the SVP.

2.5.3   No Uniform Structure for SVCs

From the point of view of both UG and F_{HL}, calling in iconicity to linearize the verbs in the SVC solves the problem only half of the way. In terms of the mapping model in (3) of Chapter 1, what iconicity accomplishes is to map R_C directly to R_L, i.e. from semantics to word order, completely skipping R_S. But human language as we know it cannot exist without a grammatically endorsed syntactic structure. Words must be grouped into constituents so as to become part of a clause. Meanwhile, UG by itself does not know how to assemble the verbs: As proven above, the semantic relation between V1 and V2 is neither a head–complement nor a modifier–modified relation, even when R_T is taken into consideration.

The dilemma, that the composite event E needs a structure to be represented linguistically but UG cannot help even after the verbs are linearized iconically, is not all bad news. At least conceptually, we now understand why SVCs have no consistent internal structure inter- and intra-linguistically. It is because UG has no dedicated algorithm for this situation. Hence, at least the ultimate source of the *varying structural relations* between verbs becomes clear. The same reasoning also reveals where and how to seek a solution: UG finishes a sentence with two mappings: from R_C to R_S and then from R_S to R_L (assuming, of course, all the needed lexical items are available for use). Take this to be the default route of sentence-generation. Now with a composite event E containing R_T, iconicity provides the abnormal mapping from R_C to R_L. What is needed is to build a legitimate R_S "backward" from R_L (namely the iconic linear order settled under the FICH), a partially reversed process of sentence-generation.

This backward step is not compatible with the most widely adopted version of UG (88a), which assumes a unidirectional transition from syntax to phonetic form (PF), but it can be implemented in Jackendoff's (2002: section 7.1) "non-directional" model, partially shown in (88b).

88.   a.   ... Syntax ⟶ PF

       b.   ... Syntax ⟶ PF

Given (88b), two components of language can communicate freely in either direction so that "the principles of the competence theory" and "the principles that the language user actually employs in speaking and understanding language" are maximally unified. (ibid.: 198; also see Culicover and Jackendoff 2005). In such a model, the channel is always open for PF information, such as the linear order of the verbs, to flow back to the syntax component, providing PF-enriched input for building R_S. The idea that different components of language feed each other is not new or rare. In his critical assessment of the lexicalist theory of word formation, for instance, Bruening (2018) discusses many examples in English (e.g. *a good-for-nothing*) and German which are most easily analyzed as "phrasal syntax feeding word formation" (p. 12). For the purpose of the SVC, we only need PF-to-syntax when it is inevitable, along the line of computational cost such that syntax-to-PF is the least costly derivational path, exercising the backward feeding only as a last resort. More on the role of cost in Chapter 4. Also note that such a model is fundamentally different from Kayne's (1994) Linear Correspondence Axiom, which I will argue against and propose an alternative to in Chapter 4 as well.

When a composite event E has its sub-events realized as verbs and R_T expressed iconically, and once the unstructured V1–V2 string is fed back to syntax by (88b), there are in fact two portions of F_{HL} that must be satisfied in order to produce a legitimate structure: the general UG principles plus particular parameter settings and the USM. The second task turns out to be more intricate than it might appear in the case of SVCs and will be tackled later. For now, let's deal with the simpler task of having the V1–V2 string meet the obvious (and straightforward) requirements of UG itself.

The only logically plausible means to reconcile the by-now determined V1–V2 sequence with a particular language's syntax is the aforementioned Chinese saying "squeeze one's feet into the shoes." The linear order of V1 and V2 is a given, which is the shoe. If the language at hand, L, is strictly head-initial, V1 must be turned into the main verb of the clause, leaving V2 to head a phrase serving as the structural complement of V1 or a postverbal adjunct if L allows it. Sranan and Kwa languages such as Buli, Nupe and Yoruba are of this kind. If L is head-initial but places all adjuncts pre-head, V2 becomes the default choice as the main verb, relegating the projection of V1 to an adjunct status. In theory, V1 also enjoys the option of serving as the main verb, but that would force V2 to head a complement, a certainly grammatical setup which nonetheless makes the outcome structurally hard to distinguish from a bi-clausal structure, especially if L has no tense morphology. Since a bi-clausal structure would fundamentally alter the very essence of an SVC, this V2-as-complement option is potentially misleading whether adjuncts precede or follow the main verb in L and thus is expected not to be favored. The expectation proves true.

First consider Chinese with preverbal adjuncts. The instrumental SVC in the language is very insistent in treating VP1 as adjunct (33–34), turning it into the main VP only when V1 is explicitly marked with an aspectual morpheme (see (42)). Clearly, the latter option acts as a last resort, especially when the nature of the instrumental SVC makes VP2 resemble a thematically saturated clausal argument containing V2 and its own patient/theme object (recall that V2 only shares a "hidden" instrumental argument with V1). On the other hand, a strongly head-initial SVC language does not have the SVC-friendly V1-as-adjunct option and must go with two other strategies in order to minimize the bi-clausal confusion. The first is to treat VP2 as a postverbal adjunct, with the complement analysis adopted only to avoid a derivational crash such as movement out of islands. This is Sranan (see (31)).[23] Another strategy for this kind of language is to turn V1 into a functional word so that VP2 is indeed the complement while the mono-clausal structure is saved. This, I suggest, explains why there is no shortage of literature on SVCs which treats some cases of V1 as a light verb. See Aboh (2009) and our discussion of it in 2.4.4 above. Logically, a language may also allow the structural options of Sranan and Chinese combined, with both preverbal adjuncts and postverbal adjuncts (and conditional complements), giving V1 and V2 all structural possibilities to choose from. We suggest that Edo, Dagaare and Gungbe fall into this type, judging from their multiple choices in the predicate cleft of SVCs examined in 2.3.3.

The previous analysis captures a fact often overlooked or even mis-treated: that the structural relation between the verbs in an SVC varies but the variations are fully expected given the grammar of the language. Our analysis also offers a falsifiable model for further investigating the syntactic properties of SVCs. In addition, like most other SVC traits analyzed so far, *structural variation* is shown to be derived from the SVP and $Void_F 1$, provided that F_{HL} adopts (88b) for inter-component communication. To complete this part of our analysis, I want to highlight the importance of UG's lack of lexical means for connecting sets of events by briefly discussing the relational words that indeed exist in languages and which one finds occasionally in the SVC literature as evidence against iconicity.

In short, once a lexical connector like *before* is used, all related grammatical behaviors such as word order and structural positioning are regulated by UG only and are therefore derived from syntax to PF in a default single pass – ultimately, this is also why the unidirectional model in (88a) is adequate for most UG-base syntactic analyses. As an example, consider (74), repeated in (89):

89. wo chu   men qian,   yiding   guanhao menchuang.
    I   go.out door before certainly shut   door.window
    'I will close the door and the window before I go out.'

Newmeyer takes this to be a problem for linear iconicity because the event of going out is meant to happen after closing the door and window but actually is expressed earlier instead. Now we know why this is not a problem.

Fundamentally, though Chinese selects the positive value for the SVP, it chooses not to do so for (89). Rather, it acts just like English by not treating this particular instance of utterance as an expression of a composite event *E* consisting of the sub-events of closing windows temporally preceding going out. Instead, what would be a sub-event in *E* is allotted the status of a standalone event characteristically expressed as a clause by UG. Or to put it differently, for (89), the SVP is given the negative value, so none of the subsequent dilemmas, choices and operations depicted in section 2.5 so far would even arise in the first place, the activation of iconicity included.

At the technical level, we know from semantics that *qian* 'before' in (89) has the meaning in (90) (we ignore irrelevant details such as how to exactly express the event in a proposition):

90. $[\![qian]\!] = \lambda x_t \lambda e_s . e > x$, where ">" = 'temporally earlier than'

That is, the basic temporal relation described by *qian* is the same as that of R_T, but the semantic types of the parties in this relation have been adjusted to become the first-order ones that UG can lexicalize. Thus, *qian* takes a proposition of type <t> – with all the θ-roles of the verb assigned and its event position properly bound by T inside the proposition-denoting clause[24] – and yields a constituent of type <s, t>, s for events and states, which is ready to undergo event-identification with the predicate of the main clause. And because *qian* acquires a UG-processible form, it projects accordingly in syntax and serves as an adjunct linearly before the main verb or even the main clause. Iconicity is not called for and is never relevant.

Other than lexically encoding a temporal relation R and subjecting the subsequent operations to UG, there is still another way to express R with a negatively set SVP, namely to simply turn to iconicity again by uttering one separate sentence after another. Because separate sentences are used, however, there is no composite event as defined in (83b-i). In fact, this option is by definition even outside UG's territory as it is beyond the level of sentence-generation (= (6a) of Chapter 1). Hence the cluster of SVC traits, such as object-sharing, are no longer present, leading to the fact that the Gricean implicature may now be reversed as expected. This brings us to the last question: Why is obligatory linear iconicity in the SVCs tied to object-sharing?

2.5.4   Argument-Sharing

Recall that once the V1–V2 string is fed to syntax, the two verbs and their proper syntactic projections must be assembled in accordance with two restrictions, UG and the USM. In fact, all linguistic constructions, SVC or not, must satisfy the USM given its generic nature. See Chapter 1 for how it is defined and positioned in F_{HL}. Assuming that there exist algorithms to encode concepts into lexical items (e.g. Jackendoff 1972, 2002), the syntax-relevant semantics of each lexical item is certainly deterministically mapped to syntactic structure via such UG mechanisms as the θ-criterion and X'-theory. Put differently, for almost all products of F_{HL} satisfying UG *is* satisfying the USM. This suggests that with respect to the R_C-to-R_S mapping, UG might be viewed as – and probably is – just the most cost-efficient embodiment of the USM (and enriched with locality conditions etc. for proper interpretations and/or computational efficiency).

But at this point of the process to derive the SVC, the USM is yet to be met because the very language-specific variations between V1 and V2 are anything but deterministic, with R_T represented either as VP2 being the complement or the adjunct of V1 in Sranan, for instance, despite the fact that these options are all good for X'-structure and the Sranan grammar. We propose that when the USM is at work while UG is not helpful, the go-to mechanism is isomorphism, regarded by Haiman (1985) as one of the two elements in iconicity. Since our concern at the moment and throughout this book is R_C, namely semantic/conceptual relations, what is needed is *relation-preserving* (aka order) isomorphism:[25]

91. Let X, Y be sets and ≤, ⊑ be the relations between the members of X and of Y respectively. The isomorphism from X to Y is the function $f: X{\rightarrow}Y$ such that $u \leq v$ iff $f(u) \sqsubseteq f(v)$

In plainer words, if ordered pairs can be defined on X and Y, then for each ordered pair from X, there exists one and only one ordered pair for Y (namely the mapping is 1-to-1, onto and structure-preserving). Applied to the satisfaction of the USM, for each pair of sub-events in E in which e_i is earlier than e_{i+1}, namely e_i R_T e_{i+1}, there should exist a consistent asymmetric structural relation R_S such that R_S holds for two constituents in syntax that present e_i and e_{i+1}, and vice versa.

Within the UG system, such a structural relation could be as simple as asymmetric c-command (cf. Kayne 1994). But c-command is not usable given the lack of consistency in the structural relation between V1 and V2. Since verbs cannot be counted on to satisfy the USM, the only hope to enforce a uniform structural asymmetry between the two verbal projections lies with their objects. And the known way to establish an asymmetric syntactic relation between objects is coreferential dependency. The relevant part of the structure is given in (92) where the structural relation between V1 and V2 may vary inter- and intra-linguistically:

92. … V1 O1$_i$ … V2 O2$_i$ …

where O2 stands for the patient/theme object of V2 in a consecutive, purposive or resultative SVC or the instrumental argument of V2 (e.g. *qie* 'cut') in an instrumental SVC (cf. Baker 1989). Logically, either O1 or O2 could serve as the head of this dependency, leaving the other as the dependent. With V1 preceding V2 as determined by iconicity, letting O1 antecede O2 is the more straightforward choice and therefore the only choice if the computationally easiest option always wins among multiple derivational possibilities (Chomsky 1995). The question now is: *What kind of O2 can guarantee a cross-linguistic deterministic O1–O2 dependency despite the varying structural relations between V1 and V2?*

O2 cannot be an anaphor, simply because O1 does not necessarily c-command O2. See the binding theory-based tests in (40b, 41b) on Chinese. For the same reason but with a reversed scenario, O2 cannot be an r-expression either – O1 can c-command O2 if V1 is the matrix verb. There is another reason why an r-expression cannot be O2, which also extends to pronouns: Neither an r-expression nor a pronoun requires coindexation inside a sentence. Within the domain of sentence-level syntax, they can be referentially independent, as is explicitly captured by Binding Conditions B and C. As such, using any of them as O2 would fail to force a dependency on O1 for principled reasons. After all, a predictable interaction between R_C and R_S means that the manner of mapping is not negotiable. E.g. a set-theoretic intersectional relation between two lexical categories is always realized as an adjunct and does not have the option of being realized as an argument. If O2 is a pronoun, then, no UG principle can force it to be coindexed with O1, thereby ruining the goal of providing an isomorphic structural asymmetry to match R_T.

This effectively leaves UG with one last candidate for O2: the phonologically null "pronominal" *e*. Historically, this *e* has been called *pro* (e.g. Chomsky 1981) or *Pro* (Huang 1989). There were also efforts in the government-binding model to equate it to pronouns and limit its distribution to the subject position (see the two works above and the references therein). If *e* were truly identical to an overt pronoun in its referential behavior, it would be obviously useless for the current purpose. Interestingly, though, the phonological emptiness separates *e* from pronouns and there exists a way to define *e* which is not only empirically advantageous to the government-binding rendition of this null element, but also capable of serving as O2:

93. *e* must have its semantic content recovered from the closest constituent with a different origin.

This definition easily retains what *pro/Pro* was meant to accomplish. The typical Romance empty subject, designated as *pro*, has its semantic content recovered from the agreement morpheme in T (part of INFL in government-binding theory). The local Spec-head relation counts as the closest. Agreement resides in T, and *pro* (= *e* in (93)) originates from inside VP/*v*P, so the two have different origins (hereafter referred to as being *heterologous*). Huang (1989) proposed Generalized Control so that the *Pro* subject of certain embedded clauses in Chinese must pick the closest c-commanding DP as antecedent. By nature, the antecedent is an argument of another verb, making it heterologous from *Pro* (= *e*) inside another clause. As Huang (1989; also see Huang 1982) noted, *Pro* cannot occur as the object because, according to Generalized Control, it must pick the subject of the same clause as the antecedent, which would lead to a Binding Condition B violation. Under (93), *e* as the object and the local subject are not heterologous, both originating with the same verb. With the general acceptance of dividing the old VP into *v*P and VP, it may appear that the subject and object are indeed heterologous, one from *v* and the other from V. But this is technicality obscuring essence. It is a fact that not every verb can have an agent argument (e.g. *arrive* and *die*), so some other factor determines whether a given verb can support *v*P or not. It is simple logic, then, that the ultimate source of agent is not *v* but is already encoded inside the basic semantics of the verb root. See Marantz (1997) and Chen and Li (2021) for evidence that the ultimate source of agentivity lies with the semantics of the lexical V. We elaborate on this topic in Chapter 4.

(93) also fares better empirically than Generalized Control. Consider these examples from Chinese:

94. a. tamen   yang   na   jige   haizi   yang-de   baibaipangpang-de.
       they   raise that   a.few   child   raise-DE white.well-nourished-DE
       'Their raising of those children made them/the children fair-skinned and well fed.'
    b. yang   na   jige   haizi,   tamen   yang-de   baibaipangpang-de
       raise   that   a.few   child   they   raise-DE white.well-nourished-DE
       Same as (a).

Both examples are based on the so-called V-*de* resultative in Chinese. Structurally, the general consensus is that the postverbal -*de* helps place a clause in the complement position of V which expresses the result of the action denoted by V (Huang 1989, Y. Li 1999). It is a unique trait of the Chinese resultatives that the matrix object can be introduced with verb-reduplication, which Y. Li (1990c) treats as the extra copy of the verb heading a VP2 left-adjoined inside the main VP1:

95. They [$_{VP1}$[$_{VP2}$ raise children] raise-DE [$_S$ Pro fair-skinned and well-nourished]].

Direct evidence for this analysis is from (94b) where *raise children* is fronted together just like a PP adjunct. Also note that, reduplication aside, the structure in (95) is the same as the defended default structure for the instrumental SVC in 2.3.1 if we view the two tokens of *raise* as V1 and V2.

Given (95), the fact that both (94a, b) are equally ambiguous becomes theoretically significant. The party that becomes well-nourished during child-raising may be either the children or the parents (= *they*). Since overt movement of VP2 does not disambiguate, one must conclude that the coreference does not necessarily hinge on c-command. But the ambiguity is predicted by (93). Take Pro in (95) as *e*. Since *e* is the subject of the embedded predicate *fair-skinned-well-nourished*, it has a different origin from *children* and *they*, both semantically affiliated with the main verb. If c-command is taken as a condition for finding the content-recoverer of *e*, the matrix subject *they* is the closest to *e* since there is no other NP closer to *e* and c-commanding it. Alternatively, if c-command is put aside, just as in the case of the Romance *pro*, the closest NP is *children* (or the copy of it given the copy theory of movement) because *children* is inside the main VP while *they* is outside, assuming the agent argument to be introduced by *v* above VP. This makes *children* the right content-recoverer. In brief, *e* operates in accordance with (93) which makes c-command a possible but not obligatory requirement.

Returning to *e* as O2, we add more information to (92) to facilitate the ensuing analysis:

96.   ... [$_{vP}$ Subj *v* [$_{VP}$ ... V1 O1$_i$ ... V2 e_i]], where
   a. Subj always c-commands *e*
   b. O1 may or may not c-command *e*.

Note first that *e* is reliant on another constituent for interpretation, thus necessitating the sought-after obligatory dependency between O1 and O2. Given the SVP, V1 and V2 together with their objects denote a composite event *E*, with *v* providing the sole agent argument for *E*. Since the sub-events denoted by V1 and V2 collectively form *E*, which has an agent, the origin of Subj is shared by V1 and V2. For one thing, this is the ultimate reason for the SVC trait of *subject-sharing* (in most cases; see below for a welcome exception). For another, *e* cannot use Subj as antecedent since the latter is not heterologous from *e*. In terms of outcome, this is identical to Huang's explanation for why *pro/Pro* never occurs as the object. But in Huang's non-SVC scenario, failing to be bound by Subj equals to a failing *Pro* because the latter would be unable to meet Generalized Control. The SVC structure in (96) is not as intolerant.

Let O1 c-command *e*. Inside VP (= the main VP), O1 originates as the object of V1 only and *e* as the object of V2 only, each finding its origin from a different lexical root and therefore heterologous from the other. Thus, O1 qualifies for recovering the semantic content of *e* if c-command is used to compute closeness. *e* also has the choice of ignoring c-command. But Subj is already disqualified for not being heterologous from *e*, so the c-commanding O1 also counts as the closest NP to recover *e*'s content since both are inside the main VP. Next, suppose O1 does not c-command *e*. But with Subj ruled out anyway, O1 is the legitimate closest constituent anteceding *e* if we discount c-command. Using c-command for closeness would leave *e* unable to have content-recovery and be bad. But c-command for *e* is only an option. As long as the no-c-command option produces a legitimate antecedent, the overall result is considered good. The conclusion: *e* not only occurs as the *pro* subject in Romance and the *Pro* subject in Chinese, but also as O2 for the SVCs which demand coindexation with O1. As *e* is phonologically empty, the structure in (97) appears as if V1 and V2 are sharing an object. *This is why object-sharing is an integral part of the SVC.*

It is worthwhile to summarize the analysis so far.

97. a. The ultimate task is to satisfy the USM in the presence of $Void_F1$, namely to structure the SVC in such a way that there is an asymmetric relation in syntax that isomorphically matches the asymmetric R_T.
    b. As the iconically linearized V1 and V2 must also meet the language-specific structural arrangement inside a clause, no deterministic mapping from R_T to syntax can be obtained between the verbs, forcing F_{HL} to rely on the objects of V1 and V2 to form an isomorphic asymmetric relation between the verbal projections. In effect, the job of completing the SVC clause is sent back to UG after iconicity helps establish R_L.
    c. Within UG, the only way to implement (97b) is to establish a dependency between O1 and O2. But no nominal form is adequate for O2 of this dependency except *e* defined in (93), which in turn explains why SVCs always appear to have object-sharing.

The specific operations may be intricate, as is common with a small set of axiomatic principles collectively generating varieties of facts, but what happens conceptually is simple: The dedicated linguistic system UG has a functional void; a more general cognitive apparatus, linear iconicity, is mobilized to help out where it can as permitted by the FICH and carried out according to the USM.

2.5.5   More Facts Explained: When and How V1 Is Ditransitive

In evaluating Carstens' structure for SVCs in 2.3.2 and Aboh's in 2.4.4, we saw that Chinese allows a ditransitive verb such as *gei* 'give' to be V1 while Kwa languages do not. If our analysis given so far, especially the part in 2.5.4 on object-sharing, indeed captures the inner workings of SVCs, the Chinese–Kwa contrast ought to be accommodated in a natural way as well. And it is.

To begin with, why is *give* even allowed in the SVC? The analysis on object-sharing in the preceding section relies on a single O1 inside the lexical VP to be the closest content-recovery constituent for *e*, aka O2. If a verb has two objects, the uniqueness of O1 would seem to disappear. How would one calculate the right object from V1 to construct the unique dependency required by the USM? Wouldn't we have too many objects from V1 to even guarantee a deterministic mapping from R_T to syntax? We start with the fact:

98. Ping'er ganggang   gei-le   Jia Lian yikuar yuebing   chi.
    Ping'er a.moment.ago give-ASP JL   a.piece mooncake eat
    'Ping'er just gave JL a piece of moon cake to eat.'

As the translation indicates, V2 actually shares both objects of V1, with the
goal argument *Jia Lian* understood to be the subject of *eat* and the theme
argument *yikuar yuebing* 'a piece of mooncake' the object of *eat*. On the
surface, this is already troublesome as one would apparently need to postulate
two *e*'s for V2, which immediately threatens the operation of finding the closest
content-recovery constituent.

The way out lies in the precise analysis of ditransitive verbs. Multiple recent
works have argued that morphological applicatives in Bantu languages are best
analyzed as a head, call it Appl. In syntax, Appl projects above the lexical root
verb V (see Y. Li 2005 and Pylkkänen 2008,[26] among others) so that when the
goal or benefactive (G/B) argument is introduced with Appl in Bantu, the
syntactic structure is something like (99):

99.

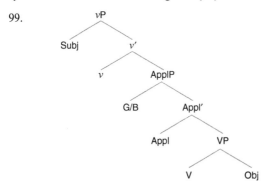

That (99) seems appropriate for ditransitive verbs is suggested by comparing
the Tswana examples (Creissels 2016) with their English translations:

100. a. Lorato   o-tlaa-kwal-a   lo-kwalo.
          CL.Lorato AGR-FUT-write-FV   CL-letter
          'Lorato will write a letter.'
      b. Lorato   o-tlaa-kual-el-a   Kitso   lo-kwalo
          CL.Lorato AGR-FUT-write-APPL-FV   CL.Kitso   CL-letter
          'Lorato will write Kitso a letter.'

Bantu languages such as Tswana and Chichewa (see Marantz 1993) exhibit
word-order variation for the G/B argument in that the latter, introduced via
Appl, must occur between the verbal cluster and the verb's original object.
What is enlightening is that the corresponding English sentences, though with
no Appl morpheme seen, display exactly the same word order. The same

pattern applies to English ditransitive verbs with the well-studied dative alternation: *give a book to Mat* vs. *give Mat a book*. The word-order variation is expected if English differs from Bantu only in having a phonologically empty Appl. Identical word-order alternations are also seen in Chinese, though they look like SVCs rather than Appl:

101. a. song yige   liwu gei Yueyue
           send   a   gift give Yueyue
           'send a gift to Yueyue'
      b. song(-gei)   Yueyue yige liwu
           send-give   Yueyue a   gift
           'send(-to) Yueyue a gift'

If ditransitive verbs have the structure (99), (98) is most appropriately analyzed as having the lexical (and ditransitive) verb *gei* 'give' as V1 and *chi* 'eat' as V2, both located inside VP in (99) in the way or ways described in the previous section (2.5.4). The relevant parts of the syntactic structure for (98) is (102), in which the two lexical verbs *give* and *eat* structurally share the same Appl and *v* heads:

102.   [$_{vP}$ Ping' er v [$_{appP}$ JL Appl [$_{VP}$ ... give a-piece-of-mooncake ... eat e]]]

    NP1   NP2   NP3

This extra goal argument *JL* from a hidden Appl gives rise to interesting complications. For easier reference, I will mark the three overt arguments in (102) as NP1, NP2 and NP3.

 First, while the agent argument NP1 is non-heterologous to the objects of V1 *give*, it is a fact that the understood agent of V2 *eat* is not NP1 but *JL*, the goal argument NP2 from *give*. At least in Chinese, there is clear evidence that this shift of agent on the part of V2 is not the enforced result of grammar but one from our knowledge of the world: After you give food F to someone X – keep in mind that this is an SVC with sub-events connected via R_T 'earlier than' – you no longer have that same F and thus cannot eat it. Meanwhile, since X has F due to the action of V1, the subsequent eating of V2 is performed by X. One naturally wonders at this point how exactly the applied argument of V1 may acquire the agentive interpretation for V2 given the widely recognized idea, also adopted here, that the agent argument is introduced by the dedicated *v*. In this view, *v* does so because agentivity is encoded in its semantics (e.g. Kratzer 1996); but the semantics of Appl is to bring in an oblique argument, not agent. We return to the applicatives in Chapter 4, assuming for now that somehow *JL* can be understood as the agent for V2.

 That pragmatics at work is substantiated by (103):

103. Ping'er tou-le   Jian Lian yikuai yuebing   chi.
     Ping'er steal-ASP JL   a.piece mooncake eat
     'Ping'er stole from JL a piece of moon cake to eat.'

This sentence differs from (98) only in having *tou* 'steal' replacing *gei* 'give' in the V1 position, with the applied argument NP2 *JL* being the source rather than the goal. Since the "direction of action" denoted by V1 is reversed, the eventual owner of the food F is indeed the shared subject of both verbs, and it is this subject NP1, *Ping'er* in (103), who is the eater of F.

Second, the pragmatically determined agent argument of V2 helps determine how e, the empty object of V2, finds its antecedent. Consider V1 being *give* first. Let e recover its content under c-command in (102). If NP3, *a piece of mooncake*, c-commands e, then it is also the closest c-commander for e. Alternatively, if NP3 does not c-command e, the goal argument NP2 is the closest c-commander by definition because AppP immediately contains VP (see (102)). But this NP2 is also the agent of *eat* and thus thematically associated with it, no longer being heterologous with e. This means that e fails for content-recovery under c-command in accordance with (93) and thus must turn to the no-c-command option. But if c-command is put aside, NP3 *a piece of moon cake* is necessarily the closest NP to e since they are both inside the VP in (102). In sum, the object of V2 *eat,* namely e, will pick NP3 with or without c-command. This explains the obligatory and consistent object-sharing reading in (98).

Next suppose V1 to be *steal*. With the agent argument NP1 from v shared by both V1 and V2, as pragmatically appropriate, e has the potential to pick either the source argument NP2 or the patient argument NP3 as antecedent, depending on whether c-command plays a role in the picking. However, common sense interferes again. NP2, *JL* in (103), is dismissed as a possible antecedent for e due to absurdity: When Ping'er steals from JL a piece of moon cake, it is natural that she eats the cake but not that she eats JL! Hence, e as the object of V2 of (103) always ends up using *a piece of moon cake* as the closest content-recovery antecedent, regardless of c-command.

This explanation of (98) and (103) also offers a natural way to understand why, according to Aboh (2009), Kwa languages do not accept a ditransitive V1 like *give* (see 2.4.4 above). The USM merely cares about a predictable dependency between the objects of V1 and V2. When V1 is ditransitive, structural determinacy and semantic congruity are simultaneously threatened. What separates Kwa from Chinese is how many UG-external aids are acceptable in order to form SVC clauses. Kwa languages insist on iconicity being the only non-UG apparatus and thus rule out ditransitive V1 "in principle." Chinese follows the same strategy by default but, with V1 being ditransitive, is willing to go further to pragmatics provided that a predictable dependency can be established between the object of V2 and one of the non-agent arguments from V1 while no part of UG is sacrificed (e.g. *e* still needs a heterologous source for content-recovery).

2.5.6 More Facts Explained: When and Why Resultative SVCs Act Differently

Of the four semantic types of SVC, instrumental, consecutive, purposive and resultative, the last one is the only type that, judging from the documented cases, does not always exhibit subject-sharing (see Miskito (7)), may take the form of a compound (Chinese (5)) and, as a compound, is not obliged to argument-share at all (see below), a very odd set of exceptions. Before demonstrating that these exceptions are predicted by the USM, however, let us recapitulate what makes an SVC resultative. As the SVP states, all SVCs express but one semantic relation among the sub-events, R_T. But when V2 denotes a change of state which can be naturally attributed to the action denoted by V1, the SVC is understood to be resultative. With this in mind, the odd behavior of the resultative SVC is explained as follows: The works of Y. Li (1990c, 1993, 1995, 1999), all on resultative compounds, are briefly recounted to introduce a semantic property and a structural one; the semantic property will be used to explain the optional subject-sharing; the structural one will be responsible for the behavioral exceptions of the compounds.

Chinese resultative compounds are known to be potentially three-way ambiguous given appropriate contexts, and thus distinguish themselves from their English counterparts:

104. Jia   zhui-lei-le   Yi.
     X   chase-be.tired-ASP   Y
     a. 'X chased Y and Y became tired.'
     b. 'X chased Y and X became tired.'
     c. 'Y chased X and Y became tired.'

Y. Li (1995) questions why the logically predicted fourth reading, that Y chased X and X became tired, is never possible, regardless of context. It is further noted that, of the three available readings, (a) and (c) have a distinct flavor of "causal roles" played by the two arguments in the clause. In both, X is the causer and Y the affected. Most noticeable is (c), where X is the patient argument of *chase* and Y is understood as the agent of *chase*. Despite a total violation of the thematic hierarchy, X the chased is interpreted as the party responsible for making the chaser Y tired, a possible scenario being that X's long-lasting stamina led Y the chaser to physical exhaustion. But this causer–affected semantics is not perceived in (b).

From this fact, Li identified an algorithm for distributing the causal roles in a resultative construction, restated below:

105. a. The structurally most prominent argument of V1 acquires the causer reading if it does not undergo the change described by V2;
      b. The affected reading is assigned to the argument of V2 which is no part of (105a).

In (104), X is an argument of V1 *zhui* 'chase' whether it is the agent or patient and not thematically related to V2 *lei* 'be tired' at all, which makes it qualify for (105a). Y is (at least) the argument of V2 *lei* and it indeed undergoes a change of state. So it acquires the affected reading according to (105b). Li also proposed that the causal-role hierarchy in (105) overrides the thematic hierarchy. Or to put it in another way, an overall causal construction C may allow us to reorganize the relevant arguments in C legitimately according to their causal roles defined in (105). On one hand, this explains the strange thematic reversal in (104c). On the other hand, the missing fourth reading is also expected. In this case, the grammatical subject X is thematically linked to V1 (*chase*) for sure, but it is also the party becoming tired and thus affiliated with V2. Hence it does not meet (105a) for being a causer. Meanwhile, Y is not even related to V2 in this intended interpretation, which disqualifies it as the affected. Since X and Y do not even enter the causal hierarchy defined by (105), the thematic hierarchy must be respected, fundamentally ruling out the fourth reading that the subject X is both the chased and the tired while the object Y is the chaser.

As part of the human language faculty F_{HL},[27] (105) provides a way to obtain the O1–O2 dependency in the resultative SVC without forcing *e* to rely on a shared subject for a necessary, hence deterministic, connection with O1. Recall that the shared subject plays a critical role in letting SVCs satisfy the USM because it is non-heterologous to *e* so that *e* can only pick O1 for content-recovery, thereby creating what appears to be obligatory object-sharing. Once R_T is equated to a causal relation (which in itself entails temporal precedence between cause and effect in our perception of the universe), (105) becomes an available mechanism to effectively exclude the subject of V1 from forming a dependency with O2. As long as O2 needs an antecedent for content-recovery, it must be coindexed with O1 (vs. the subject) in order to stay as the affected party under (105b), leaving the subject of V1 the necessarily unaffected causer. It is this extra layer of proper interpretation that implements the O1–O2 dependency separately from subject-sharing. And because (105) works only with resultatives, only the resultative SVC can be exempted from subject-sharing. Needless to say, nothing prevents this SVC from acting like other SVCs and making use of subject-sharing (see Sranan (28a) where V1 and V2 are both transitive). After all, what is actually inside E is R_T, a simple 'earlier-than' relation.

Y. Li (1993) also compares Chinese with Japanese resultative compounds and found a contrast already mentioned in (58–59) of 2.3.4: Whereas Chinese allows *hit-die*, Japanese must use *hit-kill*. The different allowance/requirement on the transitivity of V2 is associated with Chinese verbal projections being head-initial vs. Japanese being uniformly head-final. Assuming that the head of a compound must participate in thematically supporting the agent argument (essentially via *v* being licensed by the head of a compound V; see Chen and Li 2021), the head-initial *hit-die* will have V1 supporting the agent argument of the clause and exempt V2 from this responsibility (hence allowing the unaccusative *die*), but the head-final *hit-kill* expects V2 to support the agent argument thematically, forcing V2 to be the transitive *kill*.

What regulates the formation of resultative compounds in Chinese and Japanese does not end here. Li further compares these two examples:

106.   a. Chinese (Y. Li 1993 (10))
            Taotao   tiao-fan-le   Youyou.
            Taotao   dance-be.bored-ASP   Youyou
            'Taotao danced and as a result Youyou got bored.'
       b. Japanese (ibid. (12))
            John-ga   (*Mary-o)   odori-akiru-ta.
            John-NOM   Mary-ACC   dance-be.bored-PAST
            i. Without *Mary*:   'John danced and as a result got bored.'
            ii. Unavailable: 'Mary or some unspecified person danced and as a result
                                 John got bored.'

Since *tiao* 'dance, jump' is the head of the compound in Chinese, it must be thematically connected with the subject *Taotao*, leaving *fan* 'be bored' free to simply take *Youyou* as its argument. This all follows from the previous analysis (we discuss argument-sharing in compounds shortly). But Japanese is head-final, so the subject-supporting burden is on *akiru* 'be bored'. Logically, one would expect *odori* 'dance' to be freed from the same burden and thus predicated only of either the object *Mary-o* or even some unspecified dancer, essentially the mirror image of Chinese.[28] This prediction is not borne out. In fact, Li points out that Japanese resultative compounds generally behave like double-headed "coordinated" compounds in the same language, a fact that is not derivable from any existing theoretical apparatus.

As a solution, Li proposed that V1 in a resultative acts as a head due to its status in the event structure:

107.   In a composite event of two sub-events causally connected, the event of cause
       always maps to the structural head.

Two facts support (107). First, dedicated causative verbs such as *make* and *cause* encode a generic event of cause and are represented as the main verbs while the event of effect takes the form of a structural complement to these main verbs. Second, the European style of resultatives always expresses the event of cause with the verb of the clause and delegates the effect to a small clause subordinate to the verb (Williams 1980, Rizzi 1990, Levin and Rappaport-Hovav 1995, among many others). In other words, the overall head-final structure of Japanese assigns the head status to V2 of a resultative compound, but (107) makes V1 a head as well, leading to the double-headed behavior in (106b) where both V1 and V2 support the subject. In comparison, a Chinese resultative is simultaneously structurally and "causally" head-initial. Hence V2 is a non-head by any standard.

Whatever is the ultimate reason for (107), it must be part of F_{HL} and thus is expected to be available to syntactic SVCs as well. Now consider Miskito, which has a strictly head-final VP structure plus the fact that the verbs in a resultative SVC may have different argument structures, a transitive V1 and an intransitive V2 for instance. (7) is repeated below with the negative alternative added to highlight the mono-clausal nature of the resultative SVC in question (see (62a)):

108. Witin ai   pruk-an   kauhw-ri/ra.   (Miskito, Hale 1991: 37)
      he   me   strike-OBV.3 fall-PAST.1/NEG
      'He knocked/didn't knock me down.'

As already made clear earlier, (105b) lets the *e* argument of V2 (*kauhw* 'fall') be coindexed with the object of V1, *ai* 'me', for the affected interpretation, which in turn exempts V2 from the need to share the agent argument with V1 while still satisfying the USM. So far so good. But it also means that V2, as the structural head of this Miskito SVC, does *not* contribute thematically to the agent argument *witin* 'he' in (108). How is this to be understood in the overall theory of SVCs presented here?

What must be kept in mind is that one is not obliged to put (107) to work in (108) because, after all, the SVP determines that what underlies even the so-called resultative SVC is just R_T. We take R_T to be causal where it conveniently helps (as in satisfying the USM without subject-sharing) but we can always appeal to the true semantics of R_T when so doing is, again, convenient to us. Indeed, if we put (107) aside, V2 is automatically the head of the Miskito SVC, as evidenced by the tense-agreement suffix *-ri* on *kauhw* 'fall', while V1 projects its own VP and *v*P in whatever structural relation with V2 is in accordance with Miskito grammar (see 2.5.3 above), presumably something like (109):

109. $[_{TP} [_{VP2} [_{vP} \text{he } v [_{VP1} \text{me}_i \text{ strike}]] [_{V2'} e_i \text{ fall}]] \text{ T}]$

Since V2 heads the main predicate VP, T scans VP2, finds the single argument of V2, namely *e*, and agrees with it (see Chomsky's 2000 probe-goal model of syntactic licensing). As *e* is coindexed with *me* inside VP1 due to (105b) (and anticipating the discussion of (111) below), T is manifested with the first-person form *-ri*. Meanwhile, V1 projects to VP1 and then *v*P to have its agent argument expressed. No evidence is known from Miskito for the precise structural relation between this *v*P and V2. So we make the plausible assumption that *v*P is adjoined to V2', a possibility already seen in other SVC languages.

Also worth noting is that Miskito, like other Misumalpan languages, uses subject obviation, shown with *-an* '-OBV.3' in (108). Hale (1991) describes its three grammatical functions: (i) to mark the subordinate verb, (ii) to make it "anaphoric" to the main verb in terms of tense (p. 21) and (iii) to "signal not only that the subject of the dependent verb is distinct from that of the main, or final, verb but also, to some degree, the person category to which the subject of the dependent verb belongs" (p. 4–5). Function (i) confirms our structural analysis in (109), with V1 *plap* 'strike' treated as the "dependent verb." So does function (ii), since being anaphoric to the tense of the main verb, i.e. our V2, is consistent with saying that both verbs share the same T node. What is especially interesting is function (iii). Since our account of object-sharing in SVCs expresses the object of V2 as a phonologically empty *e*, a Miskito resultative SVC like (108) is short of an overt subject for the main verb V2. Meanwhile, the subject of the dependent verb V1 is overt, creating a rather confusing – indeed seemingly abnormal – scenario because typically, the overtly expressed subject would pair with the main verb. The obviative suffix on V1 helps dispel this illusion explicitly.

Hale (1991: 37) also reports that (108) is actually ambiguous between "serialization," as analyzed above, and "chaining," which is most evidently seen when V2 is negated with *-ra* 'NEG'. In the case of chaining, negation can have scope only over V2, letting (108) mean 'He struck me and I didn't fall.' This possibility also has an explanation from our theory. As is widely accepted in the UG theory of syntax, sentential negation is best represented as NegP between TP and the predicate phrase and thus with scope over everything in the latter, including both V1 and V2 in SVCs. This setup yields the "mono-clausal" interpretation given in (108). Now suppose one opts to use *-ra* for V2 only, in effect imposing (110):

110.   [$_{TP}$ [$_{vP}$ he *v* [$_{VP1}$ me$_i$ strike]] [$_{NegP}$ [$_{VP2}$ [$_{V2'}$ *e*$_i$ fall]] Neg] T] (cf. (108))

That is, the *v*P containing V1 is pushed outside the scope of Neg so as not to be affected by *-ra*. All grammatical and semantic properties of Hale's chaining variant of (108) follow from this structure.

First, (110) still qualifies as an SVC since vP and NegP each denote a set of events just as the VP in them does. For vP, see Kratzer (1996) and Chapter 4 below; with NegP below TP, Neg only provides the [+negative] feature to the overall interpretation but does not change the semantic type of VP/vP. Consequently, the iconic word order remains intact and object-sharing is still expected to guarantee an isomorphic mapping from R_T to R_S.

Second, R_T is no longer subject to the resultative interpretation. Recall from 2.5.1 that this reading depends on V2 describing a change of state plausibly caused by the event of V1. Falling is a change of state, while no falling means no change of state. This explains the chaining reading when -*ra* negates V2 only.

Third, no resultative interpretation equates to (105b) becoming unavailable, while the object of V2 still needs to be *e* in order to, hopefully, establish a USM-approved structural mapping of R_T. This is where subject obviation plays a critical role. By explicitly labeling the subject of V1 to be *different* from what triggers agreement on T, that is *e* of V2, the obviative suffix has the same effect as subject-sharing of V1 and V2 in "normal" SVCs, both excluding the agent subject from being qualified to recover *e*'s content. Therefore, *e* can only pick the object of V1 as antecedent.

This use of subject-obviation morphology to implement the needed O1–*e* dependency for V1 and V2 gives us a list of the available mechanisms for the task. Just like (111a), (111b-c) only specify relations between arguments and not any structural ones between V1 and V2:

111. a. Via subject-sharing under the heterology-based content-recovery of *e* in (93),
          which is also the default one for most SVCs;
      b. Using the causal-role algorithm in (105b), which is available only to
          resultatively interpreted SVCs;
      c. Relying on subject obviation in certain structural contexts, one such case
          being the Miskito "chaining" SVC.

As it happens, the Miskito positive SVC in (108) presents the context where both (111b-c) are available. That is, either one of these tools will be sufficient in that example to make *e* coindexed with O1 perforce. And in the absence of negation, the two options are hard to distinguish. The redundancy is evident and makes it tempting to forgo (111b).

But the temptation must be resisted. The following Tetun Fehan (Austronesian) example is from Hajek (2006: 247):

112. soldadu Indonézia buti   nia feen mate tiha.
      soldier Indonesia squeeze 3s wife die PERF
      'The Indonesian soldier strangled his wife to death.3'

In a language with a head-initial VP and without morphological subject obviation, (111c) is not around to help and the unaccusative V2 (*mate* 'die') can only rely on (111b) to guarantee object-sharing. Ridding the theory of language of redundancy has been a major characteristic of the field in the past decades, a topic to be returned to later in the chapter.

To summarize so far, (111a, b, c) and the structural mapping of causally connected sub-events in (107), all independently motivated, collaborate with the rest of UG to explain why a syntactic SVC of the resultative kind may have an unaccusative V2 while still satisfying the USM. Next, we consider the other two odd properties of the resultative SVC, both found with the compound form.

To start with, the O1–*e* strategy is not available to SVC compounds if we adopt for now the lexicalist view that compounds are words formed separately from phrasal syntax, a topic to be picked up in Chapter 4. Assuming compounds to result from direct morpheme merger and not the underlying phrasal structure of syntax plus head-movement, V1 and V2 directly merge into a word without taking any object. Y. Li (1990c) adopts Higginbotham's (1985) θ-identification to handle any "argument-sharing" in this case. For *zhui-lei* 'chase-be.tired' in (104a), for instance, the object θ-role of V1 and the single θ-role of V2 are semantically identified via set-theoretic intersection, so that the compound has the "super object θ-role" defining the set of individuals who are chased and become tired. What matters for now is that θ-identification, unlike the syntactic means of O1–*e* dependency, is unable to express an asymmetric structural relation and therefore cannot isomorphically represent the asymmetric R_T. To satisfy the USM, (107) becomes the only channel to deterministically convert R_T to an asymmetric structural R_S. And three consequences follow from this.

First, we understand instantly why only the resultative SVC can take a compound form.

113. a. ta zuo yu chi.   (Chinese)
     3s cook fish eat
     'S/He cooked and ate a fish.'

  b. *ta zuo-chi(-le)   yu.
     3s cook-eat-ASP   fish

  c. ta zuo-shu-le   yu.
     3s cook-fully.cooked-ASP fish
     'S/He had the fish well cooked.'

114. a. John-ga   sakana-o ni-te   tabe-ta. (Japanese)
     John-NOM fish-ACC boil-SUF eat-PAST
     'John boiled and ate fish.'

  b. *John-ga   sakana-o ni-tabe-ta.
     John-NOM fish-ACC boil-eat-PAST

  c. X-ga   Y-o   naguri-korosu-ta. (Same as (59b))
     X-NOM Y-ACC hit-kill-PAST
     'X hit Y and as a result killed Y.'

VP in Chinese is head-initial and O1 must occur between the two verbs in the consecutive SVC in (113a vs. 113b), in comparison with the resultative, where the semantic object of V1 follows both verbs (113c). In the Japanese counterparts (114), V1 and V2 in a consecutive SVC are separated by the suffix -te on V1, indicating the syntactic nature of the SVC. The absence of this suffix signals an SVC compound, good for the resultative but bad for the consecutive. This is so because except for the resultative, no other semantic types of SVCs subject their own R_T to the causal reinterpretation and therefore none of them can make use of (107). But without the help of this principle, there is no other apparatus either in UG or outside to guarantee a uniform isomorphic R_S between V1 and V2 inside a compound. In brief, for compounding, only the resultative SVC may satisfy the USM via (107);[29] all other types fail to meet the expectation of the USM.

The second outcome is equally straightforward. If the USM is taken care of by (107), then there is no longer need for any form of argument-sharing, which explains why Chinese resultative compounds, being head-initial as made clear earlier, exhibit the maximal degree of freedom in the distribution of the θ-roles of V1 and V2. In addition to the various readings in (104), Chinese even allows V1 and V2 to have no θ-identification at all:

115. Lele   chang-ku-le   henduo   tingzhong.
     Lele   sing-cry-ASP   many   audience
     'Lele sang and as a result many people in the audience cried.'

Lastly, the obligatory use of (107) for resultative compounds also explains a contrast between Japanese and Miskito which, at first sight, seems like a logical flaw in our analysis. Since the Miskito resultative in (108) has the option of not claiming R_T to be causal in Hale's chaining interpretation, the Japanese resultative ought to enjoy the same choice. But such a choice would wrongly allow a Japanese resultative compound to be purely head-final only and thus fail to explain its actual double-headed behavior in (106b), effectively setting us back to square one! Now we know that there is no logical problem at all. Miskito has the phrasal resultative SVC where establishing the O1–e dependency is the default means to satisfy the USM. Provided that there are grammatical means such as the obviative morphology to guarantee the needed dependency, there is no pressure on Miskito to take R_T as causal. On the other hand, the resultative SVC in Japanese takes the form of a compound and cannot rely on the syntactically formed O1–e coindexation. If (107) were not used, such

a compound could not even be formed in our theory of UG-I – in 2.3.4, we showed
that morphological headedness varies from language to language and is unable to
help establish a cross-linguistically isomorphic mapping from R_T to R_S. In other
words, the data may seem messy and their analysis intricate, but they all fall
perfectly into place in the theory presented here.

2.5.7   More Facts Explained: Revisiting Dagaare PCC, etc.

Recall from 2.3.3 that Kwa languages display a range of variations with respect
to predicate cleft. In particular, Dagaare allows focus-fronting of V1 plus the
shared object, V2 plus the shared object, and both V1 and V2 plus the shared
object. Of these options, V1+obj and V1+V2+obj are straightforward for our
analysis of the SVC because in both cases, what is fronted is a structural
constituent (VP1 or the entire VP). But V2+obj (see (52c)) is not as simple,
since in our account of the SVC so far, the overt object is grouped with V1
while V2 only takes the phonologically empty e as its object. Therefore, even
when we treat V2 as the main verb and focus-move VP2, the overt object is not
expected to go with it.

   We propose that an extra factor is at work in Dagaare that capitalizes on the
details of UG. (116) is the syntactic structure of (52c) after adapting Hiraiwa
and Bodomo's (2008) analysis to ours:

116.   [[meat eat$_{nominal}$] ... he ... [$_{VP2}$ [$_{VP1}$ roast e] [eat ~~meat~~]]]

According to H&B, phrasal cleft has the option of phonologically pronouncing
either the object in the moved verbal projection or the one in the original copy.
In (116), we ~~strike~~ the object not pronounced. Now recall that for the purpose of
establishing a coreferential dependency between O1 and O2, either one of these
objects could be e from the purely structural perspective, given how e has its
content recovered under (93) and the fact that there is no consistent structural
relation between V1 and V2 in SVCs anyway. O2 takes the e form only because
linear iconicity places the verbal constituent containing O1 before the one
containing O2, making O1 the cross-linguistically default *ante*cedent in
a coreferential dependency. It is self-evident that this setup is the simplest to
implement, with O1 being simultaneously close enough to structurally recover
O2's content and phonologically overt to antecede the gap in the natural
direction of utterance production. What happens in Dagaare, it seems, is to
allow these two aspects of the licensing job to be carried out separately. In
(116), e picks the stricken copy of O2 for structure-based content-recovery and
the overt copy of O2 as the phonological antecedent.

   There is indirect evidence that this is indeed the case. Throughout their paper
and of the multiple Kwa languages mentioned therein, H&B only associated

the V2+obj cleft with Dagaare. If this is not accidental, the option at hand must be rare. Considering that VP cleft happens to multiple Kwa languages (see the chart in (57)), it is likely that more languages of this group allow the option of treating either V1 or V2 as the main verb just like Dagaare. What prevents these Kwa languages from having the Dagaare-style V2+obj cleft is precisely their reluctance to split phonological antecedence from structural content-recovery. In other words, they want O1 to be always the true antecedent both phonologically and semantically, a conspicuously most consistent solution in a grammatical system.

The last fact to be considered with respect to argument-sharing are those cases of serial verbs which share the subject but not the object. In (76), we demonstrated with Chinese that buying newspapers and reading newspapers can indeed be understood iconically when (76a) is said alone, but are readily subject to the reversed reading when (76b) provides a different context. To our knowledge, this holds for all cases of serial verbs with only subject-sharing unless certain choices of the lexical items used to construct such a sentence impose a particular sequence of events. For instance, if one went to the fish market and bought fish, it is quite hard to reverse the event sequence even when an overt conjunctive is used. We conclude from such facts, and predict from the USM too, that a clause containing a series of verbs without object-sharing in a (phrasal) SVC language opts to not treat the sub-events as forming a composite event E as dfined in the SVP. It is precisely the lack of E that makes such examples resemble the conjunctive construction in many ways. Since they are shown not to bear on iconicity except in theoretically superficial ways (i.e. only in the sense of Grice's "be orderly"), we will not pursue them any further. For the same reason, the term SVC is reserved throughout this book for those cases of serial verbs with object-sharing.

To end this section, we briefly assess Kayne's (1994) antisymmetric syntax, which in essence defends a model of isomorphic mapping between R_S and R_L (vs. the isomorphic R_C-to-R_S mapping in the USM) by imposing the Linear Correspondence Axiom (LCA) of *earlier iff higher*. It should be obvious from the foregoing texts that Kayne's theory falls short at least for SVCs (and for coordination in the next chapter) because the same word order critically does *not* correspond to the same structural setup. We use Sranan as a case study.

From the examples (31–32) of 2.3.1, it was concluded that in the Sranan instrumental SVC, V1 is the main verb while V2 heads VP2 either as a complement or an adjunct, giving rise to the different judgments on *wh*-moving the patient/theme object of V2. For VP2 to act as the complement is fully compatible with the LCA which, minimally, needs to allow the basic head-initial structure in English anyway. Now consider VP2 in the adjunct position. (117) below represents the schematic syntactic structure of the Sranan examples in question, with X for a phrasal projection of V1 and Y a phrasal projection of V2:

117. [CP [TP Kofi [[X use O1] [Y cut O2] ...]]]

If every constituent in (117) is generated *in situ*, Y being an adjunct will correctly prevent the *wh*-form of O2 from moving into CP. But (117) is banned by the LCA because Y right-adjoins to X by hypothesis. Then Y asymmetrically c-commands both V1 and O1 (i.e. higher than them) but is linearly after them, directly contradicting the "higher iff earlier" requirement.

To avoid this problem while still producing the actual word order, X must originate after Y, in the " ... " position and thus lower than Y, and then move up the tree and left of Y. But complications arise. First and foremost, why should the pre-movement structure in (117) be even an option What is needed here is to allow the *wh*-object of *use* to move out while keeping Y as an island. But with X starting in "..." in (117) and in compliance with the LCA, two legitimate structures exist: (i) *cut* is the main verb taking the phrase of *use* as complement and (ii) *use* remains the main verb projecting to X while the phrase of *cut*, i.e. Y in (117), is left-adjoined to X. With (ii), Y is the adjunct island expected to prevent the *wh*-form of O2 from moving out and thus would yield the contrast in (31–32). But this desirable outcome would never get a chance to emerge due to (i): As *cut* can be the main verb, its object O2 should be free to move, so any extraction would automatically pick (i) as the structure to operate on. In addition, the purported and obligatory movement of X in (117) lacks clear motivation, since either (i) or (ii) is a legitimate structure for the UG model containing the LCA. Furthermore, even if X did move for some reason, it would weaken the designated status of the LCA, namely being the sole innate algorithm for the isomorphic mapping between structure and word order. Now one would have to admit that part of the word order of some natural languages is the result of iconicity.

Problems like the above as well as others to be examined later call for an alternative theory of linearization to accommodate the facts and analyses presented in this chapter and afterwards, a task to be undertaken in Chapter 4.

2.5.8   *Back to Grammaticalization*

While Newmeyer's works repeatedly denied linear iconicity in the case of SVCs (see 2.1.4, 2.2.3, 2.4.3), to the extent that we have proven differently, the obligatorily iconic sequence of V1 and V2 would fall into what he refers to as the grammaticalization of "structural options that reflect discourse-iconic principles," summarized in (6b) of Chapter 1. But what exactly is involved in such a grammaticalization?

When a language opts for not expressing a composite event inside a clause (i.e. choosing the negative value for the SVP), either a single verb encodes events of a complex structure or multiple clauses are used. This is English. But when the value of the SVP is positive, (i) UG's soft spot, $\text{Void}_F 1$ in (85), is exposed, (ii) iconicity is called in by the FICH to map R_T to R_L, and (iii) what remains unresolved by iconicity, namely R_S, is sent back to UG, which finishes the job with the aid of both language-specific grammar and (iv) the USM that utilizes isomorphism to establish a deterministic mapping from R_T to R_S, with isomorphism regarded by some scholars as a key component of iconicity. It is this back-n-forth interaction between two separate mechanisms that produces the unique set of traits in (62) associated with the SVCs. This, I contend, is how iconicity is "grammaticalized" in the case of SVCs. And this is where we advise caution about using the term "grammaticalization" casually on linguistic iconicity.

On one hand, there is indeed a single most critical factor responsible for the use of iconicity turned obligatory in the SVC, R_T. The fact that, unlike Grice's "be orderly" maxim, linear iconicity is not breakable in the SVC (see 2.4.4, especially (77)) follows from expressing R_T inside the composite event E under the general constraints of the FICH and the USM. Because iconicity is the only means to express R_T, negating it with an additional context would resemble using the word *before* to mean 'after' or 'at the same time'. In comparison, we suggest that the Gricean implicature is found only in places without an overtly expressed composite event E, including but not limited to events linked together with inherently symmetrical relations like 'and' and 'or'. See Chapter 3.

Meanwhile, simply labeling obligatory iconicity in the SVC as "grammaticalized" can be misleading because the term ends up hiding an intricate set of UG- and iconicity-based activities, each of which is of the most general nature but with its own intrinsic functional limitations/restrictions, the only language-specific decision being the SVP setting. If anything, what happens in expressing E is more like weaving iconicity into a weak spot of UG and as such, using standard algorithms to adjust each thread to accommodate how UG and iconicity make contact. In the spirit of finding exactly how UG interacts with "third-factor principles" (see Chapter 1), it is the level of detail presented in this chapter that makes a theory of UG-I concrete and specific enough for further assessment.

One last word about UG-I in the context of the SVC. The USM is defined as enforcing a deterministic mapping from R_C to R_S. In its application to R_T, a particular instance of R_C, isomorphism is used to guarantee the mapping. By definition, isomorphism is (homomorphic) bijective mapping and thus always yields a strictly one-to-one connection between two relations. At least for the linguistic data in this chapter and the next, isomorphism proves adequate for the application of the USM, making one wonder whether the USM can be revised by simply substituting isomorphism for the deterministic requirement. We leave this question for future study, focusing instead on demonstrating that as it is and perhaps subject to further optimization, our UG-I is capable of accounting for large collections of facts that have resisted exclusively UG-based analyses and it accomplishes this with a small set of highly general apparatuses such the FICH, the USM and the SVP.

2.6   Linearization vs. Fear: A Biological Analogy and a Conclusion

The essence of the UG-I account of SVCs is that iconicity helps UG where UG is incapable on its own. But this necessarily means there are two linearization algorithms available to language: the R_S-to-R_L mapping which is typically studied in the general UG framework, and the use of iconicity. In terms of their functions, this is a redundancy. Detailed argumentation has been given in this chapter that linear iconicity is a very different kind of animal from UG's default linearization algorithm because it jumps from semantics directly to word order. Still, the two algorithms overlap partially. For instance, recall how Carstens' theory only allows *take* but not *cut* to be the matrix verb (2.3.2) provided that *v*P2 is treated as the complement of V1. As we noted, her theory falls apart with examples like (45). But to the extent that Carstens' structure may hold in some cases, at least certain generally plausible implementations of UG have the power to generate part of the SVC data. A natural question is why such a redundancy exists. We suggest that it may be viewed as evidence that UG and iconicity reflect different evolutionary stages of human language, with the former evolved on top of, but not replacing, the latter.

We start by looking at the procedural differences between the two algorithms.

First, *iconicity linearizes through a "shorter" procedural route than UG does*. As made amply clear throughout the previous text, iconicity maps the temporal information in a semantic relation, R_T, directly onto the linear order of the two linguistic constituents denoting sub-events. In contrast, UG linearizes in two steps: from R_C to R_S and from R_S to R_L. See (3a, b) of Chapter 1.

Second, *iconic linearization is information-crude when compared with UG*. Iconically incurred linear order can express only the temporal relation between two sub-events, leaving all other semantic details to be determined from contextual clues that may or may not be sufficient. This is best illustrated with the single Chinese SVC example below, which can be interpreted to be either instrumental or purposive:

118. Taotao   na   zheba   dao   qie   rou.
      Taotao   take   this   knife   cut   meat

Instrumental: 'Taotao cuts meat with this knife.' or
Purposive: 'Taotao takes this knife to cut meat.'

In comparison, UG utilizes a full repertoire of lexical means to explicitly express the semantic details of each relation. (74–75) are a few examples; the entire sets of prepositions and complementizers are, in terms of functions, all for this purpose. θ-roles also participate in encoding the semantic relations between certain events.

These two differences between iconicity and UG start making sense when looked at from the perspective of evolution. Before we move further, however, a clarification is in order: Any discussion of the evolution of language, from Bickerton (1990) and Jackendoff (2002) to the multi-participant debate (Hauser et al. 2002, Fitch, Hauser and Chomsky 2005, Pinker and Jackendoff 2005, Jackendoff and Pinker 2005), is by nature speculative given our current level of understanding of the issue. The endeavor is nonetheless worthwhile simply because this potentially fruitful inquiry has to start from *somewhere*. It is in this spirit that I will offer my two cents below.

In brief, I hypothesize that linear iconicity was among the extremely limited "syntactic" tools available to protolanguage (Bickerton 1990 and Jackendoff 2002) when UG with all its lexicalized means and its hierarchical structure didn't exist yet. That linear iconicity, unlike UG, can directly operate on verbal projections is compatible with Bickerton's and Jackendoff's conjecture that protolanguage only had symbols for entities and events (and perhaps for properties) strung together via linearization. In such a communication system, utilizing the general cognitive function of iconicity to link two event symbols seemed to be the natural solution for expressing complex events. Apparently, this old trait has survived.

Interestingly, the two differences between linear iconicity and UG, in the "lengths" of procedural routes and in information-richness, form a comparison with what has been learned about the emotion of fear. Summarizing years of research, LeDoux (1996) describes two pathways from a stimulus to the amygdala, the almond-shaped body of neurons deep in the vertebrate brain for the processing and memorizing of emotions (Figure 2.1).

One pathway contains a direct link from the sensory thalamus (which processes and relays sensory information) to the amygdala. This route, called the *low road* by LeDoux, is more primitive, transmits the sensory input faster

Figure 2.1 LeDoux's neuro-roads to fear

but with much less detail. In contrast, the *high road* via the cortex is a later development, slower in speed but feeding the amygdala with much richer information due to cortical processing. An example is a hunter walking in the forest and catching a glimpse of a certain color pattern. When his body instinctively freezes with fear, it is the low road at work, instantly linking the crude representation of the visual input to his fear of a venomous snake, memorized by the amygdala. A moment later, details about the color pattern also reach the amygdala, through the high road and processed by the cortex. The initial fear may be confirmed or dismissed, depending on whether the new information includes the shape and the scaly texture of the pattern, as well as the implications of such details.

LeDoux's double-pathway system of fear is compared with our theory of linear iconicity below:

119.

Fear	Linearization in SVC
Low road is more primitive than high road	Iconic linearization is presumably more primitive than UG
Low road and high road coexist and together account for the emotion of fear	Iconicity and UG coexist and work together to linearize verbs, with possible partial overlap
Low road is shorter than high road	Iconicity is procedurally shorter than UG
Information via low road is cruder than via high road	Less semantic detail is coded by iconicity than by UG

In research, one needs to be careful about the weight of analogies, especially when LeDoux's discovery is at the hardware level whereas linguistic linearization is about software functionality. But these similarities between the two mental subsystems suggest that linear iconicity possesses certain characteristics of an evolutionary predecessor when compared with the more sophisticated UG. Whether the two linearization mechanisms we have argued for in this work can be corroborated at the hardware level may only be determined with, perhaps, more advanced brain-imaging technologies, much as LeDoux did on fear with the technologies of the time.

Back to redundancy, evolution could produce what crudely looks like a redundancy in a function F (as well as real redundancies such as the more-than-critically-needed number of nephrons in the human renal system; see Y. Li 1997) from (partially) different mechanisms. Each mechanism itself may be redundancy-free and contributes to F in its unique way. This situation is referred to by Li (ibid.)

as complementary redundancy. Fear has been shown to be of this type. I suggest that linearization by UG and iconicity is no different.

To end this chapter, I summarize the core contents below:

120. a. There is robust empirical evidence that the iconic word order among the verbs in SVCs is a fact not derivable from UG.
b. The SVCs also possess a set of other grammatical properties summarized in (62).
c. The syntactic and semantic nature of θ-relations and some properties in (120b) collectively point at Void$_F$1 in (85).
d. The SVP is defined on the mono-clausal expression of composite events (83).
e. A phonologically empty *e* is defined to both unify *pro/Pro* and accommodate facts that suggest the optional relevance of c-command.
f. (120a-b) follow from (120c-e) plus the theory of UG-I in Chapter 1.

3 The Connectors

Perhaps every language has conjunctive and disjunctive words like *and* and *or*, which will be referred to as conjunctions purely for the sake of simplicity. Some languages also have morphemes with obscure semantic contents whose only function seems to be linking two semantically "solid" constituents. These will be descriptively called *linkers* in this work. Conjunctions and linkers, collectively referred to as connectors, share two traits. (i) Lack of a categorial identity in themselves in the sense that, if they merge with a constituent of category X, the outcome is determined by X, leaving connectors apparently contributing nothing categorial. (ii) With hardly any exception, they always occur between the constituents they connect, whether the specific language is head-initial, head-final or mixed. Together, these two traits have posed a continuous challenge to analyses in the UG framework, which have kept trying without success to unify connectors with the better-understood and better-behaved lexical items in structural representation.

It is the goal of this chapter to argue that trait (i) reveals another functional void in UG, which in turn activates iconicity under the FICH and winds up with the linear positioning of the connectors, namely trait (ii). In the case of the conjunctions, this void and the UG–iconicity interaction thus incurred also give rise to a long list of syntactic properties on the part of the constituents they connect, a list which has proven resistant to a simple and uniform UG explanation up till now. The linkers are much less investigated and apparently possess fewer grammatical oddities than conjunctions. Still, their existence may also lead to facts unseen in their absence.

The overall line of reasoning is identical to how the SVCs are dealt with in Chapter 2: Much attention will be given to complex and sometimes mysterious facts involving connectors that have been resistant to an adequate account by purely UG-based efforts; a functional void is proposed and justified that puts the FICH and the USM to work, resulting in the linguistic facts in question. Specifically, the chapter consists of four sections. Section 3.1 proposes the new functional void in UG with a general justification. Section 3.2 sorts out the known and new facts bearing on coordination in accordance with the various theoretical proposals out there that such facts are problematic for, in essence demonstrating the empirical difficulty encountered by UG. An alternative theory of coordination is formulated in section 3.3 that makes use of the newly identified void and the UG-I interface defended in this work. As in the case of the SVCs, all the problematic facts of coordination are shown to follow either from the FICH and the USM or to be more properly attributed to other factors. Section 3.4 turns to linkers, using the poorly understood morpheme -*de* in Mandarin Chinese as a case study. A precise understanding of -*de* is obtained by investigating what looks like a bizarre form of minimality first reported in Chen (2017). After rejecting the existing analyses of -*de* via this fact, it will be shown that the linear position of -*de* also follows from the same void responsible for the collective behaviors associated with conjunctions.

3.1   The Void of Roots

It is a currently popular idea that categorially unspecified roots enter syntax to acquire categories from the functional environment they are placed in. Opinions differ, however, on the extent to which such bare roots participate in constructing syntactic structure. Pending a critical review of three representatives of this general approach, I will assume (1) to be another functional void of UG:

1. $Void_F2$
    Syntax does not support lexical items without any categorial specification.

where categorial specifications are defined with Chomsky's (1970) [±V, ±N] enriched by Grimshaw's (2000) concept of extended projections. So T, for instance, is categorially an extension of V and thus also has [+V, −N] plus an [nF], where $n = 0$ for the lexical verb itself and any value larger than 0 makes the category "functional" in the sense used widely in the UG literature. What $Void_F2$ states is that both V and T have structural representations (e.g. T, T′, VP) in syntax, while a lexical root without [V, N], if such elements indeed are elements in linguistic structuring, cannot participate in structure-building without extra help.

The various facts that (1) can help account for will constitute independent arguments for it. For now, I note that $Void_F2$ receives support from two related linguistic facts widely taken for granted. First, the division of lexical items into behaviorally different grammatical classes – aka lexical categories – is not totally dependent on the concept denoted by a lexical item, and second, syntactic operations such as movement only target constituents with categorial specifications. The first fact is easily illustrated with *develop* and *development*, which can both describe events (cf. *I saw Bill develop the plan.* vs. *I saw Bill's development of the plan.* See Grimshaw (1990) for the event interpretation of deverbal nouns) but act differently in grammar. There is no *a priori* reason why this must be so. Just imagine a "language" L whose vocabulary contains only lexical items encoding nothing but concepts. As long as the combinatorial mechanism is hierarchical and algorithmic and the mapping from R_S to R_L is rule-regulated, it is doubtful that L would be really inferior to actual languages in performing communicative functions (e.g. *quick develop good plan* = 'quickly develop a good plan' while *quick develop plan good* = 'quickly developing a plan is good'). Apparently, UG opts for bringing into the system certain mechanisms of classification such as lexical categories (and even finer ways like the genders of nominals) for further divisions. The second property is equally obvious: As far as we can tell, there is no evidence that any moved constituent is category-less. But why so? These two properties follow directly from (1).

$Void_F2$ is compatible with both the traditional idea that lexical items already carry categorial information independently of syntax and Chomsky's (1970) X'-theoretic model in which lexical insertion places a category-less item, e.g. *shelf*, in a categorially specified syntactic slot, e.g. N or V, so that at no stage of syntactic derivation is *shelf* ever a constituent without a lexical category. An assumption similar to (1) is also made by Chomsky (2015: 8): "Suppose further that roots alone are too 'weak' to serve as labels. Then structures of the form {K, R}, where R is a root and K a category marker, will be labeled K." That is, when K and R are merged, the end product is always of category K due to R's "weakness." Other than showing up in (2), R has no structural status:

2.

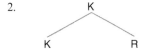

Chomsky's concern is the predictability of which element projects in Merge, a topic to be set aside in this book. Instead, let us extend the logic behind the root being unable to project in syntactic structure. Let the root be √KICK. Merging it with V simply yields the verb *kick*, labeled by V. But suppose √KICK is merged with a D first, say *it*. Either this is banned in the first place for separate reasons and thus is never generated, or {√KICK, *it*} is labeled DP, which is absurd for stating that the lexical item encoding the concept of kick plus an individual-denoting constituent is necessarily nominal in category, not to mention the off-track semantics implicated by such a structural projection, namely the product of this merger, "headed" by *it*, is individual-denoting! In sum, there is nothing √KICK can or should do in syntax except to merge with a mere categorial label. Then why bother having it represented in syntax at all? Along this line of reasoning, $Void_F2$ will be understood as preventing category-less roots from having any syntactic representation.

For sure, one can seek independent justifications for roots in syntax, of which two representative theories are examined shortly. As will become clear down

the road, however, such arguments all have a simple rendition consistent with
$Void_F2$. In addition, there is empirical evidence that the syntactic arguments
(e.g. *it*) must at least have the option of being semantically disconnected from
the root and that categorial information must exist in certain words independently of syntax. Together, a theory of UG embracing $Void_F2$ appears to be both
more theoretically consistent and empirically adequate.

3.1.1   *Distributed Morphology*

Marantz (1997) is frequently cited as the source of the bare root analysis in the
Distributed Morphology (DM) literature. It is easy to see the meta-theoretical
advantage of this approach: a maximally minimized lexicon containing only
category-less elements – the rawest building blocks – which acquire grammatically relevant categories only when inserted in a particular functional context
in syntax. But as Marantz points out at the end of this paper, "[t]he question is
not which theory is simpler or more pleasing; the question is which theory is
right" (p. 223). I concur completely with this position.

It should be noted that despite his explicit utilization of bare roots in the
specific analysis, Marantz also makes the following remark: "There's a further
issue (we won't discuss) of whether the categories reflect features of the roots
themselves or rather features of functional nodes that serve as the context for
the insertion of the roots" (p. 216). The "issue" is left unaddressed throughout
the paper. This lack of commitment aside, (3) gives the core facts (Marantz'
(12) and (13), respectively) of his theory:

3.   a.   that John destroyed the city
      b.   John's destruction of the city
      c.   the city's destruction

4.   a.   that John grows tomatoes
      b.   *John's growth of tomatoes
      c.   the tomatoes' growth

The question is why both *destroy* and *grow* have a verbal use, can be nominalized, but act differently on accepting the agent argument in the case of nominalization (i.e. (3b) vs. (4b)).

For Marantz, the contrast results from these factors in collaboration:

5.   a.   √DESTROY and √GROW are roots directly inserted in syntax;
      b.   Only √DESTROY implies agent in its semantics; (p. 217; also see Levin and
            Rappaport-Hovav 1995);
      c.   agent is projected by *v* but not by the nominal counterpart (which Marantz
            labels as D) (p. 217);
      d.   Possessors "may be interpreted in almost any kind of semantic relation with
            respect to the possessed NP" based on the meanings of the two parties (p. 218).

Because of (5c), either root can occur as the complement of the agent-projecting v and thus acquires the causative (transitive) reading in (3a, 4a). (3c, 4c) are allowed simply because the theme argument is already supported by the semantics of these roots (cf. Kratzer 1996, 2002; but also see Borer 2014 to which we return below). In the nominal context (DP for Marantz), D does not project agent given (5c). The possessor is interpreted as agent only for √DESTROY because the latter implies agentivity (5b, 5d). √GROW does not have this implication in its meaning, depriving the possessor of the possibility to acquire the agent interpretation.[1]

Of the factors in (5) for explaining (3–4), only (5a) is inconsistent with Void$_F$2. It will be shown in the next chapter that (5b-d) indeed play key roles in understanding (3–4) while (5a) can be replaced with a Void$_F$2-compliant counterpart that boasts other empirical benefits.

3.1.2   The Exo-Skeletal Model (XSM)

In a series of works by Borer (2005, 2014, 2015, among others), a theory partially similar to DM is developed that also lets roots participate directly in syntax. A major support for XSM is seen below:

6.   the form   to form   (from Borer 2015, ex. (17))
     the walk   to walk
     the chair   to chair

7.   a. a salutation   *to salutation   (ibid., ex. (22–23))
         an arrival   *to arrival
         the ability   *to ability
     b. *a crystalize   to crystalize
         *an acidify   to acidify
         *a fatten   to fatten

8.   a. math teacher   *to math teacher   (ibid., ex. (24–25))
         law enforcement *to law enforcement
     b. wallpaper   to wallpaper
         network   to network

Borer notices a pattern in these (and more) examples: While the superficially monomorphemic form of a word, plausibly taken to reflect the root, can be used directly as a verb or a noun (see (6)), a derivational affix to such a word/root stops the next "zero-affix" categorial shift. For instance, *walk* can act as a noun or a verb, but *arrival*, consisting of *arrive+al*, must be a noun and never a verb (see (7a)); similarly, *crystalize* contains *crystal+ize*, is a verb and has no use as any other category unless another derivational affix is added (e.g. *-ation*; see (7b)). Remarkably, this pattern is immune to compounding. In (8b), *wallpaper* contains two morphemes but can still be either a noun or a verb; but the compound in (8a) can only be a noun, apparently because the head of the compound, *teach+er*, contains the category-changing *-er* and thus patterns with *crystal+ize*.

This pattern, together with other empirical and theoretical considerations, provides the motivation for XSM, summarized in (9):

9. Let X, Y stand for lexical categories (e.g. V, N, A, ...) (Borer 2015: 114–115):
    a. Roots are inherently category-less but are placed in X-equivalent categorial complement space (CCS);
    b. $\{Ex(X)\}$ is a set of functional nodes with the functions of
       i. forming the Extended Projection of X, and
       ii. defining an X-equivalent CCS.
    c. $C_{Y[X]}$ is a C(ategorial)-functor such that
       i.   C is a category-changing affix,
       ii. Y is the category that C projects, and
       iii. X defines an X-equivalent CCS.

Using concrete examples while omitting the technical details that do not matter for the current illustration, let $\sqrt{\text{WALK}}$ be a bare root under (9a) and used in syntax according to (9b). (10) below is Borer's (20a):

10. a. $D \in \{Ex(N)\}$, namely it creates an N-equivalent CCS. Hence
       $[D [_{C=N} \sqrt{\text{WALK}}]]$
    b. $T \in \{Ex(V)\}$, namely it creates a V-equivalent CCS. Hence
       $[T [_{C=V} \sqrt{\text{WALK}}]]$

That is, the "verb" *walk* is simply $\sqrt{\text{WALK}}$ occurring in the complement space of T and thus becoming V-equivalent. The same logic holds with the "noun" *walk* in the complement space of D. These instances of *walk* are purely monomorphemic lexical items without any zero-morpheme derivation. In fact, they are never a verb or a noun; they simply act V- or N-equivalently due to the syntactic contexts they are placed in.

Morphological derivations take place under (9c). The noun *arrival* is formed in (11a) and the verb *crystalize*, in (11b):

11. a. $-al = C_{N[V]}$, namely it has a V-equivalent CCS but itself projects to N:
       $[_N [_{C=V} \sqrt{\text{ARRIVAL}}] -al]$
    b. $-ize = C_{V[N]}$, namely it has an N-equivalent CCS but itself projects to V:
       $[_V [_{C=N} \sqrt{\text{CRYSTAL}}] -ize]$

In this theory, the intuition that the root of *arrival* is verbal results from *-al* defining a V-equivalent CCS in which $\sqrt{\text{ARRIVE}}$ is inserted. Similarly, the root of *crystalize* is perceived as a noun as it is situated in the N-equivalent CCS defined by *-ize*.

Borer also uses the X-equivalent CCS to account for the pattern in (6–8). A root like √WALK can alternate between the nominal and verbal uses because it is category-less and thus can occur in either the N-equivalent or V-equivalent CCS. But a word like *crystalize* is already verbal because of the $C_{V[N]}$ nature of *-ize* (see 11(b)), making it no longer N-equivalent. As a result, *crystalize* may undergo further categorial change by another derivational affix, e.g. *-ation* if the latter has a V-equivalent CCS (it does), but it cannot fit into the N-equivalent CCS of D. To borrow Borer's analogy, a shapeless material may fit into a square or triangular space, but a cube cannot fit into a triangular space.

As Borer notes, "there is no need to introduce into our syntactic vocabulary category-less terminals" (p. 116) because a root acts as X-equivalent, with X being a lexical category, in the syntactic (9b) or morphological (9c) CCS. (9c) is in effect equivalent to $Void_F2$. As an example, *arriv-al* is already categorially specified to be a noun "pre-syntax," given that *-al* = $C_{N[V]}$. (9b) still lets bare roots be part of syntactic structure, but this position is weakened by one of her own claims, to be seen below.

For Borer, the ability to explain (6–8) is an advantage of XSM over DM. In the latter, "the syntax which underlies [*acidify*] and the verbal instantiation of [*form*] is identical, with the difference between them reducing to the choice of Vocabulary Items for *v*" (Borer 2015: 127). Ultimately, this means that in principle, DM does not explain why *form* also has the nominal use while *acidify* does not. Further bearing on DM is a debate between Borer (2014) and Harley on whether a bare root selects a complement. Borer examines the three arguments from Harley (no reference given) for √P composed of the root itself and its selected complement, and refutes all of them. Since this debate bears directly on the status of $Void_F2$, one of Borer's objections to Harley is recounted for illustration.

Do so and *one* substitutions are known to obligatorily target a verbal or nominal head plus its complement if the latter is present. For Harley, this is proof that there exists a root-complement constituent (see 3.1.1 above on Marantz 1997). Noting this conclusion to be "theory internal" (2014: 345), Borer points out an empirical problem with it (her (2a-b)):

12. a. my kid verbalized an adjective in the morning and yours did so (*a noun) in the afternoon.
     b. two surprising verbalizations of an adjective by a 3-yr-old child and one trivial one (*of a noun) by an adult.

Each head inside what *do so* and *one* substitute for is a derived item, *verbalize* and *verbalization*, containing multiple category-changing affixes which, in DM, are all provided in syntactic contexts. Critically, the root at issue is √VERB. While it may be semantically felicitous to associate the DP argument *an adjective* in (12a-b) with the derived *verb-al* (meaning 'have verb-like properties' (Borer 2014: 345)) and accordingly with *verb-al-ize*, etc., the same DP cannot be plausibly said to be semantically selected by the bare root √VERB. Therefore, *do so* and *one* substitutions are no automatic evidence that a root and the syntactic complement form a constituent in syntax. In fact, some of their applications such as (12) would seem to provide a counterargument for treating the first merge of a bare root to be the complement: Even if √VERB occurs in syntax, as widely assumed in DM, it must immediately merge with the category-providing *-al* to become an adjective. Only then can the object DP *an adjective* be brought into the structure.

Based on empirical and theoretical considerations of this kind, Borer concludes at the end of her paper that "[r]oots ... have no syntactic properties – they have no category, they do not take complements, and there is no evidence that they project" (2014: 356). This conclusion is what Chomsky (2015) draws on and it thus bears the same relation with $\text{Void}_F 2$ as I explicated earlier. Interestingly, it not only argues against DM and thus constitutes support for $\text{Void}_F 2$, but also reduces the overall persuasion of using bare roots as the building blocks of syntax. In general, what exactly does it mean for a root to have no syntactic property but to be given a presence in syntactic structure? How would such an element even be properly licensed or interpreted syntactically? At a more specific level, both $\{Ex(X)\}$ in (9b) for defining the syntactic CCS and $C_{Y[X]}$ in (9c) for the morphological CCS give rise to theoretical concerns.

Morphologically formed words are independently specified for category in XSM (in full compliance with $\text{Void}_F 2$). Since such words participate in sentence-formation, a syntactic CCS must be able to perform category-verification in addition to making a bare root category-equivalent. From the meta-theoretical perspective, it is not obvious what advantage such a model has over one that enforces $\text{Void}_F 2$ throughout, especially when roots are said to have no syntactic properties anyway. As for the syntactic CCS, consider as an example (10b), where a root directly functions as the complement of T. Among the syntactic properties of a verb must be included its θ-roles and the event role since there is the θ-criterion to satisfy. Meanwhile, roots are best conceptualized as representing "human concepts" in Berwick and Chomsky's (2016: 87) words. While the linguistic literature says nothing about what exactly a human concept encoded in a root might be (Progovac 2016: 993), one is surely entitled to wonder whether a concept of 'walk' already possesses the syntactic property of having an event role. An *a priori* more plausible take is to let √WALK simply encode the concept and to associate the semantic roles of its lexical realization(s) to whatever mechanism provides categorial specifications (cf. Hale and Keyser's 1993 l-syntax). In this sense, it is questionable whether (10b), the half of XSM that is incompatible with $\text{Void}_F 2$, is even legitimate because T would have no event role to operate on. In Chapter 4, we will see that independent evidence argues against letting bare roots enter syntax directly and thus in favor of Void$_F$2.

3.2 Coordination: A Large Collection of Puzzling Behaviors

Putting Void$_F$2 in reserve for now, this section focuses on going through the set of grammatical properties exhibited by coordination, a phenomenon which has triggered incessant attention, ideas and debates. The literature on it is so immense that we opt for bringing up references on each individual property as the chapter proceeds and, even then, only a subset of representative works.

The very fact that coordination spurs this high level of productivity in research points at a conclusion yet to be sufficiently recognized. In the structuralist tradition, linguistic constituents were divided into being exocentric or endocentric, depending on whether the categorial and core semantic information of a constituent C can be attributed to one of the components in C, i.e. whether C has a head or not. A representative of the exocentric type was the clause S, taken to consist of the subject (e.g. NP) and the predicate (e.g. VP) neither of which seems to determine by itself the syntactic distribution and the semantic essentials of S. Another candidate for exocentricity is coordination, though views split almost from the start (see Bloomfield 1933, Bach 1964 and Dik 1968 vs. Nida 1949 and Yngve 1960 for early divisions on the structure of coordination). At least for those who take the coordinate construction to obtain its grammatical traits from the collection of all its conjuncts and regard the role of a conjunction as merely linking these conjuncts together (e.g. [$_{NP}$ NP1 *and* NP2]), coordination is regarded as exocentric.

What is enlightening is what happened afterwards. With the introduction of Chomsky's (1970) X′-theory, and especially once the older S and S′ were reanalyzed as InflP and CP (Chomsky 1982), the clausal structure was accepted practically overnight to be endocentric because various known and new cross-linguistic facts fell into place immediately (see Sproat's (1985) and McCloskey's (1996) analyses of the VSO word order, Pollock's (1989) split InflP, and various works on cartographic syntax (Belletti 2004), for a small fraction of examples). Exactly the opposite fate was met by coordination. Even to this day and despite continual efforts to subsume it under some version of X′-theory (e.g. Munn 1993, Kayne 1994, Zoerner 1995, Johannessen 1998, Zhang 2010), the field of syntax is far from reaching any agreement on how to best describe the structure of coordination (Goodall 1987, Postal 1998, Progovac 1998, 2000, 2003, Phillips 2003, Citko 2005, Y. Li 2009, de Vries 2009, Le Bruyn and de Swart 2014, among others). This lasting indeterminacy, I contend, is enough indication that coordination is beyond a simple conversion to X′-theory. Or one would be hard pressed to explain why a consensus is so difficult to reach.

3.2.1   The Linear Position of Conjunctions

The most noticeable fact – as well as a problem yet to be resolved – about coordination is the linear position of a typical conjunction, i.e. it is located between two conjuncts regardless of whether the language at issue is head-initial (13) or head-final (14):

13. In head-initial languages
     a. I met your friends and her relatives
     b. Jean connaît Paul et   Michel.   (French, adapted from Kayne 1994)
         Jean knows Paul and Michel.

14. In head-final languages (Zwart 2005)
     a. Lagun eta ahaide-ei   agur egi-n   die.   (Basque)
         friend and relative-PL.DAT salute do-ASP AUX
         'He has greeted his friends and family.'
     b. mori   da   rdźigeni   χulōx.   (Monguor, Altaic)
         horse and donkey   hitch.up
         'Hitch up the horses and the donkeys.'

15. Mixed head-locations   (Chinese)
     women yingjing taolun   he   yujian-guo xiayibu-de   xingdong
     1PL   already discuss and predict-ASP next.step-DE action
     he   jieguo.
     and   result
     'We already discussed and predicted the next action and its consequence.'

Even when a language, such as Chinese in (15), has mixed head-locations, with head-initial VP and head-final NP, the conjunction *he* 'and' still occurs between the verbal and nominal conjuncts. This unchanging linear position of conjunctions with otherwise varying linearization patterns among languages is reminiscent of the constant word order between V1 and V2 in SVCs despite the head-initial vs. head-final variations.

   The linear location of conjunctions is best appreciated through a survey reported in Zwart (2005). In this report, NP coordination covers four syntactic constructions, illustrated with English examples (ibid.: 232, example (2)):

16. a. [John and Mary] went to the store.
     b. [John, Mary], they went to the store.
     c. [John with Mary] went to the store.[2]
     d. [John] went to the store [with Mary].

(16a) is the typical coordinate construction; (16b) involves the "summary strategy" that lists the NPs and then uses an expression, *they* in this case, to "summarize" the foregoing list; (16c, d) show the "comitative strategy" marked by *with*. Furthermore, the survey focuses primarily on monosyndetic cases, namely those examples of coordination that contain fewer conjunctive morphemes than conjuncts. Lastly, monosyndetic coordination is divided by initial and final conjunctions, schematically represented in (17) (ibid. (3)):

17. a. Initial: A & B
    b. Final: A V &

On the sample of around 150 languages, Zwart makes this observation (ibid.: 233):

> whereas head-initial and head-final construction is more or less evenly distributed ... this is not the case with initial and final conjunctions. We have conclusive data on monosyndetic noun phrase coordination in 136 languages. In 12 of those we find both initial and final conjunctions, in 4 we find exclusively final conjunctions, and in 119 we find exclusively initial conjunctions.

Collectively, we are looking at 131 languages with (17a) and 16 languages with (17b), a 8.2:1 ratio which is sufficient to beg questions on the nature of final conjunctions.

But the imbalance with respect to the linear location of conjunctions does not stop at these numbers. Zwart further notes that "languages using final conjunctions (whether exclusively or optionally) almost always employ either the summary or the comitative strategy" (p. 233). The summary strategy, including independently recognized copulas, 'together', pronouns (see English (16b)), focus markers like 'also' and 'and so on' (p. 234), are found in two of the four languages with exclusive final conjunctions and in seven of the twelve languages with optional final conjunctions. "With the exception of Tubu, the remaining final conjunction languages all use a comitative element as the final conjunction" (ibid.). The examples below illustrate these two strategies, with the key words in *italic*:[3]

18. a. Comitative (in Ket, Yenisei Ostyak)   (Zwart's (7))
        ba:t   ba:m-*as'*   dɔl'in'.
        old.man   old.woman-COM   live.3PL.PAST
        'The old man and the old woman lived.'
    b. Summary (in Baram Kayan, Western Austronesian)   (Zwart's (4))
        en   na' uvui   nah   dalo' Anyi' ji   Jau ji   Uvang ji   *pah.*
        PRT   he   call   FOC   them   Anyi   one Jau one Uvang one also
        'He called them – Anyi, Jau, and Uvang.'

In sum, a cross-linguistic survey not only indicates a disproportionately small occurrence of final conjunctions but in fact points at the strong possibility of their complete non-existence, with the apparent cases due to other grammatical reasons. In the rest of this chapter, it is assumed that there is no real final conjunction of (17b).

3.2.2   The (Suggested) X′-Compliant Properties of Coordination

The desire to bring all syntactic constructions under a uniform structural format has the obvious meta-theoretical advantage of being friendly with Occam's razor.[4] The wide-ranging success of X′-theory strengthens this approach, especially when such well-known exocentric constructions as clauses are subsumed not only smoothly but also with increasing empirical support. At first sight, a similar success would seem to be repeatable with coordination.

In the X′-tradition, an obvious move is to make the conjunction, schematically represented as &, head its own phrase &P. While technical details vary from author to author (Munn 1993, Kayne 1994, Johannessen 1998, Zhang 2010, etc.), the &P itself follows the standard X′-pattern, differing in how each conjunct is connected to the other(s):

19.

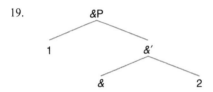

For instance, the positions 1 and 2 may each host a conjunct, or one of them does while leaving the other for another &P. In this general structural context, we consider first those facts in the literature that are considered either compatible with such a setup or as evidence for it.

Perhaps the most straightforward facts in support of treating the conjunction and the immediately following conjunct as a constituent, and thus consistent with the general X′-analysis of (19), are what Progovac (2003) collectively calls "Ross' effects":

20. a. Jeff resigned. And he didn't even explain why.
     b. Jeff bought a house last week, and the small lake behind it.
     c. Jeff sold the car, the boat, etc.

Whether *and* introduces a separate clause in (20a) (Ross 1967), is part of an extraposed conjunct in (20b) (Munn 1993) or constitutes with the subsequent conjunct the target of substitution by *etc.* in (20c) (Zoerner 1995), all these examples suggest that the conjunction and the conjunct after it form a syntactic unit.

Related to (20) is conjunction-doubling, shown below (Kayne 1994):

21. a. Jean connaît (et)   Paul et   Michel.   (French)
         Jean knows   and   Paul and   Michel
         'Jean knows both Paul and Michel.'
     b. John to   Mary (to) ga   kekkonsita. (Japanese)
         John and   Mary and   NOM   married
         'John and Mary married.'

Whereas the monosyndetic version of coordination always has the conjunction between the conjuncts, as seen from 3.2.1, conjunction-doubling, called polysyndetic by Zwart (2005) and defined as having the same number of conjunctions as of conjuncts, always displays a sensitivity to the linear location of the heads in the given language. French is head-initial and the "extra" conjunction *et* precedes the first conjunct. In a head-final language such as Japanese, however, the corresponding conjunction follows the last conjunct. Simply put, conjunction-doubling appears to align conjunctions with other heads in the same language, as predicted by an X'-treatment of conjunctions.

The nature of X'-structure is asymmetry. Hence any asymmetric property of coordination is typically viewed as evidence for some implementation of (19). Consider first the frequently quoted examples initially discussed in Gazdar et al. (1982):

22. a. You can depend on my assistant and that he will be on time.
    b. *You can depend on that my assistant will be on time and his intelligence.

23. a. Pat was annoyed by the children's noise and that their parents did nothing to stop it.
    b. *Pat was annoyed by that their parents did nothing to stop the noise and the children.

Not only are the two conjuncts in (22a) and (23a) different categorially, being NP and CP respectively, but there also exists an inherent asymmetry between them so that reversing the CP and NP in the (b) examples is downright unacceptable. This asymmetry suggests that the first conjunct (c_1) determines the categorial property of the entire coordinate construction: *depend on* expects an NP and not a CP and is satisfied provided that c_1 fits the bill. The same holds for *by* in (23). At the technical level, this prominent status of c_1 has been implemented in two ways: place it in the Spec of &P plus Spec-head agreement so that &P in (19) acquires the categorial information from c_1 (Johannessen 1998), or take the coordinate construction as c_1 itself with other &Ps adjoined to c_1 (Munn 1993).

Williams' (1978) Law of Coordination of Likes (LCL) is based on examples like (24) that seem inconsistent with the categorially mixed (22a) and (23a):

24. a. the scene [$_{PP}$ of the movie] and [$_{PP}$ of the play]
    b. *the scene [$_{PP}$ of the movie] and [$_{CP}$ that I wrote]

where the postnominal PP and CP cannot be conjoined, presumably because they are not categorially alike. But consider (25):

25. a. the shoes [$_{PP}$ in the closet] and [$_{CP}$ that I wore yesterday]
    b. the scene [$_{PP}$ about the war] and [$_{CP}$ that I wrote]

The contrast between (24b) and (25) justifies sufficient suspicion that the likeness for coordination is not measured by category but by something else, such as the conjuncts sharing identical/similar structural positions and/or having the same or compatible semantic types. In any case, to the extent that different categories are (conditionally) permitted inside coordination, (22–23) present evidence that the first conjunct enjoys a kind of prominence that other conjuncts do not, a conclusion consistent with the asymmetric structure of X'-theory.

Munn (1993) uses the bound-variable test to argue for an asymmetric structural relation among the conjuncts:

26. a. Every man$_i$ and his$_i$ dog went to mow a meadow.
     b. *Its$_i$ owner and every dog$_i$ went to mow a meadow.

Under the general assumption that QP (e.g. *every man*) must c-command *his* to license the latter's bound-variable interpretation, the contrast in (26a-b) is considered evidence that c_1 asymmetrically c-commands the other conjuncts in coordination. For Munn, the conclusion from (26) is further corroborated by another case of binding as well:

27. a. John$_i$'s dog and he$_i$ went for a walk.
     b. *He$_i$ and John$_i$'s dog went for a walk.

As an r-expression, *John* resists c-command by a coindexed constituent under Binding Condition C. Then the disparity in acceptability in (27) would follow if c_1 asymmetrically c-commands the second conjunct c_2. As such, *John* in (27a) is not c-commanded by *he* and thus can be coindexed with the latter, but *he* does c-command *John* in (27b), thereby ruining the intended coindexed interpretation.

That not all adjuncts are created equal is also confirmed by how coordination triggers agreement. If a language has the alternative subject–verb or verb–subject word orders, the former, as is known cross-linguistically, has the verb agree with the φ-features reflecting the collective effect of all conjuncts. In the latter case, however, verbal agreement may optionally (as in Russian) or obligatorily (e.g. Arabic, Benmamoun 1992) match the φ-features of c_1 only. (28) illustrates this phenomenon in Russian (Babyonyshev 1997; see Progovac 1998, 2003):

28. a. Molodaja   ženščina   i   malen'kij   mal'čik.
         young   woman-F-NOM   and   little   boy-M-NOM
         vošli/*vošla/*vošel/*vošlo v   komnatu
         entered.PL/S.F/S.M/S.N   into   room
         'A young woman and a small boy entered into the room.'
     b. V   komnatu   vošli/vošla/*vošel/*vošlo molodaja ženščina
         into room   entered.PL/S.F/S.M/S.N   young   woman-F-NOM

i   malen'kij   mal'čik.
and   little   boy-M-NOM
'Into the room entered a young woman and a small boy.'

With the subject preceding the verb in (28a), the latter must take the plural form. When the word order is reversed in (28b), however, either the plural or the singular feminine inflection can occur with the verb, the latter choice matching the (relevant) φ-features of the first conjunct *a young woman*. Whatever is the specific account of this correlation between verbal agreement and the linear location of a coordinate subject, c_1 obviously enjoys, at least under a certain structural circumstance and in terms of triggering verbal agreement, a prominence not available to other conjuncts.

The grammatical properties of coordination that are found in the literature and regarded as supporting an &P structure are listed below:

29. a. Ross' effects;
    b. Conjunction-doubling;
    c. Categorial prominence of c_1;
    d. c_1 licensing a bound-variable reading;
    e. Agreement-based prominence of c_1 in V-S order.

More rigorous assessments and/or derivations of (29a-e) will be ready once a general theory of coordination has been formulated in section 3.3.

3.2.3   Known Facts of Coordination Unfriendly to X'-Theoretic Attempts

As noted earlier, the very fact that there is not yet any general consensus on the structure of coordination, half a century after X'-theory's advent, should be regarded as a sign that something is amiss in simply trying to squeeze the phenomenon into the X'-model of syntax. Keeping this in mind, let us review the well-documented facts giving rise to the debate.

Whereas conjunction-doubling is said to support the X'-compliant &P, the linear location of the monosyndetic & between conjuncts, as established in 3.2.1, remains a mystery. In fact, (29a,b) undermine each other in head-final languages such as Japanese: If & is indeed the head of &P due to Ross' effects in (29a) and the Japanese conjunction *to* after *Mary* in (21b) is claimed to comply with the head-final word order in the language, then the Japanese &P should be head-final, leaving it unexplained why monosyndetic coordination in the language has $[c_1\ to\ c_2]$ instead of $[c_1\ c_2\ to]$ linearly comparable to the double-object construction [Obj1 Obj2 V] in the same language.

Possibly, one may put together an account of the between-conjunct *to* within Kayne's (1994) antisymmetric theory of phrase structure (KT hereafter) that distinguishes coordination from the double-object construction in Japanese. But evidence is around that KT does not work for the central concerns of this book, as seen in 2.5.7 of Chapter 2 and Chapter 4 later. For now, consider how it predicts c-command to operate.

The essence of KT is the Linear Correspondence Axiom which, in plain words, states that a structurally higher constituent, defined with asymmetric c-command, is perforce linearly earlier, and vice versa. In order for this definition to work at all for natural languages, Kayne must reinterpret X′ as a segment of XP and redefine c-command so as to ignore segments:

30.

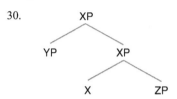

Given these revisions, YP as the Spec of XP c-commands not only the head X and the complement ZP but also anything that XP c-commands because YP is separate from "the outside" of XP only by a segment of XP, and segments are invisible to c-command by definition. To justify this outcome, Kayne brings up the contrast below (1994: 24) from Webelhuth (1992) plus the assumption in (31c):

31. a. We know whose articles those are.
     b. *We know articles by whom those are.
     c. The *wh*-phrase in interrogatives must asymmetrically c-command the [+wh] head. (Kayne's (24))

Since the possessor *whose* is in the Spec position of the *wh*-NP *whose article* in (31a), which in turn is in the Spec of CP, *whose* is able to reach beyond NP, asymmetrically c-commands C and satisfies (31c). On the other hand, *whom* in (31b) is too deeply embedded inside the NP to c-command anything outside NP. So (31b) is unacceptable because the [+wh] C of the object clause is not c-commanded by any *wh*-phrase.

But this analysis makes the erroneous prediction that the possessor of a subject (i.e. the Spec of the Spec of TP) c-commands T and the rest of the clause and therefore is a legitimate binder:

32. Whose friends admire *himself/him/the bastard.

(32) indicates the well-known fact that the *wh*-possessor *whose* does not bind anything outside the subject, thereby making the anaphor *himself* fail Binding Condition A but the pronoun *him* or the r-expression *the bastard* satisfy

Binding Conditions B and C, exactly opposite of what KT predicts. In fact, (31a-b) and (32) have a simple explanation in the "standard" model of X'-theory that prevents the Spec of XP from c-commanding beyond XP. In (31a), a *wh*-phrase in the Spec position of *whose article* triggers Spec-head agreement on N (or D as is more widely assumed now) so that the entire NP/DP inherits its [+wh] feature in (31a). (31b) is bad because *whom* is not in the Spec of *articles by whom*. As for (32), Spec-head agreement inside NP/DP is known not to apply to φ-features – otherwise *whose article* would be grammatically plural if *whose* is contextually plural! Without help from agreement, *whose* cannot be a binder precisely due to lack of c-command beyond the phrase that it is the Spec of. In brief, whatever the values of KT might be, it fails with the most basic operations of c-command, a crucial factor for determining the relation among conjuncts and the structure of coordination in general.

As a matter of fact, despite the facts we saw in (26–27) of 3.2.2 above, standard tests based on negative polarity items (NPI) and binding conditions consistently refute the possibility that the first conjunct c_1 (asymmetrically) c-commands c_2, an observation made in Progovac 2003 (and independently by this author):

33. a. Nobody chased any dog.   (ibid.: 224, ex (19, 21))
    b. *He chased nobody and any dog.

34. a. *Either John$_i$ or a picture of himself$_i$ will suffice. (ibid.: 224, ex (18))
    b. John$_i$ saw a picture of himself$_i$.

35. a. *Jeff$_i$ ignored all of the bastard$_i$'s friends.
    b. They ignored Jeff$_i$ and all of the bastard$_i$'s friends.

If c_1 c-commanded c_2, *nobody* should license the negative polarity item *any dog* in (33b), *John* in (34a) would be an equally good antecedent for *himself* under Binding Condition A, and the epithet *the bastard* in (35b) could not possibly be coreferential with *Jeff* given Binding Condition C. No example using Binding Condition B is available for independent reasons such as the binding domain for pronouns.

Since Ross (1967), coordination is well known for acting strangely with movement. Ross himself proposed the Coordinate Structure Constraint (CSC) because of the examples in (37) (pp. 98–99, with *t* indicating the structural origin of the moved phrase, aka trace):

36. CSC
    "In a coordinate structure, no conjunct may be moved, nor may any element contained in a conjunct be moved out of that conjunct."

37. a. *Which surgeon did Kim date *t* and a lawyer?
    b. *Which surgeon did Kim date friends of *t* and a lawyer?
    c. *Which surgeon did Kim date Sam and friends of *t*?

Lakoff (1986) compiled multiple types of opposite facts which in turn were attributed by Postal (1998) to such extra factors as underlyingly asymmetric structures and the use of phonologically empty resumptive pronouns in certain types of islands (p. 78). For Postal, examples like (38) must be analyzed differently from what he calls "logical coordination [where] conjunct order is semantically irrelevant" (ibid.: 53), namely the type in (37):

38.   How many courses can you take t for credits, still remain sane, and get all As in t?

But distinguishing logical and asymmetric coordination does not paint the whole picture. Compare (39a) from Lakoff (1986: 152) with (39b-c):[5]

39. a. How much can you drink t and still stay sober?
     b. . . . and drink a lot and stay sober, I can t.
     c. * . . . and drink a lot, I can t and still stay sober.

If expressing an asymmetric semantic relation in coordination makes the first conjunct in (39a) transparent to movement as Postal suggested, no phrase containing the trace t of the moved *how much*, including the first VP conjunct (i.e. *drink t*) and the entire coordinate predicate phrase, is an island. See Postal (1998: 80) for the same conclusion. Furthermore, it is also a fact that VP itself is movable, shown in (39b). It is unclear, then, why the first VP conjunct *drink a lot* cannot move in (39c). The contrast in (39) also shows that even descriptively, the CSC ought to be revised because moving a conjunct differs from moving out of a conjunct. *In the case of truly symmetric logical coordination, the two types of movement are equally blocked; but in asymmetric coordination such as (39), only conjunct-movement respects the CSC.*

The small collection of data above already poses at least two questions. The general one is how the current theory of UG can explain the CSC. There simply does not exist an X'-compliant structure with all these traits: (i) c_1, the first conjunct, is categorially superior (see (22–23) above) but (ii) unable to c-command the second conjunct c_2 for binding and NPI purposes (33–35) while (iii) neither c_1 or c_2 can be moved or (iv) allow movement out of them with conditional exceptions. As an example, suppose the two conjuncts occupy the Spec and complement positions of &P (see Kayne's (30) or the "standard" (19)). With c_1 being the Spec, it can percolate its categorial property to &P through Spec-head agreement with & and thus handle categorial superiority. But c_1 so positioned, perforce, c-commands c_2. Furthermore, short of ad hoc assumptions, at least c_2 is not expected to block movement because it is a complement. Nor is it obvious what UG principle would disqualify c_1 and

c_2 from movement themselves. The alternative structure explored by Munn (1993) faces the same c-command problem plus wrongly allowing movement out of c_1. See Progovac (2003) for relevant discussions. The partial contrast between symmetric and asymmetric coordination in (37) and (39) confounds the situation even further. One naturally wonders whether this semantic difference corresponds to any structural difference in a way that is X'-theoretic and with minimal ad hoc stipulations.

Right-node-raising (RNR, Ross 1967) is a trait of coordination inviting controversies with respect to the nature of rightward extraction (e.g. Goodall 1987, Munn 1993, Kayne 1994, Postal 1998, Phillips 2003, Citko 2005, Wilder 2008, de Vries 2009). (40a,b) below are from Wexler and Culicover (1980: 299–303):

40. a. Mary buys, and Bill knows a man who sells, pictures of Elvis Presley.
    b. *Who does Mary buy, and Bill know a man who sells, pictures of?

The basic fact is that there is an extracted constituent, e.g. the object *pictures of Elvis Presley*, which is shared by the preceding conjuncts, shown in (40a). Two intertwined questions are in need of answering about (40): How is the shared object derived and why is it that the relative clause, a well-known island, inside c_2 (*Bill knows a man [who sells]*) has no effect on this rightward extracted object but nonetheless blocks *wh*-movement? The fact that different analyses have abounded over decades is enough evidence that the phenomenon of RNR cannot be straightforwardly accommodated by X'-theory.

3.2.4   A Closer Look at Non-Constituent Conjuncts

The kind of example in (40a) – setting aside the issue of the relative clause in it for now – is assumed to involve rightward movement by Ross but will be referred to purely descriptively as having *non-constituent conjuncts* (NCCs) for the simple reason that *Mary buys*, for instance, does not form a (superficial) constituent without the shared and linearly separated object. Very different approaches have been proposed to analyze NCCs. Before assessing them, however, consider the following paradigm, with conjuncts in *italics* (first reported in Y. Li 2009):

41. a. *Her younger sister should* and *his older sister* must check this out.
    b. (?)Her *younger sister should* and *older sister must* check this out.
    c. ??Her *sisters with pink hair should* and *with blue eyelashes must* check this out.
    d. *Her sisters with *pink hair should* and *blue eyelashes must* check this out.

NCCs characteristically require prosodic help to sound appropriate or to be understandable. But even with proper prosodic support, the examples in (41) display a gradual deterioration in acceptability. The question is how to explain this gradation.

There has always been a strong tendency in syntax to equate a conjunct to a constituent. NCCs make it obvious that such an equation cannot be taken at surface value. To reconcile assumption with superficial fact, three approaches have been explored.

Certain NCCs can be handled with Larson's (1988) double-VP structure:

42. a. Jeff sent *his boss a card* and *his sister a package*.
    b. ... [$_{VP1}$ ... V [$_{VP2}$ his boss [$_{V'}$ t$_V$ a card]]]

VP2 contains both objects and the verb *sent* which is raised to the higher V position for independent reasons. When VP2 is used as a conjunct, one only hears what stays *in situ*, i.e. *his boss a card*. The analysis remains valid even when the upper VP is replaced with ApplP and vP (see (99) of Chapter 2) because the lexical verb must move up and leave behind the objects to obtain the basic word order independently of such technical details. As simple as (42b) is, though, the double-VP theory is fundamentally unable to accommodate the type of NCC in (41a). For a structure like (42b) to work, the underlying constituent must be the lowest in the tree in order to guarantee that once the head moves away, what remain are the all and only constituents in the conjunct. As the subject and the modal in (41a), namely *her younger sister should*, occupy higher positions, an NCC composed merely of these two constituents is in nature beyond the power of Larson's theory.

A novel approach to NCCs is offered in Phillips (2003). Taking sentence-generation to be a left-to-right process, Phillips makes use of the fact that as the string "grows" rightward incrementally, there exist temporary constituents. Consider (41a) again:

43. a. Her younger sister should check this out.
    b. Step $n-1$: [$_{TP}$ [$_{DP}$ Her younger sister]]
       Step n: [$_{TP}$ [$_{DP}$ Her younger sister] [$_{T'}$ should]]
       Step $n+1$: [$_{TP}$ [$_{DP}$ Her younger sister] [$_{T'}$ should [$_{VP}$ check]]]

The NCC in (41a), then, is simply based on what he calls the "snapshot" of what is formed at Step n of the derivation (i.e. TP), with the assumption that later steps "cannot 'unlicense' the syntactic relation previously established" (p. 46).

With interesting implications to be explored later on, this novel approach is nonetheless inadequate in itself for the data in (41). (44) gives the relevant derivational steps for (41c), which is highly marginal in acceptability but is perceived by multiple native speakers of English to be still somewhat better than (41d):

44. Step *n*:   [$_{TP}$ [$_{DP}$ Her sisters]]

    . . .   .

    Step *n+i*:   [$_{TP}$ [$_{DP}$ Her sisters [$_{PP}$ with pink hair]]]
    Step *n+i+1*: [$_{TP}$ [$_{DP}$ Her sisters [$_{PP}$ with pink hair]] [$_{T'}$ should]]

In no step of the derivation is there a snapshot constituent composed only of PP and the modal. The same can be said of (41b). And the core of the problem is straightforward. If the theory cannot generate any NCC in (41b) through (41d), why aren't they all equally bad?

Note that the data at hand cannot be attributed purely to processing since one must be able to syntactically generate each string of words in (41) first in order for them to be evaluated in processing for the various degrees of marginality, a task not doable if an NCC must be a constituent at some stage of the derivation of (41b-c). As shown above, these marginal NCCS are never a constituent by any means. Phillips' NCC theory also faces a meta-theoretical challenge. NCCs occur not only clause-initially and -medially but also -finally ((45a) is from Phillips (p. 41)):

45. a. Wallace gave *Gromit a biscuit* and *Shawn some cheese* for breakfast.
    b. Jeremy got books from *Boston last week* and ?(*from*) *Chicago yesterday.*

Just as the NCCs elsewhere, the clause-final ones are resistant to movement (**Gromit a biscuit, Wallace gave.*) and can get marginal. Unlike other NCCs, however, those in (45) cannot be attributed to temporary constituency because they occur at the very end of a clause and no "next constituent" will be added to restructure the snapshot. A different mechanism, be it Larson's double-VP structure plus head-movement (e.g. (42)) or something else, must be utilized for (45a). This means that NCCs all look alike and act alike but must be derived via totally different routes.

The third approach to NCCs is also the oldest one and, like the other two, it equates conjuncts to constituents. The NCC effect is accounted for by performing some syntactic operation or another on the shared element S. For Ross (1967), this operation is to literally raise S, his "right node," out of the D-structure positions and adjoin it to a higher spot, shown in (46a), a syntactic analogue to the algebraic conversion in (46b):

46. a. [X S] and [Y S] → [[X] and [Y]] S
    b. $ax + bx$ → $(a + b)x$

While we do not intend to dwell on it, one should be aware that (46a), if meant to describe a syntactic operation such as movement, does not automatically fit the current model of syntax. This is so because moving a constituent leaves either a trace or a copy behind. In (46a), then, moving S likely increases the number of S copies but certainly does not reduce it. So even if S is raised rightward, there ought to be two Ss at the adjunction site, each from an original conjunct. Unless an extra assumption is made, movement does not explain why only one shared S is heard.

In place of implementing RNR with movement, Wexler and Culicover (1980) proposed deleting the first instance of S, which is adopted by Kayne (1994) for its compatibility with his antisymmetric syntax. Leaving the evaluation of Kayne's theory for elsewhere in the book, we present arguments now against the deletion approach to NCCs. Worth keeping in mind is that both deletion and movement assume a conjunct to be underlyingly a constituent and that both operations target (a copy of) the shared element in the conjunct. Therefore, where the deletion theory is weak or incapable, at least for the purpose of this paper, RNR fares no better – despite likely different technicalities, the nature of the problem would stay the same.

The pressing question is whether deletion can account for the different degrees of acceptability in (41). By syntactic reasoning, the answer is no. As an example, the two NCCs in (41b) share the possessor *her* as part of the subjects and the VP *check this out*. If the possessor is put aside, then deleting the VP in the first conjunct is by definition grammatical, leaving us unable to explain the subtle but consistent contrast between (41a) and (41b) as both would involve the same VP-deletion. If the shared possessor is also treated via deletion, it is an equally grammatical operation in itself as *her younger sister and older brother* is fully acceptable. When each individual deletion is acceptable, the slightly marginal status of (41b) is not expected in the current understanding of syntax.

But suppose that for unknown reasons – considering how poorly understood coordination remains anyway, more required deletions in coordination translate to less acceptability. Such a theory could be formulated as in (47):

47. a. Identify the smallest constituent Z containing all the components of the surface conjunct *c*;
    b. Del_C = the total count of deletions required inside Z to yield *c*;
    c. Del_C is inversely proportional to the acceptability of *c*.

In this definition, Z stands for the underlying constituent being conjoined. The structure of the first conjunct for all examples in (41) is (48), with all irrelevant details omitted:

48.

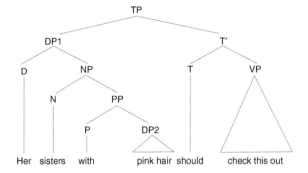

As it turns out, the theory in (47) seems capable of a quantitatively precise account for the different degrees of acceptability of the NCCs in (41).

For (41a), the NCC *her younger sister should* contains the subject DP and the model T. The smallest constituent containing both of them is TP, meaning that (40a) is underlyingly two TPs conjoined. Hence:

49. a. c = DP1 T; and Z = TP. (by (47a))
     b. Del_C = 1 = good.   (by (47b, c), with VP-deletion needed to yield 1st NCC)

The marginal or bad (41b-d) are all based on the same underlying structure (48):

50. For (40b), with c = *younger sister should*:
     a. c = NP T; and Z = TP.
     b. Del_C = 2 (deleting VP and D) = only slightly unnatural.

51. For (40c), with C = *with pink hair should*:
     a. c = PP T; and Z = TP.
     b. Del_C = 3 (deleting VP, D and N) = detectably worse.

52. For (40d), with C = *pink hair should*:
     a. c = DP1 T; and Z = TP.
     b. Del_C = 4 (deleting VP, D, N and P) = very bad.

The advantages of this theory are obvious. Both the underlying structure and the targets of deletion are constituents, conforming to the general pattern in syntax that operations are constituent-based. The theory also accurately matches the number of deletions to the gradual worsening of acceptability. But there are also several facts against it.

First compare the marginal variant of (45b), repeated in (53a), with (53b):

53. a. ?Jack got books from *Boston last week* and *Chicago yesterday*.
     b. *Jack *got books from Boston* and *ordered pencils, Chicago*.

The relevant structure for both sentences is (54), followed by the deletion-based calculations on (53a-b):

54.

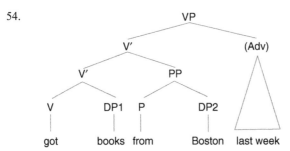

55. For (53a), with the clause-final adverbial Adv:
    a. c = DP2 Adv; and Z = VP.
    b. Del_C = 2 (deleting lower-V' and P) = slightly marginal.

56. For (53b), without Adv:
    a. c = lower-V' DP2; and Z = VP.
    b. Del_C = 1 (deleting P) = very bad.

This outcome contradicts the one in (49–50) because fewer deletions make a sentence worse now! For sure, exactly how many deletions must take place to yield the surface conjuncts depends partially on the exact structure assigned to the examples at hand. If one adopts a double-VP (Larson 1988) or one of its variants (Bowers 1993, Chomsky 1995, Kratzer 1996), for instance, the verb–object cluster *got books* may well reside inside the upper part of the structure after V-movement so that the rest of the clause for (53a) has [$_{VP}$[$_{PP}$ from Boston] t_V [last week]]. And such a structure is but one deletion of *from* away from producing the NCC in the example. But these possibilities do not improve the situation because, minimally, both (53a-b) need to delete *from* so that Del_C in them is always 1, still inconsistent with the grammaticality contrast between them.

   That the deletion algorithm (47) can be empirically problematic is further shown with a cross-linguistic comparison. Consider the Chinese counterpart of the unacceptable (53b) in (57a), with (57b) proving P to be required in the non-coordination context:

57. a. Xiren   cong   *huadian*   *mai-le*   *meigui,*   ?(cong)   *canguan*
       Xiren   from   flower.shop   buy-ASP   rose   from   restaurant
       ding-le   *fancai.*
       order-ASP   food
       'Xiren bought roses from the florist shop and ordered food *(from) the
       restaurant.'

b. Xiren *(cong) canguan   ding-le   fancai.
   Xiren from   restaurant order-ASP food
   'Xiren ordered food *(from) the restaurant.'

Regardless of the specific VP structure one adopts, the Chinese (57a) differs from the English (53b) only in placing the PP adjunct (= *from the florist shop*) on the left side of V', everything else remaining intact. Deleting the preposition *cong* 'from' makes Del$_C$ = 1 and yields the second NCC. Chinese informants agree that the sentence is somewhat unnatural but acceptable. The question is why this Del$_C$ value, identical to that of (57b) and resulting from the same P-deletion, does not make (57a) as bad as (57b) (and (53b)).

As before, the nature of this question doesn't change with a different VP structure. To obtain the word order in (57a) with a double-VP, for instance, one of the two structures below must hold:

58. a. $[_{VP1}$ V $[_{VP2}$ $[_{PP}$ from flower.shop] $[_{V'}$ bought rose]]]
     b. $[_{VP1}$ $[_{PP}$ from flower.shop] bought $[_{VP2}$ rose $[_{V'}$ t$_V$]]]

The first option places the PP inside VP2 (= the lower VP) and keeps the verb *in situ* (with the object as complement). The second option places the PP in VP1 and moves the verb to the higher V position. Either way, all one needs to produce the NCCs in (57a) is to find the smallest constituent Z containing all the words and then to delete P. With Del$_C$=1 for removing *from*, the contrast between (57a) and (57b) stays unexplained.

An interesting pattern is worth pointing out. The syntactic structure of the Chinese (57a) is hierarchically identical, and thus semantically comparable, to the English (53b), but it is linearly similar to the English (53a) for having their NCCs at the end of the clause. Apparently, it is this linear similarity, not hierarchical identity, that correlates with a slightly marginal status. In contrast, both the Chinese (57b) and the English (53b) delete the preposition in the middle of the clause – aka gapping in the coordinate context, and both are significantly worse. This correlation between the linear site of the missing preposition and the degree of acceptability seems to argue against the deletion approach to NCCs. Otherwise, why would the same P-deletion produce such a sharp contrast?

Quantificational adverbs present the third problem for the deletion theory, with the same data pattern observed in unrelated languages:

59. a. *Jack should* and *Mary must* ((?)both) put on their T-shirts.
     b. Mary must (*both) put on a T-shirt.

60. Chinese
    a. *Xiren   zuotian,   Ping'er jir   zaoshang* (dou) qu kan-guo
       Xiren   yesterday Ping'er today morning   all   go see-ASP
       laotaitai le.
       grandma PRT
       'Xiren yesterday and Ping'er this morning (both) went to see grandma.'

    b. Ping'er jir   zaoshang (*dou) qu kan-guo laotaitai le.
       Ping'er today morning   all   go see-ASP grandma PRT
       'Ping'er (*all) went to see grandma this morning.'

Quantificational adverbs like *both* and *dou* 'all' require plural subjects, shown in the (b)-examples. If each (a)-example is derived by conjoining two TPs with their own singular subjects, such an adverb is ill-formed in each underlying TP and should be as ungrammatical as in the corresponding (b)-example. A problem of the same nature is repeated by the plural possessive pronoun in the object in (59a) as coindexing *their* inside PP with a singular subject in each underlying TP simply would not work.

3.2.5   In Sum

(61) lists the (at least apparent) challenges for an X'-rendition of coordination:

61. a. Lack of consensus for decades on the precise structure of coordination;
    b. The between-conjuncts location of conjunctions across languages;
    c. Lack of c-command between c_1 and c_2 in terms of binding and NPI;
    d. Complex CSC-related facts;
    e. Non-constituent conjuncts (wrong predictions by a deletion-account, plurality issues).

In addition, even certain facts purportedly in favor of X'-theory can add complications. Take the agreement pattern in (29e) for example. The fact that c_1 triggers agreement on the preceding V certainly suggests c_1 to be more prominent than other conjuncts in some structural sense that matters in syntax. At the same time, however, the same coordinate subject S preceding V forces the latter to agree with S and not just c_1 in S. Shouldn't the structural prominence of c_1 stay intact regardless of the location of S? Babyonyshev (1997) offers an analysis based on overt vs. covert movements, to be critically evaluated in the next section.

3.3   Formulating a Theory of Coordination

The facts about coordination reviewed in section 3.2 point at different, often contradictory, theoretical conclusions, which underlies why this construction has been so recalcitrant to a uniform account, X'-compliant or not. It is against this background that an alternative theory will be formulated that not only draws on the various insights from its predecessors but also makes critical use of our theory of UG-I, demonstrating that Void$_F$2 in (1) helps us understand this large smorgasbord of facts with minimal adjustments to UG as we know it at the current stage. The starting point is a revised version of Y. Li's (2009) theory of the NCCs' gradient acceptability.

3.3.1   A Depth-Based Explanation for the Marginality Spectrum of NCCs

The failure of a deletion-based account of marginal NCCs, even as detail-catering as (47), plus the unresolved nature of right-node-raising, calls for stepping out of the familiar thinking about the phenomenon. One notion that has been occasionally made use of in the UG theory is *path* (Pesetsky 1982, Kayne 1984), namely the smallest set of nodes through which two given constituents in a tree are connected with single branches. While this particular definition of path is not of much use for understanding coordination, a variant of it provides a way to measure how closely components inside an NCC are connected. (62) defines *depth* to this effect:

62. Let c be a non-constituent conjunct with terminals $t_1 \ldots t_n$, $n \geq 1$.
    a. c = set of pairs of linearly adjacent nodes <X, Y> such that for $1 \leq i \leq j < m \leq n$,
        i.   X exclusively dominates $t_i \ldots t_j$ and Y exclusively dominates $t_{j+1} \ldots t_m$,
        ii.   there is no node exclusively dominating X and Y, and
        iii. Z is the smallest node dominating X and Y.
    b. For each <X, Y> in c
        i.   Depth$_{Z-X}$ = the number of different phrases between Z and X;
        ii.   Depth$_{Z-Y}$ = the number of different phrases between Z and Y;
        iii. Depth$_{Z-X,Y}$ = the larger of (b-i) and (b-ii);
        iv.   Depth$_C$ = the largest of (b-iii) in c;
    c. Depth$_C$ is inversely proportional to the acceptability of c.

By "different phrases between Z and X" is meant that X's own maximal projection (if different from Z) is counted out in the computation.

While (62) is elaborate so as to accommodate the most general scenarios of NCCs, the core idea it expresses is simple and intuitive: When two constituents form an NCC, the farther afield they are structurally connected, the less acceptable the NCC is. Specifically, (62a) identifies every pair of two linearly adjacent nodes (by (62a-i)) inside a given NCC that do not form a constituent (via (62a-ii), thus giving rise to an NCC). The elements in each such pair are connected through a path via the smallest dominating node, Z in (62a-iii); the number of phrases from Z to each of the two elements is counted, with the larger one determining the *depth* of the connection inside the pair; the bigger the depth, the less acceptable the given NCC becomes.[6]

(48) is repeated below to facilitate illustration:

63.

For (41a), the conjunct *c* has the terminals *her sisters with pink hair should*, where the node DP1 exclusively dominates *her sisters with pink hair* and T, *should*. So DP1 and T count as X and Y in (62a) and the smallest Z dominating them is TP. With TP = Z, DP1 = X and T = Y for (62a), the NCC in (41a) is assessed in (64) with $Depth_C = 0$ for the most acceptable NCC under (62c). (65–67) give the calculations for (41b-d), respectively:

64. a. $Depth_{TP-DP1} = 0$ (no different maximal projection from TP to DP1);
        $Depth_{TP-T} = 0$ (no phrase in between at all).
     b. $Depth_{TP-DP1,T} = Depth_C = 0$.

65. For (41b) = (?)*younger sister should*, in which Z = TP, X = NP, Y = T:
     a. $Depth_{TP-NP} = 1$ (DP1 between TP and NP);
        $Depth_{TP-T} = 0$.
     b. $Depth_C = Depth_{TP-NP} = 1$ (more marked than (41a) but still acceptable).

66. For (41c) = ??*with pink hair should*, in which Z = TP, X = PP, Y = T:
     a. $Depth_{TP-PP} = 2$ (DP1 and NP between TP and PP);
        $Depth_{TP-T} = 0$.
     b. $Depth_C = 2$ (clearly marginal).

67. For (41d) = **pink hair should*, in which Z = TP, X = DP2, Y = T:
     a. $Depth_{TP-PP} = 3$ (DP1, NP and PP between TP and DP2);
        $Depth_{TP-T} = 0$.
     b. $Depth_C = 3$ (unacceptable).

Next consider the two "extreme" scenarios for (62), starting with (68) where more than one adjacent pair of constituents in *c* are not exclusively under any node:

68. a. Her sister should try and her brother must buy this new iPod.
     b.

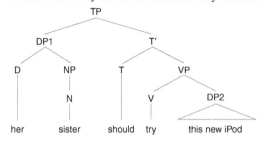

As before, TP is the node to include all the terminals in it. DP1 and T form an adjacent pair with $\text{Depth}_{\text{TP-DP1,T}} = 0$, identical so far to (64a). But the terminals in c also include *buy*, which is not dominated by T. Hence *should* and *buy* gives rise to the second adjacent pair of nodes qualifying for (62a): T and V. The smallest node Z dominating T and V is T′. The result is 0-Depth for both pairs, consistent with the acceptability of (68a).

69. a. $\text{Depth}_{\text{T′-T}} = 0$;
         $\text{Depth}_{\text{T′-V}} = 0$ (VP ≠ different phrase for V);
         $\text{Depth}_{\text{T′-T,V}} = 0$.
     b. $\text{Depth}_{\text{C}} = 0$ (both adjacent pairs DP1-T and T-V have a depth of 0).

The other end of the scenario spectrum is when no NCC is around:

70. a. You and I should try this new iPod.
     b.

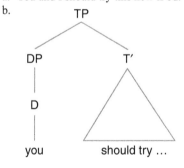

While the definition in (62) is specifically for NCCs, it is certainly possible to generalize it to all conjuncts. In (70), for instance, $i = n = 1$ for there is only one terminal, leaving no room for j+1, namely the beginning terminal of the second constituent of an NCC, because by (62a) j+1 must be larger than i (= 1) while no smaller than n (= 1 for (70)). Without the second constituent for the adjacent pair <X, Y>, none of the calculations of Depth_{C} will happen. This outcome can be easily formulated into the definition so as to be equivalent to $\text{Depth}_{\text{C}} = 0$ for acceptability. The subtle contrast between "normal" coordination like (70a) and the kind with fully acceptable NCCS such as (41a) and (68a) is attributed to using suprasegmental aids to ease the processing of a grammatical (superficial; see below) disrespect for constituency. See Chaves (2012: 477) for a similar idea on center-embedding, a grammatical outcome subject to acceptability variations depending on, among others, PF-factors. Also see 3.3.2 below. For the purpose of this book, however, we opt to focus only on NCCs.

Now we apply (62) to the three sets of data that are problematic for the deletion theory, starting with (53–54) repeated below:

71. a. ?Jack got books from *Boston last week* and *Chicago yesterday.*
     b. *Jack *got books from Boston* and *ordered pencils, Chicago.*

72.

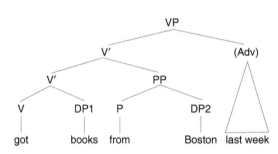

In (71a), the terminals forming the conjunct are *Boston last week*, which are all inside VP (or some V′). The nodes exclusively dominating *Boston* and the adverbial are DP2 and Adv, respectively, which together are minimally dominated by VP. That is, $Z = VP$, $X = DP2$, $Y = Adv$:

73. a. $Depth_{VP\text{-}DP2} = 1$ (with PP in between);
         $Depth_{VP\text{-}Adv} = 0$.
     b. $Depth_C = 1$.

The value of 1 matches the slight marginality of (71a) and is consistent with what we have already seen before in the evaluation of (41b). As for (71b), one may simply accept the fact, confirmed by the Chinese example (57b), that preposition deletion, at least in the context of gapping, is banned, possibly for the same reason that preposition stranding is a cross-linguistically banned operation.[7] Importantly, this explanation is entirely unavailable to the deletion theory – if P-deletion is prohibited, (71a) could not be derived by deleting P in the first place.

The contrast between the unacceptable (71b) and its slightly marginal Chinese counterpart in (57a), repeated below, can be explained in the same manner.

74. Xiren   cong   huadian   mai-le   meigui,   ?(cong)   canguan
     Xiren   from   flower.shop buy-ASP   rose   from   restaurant
     ding-le   fancai.
     order-ASP   food
     'Xiren bought roses from the flower shop and ordered food *(from) the restaurant.'

As noted earlier, the only difference between the two examples is that English has [$_{VP}$ [$_{V'}$ V DP1][$_{PP}$ P DP2]] whereas Chinese has [$_{VP}$ [$_{PP}$ P DP2][$_{V'}$ V DP1]]. This difference in word order opens up a possibility for Chinese only, namely the object of P being adjacent to V' so that an NCC can be formed according to (62):

75. a. Depth$_{VP-DP2}$ = 1 (PP in between);
        Depth$_{VP-V'}$ = 0.
     b. Depth$_C$ = 1 (slightly marginal).

The fact that an NCC can be formed this way avoids the need to delete the preposition *cong* 'from'. In comparison, the postverbal position of PP in English places P between V' and the object of P. Short of deleting P, there is no way to form the conjunct in (71b).

The last problem for the deletion theory of NCCs, the Q-adverbs and plural pronouns in (59–60), brings up the next question: If the depth theory is more adequate, what exactly is the syntactic structure it needs for an actual instance of coordination which necessarily contains more than one conjunct?

3.3.2   *The Syntax of Coordination under the Depth Theory and Its Origin*

The theory of NCCs in (62) is inherently resistant to a simple porting into X'-theory simply because (62) allows a conjunct to be a string of components that do not form a constituent and that are not derived through underlying constituents plus deletion.[8] A structurally non-constituent conjunct cannot serve as the Spec or complement in an X'-structure. On the other hand, a structure permitting multi-dominance (McCawley 1982, Goodall 1987, Blevins 1990, Moltmann 1992, Phillips 2003, D.-H. Chung 2004, Nunes 2004, Citko 2005, van Riemsdijk 2006, Henderson 2007, Y. Li 2009, 2017, de Vries 2009, Bachrach and Katzir 2009) can be adapted to work with (62) and to yield other desirable consequences. The preliminary structure is given in (76) pending major revisions:

76.

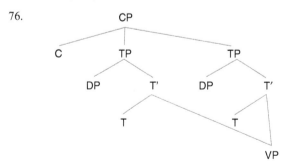

(76) directly yields the most acceptable NCC example in (41a), with each conjunct consisting of a subject DP and a modal in T. As the foregoing references show, however, this kind of structure is not new, indicating that it faces its own share of challenges. The list below gives the ones that beg for immediate attention:

77. a. A structure of this kind is by nature parallel; why does the first conjunct display superiority by single-handedly influencing categorial selection and subject–verb agreement?
    b. Where is the conjunction located and how are Ross' effects accounted for?
    c. More basically, since deletion is a convenient UG operation, why do languages even bother to have multi-dominance rather than simply letting each conjunct equal a constituent (and have a different set of behaviors)?

The first question may have a simple and intuitive answer from left-to-right structure-generation plus some sense of sensitivity to operational cost. Underlying the other two questions is $Void_F2$, to which we return later.

Phillips (2003) explicitly assumes the left-to-right process in generating sentences with coordination (see 3.2.4). While Kayne (1994) is not concerned with the direction of sentence-generation, the essence of his antisymmetric syntax is to correlate linear precedence with structural superiority, thus encoding left-to-right sentence-production into his version of phrase structure theory in UG. Driving their works is the truly universal fact, frequently put aside without any justification, that all human languages start uttering a clause from the structurally highest constituent. It is this fact that serves as a major empirical motivation for a new model of linearization in Chapter 4 which enforces left-to-right, or top-down, sentence-generation and will be derived from fundamental factors such as computational cost and the second law of thermodynamics.

One of the characteristics of the Minimalist Program since Chomsky (1995) is to favor strictly local choices and minimize the degree of lookahead in structure-building. An explicit effort in this direction is to divide a clause into multiple phases (Chomsky 2001a) so as to localize all relevant UG operations. In this general spirit, consider how coordination is to be generated. To facilitate the explication of the logic, we start with a simple case: *Jenny contacted you (and me)*.

Without coordination, left-to-right generation proceeds as follows:

78. Step 1: Jenny
    Step 2: Jenny contacted
    Step 3: Jenny contacted you

The process not only extends the terminal string linearly but also builds the underlying hierarchical structure at the same time, giving the default product of language a "vertical" dimension. In effect, *Jenny contacted you* is expressed on a *plane* defined by the linear and hierarchical dimensions. Call this the default plane P_D. Next suppose that coordination, for a reason to be spelled out shortly, creates extra planes "auxiliary" to P_D. Furthermore, let us make the hypothesis below in the spirit of the Minimalist Program:

79.   Operations on an extra plane incur extra cost.

A plausible way to understand (79) is that adding auxiliary planes means the need to keep track of multiple routes of syntactic derivation at the same time and thus to demand more computational resources. It follows from (79) that extra planes are taken as last resorts.

A direct consequence of (79) is that the first conjunct c_1 is always the one on the main plane in left-to-right structure-generation. At Step 2 of (78), if the object is not *you* but *you and me*, two options would become available: either merge *you* or merge *me* for Step 3. At this point and assuming UG to favor immediate cost-reduction (vs. waiting for a global assessment after the clause is finished), it follows from (79) that Step 3 will continue to extend the string on the default plane P_D since branching into the auxiliary plane adds extra cost at that moment and, given the two choices, staying on the default plane always wins. Once Step 3 is carried out, adding an auxiliary plane to host the second conjunct becomes the only choice for completing the coordinate construction. With no option available, cost comparison becomes meaningless, thereby legitimizing operations such as creating the auxiliary plane for the second conjunct c_2.

The structure thus obtained still parallels the conjuncts like its predecessor theories do, but c_1 is singled out for being on P_D. The categorial superiority of c_1 follows directly. The representative (22a) is repeated below:

80.   You can depend on my assistant and that he will be on time.

At the step that has *You can depend on*, c_1 is a DP and is first merged with *on*. A categorial check at this point satisfies what *on* expects and, as Phillips (2003) suggests, subsequent operations will not – actually do not have to – change the verdict. One may also opt to postpone the categorial check till the entire coordinated object is generated, namely *my assistant and that he will be on time*. But this construction, collectively, fails to provide uniform categorial information and thus offers no legitimate alternative for the purpose of categorial checking. To wit, (80) is good only because the DP conjunct on P_D is first merged with *on* because of (79). Now let CP be c_1 (see (22b)) The categorial check based only on P_D would obviously fail. Waiting for the whole coordinate construction does not help either for, again, the two conjuncts together yield no consistent category for the whole complement of *on*.

Many desirable consequences can be derived from this model of coordinate structure and these will be elaborated on later. For now, we focus on spelling out the theory itself by considering another outcome of (79). If operations involving auxiliary planes are less favored than those on P_D, then by the same conceptual principles of the Minimalist Program, we deduce that UG will minimize the amount of structure-building on auxiliary planes (P_{AUX}). Hence, the Auxiliary Plane Theorem (APT) in (81):

81. Minimize the structure on P_{AUX} by
    a. starting at the smallest P_D node N which
        i.   dominates all terminals in each conjunct, and
        ii. allows branching in accordance with X′-theory; and
    b. maximizing structure-sharing with P_D.

The plausibility of (81a-b) is self-evident as they collectively reduce to the minimum the structure – namely the nodes and branches – to be created solely on an auxiliary plane for the conjunct at issue (e.g. c_2). Concrete illustrations of the APT will be provided shortly. A welcome by-product of this theorem is to directly explain half of Ross' CSC, given in (36). (82a) repeats (37a) and (82b) is the relevant portion of its structure in our multi-planed theory of coordination:

82. a. *Which surgeon did Kim date *t* and a lawyer?

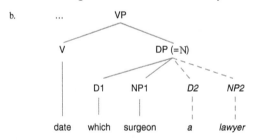

Italicized nodes and dashed branches in (82b) mark out the conjunct on the auxiliary plane. DP is the smallest node N on the main plane that dominates all terminal words in both conjuncts, and DP, by nature, permits downward branching, in compliance with (81a-i,ii). Except DP, structure-sharing does not arise with such a simple case of coordination, making (81b) essentially irrelevant. No phrasal node in the structure exclusively dominates the first conjunct *which surgeon*. Consequently, either the entire coordinate DP moves or neither conjunct moves.[9] The same logic holds with the copy theory of movement: If DP is copied, everything in DP is automatically in the copy.

A rigorous implementation of (81) also brings up a unique question: What happens when the conjuncts are not of the same category? Intuitively, if the smallest node N dominating *this surgeon and a lawyer* is a single DP (cf. (82b)), there should be a comparable N dominating *my assistant and that he will be on time* in (80). Short of equating N to &P, which is not adopted here (see 3.2 for facts against it), there is no answer readily available because such a node would have a hard time reconciling the different categorial information from its components. For instance, in order to accommodate (80), would N carry [−V, +N] from the nominal conjunct *my assistant* or [+V, −N] from the clausal conjunct *that he will be on time* (see Grimshaw 2000 for the notion of extended projections which is adopted here)?

The solution is for N to carry categorial features with variable instead of specific values when its components are categorially different. To use (80) for illustration:

83.   ...

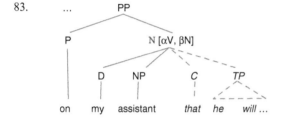

D may consider α and β to be "−" and "+", respectively, while C may reverse the values. Still carrying categorial features, N remains subject to syntactic projections and does not fall into the territory of Void$_F$2 (vs. totally category-less roots; see section 3.1). (81) is strictly implemented since N is the smallest branch-able node containing all terminals in the two conjuncts and as such maximally reduces the structure on the auxiliary plane in accordance with (79). In the rest of this chapter, N will be used when categorial inconsistencies arise; otherwise a conventional node label, such as DP in (82b), will be adopted.

Now let us reconsider example (80) in the light of (83). When left-to-right generation merges *on* with the first conjunct *my assistant*, the node representing the latter is unequivocally DP, which satisfies the categorial selection of *on*. To borrow from Phillips (2003), what is obtained at this point of derivation yields a grammatical "snapshot." Branching to the auxiliary plane brings in a CP which forces N to turn specific values of [V, N] into variables. But as Phillips proposed, post-snapshot changes do not undo the grammaticality verdict settled during the snapshot provided that the newly added structure is well formed in itself. In other words, the addition of the clausal conjunct does not alter the earlier categorial satisfaction of *on* by the temporary DP. We return to the reversed case with the clausal conjunct as c_1 in 3.3.4.

With the question in (77a) answered, we proceed to (77b,c), namely how is the conjunctive word to be treated in this theory and why does the human language faculty even support multiple planes rather than sticking exclusively to the least costly P_D? The answers to these questions are both tied to the semantics of conjunctions such as *and*, generically represented as $R_\&$. $R_\&$ is an instance of R_C (see (3) in Chapter 1) and thus must be deterministically mapped to some R_S. Conceptually, this is the same task as what R_T faces with SVCs. Differing from the asymmetric R_T, however, $R_\&$ has three properties, most clearly seen with *and*:[10]

84. a. Associative
         X [Y and Z] = [X and Y] Z
     b. Commutative
         X and Y = Y and X
     c. Unselective
         Insensitive to semantic types; e.g. *and* can group individuals, sets, sets of sets, etc.

All these properties contribute to answering the questions in (77b-c).

For $R_\&$ to be unselective of the semantic types of the entities it groups together has two closely intertwined consequences within UG. First, the situation of $R_\&$ is similar to that of R_T in the SVCs, namely it cannot be turned into a lexical item, call it *And*, with syntactic arguments because, with Void_F1 ((85) of Chapter 2), the very first-order nature of θ-roles is against the semantic unselectiveness of *And*. Specifically, *And* ought to form [x1 *And* x2], where x can be of any semantic type: <e>, <e, t>, <e, <e, t>>, *inter alia*. Except for the first type, however, all the rest would be beyond the capacity of UG containing Void_F1. It follows that the FICH should activate iconicity to assist in linguistically expressing $R_\&$ just as it does for R_T.

But there is also a difference between these two semantic relations. SVCs only have one R_T, i.e. 'earlier than', to express. The true causal relation, for instance, also contains the earlier-than relation in its semantics but is cross-linguistically encoded in a lexical word and does not compete with R_T for an iconic expression (see 2.4.2 of Chapter 2). For $R_\&$, however, there are at least 'and' and 'or'. A direct mapping from $R_\&$ to R_L *sans* any lexical clue, as the FICH does for R_T, would be disastrous. Therefore, each particular instance of $R_\&$ is forced to have an overt form in order to guarantee proper semantic interpretation. Obviously, this overt form is what we call a conjunction. Critically, conjunctions are unable to connect conjuncts with θ-roles due to Void_F1. Given UG as we know it now, the only available means to subsume a necessarily θ-less conjunction into the system is to treat it as representing a feature, call it [&], with the conjunction being but a phonological signal that at all conjuncts are connected through the specific 'and' or 'or' relation. I contend that this is exactly the nature of conjunctions.

With $R_\&$ represented as the feature [&], this automatically leads to the question of its syntactic representation. In the most general sense, there is no obvious incompatibility between [&] and the X'-expression of a conjunction. After all, ϕ-features can be projected in syntax as D/DP in the form of pronouns, the tense feature is embodied through the structure of T/TP, etc. For T to encode tense is especially enlightening because T can host and even license an argument through Case without a thematic relation with the latter. It is rather easy to imagine an analogous treatment of [&] and its conjuncts. So there must be another factor at work that forbids [&] to be X'-friendly and thereby creates many decades of debate on how to analyze coordination, totally unlike the easy absorption of, say, tense by X'-theory. This factor, I believe, is Void_F2 defined and interpreted in section 3.1 of this chapter, which brings in the second consequence of (84c).

Semantic types are partially reflected through lexical categories in UG. For $R_\&$ to be unselective of the semantic types of the entities it groups together means that the conjunction encoding $R_\&$ must be categorially unspecified so that using it does not inadvertently alter the key semantic properties of the conjoined components. For instance, $[P1_{<e,\ \triangleright}\ R_\&\ P2_{<e,\ \triangleright}]$ should yield Q of the $<e, \triangleright$ type with the categorial form of VP while $[x1_{<e>}\ R_\&\ x2_{<e>}]$ must yield y of the $<e>$ type which is categorially DP. If the lexical manifestation of $R_\&$, say *and* encoding the feature [&], is categorially unspecified, however, UG is unable to provide a syntactic structure for it because of Void_F2.[11] This is sufficient to guarantee that [&] never gets projected in syntax and the language faculty must find other means within its toolbox to associate *and* with the rest of the coordinate construction. It so happens that expressing $R_\&$ as a feature makes the task easy: Simply associate [&] with the node that dominates all the conjuncts, N in (81), so as to indicate that the conjuncts are interpreted with $R_\&$ between them. Technically, this treatment of [&] is comparable to UG handling morphological agreement on T. Let the set of bare φ-features have the option of grouping with the categorial features $[-V, +N]$, presumably due to their semantic nature. The φ-features plus the categorial features get a legitimate syntactic projection, i.e. a pronoun; otherwise they have no structural expression due to Void_F2 and can only become part of the feature set of an independently existing node, say T, with a merely PF manifestation.

Back to the FICH, lack of any structural position in syntax also interrupts default linearization through the R_S-to-R_L mapping. Just like the derivation of SVCs, this is when iconicity is called into action. $R_\&$ is a relation linking multiple conceptual entities embodied as conjuncts. If UG has no structural expression for it and does not know where to place its lexical representative *and*, iconicity is activated by the FICH and solves the problem by putting *and* iconically between conjuncts, another case of a direct mapping from R_C to R_L and skipping R_S. For SVCs, this skip is directly from R_T to R_L without any lexical and featural involvement. With coordination, $R_\&$ is treated as the [&] feature reflected by a phonological form. But both face UG's inability to implement the normal R_C-R_S-R_L mappings, an inability leading to an iconicity-determined R_L.

That [&] is associated with the N node dominating the whole coordinate structure benefits for its technical feasibility from the associative and commutative nature of $R_\&$ in (84a-b). It is these properties that exempt syntax from the need to figure out how to match the semantics of $R_\&$ with conjuncts.[12] By the same logic, there is no reason against spelling out *and* between every adjacent pair of conjuncts in compliance with iconicity, as in *Jake and Mary and Sam*. The syntactic structure of this particular example is given in (85), with proper names treated as nouns though such details have no effect one way or another on illustrating the core idea at issue:

85.

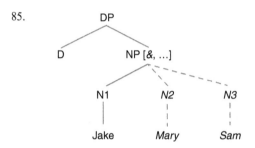

NP is the smallest node dominating all the conjuncts which are expressed on one default plane and two auxiliary ones. [&] is added to the feature cluster of NP as explicated above.

In this theory, the single-conjunction case (e.g. *Jake, Mary and Sam*) is but the result of preferring effective and efficient communication: Spelling out [&] only once reduces repetition, while marking out the final pair of conjuncts explicitly signals the imminent ending of all multi-plane operations and the returning to the default plane P_D. In some languages like English, this second part of the preference may have been grammaticalized in the simplest sense of the term: turning the processing-preferred location of a single conjunction in multi-conjunct contexts into a language-specific grammar rule. But there is nothing inherently correct about this rule. In Chinese, for instance, *he* 'and' and *erqie* 'and' can both occur on non-final between-conjunct slots:[13]

86. a. Runrun he   Lele, Youyou dou qu   xuexiao le.
       Runrun and   Lele Youyou all go   school PRT
       Literally: 'R and L, Y all went to school.'
    b. haizi   zai   jia,   erqie   wo zai   jia,   ni   ye   zai jia.
       child   be.at home and   1s be.at home   2s   also be.at home
       'The child is at home, and I'm at home and you're also at home.'

These examples are slightly more marked than having the conjunctions preceding the last conjunct – signaling the last conjunct is preferred after all, but they are both grammatical and can equally produce the same simple-sum interpretation of all the conjuncts.

When it comes to the linear location of conjunctions, -*que* in Latin is often mentioned as occurring "after the first phonological word of the last conjunct" (Bobaljik 2015: 4). For Zhang (2010: 14), data of this kind "falsify the alleged iconicity principle." But just like Newmeyer's criticism of using iconicity to account for SVC word orders (see 2.4.3, Chapter 2), Zhang's conclusion is simultaneously valid and invalid, both for the same reason. Neither Zhang nor the previously existing view she objects to is aware of a critical fact about iconicity that is being elaborated on in the current work: Up to the level of clause-formation, iconicity is brought in by the FICH and thus is strictly conditioned in its use.

As is made clear by Embick and Noyer (2001) and Bobaljik (2015), the positioning of -*que* in Latin is heavily PF-sensitive (also see Sadock 1985 and Marantz 1989). In the examples below, phonologically light prepositions such as *in* 'in' do not count as the first word of the last conjunct:

87. a. circum-que ea   loca   (Latin, Embick and Noyer 2001)
       around-AND those places
       'and around those places'
    b in   rēbus-que
       in   things-AND
       'and in things'

Within the theory presented here, $R_{\&}$ may only be treated as the [&] feature. When this feature is lexicalized as *and*, the lack of structural expression requires help from iconicity for linearization. But when the feature takes the form of -*que*, the task of its linear positioning is allocated to Latin morphophonology, a proper part of UG. The FICH becomes irrelevant and iconicity is not activated at all. As long as -*que* is with the last conjunct, it signals the end of the multi-plane structure just as *and* does. To use the location of -*que* as evidence against iconicity is no different from negating iconicity through European verbal morphology for subject agreement, with a relational morpheme not placed iconically between the subject and the verb. In each case, UG is operational and leaves no motivation for iconicity.

The last piece of our theory is in dealing with the conjuncts. If *and* (or -*que*) only reflects a feature without syntactic representation, UG is not given enough foundation to properly position the conjuncts. In fact, this is precisely what drives an incessant effort to assign &P to coordination (see (19)): Doing so would automatically make the Spec and complement positions available to conjuncts. But if UG cannot assemble conjuncts via the standard X'-apparatus because there is nothing like &P to help position them, the situation at this point of syntactic derivation is, by nature, identical to what happens with SVCs: A particular R_C encounters some functional void of UG so that the elements which R_C connects cannot map to a legitimate R_S. Again, we expect isomorphism ((91), Chapter 2) to lend a hand as required by the USM. For SVCs, R_T is asymmetric, matched by the asymmetric dependence between the overt object of V1 and the e object of V2. For coordination, $R_\&$ is symmetric as stated by the Commutative Law in (84b). Given the fact that the X'-template is inherently asymmetric (see Larson 1988, Kayne 1994), the only way to have a structural symmetry is by creating parallel planes. In sum, the multi-plane structure of coordination results from $Void_F 1-2$ in UG. It is not favored due to (79) but the way the overall human language faculty has evolved leaves us with no other option when $R_\&$ needs a linguistic expression.

The complete theory of coordination is summarized as follows:

88. Let a coordinate construction C consist of conjuncts $c_1 \dots c_n$.
   a. c_1 is on the default plane P_D due to left-to-right structure-building and the operational cost factor (79).
   b. All c_i, $1 < i \le n$, are on auxiliary planes as required by the USM.
   c. The smallest node N dominating $c_1 \dots c_n$ and capable of branching is where all the planes in C start according to the APT in (81).
   d. $R_\&$ is represented as the [&] feature in N because of $Void_F 1-2$ and the semantics of $R_\&$ that prevents it from having any θ-role or lexical category.
   e. The lexical form of $R_\&$ is linearized either by UG or by iconicity otherwise.

3.3.3   Application 1: The NCCs

The multi-plane theory of coordination in (88) has already explained four traits of coordination: immovable individual conjuncts (= half of the CSC), the between-conjunct location of conjunctions, the categorial superiority of c_1, and why languages even support a multi-plane structure for coordination. The theory also extends naturally to NCCs and related data. Prior to doing this, though, we note that much of the theory is built on the lexicalizations of $R_\&$ being categorially unspecified. A quick proof is due.

As stated in section 3.1 above, a lexical item has a categorial specification when it carries the feature cluster in the form of [±V, ±N]. European conjunctions demonstrate this lack of categorial information clearly because *and*, for instance, has no effect on the category of its conjuncts. But there are languages in which conjunctions appear to be sensitive to the category of what they conjoin. It may be tempting to interpret this category sensitivity as the conjunction itself bearing a category. In the Chinese examples (86a-b), for instance, *he* 'and, with' links nominals while *erqie* 'and, also, but also' is for clauses. More examples that seem to pair these conjunctions with conjuncts of particular categories can be found in Huang et al. (2009) and Zhang (2010), among others.

It must be pointed out, however, that having a categorial requirement on what to conjoin is logically separate from the conjunction having a category in itself – it is certainly possible, even theoretically preferred, that the two Chinese conjunctions *he* and *erqie* are simply the same &-feature spelled out differently depending on the category of the node the feature is associated with (cf. (85)). Such an analysis of the Chinese conjunctions not only minimizes their differences from how conjunctions work in many languages but also receives support from other facts in Chinese.

Consider *erqie* first. One way to distinguish V from A in the language is how a DP object is represented. While VP is head-initial, shown in (89a), AP is head-final because a DP object, as expected, relies on a preposition to provide syntactic licensing (aka a Case), and PPs in Chinese are necessarily pre-head, as reflected by the contrast in (89b-c):

89. a. ta   mudu   erqie baodao-le naci   shigu.
       3s   witness   and   report-ASP that   accident
       'S/He witnessed and reported that accident.'
    b. ta   wei   zhege chengji   gaoxing erqie   zihao.
       3s   for   this   grade   glad   and   proud
       'S/He is glad about and proud of this grade.'
    c. *ta gaoxing erqie zhihao   zhege   chengji.
       3s glad   and   proud   this   grade
       Intended reading: Same as (89b).

Relevant to the current concern is that these examples also use coordinated predicates. Clearly, the V or A category of the conjuncts, shown via the corresponding behavior, is intact and thus independent of *erqie*, proving *erqie* unspecified with respect to V and A.

As for the purported nominal conjunction *he*, Shengli Feng (p.c.) made the observation that it becomes compatible with verbs once the context is somewhat less casual, a register usually accomplished with disyllabic synonyms in modern Mandarin Chinese:

90. a. *ta yijing   du   he ping-guo   naben shu.
       3s already read   and comment.on-ASP   that   book
       'S/He already read and commented on that book.'
    b. ta   yijing   yuedu he pinglun-guo   nabu   zhuzuo.
       3s   already read   and comment.on-ASP   that   book
       = a more formal version of (90a).

In fact, *he* can replace each instance of *erqie* in (89a-b) where disyllabic forms of the verbs and adjectives are used. In conclusion, the factors behind the proper use of different conjunctions in a given language certainly deserve sorting out, but there is no compelling evidence against treating conjunctions as categorially unspecified. Also see section 3.4 below for the adverbial marker *-de* in Chinese, which can be proven to be category-less in itself but sensitive to adjectival stems nonetheless.

With this substantiation of the coordination theory in (88), we now apply it to (41c), a highly marginal case of NCCs. The example is replicated in (91a) and its structure in the multi-plane theory of coordination is given in (91b):

91. a. ??Her sisters with pink hair should and with blue eyelashes must ... .

b.

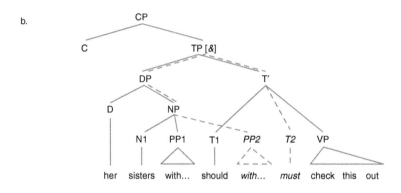

The smallest node N in question is TP containing the PP inside the subject and the modal in T. So the auxiliary plane P_{AUX} starts at TP. The APT also minimizes structure-creation on P_{AUX} through node-sharing with P_D under (81b). The parallel branches and the nodes they connect indicate the partial structure made use of by both planes. Also note that the depth computation for NCCs is done directly with such a structure. Take the second conjunct in (91) for example. With the dashed lines connecting PP2 and T2, it is straightforward that $Depth_{TP-T2} = 0$ and $Depth_{TP-PP2} = 2$ because of the NP and DP nodes on the path. Hence the total depth of the conjunct is 2, explaining the high degree of (91a)'s marginality.

Apart from the gradient marginality in (41) accounted for above, this kind of NCCs is just right-node-raising (RNR). In our theory, RNR is simply the shared lowest constituent on P_D, VP in (91b). There is no movement whatsoever involved nor anything different from the shared constituents elsewhere in the tree. It follows, as already noted by others (e.g. de Vries 2009: 351 and the references cited there), that "RNR is apparently insensitive to island conditions," as shown with the example of (40a) earlier.[14] Another advantage of this *in situ* analysis of RNR is to rid UG of a case of generally dubious rightward movement. At the same time, movement involving the shared constituent – "the right node" – is still prone to islands. The structure of (40b) is given below, with irrelevant details put aside:[15]

92. a. *Who does Mary buy, and Bill know a man who sells, pictures of?

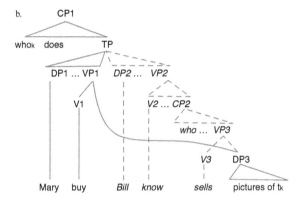

The unacceptability follows from the shared DP *pictures of t* being multiply dominated by both the main VP1 on P_D and the VP3 inside the relative clause CP2 on P_{AUX}. So there is at least one route of dependency between *who* and its trace t_k that is ungrammatical. Compare this scenario with the categorial superiority (22a/80) treated in 3.3.2. There, left-to-right generation encounters the conjunct on the default plane first and thereby enjoys the option of satisfying the preposition *on*'s categorial selection at that point of derivation. In (92b), however, both conjuncts are already created in the left-to-right process by the time the movement of *who* gets evaluated with respect to *t*. At this point of derivation, even a snapshot has the entire coordinate structure and no part of it can be ignored, just as no conjunct of a preverbal coordinate subject can be ignored in determining the agreement on the verb in the Russian example (28a) (see 3.3.4–5). If one of the conjuncts contains an island, the movement is ungrammatical on that plane.

The multi-plane structure also explains why a coordinate subject with singular conjuncts licenses subsequent adverbs and pronouns requiring a plural subject. To avoid excessive details, we will use the bracket notation for syntactic structure from this point on where no unclarity arises. If the end of the conjunct does not coincide with the end of a constituent, a curly bracket is used.

93. a. Jack should and Mary must both put on their T-shirts. (= (59a))

b. ... $\begin{bmatrix} \text{Jack} \\ \text{TP Mary} \end{bmatrix} \begin{bmatrix} \text{should} \\ \text{T' must} \end{bmatrix}$ [vp both put on their T-shirts]]]

As VP is dominated by the shared T' node, *both* and *their* inside VP have structural access to the two subjects in the Spec of TP via c-command, and again, neither one can be ignored. Taking *Jack* and *Mary* together into semantic interpretation translates to a plural subject.

3.3.4   Application 2: More on the Prominence of c_1

The tests with Binding Conditions A and C and NPI in (33–35) prove unequivocally that c_1 does not c-command the conjuncts after it. For the multi-plane theory of coordination, this can come naturally since there is no conceptual or theoretical reason why c-command must happen across planes. What appears to complicate the otherwise straightforward conclusion is the examples involving bound variables and r-expressions discussed in Munn (1993) (see 3.2.2):

94. a. Every man$_i$ and his$_i$ dog went to mow a meadow. (= (26a))
     b. *He$_i$ and John$_i$'s dog went for a walk.   (= (27b))

With the intended coindexations, (94a) seems to prove c_1 'every man' to c-command c_2 and hence the pronoun *his* in it while the unacceptable (94b) is taken to result from a Binding Condition C violation, suggesting that c_1 *he* c-commands *John* in c_2.

But this is where I share with Progovac (2003) that both cases in (94) are misleading. For bound variables, Progovac mentions (95a)[16] and we add (95b):

95. a. John criticized every senator$_i$ in private while praising the bastard$_i$ in public.
                  (ibid.: 243; see Hornstein and Weinberg 1990)
     b. From every candidate$_i$, we've heard his$_i$ promises to save the dinosaurs.

The epithet *the bastard* in (95a) is coindexed with the quantifier phrase (QP) *every senator* and thus has the bound-variable interpretation. But as the sister of V, QP does not c-command the epithet inside the higher-adjoined adverbial clause. As a matter of fact, since epithets are r-expressions regulated by Binding Condition C, they must not be c-commanded by their antecedents. So the very fact that (95a) is acceptable (to some speakers) is evidence that the bound-variable interpretation is not dependent on c-command at least at some stage of derivation, in overt syntax for instance, so as to create a chance for the epithet to be regarded as obeying Binding Condition C. In (95b), no matter where the *from*-PP originates and ends, the QP *every candidate* is inside this PP and cannot c-command the coindexed pronoun *his*. But the coreferential reading is easy to obtain.

The lack of obvious c-command between QP and the bound variable is not limited to English. In 2.3.2 of Chapter 2, multiple Chinese examples were given to make the same point, of which two representative groups are repeated here:

96. (?)meige xin   xuesheng$_i$ dou jiandao-le tade$_i$ laoshi.
    every new student   all meet-ASP 3s.POSS teacher
    'Every new student met his/her teacher.'

97. a. (?)women [$_{PP}$ cong meiwei   houxuanren nali] dou tingdao-le ta$_i$
      1PL   from   every   candidate   there all hear-ASP   3s
      dui gongzhong de   xunuo.
      to   the.public DE   promise
      'We heard from every candidate his/her promises to the public.'
   b. (?)[$_{PP}$ cong meiwei   houxuanren$_i$ nali], women dou tingdao-le ta$_i$
         from every   candidate   there 1PL   all hear-ASP   3s
      dui gongzhong de   xunuo
      to   the.public DE   promise
      'From every candidate, we heard his/her promises to the public.'

Due to the availability of the *pro*-strategy and the monomorphemic – and thus long-distance – anaphor *ziji* 'self', it is not always natural to use an overt and sentence-internally coreferential pronoun in Mandarin Chinese. With this in mind, (96) is the control sentence in which the QP subject c-commands the pronoun inside the object. In (97), a QP is placed inside a PP headed by *cong* 'from'. Whether this PP is between the subject and the verb, the default position for typical adjuncts, or is topicalized in (97b), the bound-variable interpretation is no less acceptable than in (96). Just as in English, for QP to be inside a phrase does not seem to affect its ability to license a coindexed pronoun. That *cong* 'from' blocks its object from c-commanding outside PP is confirmed if the bound pronoun *ta* '3s' is replaced with an epithet such as *neige jiahuo* 'that fella'. Then coindexation between the QP subject and this epithet is totally impossible in (96) as expected under Binding Condition C, but can still yield a legitimate reading for (97a-b), proving that the object of *cong* 'from' indeed does not c-command the rest of the clause.

Collectively, the data above pose a question on the exact licensing condition for bound variables. As Hornstein and Weinberg (1990) noted, quantifier raising (QR) at LF could provide the needed c-command for the coindexed pronouns. E.g. as long as the QP at issue is covertly raised to adjoin to the topicalized PP in (95b, 96–97) and provided that segments do not block c-command, *his* would be c-commanded by this QP. Meanwhile, a QR'ed and thus c-commanding QP would bind the epithet *the bastard* in (95a), leading to a Binding Condition C violation. In addition, making segments invisible to c-command is a theoretical exception that should and can be removed, as will be shown in Chapter 4. No matter what the final solution to this problem is, however, the data above provide unequivocal cross-linguistic evidence that in overt syntax, bound variables do not need a c-commanding QP for licensing. Consequently, (94a) is no evidence at all that c_1 c-commands c_2.

As for the unacceptable (94b), Progovac (2003: 243) proves that c-command can be simply irrelevant:

98. a. *He$_i$ and John$_i$'s dog went for a walk.   (= (94b))
     b. *He$_i$ finally arrived. John$_i$'s dog went for a walk.

Located in two separate sentences, *he* in (98b) cannot possibly c-command anything in the second part of the utterance. Whatever is the ultimate reason for *John* to be unable to refer back to *he* in (98b) will apply to (94b/98a). In fact, a uniform account of (98a-b) is made easy (see below) in the multi-plane structure of coordination because it is more intuitive to compare conjuncts on different planes with two separate clauses than to compare the Spec and complement of an &P with the latter.[17]

The conclusion so far is that conjuncts do not c-command one another for the purposes of Binding Conditions A and C and NPI while bound variables are no proof for the matter at hand. Lack of c-command between conjuncts can be accomplished easily within the multi-plane theory of coordination with the definition of c-command in (99):

99. Let X, Y be sister nodes on the same plane. Then
     X c-commands Y and all the offspring nodes of Y.

Other than requiring the sisters to share the plane, (99) is simply another way to state exactly the same content as the standard "first-branching" definition of c-command. It may be possible to derive the "same-plane" condition from more fundamental elements of UG. Consider the idea (though not the exact formulation) of Epstein (1999) that c-command is computed from Merge. In the left-to-right model adopted here, let X in (100) be the constituent – not Phillips' (2003) snapshot but the actual constituent ending the string at Step i – at which the existing structure is to be extended by adding Y:

100. Step i ... X
     Step $i+1$ ... [$_Z$ X Y]

For Y to merge with X on the same plane is the default scenario according to the APT (see (79, 81)) and defines c-command. In comparison, for Y to bring in another plane can be reasonably thought of as entailing not merely Merge because the operation, call it O, also simultaneously creates an extra plane. If O is not identical to Merge, no c-command comes into existence. Meanwhile, every W inside an already c-commanded Y inherits the trait from Y regardless of the plane that W is on. We leave this line of reasoning for future pursuit (but see section 4.3 of Chapter 4), concentrating instead on demonstrating how (99) works with coordination.

The same-plane requirement directly rules out any binding relation between conjuncts, explaining the unacceptability of anaphors, epithets and NPIs in the second conjunct. Meanwhile, it also accommodates (101):

101. Jeff$_i$ [$_{T'}$ burned [$_{DP}$ a book by Sarah and an article about himself$_i$/*the bastard$_i$]].

With T′ the sister node to *Jeff*, the rest of the sentence, including both conjuncts in the object DP, serves as the offspring of T′ under (99). It follows that *Jeff* c-commands *himself* legitimately and *the bastard* is illegitimate inside c_2. Assuming bound variables to need c-command by a quantifier Q in some sense, (99) also provides the structural basis. Consider the LF structure of (94a) after QR where *every* adjoins to the immediately dominating DP. For such a DP-internal movement, whether DP is an island is irrelevant.

102.

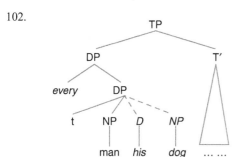

Once raised, *every* becomes a sister to the lower DP node and both are on P_D, so *every* c-commands the lower DP and all its daughter nodes, including *his* on the auxiliary plane. Hence *every* c-commands D at LF, which is sufficient for licensing the bound-variable reading of D à la Hornstein and Weinberg.

Progovac's example in (95a), I venture to suggest, indicates an expedient solution on the part of an epithet E in this particular context. The bound-variable part of E, due to its need for an antecedent, indeed requires c-command, as is typical of any obligatory dependencies in syntax. Ultimately, this is the reason why a licensing quantifier cannot be too deeply embedded, a topic demanding further investigation of its own. Meanwhile, the r-expression part of E considers itself to satisfy Binding Condition C by looking only at the pre-QR location of the binder B. If B does not c-command, the r-expression in E is licensed. This kind of excuse may not be to the taste of every speaker (see note 16), but it becomes totally unavailable when B is located in a c-commanding position to begin with, making E bad pre- and post-QR alike.

Behind this LF-account of bound variables is the fact that neither side enters this relation out of its own inherent quality. The raised quantifier *every* has its own trace to bind while *his* can always have a context-determined referent. Compare this with NPI (cf. (33b)):

103.   * $\begin{bmatrix} \text{nobody} \\ \text{\tiny DP} \ \text{any dog} \end{bmatrix}$ went to the park.

It is in the lexical nature of *any* to be an NPI in need of licensing by a negative c-commander. With Chomsky's (2000) probe-goal theory for structural dependencies, *any* must carry an unvalued feature, call it [NPI] just for the sake of easy reference, that prompts it to agree with some licenser (e.g. Giannakidou 2000). Since this feature must be valued prior to *any* being sent to LF for interpretation, the agreement must happen in overt syntax. In other words, the licensing of *any* under c-command must happen before LF when *nobody* still resides inside c_1 and is unable to c-command any other conjunct. To wit, NPIs require c-command in overt syntax, bound variables do not.

If left alone, this analysis of the interaction between coordination and bound variables would also predict, incorrectly, that a quantificational c_2 equally licenses a bound variable in c_1:

104.   *His$_i$ dog and every man$_i$ went to mow a meadow. (Progovac 2003: 244)

But as has already been observed in the literature (ibid. and the references therein), raising *every* over *his* creates a context of weak crossover, for which different analyses exist (e.g. Koopman and Sportiche 1982, Bautista 2014.).

    Another set of facts bearing on the unequal statuses of conjuncts is subject–verb agreement, already brought up with Russian data in 3.2.2. The English examples below from Progovac (2003: 246) exhibit a very similar pattern:

105.   a.   A man and three children *is/are at the front door.
        b.   There is/??are a man and three children at the front door.
        c.   There *is/are three children and a man at the front door.[18]

Briefly, when the coordinate subject precedes the verb, the latter agrees with the entire subject put together, but the verb–subject order triggers agreement with the first conjunct only. (105) differ from their Russian counterparts in (28) earlier only in that the verb may agree with the entire postverbal subject as well in Russian but is given question marks in the English (105b). Still, if the judgments are accurate, the marginal plural form *are* in (105b) vs. the starred singular form *is* in (105c) generally matches the contrast in the corresponding cases in Russian.

    As Progovac (2003) reports, Babyonyshev (1997) offers an analysis of this correlation between agreement and the linear positions of the subject and the verb with the &P treatment of coordination. In brief, the subject–verb order results from the subject moving overtly to the Spec of TP, which naturally triggers agreement with whatever φ-features the entire subject carries. In contrast, the postverbal subject stays *in situ* (e.g. in the Spec of vP), lending itself to covert feature-movement. This LF movement may involve either the whole subject or only the first conjunct, with independent UG restrictions (e.g. some version of minimality) blocking the second conjunct. As a result, the verb either agrees with the subject as a whole or with c_1 only. The same reasoning extends to the English examples in (105) as long as the marginal status of targeting the whole subject DP for covert movement is put aside.

Babyonyshev's analysis is technically plausible but is undermined by an independent fact. Combining the *there-be* construction with Ross' CSC gives the following test:

106. a. There is a picture of Sam in the book.
      b. Who is there a picture of *t* in the book?
      c. There is/?are a picture of Sam and three drawings by me in the book.
      d. *Who is/are there a picture of *t* and three drawings by me in the book?

(106a-b) show that the postverbal DP does not block movement. The singular agreement in (106c) means to Babyonyshev that the relevant features in c_1 can and do move up covertly. Exactly the same context, however, blocks overt movement out of c_1 in (106d), as expected from the CSC (see 3.3.5 below). This result contradicts the purported derivation of (106c): If movement out of c_1 is banned, how could feature-movement be out of the same conjunct to trigger the singular agreement?

Whatever may be the potential of the movement-based accounts of the agreement patterns across many languages – see Progovac (2003) for some references – the facts have a simple explanation in our multi-plane theory. With a preverbal coordinate subject, all conjuncts are already created in the left-to-right process by the time T is added to the derivation so that T can only agree with them all together. If T is generated before the subject, on the other hand, there is a point of derivation where T is merged only with c_1 on the default plane due to (79), which triggers the V–c_1 agreement. The other option is to delay agreement till all conjuncts are created, which naturally leads to V agreeing with the entire postverbal coordinate subject. Then other (likely non-UG) factors chip in to create finer contrasts such as (106c). In other words, the superior status of c_1 in subject–verb agreement is the same as that in categorial selection: left-to-right sentence-generation in a multi-plane structure.

Speaking of c_1's superiority in categorial selection in *depend on DP and CP*, the analysis provided earlier is that DP as c_1 has a chance in left-to-right sentence-generation to satisfy the categorial selection of *on* all by itself. The remaining question is what makes the clausal c_1 unacceptable once N is defined as the smallest dominating node of all conjuncts with the values of [V, N] changed to variables. For this purpose, consider first a similar case except that either CP or DP is an independently good object. Still, the licensing of the first conjunct also differs from that of the second conjunct.[19] Their multi-planed derivation is represented schematically in (108):

107. a. Jack announced *his year-end report on the stock market* and *that he intended to retire.*
      b. *Jack *announced that he intended to retire* and *his year-end report on the stock market.*

108.   Step *n* :   ··· [VP announced c_1]

       Step *n* + 1:   ··· $\begin{bmatrix} \text{announced} & \begin{bmatrix} c_1 \\ {}_N \ c_2 \end{bmatrix} \\ {}_{VP} \end{bmatrix}$

First, let c_1 be DP and c_2 be clausal (i.e. (107a)). If Step *n* is where grammaticality is evaluated, DP is categorially compatible with *announce*. Waiting for CP at Step *n*+1 would create the conjoined DP and CP whose dominating node N can only be [αV, βN] for categorial specification. Whether these value variables in N can meet the categorial selection of *announce* (see below), we know for sure that at least Step *n* can guarantee a legitimate derivation for (107a), as made clear previously. But inside the theory of UG, there is another critical factor to consider before we move further on in analysis: that DPs need Case but CPs do not. When c_1 is DP, V/*v* provides the Case for DP, making Step *n* good both categorially and Case-wise. At Step *n*+1, however, the N constituent consisting of both the nominal *his year-end report . . .* and the clausal *that he intended to retire* is unable to be evaluated for Case because part of it – such as the D head – needs Case while the other part, i.e. the C head, does not. The dilemma is not solvable as long as the object of *announce* is the whole N, making the licensing at Step *n* the only legitimate choice in the derivation. The later addition of the clausal conjunct still brings in the trouble but, as already stated, a good past verdict will not be undone if Phillips' snapshot mechanism is part of UG's left-to-right structure-generation. For sure, relying on the grammatical evaluation at Step *n* settles the Case-based calculation and leaves the clausal conjunct at Step *n*+1 no part of the Case factor. But clauses do not need Case anyway.

Now let c_1 be the clausal conjunct and c_2 the nominal one (= (107b)). Step *n* is still legitimate. Categorially, *announce* accepts a CP complement as well; Case-wise, CP does not care. Proceeding to Step *n*+1, again the coordinated CP and DP lead to N with categorial uncertainty and conflicting demands for Case. The situation looks identical to (107a) but actually is not. Because the N node poses a problem with grammatical licensing, Step *n* is again the only point of derivation to rely on in order to make the construction legitimate. However, this also means that the later-added nominal string *his year-end report on the stock market* is not given any chance to obtain a Case. In brief, a clausal c_2 can afford to be ignored because its grammatical status does not rest on Case, but a nominal c_2 cannot afford this exemption. Thus, the ungrammatical (107b) is explained. Exactly the same logic applies to *depend on*, in addition to the fact that [*on* CP] is not a good default-plane derivation to begin with.

To end this discussion of categorial disparities inside a coordinate structure, consider N with [αV, βN] one last time. Given the logic adopted here, using such a node to represent, say [N D NP and C TP] (see (83)) is legitimate when looked at from the inside. For instance, D has its own categorial specification [−V, +N], and taking an NP complement on the same plane is the expected norm. Also, as long as the variables α and β can accommodate D's own "−" and "+" values – and they obviously can – N is viewed by D as a good projection. Whether N with [αV, βN] is viewed as satisfying the categorial selection of *announce* from outside N is unclear in the theory of UG as we have it. One may regard this scenario as bad because N cannot provide the precise categorial information expected by *announce*; or one may argue that the categorially very variable nature of N gives the node the ability to satisfy any categorial selection. I am not aware of any way to choose between these independently plausible options. Fortunately, there always appear to be other UG factors that can distinguish between the good and bad examples with categorially different conjuncts. For the type in (22) and (107), Case is sufficient, as demonstrated above. For Bowers' (1993) type of conjoined predicates before PredP, the only impossible combination is between VP and another non-verbal predicate (cf. Zoerner 1995):

109.   a. Jim considers Robin [ugly, a dolt and of no help].
        b. *Jim considers Robin [ugly, a dolt and always intrude on others].

But independently, VP needs T to bind its event position while other categories do not (Higginbotham 1985). Since verbs like *consider* cannot provide this event-binding for their small clause complements, (109b) is ruled out.

3.3.5   Application 3: Last-Conjunct Agreement

Bošković (2009) reports a "rather rare" (p. 455) last-conjunct agreement (LCA) in Serbo-Croatian (SC):

110.   a. Juče   su   uništena/?uništeni   sva sela   i
           yesterday   are   destroyed.PL.NEUT/PL.MASC   all villages.NEUT   and
           sve   varošice.
           all   towns.FEM
           'All villages and all towns were destroyed yesterday.'

b. Sva sela   i   sve varošice   su (juče)
   all villages.NEUT and all towns.FEM are yesterday
   uništene/uništeni.
   destroyed.PL.FEM/PL.MASC

(110a) appears to be the familiar first-conjunct agreement (FCA) already seen in Russian, Arabic and (to some extent) English. When the subject precedes the verb, as in (110b), the verb (in its participial form) may also optionally agree with the last conjunct. This is not only a relatively rare phenomenon but also unexpected from the analysis given above.

The SC verb agreement with a coordinate subject has further complications. The overall pattern is stated in (111).[20] See Bošković (2009) for concrete data.

111. a. Number is always plural in the verbal agreement.
      b. FCA in gender happens only when the first conjunct is plural.
      c. LCA happens only when
         i.   all conjuncts are plural, and
         ii. no non-last conjunct has a masculine or semantically feminine gender.
      d. When all conjuncts have the same feminine gender, the verb is also feminine.
      e. The default gender is masculine.

Bošković's own analysis is built on a critical SC fact in (112) plus various theoretical apparatuses, among them being the &P structure for coordination, the general and language-specific feature-based operations (Match, Value, Delete, etc.) within the Minimalist framework, and a division of SC φ-features in terms of interpretability.

112. a. ?Knjige$_i$ je Marko [t$_i$ i   filmove] kupio. (ibid. (30))
         books is Marko   and movies   bought
         'Marko bought books and movies.'
      b. *Filmove$_i$ je Marko [knjige i   t] kupio. (ibid. (31))
         movies is Marko books   and   bought

Assuming the first conjunct c_1 to be in the Spec position of &P, (112) is taken as evidence that c_1 is susceptible to movement. It follows that when &P is the subject originating in the Spec position of vP, both c_1 and &P are equidistant to whatever functional head F is relevant here. When &P stays *in situ*, yielding the verb–subject order after V moves up, F has equal options to agree with c_1 or &P in (110a). If F triggers subject-movement, it is again both &P and c_1 that are equally qualified. Since only one of them can actually be moved, the indeterminacy stalls the attempt. Bošković proposes that this failed first attempt nonetheless deletes the (uninterpretable) gender feature in c_1 (his definition (31)) and thereby makes c_1 invisible to subsequent attempts by F to identify the target of movement. As a result, F finds &P and c_2 in the second round but, based on (112b), c_2 cannot be extracted out of &P, effectively leaving &P to be the only target for movement. Meanwhile, provided that agreement is part of the process of movement (ibid. definition (29)), for F to be able to see c_2 is sufficient to make F agree with the gender feature of c_2, explaining why the raised subject before V exhibits LCA. This line of analysis aided by other tools/assumptions accounts for the data pattern in (111).

Since c_1 is proven to not c-command c_2 in 3.2.3 earlier, the &P structure is no longer valid for explaining coordination. Furthermore, there is one more fact, noted by Bošković (ibid., example (8)), that actually questions his analysis:

113. Sve banje,   sve varošice,   i   sva sela   su
    all spas.FEM all towns.FEM and all villages.NEUT are
    uništena/*uništene.
    destroyed.PL.NEUT/*FEM
    'All spas, all towns and all villages were destroyed.'

The key assumption in (113) is that &P allows multiple Spec positions to host more than one non-final conjunct and that all such positions are equidistant to F for the purpose of movement. Thus, the first two attempts by the F-head to identify a unique target of movement in (113) both fail, for each round finds &P and one of the non-final conjuncts to be equally qualified. Only the third attempt has &P and the immovable last c_3, resulting in the subject–verb order plus LCA.

But in note 22, Bošković observes that "when there are more then [sic] two conjuncts, extraction of any conjunct is banned." If no conjunct can move, the first attempt by F should succeed because the only movable constituent is &P while F agrees with c_1 in gender. We would predict, contra (113), that a tri-conjunct preverbal subject may trigger agreement with the first conjunct. In response to this problem, Bošković separates multiple Specs as in (113) from one Spec, assuming in note 22 that what bans movement in the former case "is not taken into consideration when determining potential pied-pipers," namely the conjunct that would help move the entire subject. What remains unclear is why this is so. Movement is the operation in both scenarios, and the conjuncts in Spec positions are the targets in both scenarios. If the actual (marginal) movability of c_1 in (112) is considered the empirical basis on which to create the unsolvable competition between c_1 and &P, it just seems ad hoc that the immovability of any individual conjunct in (113) is discounted.

Now consider an account of SC agreement in (111) with the multi-plane theory of coordination defended in this chapter. To begin with, given the left-to-right sentence-generation plus the default and auxiliary planes, the overall pattern in (111) is expected in a conceptually simple way. As pointed out by Bošković, number is a φ-feature that is semantically interpretable and SC is sensitive to the semantically interpretable φ-features, a clearly language-specific trait not found in, say, Russian (cf. (28b)). When the verb in the F position precedes the coordinate subject, there is a stage n of derivation with V and c_1 on P_D only and where grammaticality can be evaluated. If this stage n is judged well formed and FCA results, the verdict will not be reversed unless forced by semantic considerations to be discussed shortly. In contrast, the preverbal subject means that by the time the verb in F is reached, the entire coordinate subject has already been generated. Regardless of how SC enables LCA, then, agreement necessarily has all the conjuncts in the subject to consider for grammatical assessment. And this is exactly what (111) looks like: FCA in (111b) is significantly less conditioned than LCA in (111c) because the latter has more conjuncts and their φ-features to worry about.

Specifically, FCA is implemented as follows:

114.

Stage n: ... V [vP c_1

Stage $n + 1$:   ... V $\begin{bmatrix} \begin{bmatrix} & c_1 \\ _{vP} \lfloor_N & c_2 \end{bmatrix} \end{bmatrix}$

Let c_1 have the plural number and any gender. V obtains these φ-features (via F) from c_1 at Stage n and satisfies that part of UG which requires agreement. The addition of c_2 at Stage $n+1$ does not affect the plural agreement since (i) the default-plane computation has already been judged good and (ii) V is plural from c_1 already, while c_2, whether plural or singular, still leaves the entire subject N plural. Gender is mostly semantically null (= uninterpretable) and thus the gender of c_2 is ignored. Put together, V agrees with c_1 to yield FCA. It also covers the cases when c_2 has the same gender as c_1 as the result is simply invisible (see below for the feminine gender in (111d)).

Now suppose c_1 to be singular. C_2 necessarily alters the number value at Stage $n+1$. Since number has semantic content, the agreement between V and c_1 must be retracted due to the SC-specific sensitivity to interpretable φ-features, which in turn prompts the second attempt at verbal agreement, this time with the whole subject. In SC, this means a plural number and the correspondingly readjusted default masculine gender. Hence (111b) is fully derived. Short of other yet unconsidered factors, this logic also predicts that, if c_2 differs from c_1 in carrying a semantically interpretable gender feature (in SC), such as *žene* 'women.FEM', where the noun is itself inherently feminine, there should be no FCA either because the default-plane agreement cannot survive the interpretable feminine gender of c_2 which alters the collective gender property of the coordinate subject. But no data are given by Bošković to verify the prediction.

The structure for LCA is (115):

115. ... $\left[\begin{array}{cc} \left[\begin{array}{cc} c_1 \\ _N\ c_2 \end{array}\right] & V \end{array}\right]$

Since LCA is rare, there must be some extra and abnormal factor at work. Bošković correlates the phenomenon with the extraction of c_1 in SC. Absent of cross-linguistic substantiation and with the unresolved tri-conjunct data in (113), I will pursue a different route:

116.   SC allows F/V to agree with the immediate element that is structurally qualified for the operation.

The general requirement for structural qualification limits the candidates to those in, for instance, the Spec position of FP, while excluding constituents inside them, as is normal of the UG system. If one looks at the entire subject constituent S, S is immediately before F/V if preverbal or immediately after F/V if postverbal. But for individual conjuncts, the last conjunct before F/V is immediate to the latter and so is the first conjunct after F/V. That is, (116) properly includes what creates the much more common FCA and, in a sense, turns the spirit of the latter's default structural environment around to include the conjunct immediately before F/V.

(116) may be attributed to a processing factor fossilized into SC syntax, or it might be a language-specific attempt to make full use of the multi-plane structure of coordination (or possibly a combination of both). Regardless, the last conjunct in a subject–verb structure is also the one on the auxiliary plane from which to return immediately to the default plane so as to generate F. Given the implementation of the multi-plane structure with shared branches, SC allows the (116)-sanctioned structure for LCA to be literally represented as below:

117.   ...

That is, SC implements (116) by calculating a path from c_2 on the auxiliary plane back to F, the next constituent merged with DP on the default plane in the left-to-right process, thereby giving F access to c_2 individually, in a way similar to how F accesses the default-plane conjunct in the FCA context (114).

But (117) differs from (114) in a fundamental way. In (114), there exists a state of derivation, Stage n, where there are only F/V and c_1 for grammaticality calculations. In (117), though, F may access c_2 individually through the dashed path but it cannot be blind to the presence of c_1 and the entire DP that are already generated by now. Plausibly, any ϕ-feature of c_1 and DP, be it grammatical or semantic, that contradicts that of c_2 is enough to disqualify c_2 as the ϕ-feature representative for subject–verb agreement. What is critical here is the standard for determining feature-contradiction. Given the SC data summarized in (111c) and Bošković's analysis, the language seems to maintain a prominence ranking among its ϕ-features:

118. semantic ϕ > masc. > fem./neut.

With FCA, since grammaticality is already settled between F/V and c_1 on the default plane, only semantic inconsistency could motivate the second round of agreement. Hence, all the purely grammatical uninterpretable gender values from which FCA is immune are lumped together. For LCA, grammaticality cannot be determined by c_2 alone when the entire coordinate subject is around, so all interpretable or uninterpretable ϕ-features in and of DP may play a role in evaluating LCA, in accordance with the ranking in (118). No feature value of a lower rank can represent that of a higher one.

Starting with number, a "semantic ϕ" in (118), let the value of c_1 be α and the value of c_2 be β. If they are different, the agreement between c_2 and F on β cannot represent α, forcing the second attempt at subject–verb agreement, which yields the necessarily plural number and the default masculine gender. If α and β are both singular, then β cannot represent the number value of the whole subject DP; again plural number and masculine gender result. It is only when both α and β are plural that V's agreement with c_2 on β can represent both c_1 and DP. And only if V can keep β will V's agreement with c_2 on gender have a chance to survive in the form of LCA. This explains (111c-i). As for gender, LCA becomes possible only when the feature value of c_2 is not lower than that of c_1. In (110b), for instance, the two conjuncts have the neuter and feminine genders, respectively. Since the two values have the same ranking, LCA may happen with c_2 having either of them. In contrast, if c_1 has the higher-ranked masculine or semantically interpretable feminine gender, c_2 with a lower-ranked gender fails to be the representative and once more agreement takes the form of the plural number and default masculine gender, leading to (111c-ii).

The theory, as is formulated, also makes three specific predictions. If c_2 is masculine while c_1 is neuter or feminine, LCA is possible since masculine is ranked higher than the other two. If c_2 is masculine and c_1 has the interpretable feminine gender, the verbal agreement is also masculine because the interpretable gender will impose a recalculation of agreement and thereby yield the default masculine gender. On the surface, however, this outcome looks the same as LCA. Lastly, if c_2 has an interpretable gender, LCA is allowed simply because it prevails over all other gender values lower than it in ranking. No data are given in Bošković (2009), and the theory presented above may need minor adjustments depending on how these predictions pan out.

The last fact with SC verbal agreement is (111d): When both conjuncts are feminine, V is always feminine in gender regardless of the linear relation between the subject and the verb and the number value of each conjunct. Bošković takes this to mean that the uniform feminine gender always percolates to &P and reasons that "feminine gender is sometimes semantically grounded" and that "only interpretable features can be present at the &P level" (p. 485). It is totally plausible that the semantic features of the conjuncts are retained in the coordinate subject, which would follow directly from my analysis above. Since feminine gender is semantic only "sometimes," however, (111d) still awaits a coherent account in which, I suspect, pure reference to semantics is inadequate.

3.3.6   More Factual and Theoretical Facets of Coordination

One of the reasons that coordination is difficult to analyze is that some facts look like they lie at the very UG basis of the phenomenon but actually do not. Consider (119) from Progovac (2003: 259):

119.   a.   John read the book and quickly
     b.   *John read quickly and the book

On the surface, the contrast in (119) parallels the *depend-on* examples seen earlier, namely one sequence of the conjoined elements is good while the other is not. It is tempting, therefore, to subject them to the same analysis. But a closer look reveals a fundamental distinction. Though DP and CP after *depend on* are of different categories, both are semantically well-formed arguments in themselves, i.e. with full internal thematic saturation. This level of semantic identity leaves those examples only with syntactic licensing such as Case and category to worry about. In (119), on the other hand, *the book* is an argument of the verb *read* with a function application to perform between them for proper semantic interpretation, whereas *quickly* is a Davidsonian predicate of events and requires event-identification to be semantically connected with *read*. If *the book* and *quickly* were to form a coordinate structure – dominated by N in our notation, there would be no legitimate semantic relation between *read* and this N, regardless of how syntactic licensing works. In other words, it is unlikely that (119) simply conjoins a DP and an adverb, just as the coordination of AP and VP is unacceptable in (109b). It also happens that (119) patterns cleanly with (120):

120.   a.   John read the book and did so quickly.
     b.   *John read quickly and did so the book.

It seems more plausible, then, to attribute (119) to some form of identity-deletion of V' instead of worrying about an object and an adverb being ungrammatically coordinated in a certain order.

The Ross' effects reviewed in 3.2.2 remain a poorly understood case. Example (20b) is repeated in (121):

121.   Jeff bought a house last week, and the small lake behind it.

The "right-extraposed" string *and the small lake behind it* is often viewed as direct evidence for &P, but it is equally compatible with treating *and* as reflecting the [&] feature associated with the topmost node of the subsequent adjunct and linearly positioned between the conjuncts. As for the separation of the two conjuncts *a house* and *the small lake behind it*, the &P structure does not automatically account for it. As an example, the most popular implementation places the conjuncts in the Spec and complement positions (see (19)). It is not clear by what independently motivated mechanism the &' node dominating *and the small lake behind it* could be extraposed rightward. Whether X' moves or not remains unclear and theory-specific, but where else does movement strand just the Spec of XP? I admit to not understanding the precise nature of the phenomenon, merely noting that in the multi-plane theory, it is possible that the extraposed conjunct results from a delayed creation of the auxiliary plane, namely completing the initial clause on P_D before branching at the N node for the second conjunct and thereby yielding the right-extraposed word order from the left-to-right process of structure-generation. I suspect that de Vries' (2009) algorithm of top-down depth-first tree traversal for computing the linearization in multi-dominance contexts could be revised to implement the possibility of the delayed creation of auxiliary planes, but will leave it to future investigation. Also worth emphasizing is that in the multi-plane theory, the first part of (121) is exclusively on P_D with NO coordination, so the DP node for the object does not carry [&] yet. It is only when the delayed addition of the second conjunct starts that [&] is introduced. This operational sequence not only complies with *and* necessarily associated with the "extraposed" conjunct but also suggests that the overt signal of [&] accompanies the creation of a new plane, an intuitively natural strategy.

Another instance of Ross' effects is *etc*. Like (121), it is often regarded as supporting the constituency of *and* plus the subsequent conjunct. Such a conclusion does not contradict treating *and* as a mere phonological label of [&] on the added conjunct. Meanwhile, it should be borne in mind that logically, *etc*. is only consistent with the constituency account but is not a compelling argument for it. After all, *gonna* replaces *going to* even though the latter expression is but a phonologically adjacent string of words without exclusive structural constituency.

Conjunction-doubling is one more phenomenon frequently included in the study of coordination (see (21)) that strives for an X'-theoretic account. But such efforts typically overlook several facts. In Zwart (2005), conjunction-doubling is called polysyndetic coordination since it is not limited to two conjunctions. To facilitate discussion, the "doubled" conjunction will be called the edge-conjunction to reflect the fact that it always occurs at the left or right edge of the coordinate construction. Based on Zwart's survey of 162 languages, "it is perhaps significant that in all cases where polysyndetic coordination alternates with monosyndetic coordination, [the latter] appears to present the unmarked case" (p. 238). Indeed, judging from my own investigation of French and Japanese, there is no significant contrast between [A, B & C] and [A & B & C] in terms of naturalness, but every native speaker consulted finds [& A & B (& C)] in French and its mirror image in Japanese a considerably more marked form, some even hesitating before accepting it. This outcome is also reflected tacitly in Zwart's report in which [A, B & C] and [A & B & C] are lumped together under the monosyndetic type vs. the polysyndetic type with the edge-conjunction.

The cross-linguistic contrast is further highlighted by how Zwart words his report: "A number of head-final languages in the sample show polysyndetic noun phrase coordination of the type A & B &" (p. 238). The footnote (fn. 14) on this remark lists 20 languages with this property, out of 52 consistently head-final languages in the survey. Noticeably, no mention of polysyndetic cases is made on the 67 cleanly head-initial languages investigated, possibly indicating that the phenomenon is so uncommon in this latter group as to deserve no attention. In sum, in the 119 languages where the linear location of the head is consistent, only one-sixth of them are found with polysyndetic coordination. It ought to be obvious, then, that, minimally, edge-conjunctions should not receive exactly the same treatment as the in-between conjunctions.

Zwart further observes that "where the two conjunctions used in polysyndetic coordination are not identical, the final conjunction is a summary or comitative element" (p. 238), and quotes Murane (1974) for (122):

122. nenip Bure ge   nenip Dukuik dere   (Data, Trans New Guinea)
     bird   Bure and bird   Dukuik two
     'the Bure bird and the Dukuik bird'

Recall that similar strategies are used with what appears to be the counter-iconic location of conjunctions like A B & (see examples (18a-b) and the discussions thereon). The summary word *dere* 'two' is certainly reminiscent of *both* in English (cf. *both the Bure bird and the Dukuik bird*) while string-final comitatives are good candidates for postpositions. Together, the two strategies further reduce the number of languages with real polysyndetic coordination and emphasize how marked the phenomenon is.

Having an edge-conjunction is not only a grammatically marked form. My French and Japanese informants all noted, most of them without prompt, that this use of the conjunction always carries extra semantic flavors and/or is appropriate only in certain discourse contexts. Theory-independently, this fact conforms with the rarity of true polysyndetic coordination.

With all these facts in mind, an account suggests itself. The phenomenon is both typologically and intra-linguistically unpopular; the edge-conjunction is associated with extra semantic content; some cases might involve superficially look-alike strategies (e.g. comitative and summary morphemes). Thus, true polysyndetic coordination, namely those cases which use the same conjunctive form in all spots, can be analyzed as follows. (i) Because the &-feature is associated with N that dominates all conjuncts, it is grammatically possible that the feature, once present, is phonologically manifested on all planes. (ii) Since all between-conjunct positions are already taken by "normal" conjunctions under iconicity, the edge-conjunction can only occur at one side of the entire coordinate construction (which immediately explains why no polysyndetic examples are reported in the literature with partly missing in-between conjunctions: [& A, B & C]). But this edge-solution is anti-iconic for not being between conjuncts and thus lacking in any grammatical or extra-grammatical ground for justification in its linearization. (iii) To resolve the dilemma, the semantics of the conjunction is brought into consideration, i.e. $R_\&$, which is a relation. It cannot possibly be analogized to verbs because verbs necessarily denote events, but $R_\&$ does not; adjectives and nouns define sets of entities and are fundamentally different from the semantic nature of $R_\&$ (which defines a set of pairs of anything), so no analogy here makes sense. The only lexical category which is in nature relational is adpositions (see Hale and Keyser 1993 for assigning P to the semantic class of "interrelation"). Consequently, the linearization of the edge-conjunction is forced to mimic an adposition in the given language in order to solve the linearization dilemma through UG, namely trailing the coordinate structure like a postposition in Japanese and preceding it like a preposition in French.

In fact, this may be why, according to Zwart, one form of polysyndetic coordination is to use comitatives at the edge – if one pretends that the conjunction is a postposition in a head-final language, one might as well simply use a real postposition instead. Furthermore, the adposition-analogy is by nature a stopgap, a make-do strategy because, fundamentally, the edge-conjunction is just a phonological embodiment of the &-feature in N. It follows that polysyndetic coordination is rare and marked. Its use had better offer something that iconically linearized conjunctions do not. Hence the extra semantic flavors of the edge-conjunctions. To this end, the edge-conjunction can be compared with Ross' right-extraposition in (121), which also has a conjunction at one side of the string at issue (*and the small lake behind it*).

From what I can tell, the latter is not as marked a phenomenon as polysyndetic coordination. This is so because, despite the extraposition separating the conjuncts, *and* remains iconically positioned between them and in contrast with the edge-conjunction which is neither really UG-authorized nor iconically compliant. Lastly, we predict, pending further assessment, that those instances using independently verifiable comitatives should be more natural than the true polysyndetic cases with the same conjunction all the way through.

An entirely different phenomenon associated with coordination is the abnormal Case that has been observed and investigated by a few authors (e.g. Schwartz 1985, Zoerner 1995, Johannessen 1998). The examples below are all quoted from Progovac (2003: section 1.6; also see the references therein):

123. a. Them and us are going to the game together.
      b. She and him will drive to the movies.
      c. I really wanted my mother to live with I, him and Michael.
      d. Robin saw he, she and me.

The difficulty here lies in lacking a sufficiently clear and uniform pattern. Case deviation happens to both conjuncts in (123a), to the last one in (123b), to the first one in (123c) and the first two in (123d). No attempt will be made in this book to analyze them because it remains unclear what to base an analysis on.[21] Still, it may not be coincident that abnormal Cases occur with the multi-plane structure of coordination. LCA and FCA both deviate from the standard subject–verb agreement and, as shown above, they are derivable from the conjuncts on different planes. Possibly, multiple planes also create the structural context for grammatical flexibility or a functional gap in Case manifestation, opening up the window for other facts to determine acceptability. See Progovac (ibid.) for "draw[ing] the line between grammaticality and acceptability" in this regard.

Ross' CSC in (36) covers two scenarios, the immovability of a single conjunct (37) and no extraction out of a single conjunct. The first kind, part of which Postal calls "logical coordination" where the conjuncts can be freely swapped, has a robust factual base and was shown in 3.3.2 to follow from my multi-plane theory. The second scenario, call it S2, appears much more complex than the CSC describes, already noted by multiple authors (see (38–39) and the references therearound, especially Postal 1998). The very fact that no conclusion has been reached for decades on the structural mechanism behind S2 may be regarded as a prompt to look beyond syntax for an explanation. It is in this sense that Chaves' (2012) pragmatic-semantic approach to S2 is briefly recounted below as a plausible alternative.

Drawing on the preceding works, Chaves divides coordination according to the "symmetric and asymmetric readings" (p. 469). Multiple arguments are presented that even S2, the asymmetric variant of coordination, does not behave like a subordinate structure in other aspects of grammar, proving that the familiar asymmetric structure separating islands from non-islands is an unlikely place to find explanation. Chaves further demonstrates the role of pragmatic and processing factors in sentence acceptability for coordination and beyond. Directly pertinent to the current concern is Kuno's (1987) observation through examples like (123) that extractability rests on the "relevance" between the moved constituent serving as the topic and the rest of the sentence:

124.   a.   Who did you write a book about *t*?
       b.   Who did you lose a book about *t*?

As Pustejovky (1995) puts it, *who* as Kuno's topic is also a "shadow argument" in the semantics of *write* and thus there exists a straightforward relevance between the *wh*-moved *who* and the event described by the rest of (124a). In contrast, the event of losing a book in (124b) is unrelated to the subject matter of the book, leaving the sentence pragmatically incoherent and thus less acceptable.

Chaves moves on to propose the Fill-head Relevance condition (2012: 490). (125) is the part of his definition sufficient for the present purpose of illustration:

125.   R(x, e) holds iff x is a coherent argument of event e.

Where R is "a pragmatic predicate ... that requires that [a moved constituent] x must be pragmatically relevant/coherent in the event described by the sister phrase e" (ibid.). Given the understanding that the symmetric coordination of event-denoting conjuncts creates event pluralities (Bach 1986, Eckardt 1995, Link 1998, etc.), Chaves reasons that $R(x, e_1+e_2)$ entails the distributive $R(x, e_1)$ $\land$ $R(x, e_2)$. That is, the extracted x must be pragmatically relevant to each event-denoting conjunct, which explains why in strict symmetric coordination, only Williams' (1978) across-the-board (ATB) movement (e.g. *which city does Fred like* t *and Mia despise* t?) is acceptable. Asymmetric coordination, on the other hand, has *and* interpreted pragmatically as 'earlier than' or 'cause' (cf. R_T interpreted as 'cause' in the resultative SVC), in compliance with the Gricean maxim of "be orderly" in our theory. Such an interpretation of *and* no longer produces event plurality and hence "cannot force distributivity, and consequently, R does not have to distribute, thus explaining why ATB extraction is not obligatory in asymmetric coordination" (Chaves 2012: 491). Chaves further points out that since 'earlier than' and 'cause' are available only for events, nominal coordination is not known to allow extraction out of only one conjunct (p. 505).

In conclusion, the multi-plane structure defended in this chapter, though asymmetric in the sense that c_1 is on the default plane and thereby participates in grammaticality calculation in a way that other conjuncts do not, is otherwise treating all conjuncts in a parallel fashion. Thus, it is unlikely that it can provide a structurally based explanation for both scenarios of the CSC. If Chaves' pragmatic-semantic account of the phenomenon eventually proves to be on the right track, this inability of the multi-plane model may turn out to be an advantage, for it would correctly assign this cluster of facts to other components of language or the interface between language and another general cognitive facility and thus avoid redundancy in a principled manner.

To end this section, we consider two objections by Zhang (2010) to the parallel structure analyses of coordination. One of them is that "the multiple dimensional analysis ... depends on the linearization of multiple dimensional structures, a more complex operation than linearization of two-dimensional structures." Zhang sees "no advantage to the more complex multiple-dimensional approach" if the goal of explaining relevant facts "can be met by the simpler two-dimensional approach" (p. 167). But the two-dimensional structure that Zhang adopts, the X'-style phrase with the conjuncts in the Spec and complement positions and the conjunction in the head position (see her Chapters 2 and 3), cannot explain why c_1 does not c-command c_2 for binding, a straightforward fact seen in 3.2.3 in English and below in Chinese:

126. wo ganggang   dafa-le   *Xue Pan$_i$* he   *zhege hundan$_i$*
      1s a.moment.ago send.away-ASP XP   and this   bastard
      dailai de hupenggouyou.
      bring DE scoundrel.friends
      'I just sent away XP and the scoundrel friends this bastard brought along.'

The example is perfect with the epithet *zhege hundan* 'this bastard' inside c_2 and coindexed with c_1 *XP*. When basic facts are not covered, theoretical simplicity is groundless to determine.

Zhang's second objection (ibid.) is based on the long-known fact that when a single relative clause (RC) modifies both conjuncts, the latter must have identical determiners. The examples below are among those quoted by Zhang from Moltmann (1992) (the brackets are mine):

127. a. *[the father of John and a woman [RC who know each other well]]
      b. *John saw the man and Mary saw a woman [RC who met last year].

128. John met a man and [DP the woman [RC he saw yesterday]].

The definite and indefinite determiners result in unacceptability with a shared RC in (127) but are good when the RC is for one conjunct only in (128). In (127b) for instance, the shared RC is multiply dominated by the separate DP nodes for *the man* and *a woman* in a structure where conjuncts are placed on different planes (or dimensions). Since these two DPs do not form a constituent, "additional constraints are required to cover facts [like (127–128)]" (Zhang 2010: 167).

Now consider how Zhang covers these facts. For her, the examples in (126) are unacceptable because

[*the man* and *a woman*] do not provide a consistent set of specificity features for the RC, which takes the combination of the two nominals as its Head (its semantic subject). If the Head of an RC does not exhibit consistent specificity features, there cannot be any predication relation between the Head and the RC. (p. 159)

Critical in this reasoning is that the DP conjuncts involved are always from a "coordinate complex" which together acts as the head of the RC. From (128), we know that a coordinate structure does not in itself require the conjuncts to have identical determiners. So the quotation above is right in placing the burden on the relative clause for enforcing identical determiners. As a matter of fact, this can be automatically accomplished in a multi-plane structure. First, one must assume, regardless of the specific theories of coordination, that the *wh*-operator, *who* in (127), is coindexed with all the conjuncts put together serving as its head because this is a semantic requirement, similar to what happens to the interpretable number feature in Serbo-Croatian verbal agreement but in a more fundamental manner. If the conjuncts have different specificity/definiteness values, the single *wh*-operator will end up with conflicting values of the same semantic feature, which is enough to crash the derivation due to semantic contradiction (and possibly valuation failure at the grammatical level). None of these belongs to "additional constraints," as Zhang phrases it, but rather is out of the core nature of UG. As a matter of fact, this reasoning follows straightforwardly from the multi-plane structure since all conjuncts are equally visible to the RC by definition. In contrast, one must invoke an extra mechanism to guarantee that the complement conjunct of &P also has its specificity visible to an RC which is only structurally affiliated with &P.

It is worth noting, especially in light of Zhang's first and simplicity-based objection, that the multi-plane model in this chapter, once established, handles shared constituents in coordination without extra stipulations. In comparison, Zhang's X′-theoretic coordinate complex relies on several construction-specific assumptions for the data: (i) for examples of the (127b) type, the head of this complex "is realized by a null conjunction" (p. 156) since the overt *and* is for the clausal conjuncts (see (iv) below); (ii) "the two DP conjuncts are separately re-selected by two verbs" in the two preceding clauses (ibid.); (iii) the null head in (i) differs from *and* by having "its own categorial features, and thus it does not get categorial features from any conjunct" (p. 163); (iv) the underlying structure for (127b) has two coordinate complexes, one with two TP conjuncts and the other with two DP conjuncts, and the RC at issue adjoins to the latter "DP" complex, while this whole structure is further adjoined to the former "TP" complex (p. 163, tree (6.59)); and finally, (v) each DP conjunct sideward-moves to the object position of the verb inside one of the

TP conjuncts (p. 162, tree (6.57)). An analysis with all these extras does not
seem simpler at all.

3.4   The Linkers

The term "linker" is borrowed from Chung (1991) (also see Chung and
Ladusaw 2004) and is to be distinguished from the use of this word in den
Dikken (2006), to which I will return later in the section.

3.4.1   Cross-Linguistic Facts

As part of her data to set up the structure of DP in Chamorro (Austronesian),
Chung (1991) provides these examples (her (20–22a)), with L for linkers:

129. a. i   lingguahi-n Chapanís
          the   language-L   Japanese
          'the Japanese language'
      b. patgun   dángkulu
          child   big
          'a big child'
      c. i   lepblu ni   yä-ña   si   Juan
          the book   c   like-3s   Juan
          'the book which Juan likes'
      d. ospitát   nai   siña   hit   man-ma-asisti
          hospital c   can   we   PL-PASS-assist
          'hospitals where we can be helped'

130. a. i   Chapanís na   lingguahi
          the Japanese L   language
          'the Japanese language'
      b. dángkulu na   patgun
          big   L   child
          'a big child'
      c. i   ya-na   si   Juan   na   lepblu
          the like-3s   Juan   L   book
          'the book which Juan likes'
      d. todu ädyu siha i   ti   man-ofisiát   na stickers pat decals
          all   that PL   the not PL-official   L   stickers or decals
          'all those stickers and decals that are not official'
      e. i   ginin Tinian na   taotao
          the from   Tinian L   people
          'the people from Tinian'

In these examples, Chung notes (p. 97, footnote 5) that "[m]odifers are joined to
N by the linker. When the modifier precedes, the linker is realized as *na*; when
the modifier follows, the linker is -*n* after a vowel and null otherwise."

To recapitulate our earlier characterization of linkers, they have obscure semantic and categorial content – therefore labeled as L rather than any familiar category – and they occur between the constituents they connect. When the modifier M is postnominal, as in (129a), L precedes M; when M is prenominal in (130), L follows M. Also worth noting is what happens with relative clauses. The prenominal form has no overt complementizer but uses the linker *na* (130c), while the postnominal one has the complementizer *ni* 'which' (129c) and *nai* 'where' (129d), which happen to have the same /n/ consonant. One cannot help but speculate that these so-called complementizers are actually composed of the postnominal linker *n* just like (129a) plus the vowel that signals the semantic content of a given C (or Spec of CP). In this sense, the postnominal linker manifests itself as *n* as long as there is an adjacent vowel support. A more subtle implication of this *n* will be considered later on. Furthermore, the Chamorro linkers are insensitive to the category of the modifier, which can be a DP, an AP, a CP or a PP.

Mandarin Chinese has a very similar counterpart in the form of the mysterious morpheme -*de*, which is labeled as L pending further justification:

131. a. Yueyue   -de   gushi
         Yueyue   -L   story
         'the story by/about Yueyue'
      b. dongren-de gushi
         moving-L   story
         'a moving story'
      c. guanyu konglong-de gushi
         about   dinosaur-L   story
         'a story about dinosaurs'
      d. Yueyue jiang-guo-de gushi
         Yueyue tell-ASP-L   story
         'the story that Yueyue told'

132. a. Lele chuhuyiliao-de/zhishuang-de chengren-le (zheci shiwu).
         Lele unexpected-L/candid-L   admit-ASP this   fault
         'Lele unexpectedly/candidly admitted (this mistake).'
      b. Lele chengren-de   hen   chuhuyiliao/zhishuang.
         Lele admit-L   very   unexpected/candid
         'Lele admitted it unexpectedly/candidly.'

In modern Mandarin Chinese, -*de* is phonologically indistinguishable whether the modifier it introduces is for a noun (131) or a verb (132) or whether in the latter case, the modifier is preverbal (132a) or postverbal (132b). Furthermore, the linear location of -*de* is always between the modifier and the modified. If the modifier has the option of occurring on either side of the modified, which is possible only with Chinese verbs, -*de* is adjusted accordingly.

It must be made clear at this point that the prenominal, preverbal and postverbal instances of -de are all given different written forms in official orthography so as to reflect their (superficially) different grammatical functions. And the fact that all three uses of -de share the same phonological form is not necessarily significant. In fact, many dialects of Chinese use different words for the three contexts in (131–132). Cantonese, for instance, has *ge*, *gam* and *dak* respectively in the corresponding contexts of (131), (132a) and (132b). This is no different in nature from Chamorro using *na* for the prenominal constituents and $n/\emptyset$ for the postnominals. What remains unchanged is the grammatical traits they all share: semantic and categorial obscurity plus the in-between location. A more fundamental similarity among these linkers from Mandarin Chinese and Cantonese will be demonstrated and treated in 3.4.4.

Given these facts, the essence of the explanation becomes straightforward in the theory of UG-I defended in this book: Linkers have no categorial specification and therefore have no legitimate syntactic representation under $Void_F2$, which in turn halts at least the R_S-to-R_L mapping. To linguistically manifest whatever information is encoded in a linker, iconicity is brought in, placing a linker where it should be, namely between the constituents it links in the same way that conjunctions are positioned. The questions from the UG side are: Exactly what type of information does a linker carry so as to deprive it of any categorial property and, more generally and fundamentally, what justifies the claim that linkers exist in the human language faculty anyway? These questions must be properly addressed before linkers are entitled to escape the jurisdiction of UG and to solicit help from iconicity. To this end, the rest of this section will take a closer look at -de in Mandarin Chinese (MC), and *de*'s counterparts in Cantonese where relevant, so as to learn more about linkers.

3.4.2   What -de *Is and Does in Mandarin Chinese (Preliminary)*

Chen (in press) discovers an interference pattern in MC not known in any other language.[22] The pattern is given in (133), while the relevant facts in MC are summarized in (134) (cf. Chen's (1), (2), (58)):

133. Let A stand for adjectives in MC. Then
      $[_Y \ldots (*A_1\text{-}de) \ldots V\text{-}de \; A_2]$,
      where A_2 has the scope Y and is unacceptable if A_1 belongs to a lower adverb class than A_2.

134. a. Adjectives plus -de can occur either before or after V to modify V;
      b. Each clause can host no more than one postverbal adjective;
      c. A_2 is a syntactic predicate while A_1 is not.

For easier reference, the preverbal A-*de* modifier will be called an adverb and translated with the English form of A-*ly* until the nature of -*de* is made clear; -*de* accompanying the postverbal adjective is simply glossed as -*de* for now to avoid premature theoretical commitment. Chen (2017) also shows the adverb classes in MC to be generally consistent with Cinque's (1999) adverb hierarchy.

(134a), already demonstrated in (132), also serves as the base for illustrating (134b):

135. a. Lele chuhuyiliao-de zhishuang-de   chengren-le. (cf. Cheng's (12))
          Lele unexpectedly   candidly   admit-ASP
          'Lele unexpectedly admitted it candidly.'
      b. Lele chengren-de   hen zhishuang (*-de hen   chuhuyiliao).
          Lele admit-DE   very candid   -DE   very   unexpected
          'Lele admitted it candidly (unexpectedly).'

The two preverbal adverbs, in the evaluative (Ev) and subject-oriented (So) classes respectively, can co-occur when the linear sequence complies with the hierarchy reported by Cinque (1999). But the postverbal context only permits one of them and never both.

That the postverbal adjective acts as a syntactic predicate, as stated in (134c), can be seen through (135) as well. From (131), (132a) and (135a), we see that as pre-head adjuncts, Chinese adjectives can be all by themselves. In contrast, their postverbal use in (132b) and (135b) require some degree element such as *hen* 'very', making them identical to adjectival predicates in syntactic behavior:

136. a. Lele hen zhishuang.
          Lele very candid
          'Lele is candid.'
      b. Lele de   jueding   (hen) chuhuyiliao.
          Lele DE   decision   very   unexpected
          'Lele's decision is unexpected.'

In both (135b) and (136a), the default interpretation of *zhishuang* 'candid' must be accompanied by *hen* 'very', itself the default degree word in MC. Absent of any degree word, these sentences are "infelicitous out of the context and felicitous in a context in which there is a salient standard of comparison" (Grano 2012: 515–516), as is widely known in Chinese linguistics. Independent reasons make *hen* optional for quadrisyllabic words which are treated as idioms of historical origin. Still, *hen* is often automatically added by native speakers in (136b) and (135b). See Grano (ibid.) and Liu (2013) for syntactico-semantic accounts of this phenomenon. What matters for the current purpose is the fact itself: that the postverbal adjective modifier, A_2 in (133), patterns with the same adjectives serving as the predicate of a clause.

Chen (in press) presents another fact in support of A_2 being a syntactic predicate, its *wh*-form. The examples are her (49–50):

137. a. Runrun zenme/zenmeyang wanr   shouji?
        Runrun how/how   play.with   smartphone
        'How does Runrun play with smartphones?'
     b. zhebu   shouji   *zenme/zenmeyang?
        this   smartphone   how/how
        'How is this smartphone?'
     c. zhebu   shouji,   Runrun   wanr-de   *zenme/zenmeyang?
        this   smartphone   Runrun   play.with-DE   how/how
        'How well does Runrun play with smartphones?'

While both *zenme* and *zenmeyang* can occur preverbally, only the latter is permitted as the syntactic predicate in (137b) and as the postverbal A_2 in (137c), unequivocally indicating that the latter two have the same grammatical status. Also note a semantic difference between the preverbal 'how' interpretation and the predicative/postverbal 'how well'. We return to this contrast after an analysis of *-de* is presented.

With (134a–c) established, the novel interference effect in (133) is illustrated with the same two adjectives *chuhuyiliao* 'unexpectd' and *zhishuang* 'candid'. See Chen (2017) for a much larger set of adverb classes in this regard.

138.   *Lele zhishuang-de chuhuyiliao-de chengren-le (zheci shiwu).
        Lele   candidly   unexpectedly   admit-ASP   this   fault
        *'Lele candidly unexpectedly admitted this mistake.'

139. a. Lele   chuhuyiliao-de chengren-de hen   zhishuang.
         Lele   unexpectedly   admit-DE   very   candid
         'Lele unexpectedly admitted it candidly.'
      b. *Lele   zhishuang-de   chengren-de hen   chuhuyiliao.
         Lele   candidly   admit-DE   very   unexpected

The acceptable preverbal Ev-So sequence in (135a) vs. the unacceptable So-Ev sequence in (138) follows from Cinque's (1999) adverb hierarchy in which the Ev class is structurally higher than the So class. What is not as straightforward is the contrast in (139). Recall that the postverbal A_2 is a syntactic predicate and unique per clause. On one hand, there is a unified explanation for this distributional contrast between preverbal and postverbal adjectives. With rare and irrelevant exceptions (see Huang et al. 2009, Deng 2013), MC puts all adjuncts left of the head they modify, which in turn forces A_2 to occupy the complement position with respect to the main verb. Since there can be only one available complement position under the binary-branching structure, no more than one A_2 can be hosted. Furthermore, if A_2 is a complement, it is no surprise, at least in principle, that it acts differently from an adjunct. But the smooth explanation of A_2 in these aspects makes the rest of its behavior mysterious: Why should a syntactic predicate interact with a preverbal adverb to produce (133)?

Chen's empirical justification for attributing this mystery to -*de* is that the preverbal PP and CP adjuncts both reject -*de* and are unable to trigger the interference effect at issue. I echo this choice of the culprit with the -*de*-less postverbal adjectives:[23]

140. a. Lele (*chuhuyiliao-de) chengren zheci shiwu hen   zhishuang.
          Lele unexpectedly   admit   this fault very candid
          Literally: 'It was candid of Lele to (unexpectedly) admit this mistake.'
      b. Lele (zhishuang-de)   chengren zheci shiwu hen   chuhuyiliao.
          Lele candidly   admit   this fault very unexpected
          'For Lele to admit (this mistake) candidly is unexpected.'

Remarkably, (140) displays exactly the opposite of (139): Whereas Ev-So is good in (139a), it is bad in (140a); and where So-Ev is bad in (139b), it is good in (140b). If the presence/absence of the DP object *zheci shiwu* 'this fault' is put aside for the moment, the only difference between these two apparently conflicting patterns is whether the postverbal adjective is accompanied by -*de*. An explanation for this contrast, including the status of the DP object, will be offered after Chen's own analysis of (139) has been introduced. For now, the contrast between the two patterns is direct evidence that, in some manner, -*de* is responsible for (139), the manifestation of the interference effect in the context of (133).

Chen's analysis treats -*de* as manifesting a modification feature plus Cinque's theory of adverbs in which each adverb is uniquely licensed by a functional head. Such an analysis would work well for the purpose of analyzing linkers in this section. To maximally synchronize the contents of the whole book, however, I will present a slightly revised account of -*de*:

141. a. -*de* signals an agreement on the μ-feature, [μ:*val*], between the adjective used as a modifier and the modified constituent;
      b. *val* is the categorial label of the modified constituent (e.g. N, T, v, ...);
      c. μ-agreement happens between two constituents with the μ-feature:
          i.   The constituent consisting of A and -*de* carries [μ:__] as the probe, and
          ii. Any constituent of category *cat* may optionally carry [μ:*cat*].

(141c-i) follows from the probe-goal mechanism, the intuition being that a modifier must find the right constituent to modify. There is no *a priori* necessity for (141c-ii), but there is nothing inherently implausible about it either. A constituent X is always subject to modification. If it is indeed modified, agreement happens due to probing on the part of the modifier and a legitimate structure results. Having no modifier trashes the derivation since μ has no proper interpretation in X (e.g. because μ is uninterpretable with

A alone). However, X always can, and logically should, have the option of not having μ. The option fails in the presence of a modifier but succeeds if there is none. It is also possible that the shared μ-feature underlies the semantic operation of predicate modification (= Higginbotham's 1985 θ-identification) on the two parties and syntactically singles out Chomsky's (2001a: 18) Pair-Merge, an effort to find "a really satisfactory theory of adjunction." (ibid.: 17). But I will not pursue this subject matter any further.

The application of (141) to preverbal modifiers in MC proceeds as follows. Furnishing an adjective with -de creates an adverb adv with [μ:__], thereby motivating the probing operation in syntax (Chomsky 2000, 2001a). Let the modified constituent C be of category cat to which adv adjoins. Obviously, C must choose the option of having [μ:cat] so that probing by adv finds the closest goal in C and agrees with it in the form of [μ:cat], enabling Davidsonian semantics (i.e. λe.**adv**(e) ∧ **C**(e)). With more than one preverbal adverb adv1 and adv2 of different classes, either they modify the same constituent or different ones, the latter case merely being the single-adverb scenario happening twice in different locations. The fully expressed post-agreement and well-formed structure for the former case is (142) with the standard X′ representation:

142. ... [C′ adv1[μ:C] [C′[μ:C] adv2[μ:C] [C′[μ:C] C ...]]]

Each adv probes the sister C′, shown with arrows, and acquires the same cat value. Other parts of semantics force adv_1, of a higher class, to scope over the lower-classed adv_2 for proper interpretation.

The syntactic environment changes drastically for the postverbal adjective in the complement position (see the discussion after (139)):

143.   ... [... V-de A]

Given the θ-criterion and the fact that A is meant to be a predicate of events, A either takes for its thematic argument a preceding constituent, i.e. some (extended) projection of V, or modifies some such constituent via predicate modification. As it turns out, the first possibility is realized with the -de-less case in (140) to which we return below. Critical for now is that this option, at least its default implementation in UG, would yield a totally different structure, with the brackets in (143) representing an (extended) projection of A (vs. a projection of V) since V would now be (part of) the subject argument of A, which in turn would make -de mysterious. The second option essentially treats A as an adjunct for thematic purposes. But this outcome runs counter to Chinese syntax, which places adverbial (and adjectival; see (131)) modifiers before the modified. Chinese overcomes this impasse by giving A a phonologically empty subject and creating an operator O with it, the latter being the same strategy as for tough-movement:

144. a. ... [... V-*de* [$_{SC}$ O$_i$ [$_{SC}$ t$_i$ A]]]
      b. ... [*tough* [$_{CP}$ O$_i$ [$_{TP}$ ... V t$_i$]]]

With t_i receiving the θ-role of A, the θ-criterion is satisfied. O$_i$ recreates a semantic predicate out of this small clause (SC). As *tough*-movement indicates, a predicate induced with a syntactic operator can delay its semantic/ thematic saturation by the matrix subject (in the initial " ... " position in (144b)) till after merging with *tough*. Similarly, the SC predicate in (144a) can merge with V first and worry about event-identification separately, via the same [μ:__] encoded in -*de*. If V picks the option of having μ, agreement happens. Whether this agreement complies with the semantic expectation of A is another story. A may be of the VP modifier and thus is a good match. But A may actually be for clauses (or of the propositional type in Ernst's (2002) terms; see below). The agreement with V carrying [μ:V] would lead to a semantic mismatch and trash this particular derivation. But there may always exist some head H up the clausal tree picking the option of having [μ:H] which is not only the closest head with [μ] but also the right one. This is how the postverbal A in (144a) gets licensed. Also, because the postverbal A is structurally a predicate with a subject (= t_i in (144a)) and not an adjunct, it acts like a syntactic predicate and its *wh*-form patterns accordingly, shown in (137).

Chen's case of interference has the schematic structure below:

145.   ... [... H ... [adv$_{[μ:val]}$ ... V-*de* [$_{SC}$ O$_i$ [$_{SC}$ t$_i$ A]]]]

The preverbal *adv* may modify V′ or some F′, F being a functional head above VP, with the help of -*de*. To the extent that this mediation is successful, there is now a pair of constituents, *adv* and its modifiee, both carrying [μ:*val*]. This is enough to prevent A from modifying any node H further up the tree. For A, the closer constituent both with [μ] and structurally available for μ-agreement (i.e. with c-command) is *adv*, but the *val* that *adv* provides is of the wrong kind for the context. A can also agree with any head, say V, lower than *adv* and optionally having the μ-feature. But such an agreement would, by hypothesis, provide the wrong *val* as well and thus be of no help. This explains half of the situation for the interference effect. The other half is for A to modify the same type of constituent that *adv* does but to belong to a higher semantic class than *adv*, the postverbal counterpart of (142). Agreement-wise, the outcome is legitimate. But A is unequivocally c-commanded by the preverbal *adv*, there being no plausible covert movement to lift A structurally above *adv* for the intended wide-scope interpretation. Logically, this is no different from swapping *adv$_1$* and *adv$_2$* in (142) against their semantic classification and thus incurring unacceptability. In sum, as long as A belongs to a higher class than *adv*, it simply cannot be duly interpreted. Hence the interference effect.

Next, consider the -*de*-less postverbal adjectives seen in (140), which is behaviorally opposite to the interference effect at issue. If -*de* indeed serves to mark A as a modifier (whether directly in preverbal adverbs or indirectly for the postverbal SC), we predict that A without -*de* is not used for modification.[24] This prediction explains (140) immediately when coupled with another well-documented fact in MC: The predicate of a clause can be a subject–predicate construction in itself:

146.　a.　zhege　　chengshi　　jiedao　　hen　　　　zhi.
　　　　　　this　　　city　　　　streets　　very　　　　straight
　　　　　　Literally: 'This city, the streets are straight.'
　　　b.　nage　　bingren　　zuotian　　zuobian-de　　leigu　　teng.
　　　　　　that　　patient　　yesterday　　left.side-DE　　rib.bone　　painful
　　　　　　Literally: 'That patient, the left side of the rib bones ached yesterday.'

Whatever licenses this construction, applying it to (140) allows the structure in (146):[25]

147.　　[*Lele* [$_X$ [$_{YP}$ ... A$_1$-*de* ... V (obj)] A$_2$]]

where X consists of YP (= *v*P or some higher FP) as the subject and A$_2$ as the predicate. It is X as a whole that is predicated of *Lele*. See Heycock (1993) for an analysis of the similar fact in Japanese.

Let A$_1$ be So and A$_2$ be Ev (= the acceptable (140b)). We know as a fact that Ev is a higher class than So. Whether they modify the same functional head or not, (147) comes out fine because the basic semantics of the subject–predicate structure in X is such that A$_2$ "has the scope" over its thematic argument containing A$_1$, just as how Ev and So are to be interpreted relatively to each other (cf. *Admitting mistakes candidly* (*by someone like Sam*) *is unexpected.*). Next suppose A$_1$ to be Ev inside the subject and A$_2$ to be So and the predicate, namely the unacceptable (140a). As the foregoing logic dictates, such a sentence expects So to have a scope reading over Ev, contra their classes.

Another grammatical fact has been buried in all the examples since (132b): While Chinese has the default VO order, the object must be either contextually omitted or moved elsewhere in the presence of the postverbal -*de*, in effect enforcing the V-*de* A string with no constituent in between. In comparison, the -*de*-less postverbal A in (140) shows no such eccentricity. The rejection of an overt object follows from three independent factors at work. First, as long as the postverbal A is to be used as a modifier, -*de* is needed to mediate this modifier relation. Second, -*de* is a prosodic enclitic to a [+V] host (i.e. [+V, ±N] = A, V) and thus must be linearly adjacent to such a constituent before it. Third, [μ] simply expresses a modificational relation and thus is not inherently associated with any categorial features. A more detailed examination of [μ] is postponed till the final subsection. It suffices for now that a category-less feature has no structural representation under Void_F2 and thus is sent to iconicity for linearization. And the solution has already been alluded to earlier: Since -*de* links the modifier to the modified, it is placed between the two linked constituents. When all these factors collaborate, the only option left for MC is (148):

148.   ... V (t) [-*de* A]

The brackets indicate the A-headed small clause that has the μ-feature added through -*de*, much like a Case feature being part of a DP argument, the φ-features being part of T or [&] being part of N. -*de* precedes A as dictated by iconicity. And any postverbal object of V must be displaced so that -*de* as a morphological enclitic is next to a [+V] host, V in this case. In contrast, -*de* is not even needed when the postverbal A takes what precedes it as the subject. Nothing prevents the verb inside this subject from having its own object, seen in (140).[26]

3.4.3   On Alternative Analyses of -de

The very obscure categorial and semantic nature of -*de* has inspired many efforts to analyze it (Simpson 2002, den Dikken 2006, Zhang 2010, Larson 2018, to name a few recent works). Larson treats -*de* in the preverbal adverbs as being "concordial" similar to adjectival agreement with nouns in European languages. This is conceptually close to Chen's association of -*de* with the unvalued [μ__] seeking agreement with the modified constituent. Zhang unifies -*de* with conjunctions through the same X'-theoretical structure, both heading their own phrases. As Chen demonstrates, however, Larson's and Zhang's theories are both empirically flawed. Larson's is based on the assumption that Chinese adjectives all contain a nominal element and thus are regulated by Case assignment which ultimately results in the preverbal A-*de* form. The Chinese fact proves otherwise. *Zhishuang* 'candid', for instance, is composed of *zhi* 'straight, direct' and *shuang* 'forthright, frank'. With these meanings, neither morpheme is used as a noun diachronically or synchronically, but the whole word still requires -*de* to act as a preverbal adverb. In Zhang's analysis, the X' representation of -*de* appeals repeatedly to tests that ignore major differences between the nominal and verbal contexts.[27] As an example, she justifies the claimed constituency of -*de* and the modified element after -*de* with the fact that the modified noun can elide: A-*de* (N), the logic being that -*de* as the head licenses the empty nominal complement. But extending the test to [A-*de* V] shows that no ellipsis to V/VP is allowed. By Zhang's logic, then, at least -*de* in the adverbial context should not head its own head-initial phrase. Also worth keeping in mind is that [*the rich* ∅] in English is good too, without anything like -*de*. See Chen (in press) for more factual and theoretical counterarguments.

There are also works that do not directly talk about -*de* in the clausal context but nonetheless bear critically on the subject matter. Den Dikken (2006: 1) identifies two kinds of functional heads which he calls relators (R) and linkers (Ln):

The former mediate the relationship between a predicate and its subject in the base representation of predication structures; the latter connect the raised predicate to the small clause harboring its subject in so-called Predicate Inversion constructions.

Defined within Chomsky's Minimalist theory, these heads are given the structures in (149) and (150). Only structures directly relevant to the current concern are shown, with den Dikken's explanation that the F-head, referred to as the linker (Ln in (150)), "provides the *link* between the raised predicate and the small clause that it came from." (ibid.: 116, 241):

149.   a.   Movement of the head of a phase to a higher F *extends the phase* to FP.
             (den Dikken 2006: (79))
       b.   [$_{RP}$ subject [relator [predicate]]]   (ibid. (80a, c))
       c.   [$_{FP}$ predicate$_j$ [F+R$_i$ [$_{RP}$ subject [t$_i$ t$_j$]]]]

150.   [$_{DP}$ D (. . .) [$_{FP}$ XP$_i$ [Ln=*de* [$_{RP}$ NP [R t$_i$]]]]]   (ibid. 241)

In these structures, RP is the "small clause" headed by the relator R. It should be obvious that den Dikken's linker is a different concept from the one used in the current chapter, but he does apply it to the Chinese -*de* that introduces modifiers to nouns, shown in (150) where the raised predicative XP ranges over AP, PP, (superficial) DP and relative clause (see (131) earlier).

Not all syntactic tests, movement across islands for instance, are available for the nominal context, at least not in Chinese, so as to effectively assess (150) with its claimed syntactic properties (e.g. that NP in the Spec of RP is "'frozen' in syntax" (den Dikken 2006: 83) for various purposes). Still, facts about Chinese DPs raise doubts about (150). Despite the popular practice of applying a strictly head-initial structure to Chinese DPs (see the references in note 61), most without independent justification, explicit arguments have been made in the recent literature in favor of a consistent head-final DP structure.

The examples in (151) are adapted from Y. Li (2015) and are to be compared with (152):

151.   a.   shengming   [$_{CP}$ zhege   hetong   zuofei]
             announce   this   contract   become.void
             'announce that this contract becomes void'

b. *jinxing [x   shengming   [cp   zhege   hetong   zuofei]]
carry.out   announce   this   contract   become.void
Intended reading: 'carry out the announcement that this contract becomes void.'

c. jingxing [x [cp zhege hetong   zuofei]   -de shengming]
carry.out   this   contract become.void -DE announcement
Same as (151b).

152. a. wo   hen   gaoxing [cp nimen chenggong-le].
1s   very   glad   2PL   succeed-ASP
'I am glad that you succeeded.'

b. *wo   hen   gaoxing [dp nimen-de   chenggong].
1s   very   glad   2PL-DE   success
Literally: *'I am glad your success.'

c. wo   [pp   dui [dp nimen-de chenggong]] hen   gaoxing.
1s   P   2PL-DE   success   very glad
'I am glad of your success.'

(151a) is the default word order of a Chinese VP, with the CP complement after the verb. *Jinxing* 'carry out, put in action' is a verb known for requiring a nominalized event-denoting object (e.g. Fu 1994), namely X in (151b, c). Under this verb's categorial demand, the head–complement word order inside X is no longer possible; instead, the CP complement must be placed before *shengming* 'announce, announcement'. If Chinese DP/NPs have an underlying head-initial structure, the obligatory word order shift in (151) would be a mystery for lack of any non-ad hoc motivation, as is made clear by comparing the case with adjectives in (152). Despite the fact that A, like N, is [+N] and thus unable to provide a Case for its object, the CP complement is still post-adjectival since CPs do not need Case. In contrast, a DP object relies on a preposition, *dui* in (152c), for Case (cf. *of*-insertion in English), and other parts of Chinese syntax require all PPs to be pre-head. Following the same logic, why do (151b, c) differ from (152a) in acceptability? Shouldn't CP, in no need of Case, stay put in a head-initial structure?

The apparent inconsistency in how N and A linearize their CP complements follows automatically from recognizing that Chinese simply chooses to have a head-final DP, possibly under influence of the head-final Altaic languages it has been in contact with for millennia. Further corroborating this conclusion are the recent works (Y. Li 2015, Her 2017, Her and Tsai 2020) which argue that another important part of the Chinese DP, the numeral-classifier portion of the nominal system including NumP and the numeral-internal *n*-base arrangement (e.g. *wu-shi* 'five-ten = 5×10^1'), is consistently head-final. That is, a complex numeral is base-final, the numeral-classifier constituent is classifier-final and NumP is Num-final. Also see He and Tan (2019) for related discussions. Adding to all these the head-final NP seen through (151–152), one must wonder whether any evidence exists for R and Ln to stay or appear head-initial as claimed in (150).

In addition, the CP complement before N is obligatorily trailed by -*de* (see (151c)), like all other DP-internal prenominal constituents. But this -*de* is by definition not a linker in den Dikken's theory because the CP it "links" is a thematic argument and not a predicate (see the quotation above (149)). So even if we adopt the head-initial structure for nouns to have [$_{NP}$ N CP] plus raising CP before N, the derivation cannot be subsumed under the relator-linker theory since the use of -*de* in this case does not play the role of a linker as defined. In other words, one would be forced to distinguish two -*de*'s before N even though they have identical grammatical behavior. On the other hand, there is a natural and uniform analysis of the nominal -*de* that also complies with native Chinese speakers' intuition about this morpheme. We postpone till 3.4.4 the precise formulation of this -*de* and its unification with Chen's verbal -*de*. For now, simply imagine that the nominal -*de* encodes a generic asymmetric relation R_A between the nominal head and everything else. R_A can be a relation of modification, thereby connecting N with an AP or a relative clause; it can also be thematic so as to signal the link between the nominalized *shengming* 'announce' and its CP object in (151c); finally, it can represent a totally contextually determined relation as in *Yueyue-de gushi* 'Yueyue's story' in (131a), which may be either a relation of possession so that Yueyue tells the story or one of aboutness in which Yueyue is the heroine. See Marantz (1997) on the semantic flexibility of the possessor, recounted in (5d) of this chapter. The analysis postulates but a single -*de* and does not hinge on an elaborate structure which conflicts inside and out with the uniform head-final word order of Chinese DPs.

There are also reasons, more direct in this case, against extending the relator-linker theory to the preverbal and postverbal -*de*'s. According to den Dikken, adverbs occur in three contexts (his (52), p. 41; also partially repeated on p. 142) which I simplify to set aside irrelevant details:

153.   a. [$_{RP}$ *v*P$_i$ [R AdvP]] (…) t$_i$
       b. [$_{RP}$ *v*P [R AdvP]]
       c. [$_{RP}$ AdvP [R *v*P]]

Of these, (153a-b) have a postverbal adverb while (153c) has a preverbal one. This structural disparity is based on his observation that scope-wise, only the postverbal adverb is ambiguous, which plausibly results from either AdvP c-commanded by *v*P throughout the derivation, as in (153b), or c-commanding at least a copy of *v*P in (153a). No further explanation is found in the book on what "(…)" is and where exactly the trace of *v*P is located in (153a). What matters is that *v*P and AdvP may alternate in the Spec and complement positions despite their unchanging semantic relation in which AdvP is predicated of vP.

This structural flexibility might seem to be exactly what Chinese needs if, putting aside that -*de* is taken to be a linker for nominals in (150), -*de* is treated as the relator in the R position of (153). Immediately, one would generate A-*de* V from (153c) and V-*de* A from (153b). Multiple problems arise, however.

First consider the theoretical implications of (153b). As the quoted extract before (149) makes clear, a relator "mediate[s] the relationship between a predicate and its subject." While adverbs are widely taken to be event-predicates, one must distinguish this semantic characterization of adverbs from their actual implementation in language. Compare (154a) with (154b):

154. $[\![\text{Adv}]\!] = \lambda e_s.\textbf{Adv}(e)$
       $[\![v\text{P}]\!] = \lambda e_s.\textbf{vP}(e)$ (ignoring the exact meaning of vP)
       a. Adv as modifier:
           $[\![v\text{P Adv}]\!] = \lambda e_s.\textbf{vP}(e) \wedge \textbf{Adv}(e)$ (event-identification)
       b. Adv as predicate (see the explanation below):
           $[\![v\text{P Adv}]\!] = \exists e_s.\textbf{vP}(e)[\textbf{Adv}(e)]$ (function application)

(154a) is standard Davidsonian semantics that calculates the intersection of the two sets defined by vP and Adv, respectively. The result remains a set of events. Adv is indeed a semantic predicate, but it is an adjunct (or Spec for some people) in syntax. Now suppose Adv is a structural predicate to vP, i.e. in the complement position of some functional head F while vP is the subject of Adv in the Spec of FP, as in (153b). The semantic relation of the two constituents changes completely, with the vP subject denoting a member (or a subset) of the set defined by Adv. An existential closure at the edge of vP (see Diesing 1992) "saturates" the event position of vP to qualify it as an argument, resulting in a proposition meaning something like 'some events described by vP are Adv' (cf. *Some* N *are* AP.), shown in (154b). In other words, the semantics of (153b) is not that of modification if the syntactic structure of predication acts the way we understand it.

The problem at issue is not merely theoretical. In reality, adverbs are not known to even serve as the structural predicate of any clause, small or not. The closest to (153b, 154b) is actually the Chinese -*de*-less postverbal adjective A in (140), analyzed in (147) in which A sits in the predicate (= complement) position and acts as a predicate, taking some functional extended projection of the preceding V as its subject. Which brings us to the empirical reason against applying the relator-linker theory to -*de* in the clausal environment. If vP or some FP containing vP is indeed the legitimate subject of a predicate X, an adverb inside the subject should be compatible with the adjectival predicate corresponding to a higher class, as we saw in (140) and the analysis through (147). But (140) is -*de*-less and exhibits the opposite acceptability pattern to the

[V-*de* A] construction in (139). Hence, independently of how these two con-structions in Chinese are analyzed, [V-*de* A] is the wrong fit for (153b) if -*de* is treated as R. In addition, the RP structures in (153) must allow recursion – and they do for den Dikken (2006: 73) – so as to host more than one adverb per clause. Then there would be no means, beyond ad hoc and extra assumptions, to prevent (153b) from being inserted recursively in the Spec position of (153b) and thereby producing multiple postverbal adjectives, directly contradicting the facts in Chinese (see (134b, 135b)).

As the last point, the relation between the past few pages and den Dikken's theory deserves clarification. The copulas, the prepositions or postpositions and French idioms such as *un/une drôle de N* 'a funny of N' uniformly treated in the relator-linker theory all have lexical categories. Copulas, for instance, are linkers in an intuitive sense. But they are also verbal for their association with tense, and as expected from both UG and our theory of the UG-I, their linearization is fully UG-compliant (e.g. Japanese and Korean copular are cleanly head-final). Similarly, *de* in French can provide a Case, so it should be [−N]. These words are outside the concerns of this book. Meanwhile, when a lexical item performs the linking function but is obscure in lexical category, its linearization is no longer predictable by any UG principle or parameter setting. If we get a chance to look at such words in depth as we have done here with -*de*, it becomes clear that they are not den Dikken's relators and linkers despite possible superficial similarities. It is precisely these category-less words that become part of the empirical foundation for the UG-I theory in this book.

Whereas den Dikken offers a short but dedicated syntactic analysis of the nominal use of -*de* in Chinese, Ernst's (2002) theory of adverbs has references to the verbal -*de* only as side notes, recognizing the different historical origins of the preverbal and postverbal instances (p. 488; see 3.4.4 below), taking the morpheme to be a clitic (pp. 221–222) and assuming both uses to "act as adverbializers" (p. 488). These remarks are clearly consistent with the analysis adopted here. What deserves more attention is Ernst's semantic theory of adverbs on the basis of his fact-event object (FEO) calculus:

155.   a. The FEO hierarchy (Ernst 2002: 53)
           Speech-Act > Fact > Proposition > Event > Specified Event
       b. Adverbs are predicates of FEOs. (ibid.: Chapter 2)
       c. An FEO type may be freely converted to a higher FEO type but not to a lower one. (ibid.: 50)

This calculus appears to offer an alternative solution[28] to the interference effect in the [V-*de* A] construction in (139) and thus to challenge the critical reliance by Chen and in the current chapter on -*de* for explaining the fact. If -*de* is out of the picture, the empirical basis of my theory of the linkers would be undermined.

The schematic structure of example (139) for implementing the FEO is given in (156):

156.   ... A_1-*de* [$_X$ V-*de* A_2]   (vs. (145))

Let A_2 belong to some higher FEO type (e.g. Proposition) and V denote a lower type (e.g. Event). If -*de* is put aside, merging V with A_2 results in the constituent X in (156). In the FEO calculus, this means that the Event type of V is converted to the Proposition type because the semantics of A_2 demands the latter. This upward conversion is legitimate according to (155c). Further merging X with A_1 in (154) will be permitted if A_1 is of an even higher FEO type but prohibited if A_1 is of a lower type since that would convert the proposition-denoting X downward in violation of (155c).

I take it for granted that adverb classes and their distributions have an inherently semantic foundation. But the FEO calculus in (155) is no solution to the collection of the Chinese facts at hand for at least three reasons.

The first is simply factual: that the occurrence of -*de* correlates with a set of syntactic properties in (134), including that its postverbal use is paired with A being a syntactic predicate. These facts are sufficient to dismiss a simplistic treatment of the postverbal A-*de* as a simply adverbialized adjective on a par with the European bound morphemes like -*ly* and -*ment(e)*.

Second, (155) as defined is inadequate for the relevant facts. There is robust evidence (Cinque 1999 on a wide range of languages; Li et al. 2012 on English and Russian, Chen 2017 on Chinese) that many more than five adverb classes have "rigid ordering," a term used by Ernst (2014: 119) on those classes whose linear locations (and thus hierarchical locations) are constant with respect to other adjacent classes. As an example, both Ev and So have rigid ordering since swapping them results in unacceptability (e.g. (135a) vs. (138)). Therefore, the five FEO types in (155a) are simply unable to accommodate the sixth rigid adverb type which would have to belong to one of the five types and thus be counterfactually swappable with adverbs of that type. Such facts made Ernst admit that "there are some problems and exceptions" in his theory (ibid.: 121). There is an easy fix to this problem: Simply postulate as many FEOs as there prove to be rigidly ordered adverb classes. In effect, an FEO calculus so revised would converge with Cinque's adverb model, a direction which Ernst is presumably unwilling to go considering that his work comes after Cinque's by a few years. While I side with Ernst for keeping the syntactic structure and the semantic types minimal, his theory is simply incapable of handling adverb classification and distributions. Specifically, if two adverb classes modify at the same syntactic level, say v', one must look beyond the limited number of FEO types to account for any interaction between them.

Third, there is a more fundamental issue when the FEO calculus is applied to the Chinese adverb interference in (139). Where it seems to work results from the unidirectional conversion stated in (155c) that the FEO type of an (extended) projection of V can be lifted on the FEO hierarchy but never lowered. So stated, it looks like a purely semantic constraint, but the theory of semantics has no qualms in itself about applying lambda abstraction to (157a) to create (157b):

157.   a. **sing**(e)
        b. λe.**sing**(e)

(157a) is an open statement but still propositional in terms of FEO types, and it can be easily converted into an event-denoting predicate in (157b), a downward operation by the FEO hierarchy (155a). The plausibility of the unidirectional FEO conversion, then, must be rooted in its actual syntactic manifestation: that a higher FEO type of adverb is also structurally positioned higher than any lower FEO type of adverb, as is expected from deterministic R_C-to-R_S mapping. Now consider the evaluative adverbs, traditionally called sentential adverbs. In modern syntactic parlance, they are "rigidly" placed in the TP region of a clause. On the FEO hierarchy, they belong to no lower than the Proposition type. If an Ev adverb such as *chuhuyiliao* 'unexpected' occurs in the complement position of V and converts the event-denoting V to the proposition-denoting X in (156), the otherwise consistent match is broken between the internal structures of a natural language clause and the FEO types they correspond to. The question now is whether this postverbal Ev modifier is subject to any grammatical licensing. If it is not, why must it occur in the TP region in preverbal contexts rather than acting optionally like a VP-adverb by simply converting VP into a higher FEO type? If it is, however, its occurrence as the structural complement of V necessarily means that it cannot be properly interpreted in that spot yet and extra help must be solicited to connect it to the functional head of the matching FEO type. But this is precisely what Chen's theory and my revised one do: A string of UG apparatuses, including the [μ]-embodying *-de*, collaborate to have *chuhuyiliao* 'unexpected' probe up the tree for the right licensing head.

3.4.4   What *-de* Is and Does in Mandarin Chinese (Final)

Proving apparently competing analyses to offer no solution to the interference pattern in (139) (especially when compared with (140)) further validates treating *-de* as playing the role of signaling modification. As a matter of fact, letting -*de* encode [μ] lends itself to a unified account of all uses of -*de* in Chinese and possibly beyond:

158.   -*de* signals an asymmetric semantic relation R_M, hence an instance of R_C, for a generalized sense of *modification* or providing *more* information; R_M is represented as the feature [*m*] for syntactic computation:
   a.   In the nominal context, [*m*] retains its generic nature, with its specific content contextually determined.
   b.   In the clausal context, [*m*] = [μ], namely the narrow relation of Davidsonian modification by adverbs.

(158b) is the essence of Chen's theory of -*de* and the revised version in (141). With (158a), all adjuncts are mediated to the nominal head by -*de* in the same way as its verbal use, resulting in predicate modification. For a DP possessor or an XP complement, [*m*] can be literally interpreted as [θ:__] to be valuated by N for the theme/patient reading or from *n* for the possessor reading (cf. agent from *v*; see Chapter 4 below).

Viewed this way, the generic R_M seems to be treated in accordance with the particular lexical and/or morphological means of a given language L. (i) If L has morphological case and agreement/concord, R_M is encoded in such affixes (e.g. the genitive Case for possessor or object interpretations) and gets linearized morphologically by UG, much like the conjunctive -*que* in Latin. (ii) In the absence of these means, "analytic" lexical items may be used to encode R_M; Chinese clearly belongs to this kind. In this scenario, the lexical manifestation of R_M has no inherent categorial property, encounters Void$_F$2 as explicated before, and relies on iconicity for linearization. (iii) Lastly, it is possible for R_M to be included in the semantic content of pre- or postpositions. At the bottom of it, both (i) and (iii) are possible because R_M is an asymmetric relation and thus, unlike $R_\&$, has the potential to become part of the overall semantics of a lexical item given the inherently asymmetric structure of UG.

Option (iii) underscores a point made with SVCs already: What looks iconic may be only the particular parameter setting of UG in a given language. In a head-initial language like English, for instance, the [N [$_{PP}$ P DP]] sequence looks iconic with P between N and DP and linking them. But this is UG at work whether P contains [*m*] or not. In a similar fashion, the English adverbializer -*ly* is possibly a form of option (i), with the suffix signaling [*m*] plus semantic type-shifting/-specifying so as to let adjectives be predicated of events. As the lexicalization of [*m*] is subsumed under English morphology, UG regulates its linearization so that -*ly* is suffixal whether the adverb is pre- or postverbal.

Why the separation of (158a) and (158b) exists remains unclear, and this is not unique to Chinese. In English, for instance, AP, PP and CP can all modify

N directly (vs. the necessary use of -*de* in Chinese), but only A requires -*ly* in the clausal context, patterning with Chinese adverbial A-*de* to a T. If we put this mystery aside, an interesting argument can be made to solidify the iconic treatment of -*de*. Assuming [±V, ±N] for exclusive categorial specification (Grimshaw's [F] being irrelevant here), only four lexical categories, namely V, N, A, P, can be defined, there being no separate category Adv. Thus, -*de* cannot possibly carry an "adverb category." It is plausible and even possible that -*de* may convert whatever is the semantic type of an adjective to <e, t> so as to perform event-identification with verbs. But this operation does not convert A to V because, as our linguistic knowledge tells us, the adverbial A-*de* does not acquire the ability to act as the predicate of a finite clause. Similarly, the -*ly* adverbs in English do not get suffixed with tense. Therefore, -*de* does not verbalize A. In effect, this is proof that whatever -*de* contributes is not categorial despite the fact that it only pairs with adjectives in the clausal environment. On one hand, this conclusion allows [μ] to mean literally 'modification by A', which enables any probing by [μ:__] to ignore adverbial modifiers of other categories (Chen 2017).[29] On the other, since -*de* remains category-less in itself, the FICH still needs to call in iconicity to linearize it, as our theory predicts.

Finally, adopting (158) offers a way to understand the forms of linkers across languages. In Mandarin Chinese, both the nominal and verbal uses of -*de* end up having the same form because they both encode [*m*]. But a language or dialect may choose to distinguish the various uses according to the types of syntactic environment each occurs in. Cantonese, for instance, uses three different morphemes for the prenominal, preverbal and postverbal cases:[30]

159. a. geize-ge   mantai, keoi wuidaap-dak hou mingzi/faaicuk.
        reporter-GE question 3s   answer-DAK   very wise/quick
        'The reporter's question, s/he answered wisely/quickly.'

    b. keoi hou faaicuk-gam mingzi-gam wuidaap-zo geizi-ge   mantai.
       3s   very quick-GAM   wise-GAM   answer-PERF reporter-GE question
       *'S/He quickly wisely answered the reporter's question.'

    c. keoi hou mingzi-gam faaicuk-gam wuidaap-zo geize-ge   mantai.
       3s   very wise-GAM   quick-GAM   answer-PERF reporter-GE question
       'S/He wisely quickly answered the reporter's question.'

    d. geize-ge   mantai, keoi hou faaicuk-gam wuidaap-dak hou mingzi.
       reporter-GE question 3s   very quick-GAM answer-DAK   very wise
       'The reporter's question, s/he quickly answered wisely.'

    e. geize-ge   mantai, keoi hou mingzi-gam wuidaap-dak hou faaicuk.
       reporter-GE question 3s   very wise-GAM answer-DAK   very quick
       'The reporter's question, s/he wisely answered quickly.'

As mentioned earlier, Cantonese uses -*ge* (e.g. *geize-ge* 'reporter's'), -*gam* (e.g. *hou mingzi-gam* 'very wise-ly' and -*dak* (e.g. *wuidaap-dak* … 'answer-DAK') before N, before V and after V, respectively.

(159a) corresponds to V-*de* in MC. With one exception for the adjective *faaicuk* 'quick', all eleven informants find the example acceptable ("very natural," "natural" and "OK"). When a sentence contains more than one modifier, its acceptability deteriorates drastically. So even when both adjectival modifiers occur preverbally, the default order of Chinese adjuncts in general, eight people find (159b) unacceptable ("somewhat unacceptable" and "totally unacceptable") while five people find (159c) so. Still, the difference matches the understanding that Ev is by default higher than So so that (159c) should be somewhat better, especially given that three informants find (159b) "totally unacceptable" but no one reports this judgment on (159c). Against this background, when the two modifiers are distributed on both sides of V, eight people take the So-V-Ev sequence in (159d) to be unacceptable while six people dislike the Ev-V-So sequence. And again, the latter case receives no "totally unacceptable" grading at all. While the contrast is not as sharp as Chen observed in MC, the general pattern remains consistent with MC: When Ev is positioned lower than So, the acceptability worsens whether Ev is pre- or postverbal.

Now consider how the three linker forms in Cantonese can be understood through (159). First, the nominal use -*ge* is separated from the preverbal use -*gam* to reflect (159a-b). Furthermore, the postverbal -*dak* may be taken as a phonological indication that in Cantonese, this morpheme encodes the μ-feature and the operator that helps the postverbal A to carry [μ] legitimately. The structure in (145) is repeated below, with the preverbal modifier and the Cantonese linkers added:

160. ... [A-[μ] ... V[μ] [sc O$_i$ [sc t$_i$ A]]]

       -gam   *-dak*

Chamorro opts for a partially different strategy, with [m] encoded in both *na* and *n* to reflect the preverbal and postverbal distinction. Furthermore, the linker *n* is phonologically dependent on an adjacent vowel either from the preceding N or the manifestation of the immediately following *wh*-operator. That is, *ni* and *nai* in (129c-d) are the Chamorro counterparts to -*dak* in (160), with the vowels signaling the difference in the semantic restrictor part of the operator.

4   From the External Argument Onward

Newmeyer's (1992) division of the UG–iconicity relationship is repeated below:

1. a. Iconicity affecting the finished products of UG;
    b. Grammaticalization of iconicity-motivated options into UG;
    c. Part of UG being iconic.

With the contents of the previous two chapters behind us, a more precise understanding of these scenarios becomes possible.

As stated back then, (1a) happens characteristically above the sentence level. An exception to this otherwise correct generalization is the interpretation of the linearized conjuncts that are typically clause-internal but encode an inherently symmetric relation, rendering the actual linear realization of conjuncts susceptible to (1a). The exceptions to the CSC ((38–39) of Chapter 3) represent such a case where the linear sequence of the verbal conjuncts is treated iconically to express temporal sequence, thus exempting them from the event-plurality semantics that holds for parallel events (see 3.3.6). In the broad sense of the SVCs, those examples with only subject-sharing (2.5.7) are of a similar nature. Without shared objects, there is no principled way in such a context to let the expression of R_T satisfy the USM. To solve this impasse, I surmise that R_T is treated as $R_{\&}$ so as to give the two verbal projections a parallel structure and then take advantage of the iconic interpretation of their linear order. But as seen in (76) of Chapter 3, the iconic interpretation in this case may be natural but it is not mandatory. At least when it comes to word order, then, the more precise statement of (1a) is (2):

2. Iconicity operates on the products of the human language faculty F_{HL} only when linearization results from neither (a) nor (b):
    a. UG's inherently asymmetric structure (= R_S);
    b. the joint effort of the FICH and the USM.

(2a) specifies the familiar territory of UG where no extra appeal to iconicity is needed at all. But even when UG is not calling the shots, the FICH and the USM may enforce an iconic word order, as stated in (2b). Both scenarios result from some mechanism internal to F_{HL} and are thus not subject to influence by factors external to F_{HL}. It is only those cases of linearization that are neither required by UG nor dictated by the FICH plus the USM that lend themselves to Grice's "be orderly" maxim and may be contextually reinterpreted.

(2) obviously covers separate sentences, allowing them to have "statistical" iconicity (van Langendonck 2010). Coordination is also in the domain of (2). First, the sequencing of the conjuncts is not a product of UG's asymmetric X'-structure (because $R_{\&}$ is symmetric and isomorphism must be respected). Second, the FICH-incurred iconicity only takes care of the conjunctions while the USM responsible for mapping $R_{\&}$ to a parallel R_S says nothing about R_L. The conjuncts linearize only as the outcome of left-to-right structure-generation, a topic to return to in section 4.3 later. The bottom line is that the linear order of conjuncts results neither from UG nor even from the FICH, giving room for (2) to take effect. With respect to linear iconicity, then, (2) is more accurate than (1a) in specifying the relation between iconicity and the products of F_{HL}.

Regarding (1b), we surely share the spirit of Newmeyer's view that certain iconicity-motivated grammatical behaviors are rule-governed and obligatory just like those from UG. Two major differences have become clear, though.

The first concerns the exact status of such "grammaticalized" iconic operations in our theory of language. For Newmeyer, (1b) "poses no challenge to generative grammar, because the autonomy of grammar is compatible with system-external triggers for system-internal changes" (p. 789). Judging from the wording, he seems to consider what we call UG to be the host for iconicity-favored rules. In my UG-I theory, the picture is different: UG contains precisely identified functional voids ($Void_F1$, $Void_F2$) which prompt help from iconicity to linearize certain constituents in sentence-generation. While the use and effect of iconicity thus invoked are obligatory and rule-like, iconicity itself does *not* internalize into the UG system. It simply collaborates with UG through a chain of fully predictable and intricately interactive operations so as to help complete a particular task that UG alone cannot do. This is why, from the very start, we distinguish UG from F_{HL}, with the latter a "superset" of the former in function and in apparatus. Which also highlights the second difference between the UG-I theory here and Newmeyer's: A substantially detailed model of UG–iconicity interaction is formulated throughout the past chapters so that the "grammaticalization" of iconicity changes from a generic cover term to logically and empirically specific steps of linguistic computation that can be properly assessed.

Whereas (1b), or our revision of it, focuses on incorporating operations based on the general cognitive function of iconicity into the dedicated linguistic system F_{HL}, (1c) claims part of UG to be iconic in itself, or as Newmeyer puts it, "grammatical structure is an iconic reflection of conceptual structure"

(p. 789). In fact, this idea is most directly expressed in Haiman's (1985) inclusion of isomorphism into the linguistically pertinent diagrammatic iconicity. As seen from the foregoing analyses of the SVCs and coordination, isomorphism has played a vital role in implementing the USM when the default R_C-to-R_S mapping by UG is arrested because of the latter's functional voids. At least by certain theories of linguistic iconicity, then, what (1c) is meant to capture is already manifest in part of our UG-I theory.

This conclusion is embraced willingly here while a clarification is no less important. One might want to argue that the basic structure provided by UG, such as the X'-pattern that enables c-command, isomorphically expresses asymmetric semantic relations such as "argument-of" or "modifier-of," but that is not where the focus of this book lies. Instead, we are interested in those parts of language where F_{HL} does not act like its typical UG-dominant self. With the SVCs, this abnormality takes the form of using an asymmetric dependency between the objects of the verbs to reflect the asymmetric R_T so as to keep the R_C-to-R_S mapping isomorphic. For coordination, the multi-plane structure is more costly and always avoided until UG runs out of cheaper means to express $R_\&$. It is in these cases that we get a chance to glimpse those fine details of F_{HL} which are otherwise overshadowed by its by-far more dominant "normal" behaviors.

Out of the same motivations, this chapter looks closely at the external argument, so named by Williams (1981) to single out the subject of transitive and unergative verbs from other arguments. Purely for the sake of clear explication, by "external argument (henceforth Arg_E)" we mean the structural constituent serving as the subject of the above-mentioned verb types. At least for the facts that concern us in the chapter, the θ-role that Arg_E receives is agent. After examining the documented evidence for Arg_E, we justify and try to answer in section 4.1 the question of why it must act externally to verbal projections. A few theoretical implications are explored in 4.2, followed in 4.3 by another aspect of Arg_E and other comparable constituents in a clause: their linear distributions in a typological perspective. An alternative theory of linearization will be proposed which works naturally with our model of the UG–iconicity interface as well as a novel data pattern. The theory combines the insights of both the conventional parameter-oriented theory of linearization and Kayne's (1994) antisymmetric syntax. Reasons will be given why such a linearization theory, though itself independent of iconicity, is nonetheless vital to the overall validity of our UG-I theory.

4.1   Why External?

Before attempting an answer to this question, we look at some evidence accumulated over the past decades that the Arg_E of a transitive or unergative verb is structurally separate from the direct projection of the latter.

4.1.1   Sampling the Facts behind Arg$_E$

At the level of word formation, an English N-V-*ing* compound requires N to be understood as the object of V and never the subject. For instance, *janitor-cleaning* only has the funny reading of cleaning janitors and not the more sensible meaning of janitors doing cleaning. The morphological phenomenon of noun-incorporation (see section 4.2), exhibits the same asymmetry. Syntactically, the object can form an idiom with the verb in exclusion of the subject but not vice versa (Marantz 1984), and the past participles in French complex past tense agree with both the raised object of a transitive verb and the subject of an unaccusative verb but not with the subject of transitive and unergative verbs. In all these cases, the object apparently has a bond with a verb in a way that the subject does not.

There is also semantic evidence that the subject and object are fundamentally different in their relations with verbs. Consider this example from Kratzer (2002: Section 3.1) with respect to cumulativity defined in (3), with R defining a thematic relation:

3. $\lambda R \forall e \forall e' \forall x \forall y.[R(x)(e) \ \& \ R(y)(e')] \rightarrow R(x+y)(e+e')$ (Kratzer's (1))

If X, Y, Z and W each did a different action (e.g. X bought a bush, Y dug a hole in the ground, Z placed the bush in the hole and W shoveled soil back in the hole) that collectively form the action of planting the bush, then X, Y, Z and W planted the bush, with 'plant' = 'buy'+'dig'+'place'+'shovel' in accordance with (3). But it is simply nonsense to say that these people planted the flower, the hole and the soil. Clearly, if R in (3) is the subject-of relation, R is as cumulative as the sub-events while the object-of relation is not and thus is not describable by (3). That is, the agent argument of a verb is independent of the verb's semantic details so that if each individual is the agent of a sub-event such as digging or buying, s/he is among the collection of the individuals that together serve as the agent of the summative event of planting. In contrast, the theme argument, i.e. the object, is tied to the semantics of a specific verb like *dig* and thus is not automatically compatible with a different verb like *plant*.

The grammatical status of Arg$_E$ receives further support from a less known but rather unique fact in Chinese. It is well documented that the subject and object of activity verbs in Chinese can receive liberal thematic readings (Xing 1991, Guo 1999, Lin 2001, Yang 2007, Huang et al. 2009, Sun 2010, Sun and Li 2010, Chen and Li 2016, Zhang 2018, among many others). Zhang (2018) refers to such an object as a "noncanonical object." We generalize the term to both arguments.

What is of particular interest for the grammatical status of Arg_E is that the agent argument acts differently from all other arguments, canonical or not (Chen and Li 2016):

4. a. location > purpose?
    zhejia   canguan   (*yuchun-de) chi paichang.
    this   restaurant   foolish-DE   eat extravagance.
    'In this restaurant, one dines to display extravagance.'
   b. purpose? > location
    paichang   (*yuchun-de) chi   zhejia   canguan.
    extravagance foolish-DE   eat   this   restaurant
    'For showing off extravagance, one dines in this restaurant.'

5. a. theme > instrument
    mifan   (*yuchun-de) chi zhege xiao   wan.
    steamed.rice foolish-DE   eat this   small   bowl
    'One eats steamed rice with this small bowl.'
   b. instrument > theme
    zhege   xiao   wan   (*yuchun-de) chi mifan.
    this   small   bowl   foolish-DE   eat steamed.rice
    'One uses this small bowl to eat steamed rice.'

6. a. agent > purpose?/location
    qiongren   (yunchun-de) chi paichang/   zhejia changuan.
    poor.person   foolish-DE   eat extravagance/ this   restaurant
    'Poor people foolishly dine to display extravagance/at this restaurant.'
   b. *purpose?/location > agent
    *paichang/   zhejia   canguan (yunchun-de) chi   furen
    extravagance/ this   restaurant foolish-DE   eat   rich.person
    Intended: Comparable to (6a).

(4) and (5) illustrate noncanonical arguments used as the subject or object of a clause. The unacceptable subject-oriented adverbial *yuchun-de* 'foolishly' in these examples indicates that the subject position is indeed occupied by the overt preverbal DP rather than a phonologically empty agentive *pro*. Critically, location, purpose, instrument and theme are swappable between the two argument positions provided that each sentence is put in the proper discourse context (see 4.2 later). When the subject is the agent, the object can accommodate any of these interpretations, as is partially shown in (6a). But reversing them like (6b) is impossible regardless of context. See Chen and Li (2016) for more examples with the same disparity pattern.

With an account of the phenomenon postponed till 4.2, (4) through (6) prove that the "factors" of an event which we name as location, instrument, theme, etc. may all enjoy an equal status with respect to the lexical verb at least under certain conditions. It is this equal status that allows them to swap freely between the two argument positions. The agent argument is in a class by itself in this regard and does not mingle with the rest. Specifically, let agent be introduced into syntax by v (Chomsky 1995; also see Kratzer's (1996) Voice) whereas all the others are affiliated in some sense with the lexical verb. In the absence of v, syntax views "the others" as having the same distributional status, limited only by the number of independently licensed host positions per clause, *viz.* the subject and object positions. The presence of the agent argument entails the presence of vP outside VP, enough to keep this Arg_E external to VP, as seen in (6).

Marantz' (1997) observation that *destruction* and *growth* behave differently with respect to an agentive possessor reveals more about the nature of Arg_E. His examples, given in (3–4) of Chapter 3, are repeated below:

7. a. that John destroyed the city
   b. John's destruction of the city
   c. the city's destruction

8. a. that John grows tomatoes
   b. *John's growth of tomatoes
   c. the tomatoes' growth

As Marantz notes, the ungrammaticality of (8b) can be explained if the root √DESTROY contains an element of agentivity in its meaning while √GROW does not. If v is the mechanism for supporting the actual agent argument, the semantic difference between these two roots has no effect on clauses having an agentive subject. But the corresponding nominal context does not provide an agent in itself. The possessor *John* in (7b) acquires such a reading because agentivity is a semantic element of √DESTROY. No such interpretation is available from √GROW in (8b). Putting aside certain technical details for now, (7–8) indicate that the realization of the agent argument needs to be implemented by some extended verbal projection separate from the lexical portion of the clause, be that V or the root. Chen and Li (2021) reach the same conclusion based on how subject-oriented adverbs and subject-depictive small clauses act contrastively in Chinese passive constructions: Certain lexical verbs contain agentivity in their meanings while the agent argument itself comes into existence only through v.

4.1.2   Understanding the Structural Origin of Arg_E

While the bipartite expression of agentivity fits into the vP–VP separation perfectly, it also raises a question:

9. If agentivity is already part of the semantic content of some V, why must the agent argument be expressed separately via v instead of, say, as just another "internal" argument of V?

To better appreciate this question, consider Kratzer's (1996: 121) semantic solution to Marantz' (1984) subject–object asymmetry with idioms (with minor notational changes; no distinction is made between Voice and v):

10. a. $[\![\text{feed}]\!] = \lambda x \lambda e.\textbf{feed}(x, e)$
    b. $[\![\text{the dog}]\!] = \textbf{the dog}$
    c. $[\![\text{Voice}]\!] = \lambda x \lambda e.\textbf{agent}(x, e)$
    d. $[\![\text{Mittie}]\!] = \textbf{Mittie}$
    e. $[\![\text{Mittie feed the dog}]\!] = \lambda e.\textbf{agent}(\textbf{Mittie}, e) \wedge \textbf{feed}(\textbf{the dog}, e)$

The essence of this analysis is that the semantics of the verb *feed* contains the theme argument through the variable x in (10a) but not the agent argument. It follows that the choice of object may influence the exact meaning of the verb and result in Marantz' verb–object idioms, but being a semantic outsider, the subject has no such power. Kratzer's cumulativity argument recounted earlier corroborates such divided sources of argument-introduction from a different angle. Now, however, agentivity is shown to be in the meanings of some verbs. Why is it, then, that even these verbs still treat the agent argument to be Arg_E?

It should be made clear that the problem cannot be solved by simply postulating the internal structure of a lexical verb to contain a generic light verb that implicates agentivity but does not in itself bring in the agent argument (e.g. the VP-taking V paraphrased as 'bring about' in Hale and Keyser's (1993) lexical relational structure). It might appear that such a light verb would free the lexical root from the agentivity-implicating burden and thus nullify the question in (9). Not so, for there are non-agentive verbs which, unlike *grow* in (8), are incompatible with an agent argument all by their superficial selves (e.g. *die*, *arrive*, *faint*, ...). One must admit that, ultimately, it is the lexical root, or the concept the root encodes, that determines whether it can support agentivity. Or to borrow Hale and Keyser's (2002: 190) words for another lexico-semantic trait of verbs like *arrive*, the said trait exists because of "a particular lexical feature of the verbs of interest here". Also recall (7–8). If every lexical root/verb were equally devoid of the agentivity element, it would be difficult to see how *destruction* and *growth* could be distinguished.

The question in (9) can be further sharpened by examining the behavioral patterns of words formed of a nominal component and a verbal one. It is well known that noun-incorporation, a morphological phenomenon, displays the subject–object asymmetry (Baker 2001: 90–93):

11. a. Owira'a   wahrake'   ne   o'wahru.
       baby   ate   the   meat
       'The baby ate the meat.'
    b. Owira'a   waha'wahrake'
       baby   meat-ate
       Same as (11a).

c. *Wahawirake' ne   o'wahru.
   baby-ate   the   meat
   Intended: same as (11a).

(11a) is the "plain version" (ibid.: 90) with the subject and object expressed as separate DPs. In (11b), the noun for 'meat'[1] is incorporated into the verb. The same operation cannot happen to the subject noun, shown in (11c). This asymmetry is also observed with English N-V-*ing* compounds, as mentioned earlier with the example of *janitor-cleaning*. It has been controversial from early on how best to analyze this asymmetry (see Sadock 1985, Baker 1988, Rosen 1989 and Y. Li 2005 for four different views). What matters for now is the existence of the fact itself.

It is not true, though, that a nominal morpheme interpreted as Arg$_E$ cannot form a word with a verb. In English -*er/-or* and -*ant* do exactly that, and a much larger set of morphemes have this function in Chinese:

12. a. operat-or   defend-ant   teach-er …
     b. huli-yuan   ji-zhe   xiuli-gong
        tend-member report-person   repair-worker
        'nurse'   'journalist'   'repairman'
        jianju-ren   yasuo-ji   yiliao-shi
        inform-person compress-machine medically.treat-master
        'informant'   'compressor'   'therapist'
        daoqie-fan   zhizao-chang   zhihui-guan … …
        steal-criminal create-factory   command-officer
        'thief'   'manufacturer'   'commanding officer'

The difference between noun-incorporation and (12a-b) is summarized in (13):

13. Let a word W be composed of N and V.
     a. If N = theme, W denotes what V denotes, namely events;
     b. If N = agent, W denotes what N denotes, namely individuals.

"Theme" is used here as a generic label for the thematic role of the object.

The division in (13) repeats the question in (9) from another angle. When N is theme, the N-V (word order being irrelevant) cluster is a projection of V whether word formation takes place in syntax or elsewhere and therefore still denotes events. If N is agent, its external nature prevents N from being part of V's projection so as not to become an internal argument like theme. Hence W can only pick N as the head and denote what N does. At this semi-technical level, the contrast in (13a-b) is "accounted for." But why must agent stay external to V in word formation?

A note of clarification at this point: Whether (13) can be derived with head-movement in syntax along the lines of Baker's (1988) analysis of morphological incorporation – we will argue later that it cannot – is not at issue here. As Baker shows clearly, the structural asymmetry provided by syntax can indeed distinguish the subject from the object and thus possibly be made use of. But this very structural asymmetry presumes the subject being Arg_E, the very locus of the problem put under the spotlight by (9).

Now consider the semantic aspect of the words in (12). Suppose -er to be a nominal variant of Kratzer's Voice (which I will refer to as v for consistency), both introducing agent and both merging with a verbal projection. A direct conversion from the verbal v to the nominal -er gives (14). Similarly, the collection of Chinese counterparts of -er in (12b) should have (15).

14. a. $[\![$-er$]\!] = \lambda x \lambda e.\mathbf{agent}(x, e)$ (cf. (10c))
     b. $[\![$teach-er$]\!] = \lambda x \lambda e.\mathbf{teach}(e) \wedge \mathbf{agent}(x, e)$ (cf. (10e))

15. $[\![$-zhe/-yuan/-ji/-guan/ ... $]\!]$
     $= \lambda x \lambda e.\mathbf{agent}(x, e) \wedge \mathbf{person/member/machine/officer/} \ldots (x)$

Zhihui-guan 'command-officer', for instance, defines a set of officers who act as the agent of some event of commanding or another. But what forces teacher and zhihuiyuan 'commander' to be nominal and denoting individuals?

The question is sharpened by two more facts. First, (12b) is but a small sample of such V-N words in Chinese that are easy to come by (e.g. ming-qin 'sing-fowl →
songbirds', shashang-dan 'kill.injure-bomb → anti-personnel bomb', jian-chen 'expostulate-courtier → expostulatory courtier', ganzao-qi 'desiccate-instrument → desiccator'). The "nounhood" of these words can only come from the final and agentively interpreted morphemes which are simply among common nouns in Chinese. In fact, many of these nouns also form V-N words with N interpreted as theme and the compound word itself denoting events:

16. Cai-yuan,   kai-ji,   zun-shi,   chai-dan, ...
     reduce-member   turn.on-machine   respect-teacher   defuse-bomb
     'lay off employees' 'turn on a machine' 'respect teachers' 'dispose bombs'

It does not follow from any principle in UG or the theory of semantics that adding '$\mathbf{agent}(x, e)$' to the meaning of such a noun necessarily renders the resulting V-N word an individual-denoting nominal. Second, it is known that the interpretation of nouns is no less dependent than verbs on situations. The example below is from Enç (1986):

17. Every fugitive is now in jail.

By definition, a criminal already in jail is no longer a fugitive. Since (17) is semantically felicitous, the noun fugitive must be evaluated in a situation different from that of the predicate of the sentence. To this end, a situation variable, e in Kratzer's notation, is taken to be part of the semantics of even common nouns. See Schwarz (2012), among others, for defending this view while exploring how exactly this variable is saturated DP-internally. On one hand, for common nouns to have a situation variable maximally unifies the semantic representation of nouns, making them $<e, <s, t>>$, for instance, no matter whether they occur in (12) or (16). On the other hand, why '**agent**(x, e)' can single-handedly distinguish the individual-denoting (12) from the event-denoting (16) and noun-incorporation as summarized in (13), or more generally why the structural expression of Arg_E must be "external" to any projection of V, namely (9), is brought under the spotlight for an explanation.

I suggest that the explanation is what Haiman (1983) refers to as the iconicity of independence, i.e. "the linguistic separateness of an expression corresponds to the conceptual independence of the object or event which it represents" (p. 783). The literature in and outside the UG framework on lexical semantics has always expressed or implicated the intuition that Arg_E is not just structurally external to the verbal projection but also semantically/conceptually so. Jackendoff (2002) identifies this role in his lexical decomposition of verbs as instigator. Hale and Keyser (1993) paraphrase the agent-implicating light verb to be 'bring about'. And there has been a long tradition in the UG framework since Generative Semantics to refer to the subject of many verbs as causer. All these labels converge on the perception that the party denoted by Arg_E exists independently of the event e expressed by the verb so as to bring about, instigate or cause e. In fact, Dowty explicitly names "independent existence" to be one of his five "Proto-agent entailments" (1991: 572–573).

Combining this insight from the existing literature with the UG-I theory of this book gives the following step-by-step answer to the question in (9).

A. In our conceptualization, certain events e happen due to an external factor f, a party separate in existence from e but responsible for e's advent. To facilitate explication, let us call the relation between f and e 'agent-of', another instance of R_C. At least with certain lexical roots, 'agent-of' is a must due to the implicated agentivity in their own semantic content which is responsible for Marantz' *destruction* vs. *growth* disparity and for Chen and Li's preverbal adjuncts in Chinese. We postpone this topic till later.

B. The 'agent-of' relation is asymmetric, and mapping an asymmetric R_C to an asymmetric R_S is what UG is programmed to do. The obstacle here is that UG has available more than one asymmetric R_S to choose from with respect to the event-denoting V, though none of them is a self-evident fit for 'agent-of':[2]

18. a. Since f exists independently of e, 'agent-of' is not in the meaning of the e-encoding V. Therefore, 'agent-of' cannot be converted to a θ-relation with V which UG can map to the Spec or complement position in VP.
   b. Nor is 'agent-of' a relation of modification R_M (cf. section 3.4 of Chapter 3) that UG expresses with adjunction inside VP.

In sum, UG is at a loss with how exactly to map the R_C of 'agent-of' to any R_S.

C. The two functional voids of UG in the previous chapters both describe a lack of apparatus on UG's part to perform a certain function. (18) is the opposite, with too many options of which none is better or worse than the rest. So I will refrain from calling (18) Void$_F$3. Regardless, the situation creates a dilemma which is sufficient to activate the FICH. The iconicity of independence is appealed to: Because the factor f is external to the event e, the linguistic manifestation of f is placed outside the structural representation of e. Once 'agent-of' is paired with a structural head H of the semantic type $<e, <s, t>>$, UG is equipped to take over the rest of the task by merging H with whatever is the maximal projection V_{max} of V at the level of derivation in question. The H-V_{max} structure also satisfies the USM, for the asymmetric 'agent-of' external to e is indeed mapped isomorphically to H being the structural head and outside the projection of V. Two specific scenarios arise at this point.

D. If f is introduced into the event-denoting context, namely in a clause, VP = V_{max} and whatever lexical means brings in f must both stay structurally outside VP and act in itself as part of event-denoting extended projections of V. The result is v with the semantics of (10c) and the structure of vP so as to accommodate the actual agent argument (= Arg_E) by means of its Spec position external to VP.

E. Since f is ultimately about the external participant of events, it is a simple logical option that f be lexicalized as an individual-denoting morpheme, namely a nominal such as -er. If -er must stay outside any projection of V, its merger with V, no matter how that is implemented, must not let V project, or -er would end up structurally internal to V's projection in violation of the USM. But for the V-er cluster to be nominal means that -er is the head; if the head is individual-denoting, so is V-er.

In brief, the "conceptual independence" of the external factor f from the event e it brings about or instigates obtains the iconic "linguistic separateness" through the structurally defined Arg_E, resulting in an instance of the iconicity of independence. As briefly noted above, this instance of the UG–iconicity interaction differs from the cases of the SVCs and connectors. With a view to maximizing theoretical explicitness, we compare the two types more closely.

First and foremost, unlike the SVCs and coordination, where UG relies on iconicity for linearization and must improvise with an inter-object dependency or a parallel structure for R_S, every apparatus employed for Arg_E comes from the core design of UG: the combinatorial algorithm to build hierarchical structure (see (1) of Chapter 1), the extended projections of categorially specified lexical items (see Miyagawa et al. 2014 for an evolutionary account of this property of language), the way morphologically complex words are headed and how extra syntactic arguments are introduced via extra heads (see (10)/(14) and below). Second, unlike the other cases that enlist isomorphism for R_S and linear iconicity for R_L, the solution to structurally expressing Arg_E applies both isomorphism and iconicity (of independence) to create R_S: For Arg_E to be encoded though a head outside a verbal projection is simultaneously iso-morphic and iconic. Lastly and to repeat what was pointed out earlier, whereas $Void_F1$–2 both involve UG lacking a certain means to finish the job (no lexicalization of R_T and no structural projection of category-less lexical items), (18) indicates the Arg_E problem to arise from excessive R_S options on the part of UG.

It is because of these differences that I find it still plausible to consider certain forms of iconicity to be viewed as being encoded in UG, namely (1c) at the start of this chapter – after all, both v and -*er* act exactly like other functional and/or morphological heads in the UG system without any of the structural improvisation found with the SVCs and coordination. Classification aside, however, the central claim of this book should be emphasized: that our overall understanding of language benefits from an algorithmic investigation of the UG–iconicity interface as articulated here. Specifically, the line of logic leading to the final answer to (9), as well as the underlying mechanism thus revealed, is of exactly the same nature as in the previous chapters:

19. a. Identify a linguistic phenomenon P with the careful proof that there is no explanation in the theory of UG as we know it.
    b. On the basis of the FICH, seek a coherent solution with some form(s) of iconicity regulated by the USM, making explicit each step of the process leading to an explanation of P.

(19) simply repeats the research algorithm in (5) of Chapter 1 which guides all the contents of the book so far.

4.2   More Facts and Their Implications

It is typical of a linguistic analysis to have implications beyond its immediate concerns. The theory of Arg_E above is no exception. A range of facts will be given a unified account in this section to further solidify the iconicity-based approach to Arg_E.

4.2.1   -ee vs. Noncanonical Arguments

There is a three-way contrast among the noncanonical arguments (NCA here-after) in Chinese, the yet undiscussed -*ee* in English, and the agentive affixes in both languages.

First, one use of -*ee* as in *employee* and *appointee* seems to have the morpheme denote the semantic object of the verbal root. This semantic

relation with V would nullify any need for the iconicity of independence for
-*er*. At the same time, however, *employee* refers to individuals and not to
events, grammatically patterning with -*er* for making the V-*ee* form individual-denoting (and thus different from noun-incorporation). Fortunately, there
is reason to believe that -*ee* does not represent the theme argument. *Donatee*
and *grantee* refer to the parties receiving or benefiting from the said events.
Even when this use of -*ee* is perhaps associated with [+human], these
examples at least dissociate the morpheme from a simple denotation of
theme. For *standee*, which would seem to associate -*ee* with an agentive
reading, *Random House Webster's College Dictionary* paraphrases it as "a
person who stands, as in a public conveyance, usu. because all seats are
occupied." In other words, *standee* refers to those on whom standing is
imposed, in effect a malfactive. Thus, an employee at least does not have
to be a person who is employed. Instead, s/he is one to whom employment is
given or with whom employment exists; the same applies to *appointee*,
absentee, etc.

The semantics of -*ee* suggests this analysis: Just as -*er* is the nominal variant
of the agent-introducing *v*, -*ee* is the nominal form of the applicative which is
UG's way to bring in extra ([+human]) arguments. The examples below
illustrate the phenomenon of applicatives in Chichewa (Bantu; Baker 1988:
229) and English:

20. a. Ndi-na-tumiz-a   chipanda cha   mowa   kua mfumu.
         1s.SUBJ-PAST-send-ASP calabash of   beer   to   chief
         'I sent a calabash of beer to the chief.'
     b. Ndi-na-tumiz-ir-a   mfumu chipanda cha mowa.
         1s.SUBJ-PAST-send-APPL-ASP   chief   calabash   of   beer
         'I sent the chief a calabash of beer.'

21. a. Sam made a pizza for her friend.
     b. Sam made her friend a pizza.

In (20), the goal argument *mfumu* 'chief' is either associated with the preposition *kua* 'to' or the applicative suffix -*ir*, a variation accompanied by the
characteristic word order change. The same word-order alternatives are found
with the goal and benefactive arguments in English (see the translations of (20)
and the examples in (21)). It is thus plausible to think of English as having
a zero-form applicative morpheme.

Multiple works have converged on treating the applicative morpheme as
a head, Appl, sitting outside the lexical VP (Marantz 1993, Baker 1996, Y. Li
2005, Pylkkänen 2008) which introduces an extra argument. Adopting this
analysis, the semantics of Appl (from Pylkkänen) and its nominal counterpart
-*ee* pairs well with that of *v* and -*er* in (10c) and (14a):

22. a. [[Appl]] = λxλe.**Extra-Arg**(x, e)
    b. [[-ee]] = λxλe.**Extra-Arg**(x, e)

While (22a) is combined with VP to yield an extended projection of V, (22b) terminates a verbal projection and yields an individual-denoting nominal.

A question arises with both a theoretical facet and an empirical one. Theoretically, if the agent argument stays external to VP for denoting an external factor to events, what forces an applied argument – goal, benefactive, etc. – to be represented outside of VP? Note that this "external" status of the applied argument is critical, or V-*ee* would end up with the unwanted semantic similarity to noun-incorporation. On the empirical side, we know that the applicative strategy can, in some languages, introduce multiple kinds of arguments, as seen in Kichaga (Bresnan and Moshi 1993: 49):

23. a. N-a-i-ly-a   k-elya.
       FOC-AGR-PRES-eat-FV   food
       'He is eating food.'
    b. N-a-i-lyi-i-a   m-ka   k-elya.
       FOC-AGR-PRES-eat-APPL-FV   wife   food
       'He is eating food for/on his wife.'
    c. N-a-i-lyi-i-a   njaa   k-elya.
       FOC-AGR-PRES-eat-APPL-FV   hunger   food
       'He is eating food because of hunger.'
    d. N-a-i-lyi-i-a   ma-woko   k-elya.
       FOC-AGR-PRES-eat-APPL-FV   hand   food
       'He is eating food with his hands.'
    e. N-a-i-lyi-i-a   m-ri-nyi   k-elya.
       FOC-AGR-PRES-eat-APPL-FV   homestead   food
       'He is eating food at the homestead.'

(23a) is the base form, with (23b-e) for an added benefactive/malfactive, reason, instrument and location, respectively. On one hand, it is hard to miss the similarity between this range of applicative choices and what are available with the noncanonical arguments in Chinese. On the other, the latter phenomenon clearly treats the instrument, location, purpose, etc. to be "internal", swapping freely with the theme argument.

Adding the behaviors of -*er*, -*ee*, Appl and NCA together gives what looks like self-contradictory behaviors among these cases:

24. Given that -*ee* and NCAs are all comparable to applied arguments,
    a. -*ee* resembles -*er* by letting V-*ee* denote individuals and because ApplP is external to VP,
    b. but NCAs resemble the theme argument for free swapping between the subject and object positions, unlike the agent argument.

When applied arguments, *-ee* and the NCAs all embody "oblique" arguments but appear to exhibit contradictory behaviors, does there exist a unified account of them all?

Our answer to this question is positive and draws on Pylkkänen's (2008) division of high and low applicatives. As she observes, not every language allows the applicative to happen to an unergative verb: Kichaga does (Bresnan and Moshi 1993: 50) while English does not (Pylkkänen 2008: 11):

25. a. N-a-i-zric-ia   mbuya.
       FOC-1S-PRES-run-APPL-FV   friend
       'He is running for a friend.'
    b. *I ran him.
       Intended reading: 'I ran for him.'

For Pylkkänen, this distinction is tied to whether the applicative affix has a built-in requirement for the applied argument to hold a relation with the theme argument of the lexical verb. The high applicative in Kichaga does not, with the meaning in (22a). Hence it is compatible with transitive and unergative verbs alike. In contrast, the low (and coincidentally zero-formed) applicative in English contains a semantic component that links the applied argument to the object of the verb, forcing the latter to be transitive. I will adopt this distinction of high and low applicatives and note emphatically that the high applicative brings in an extra party which, unlike theme, is not encoded in the semantics of the lexical verb.

With the division of high and low applicatives, we propose (26):

26. In Chinese and English, a high applicative is used only with operations whose nature disables the low applicative.

(21) and (25b) prove English to have a low applicative. The discussion of ditransitive verbs in 2.5.5 of Chapter 2 illustrates the same in Chinese. Plausibly, (26) is rooted in the complementary distribution of the high and low applicatives: In a language defaulting to the low option, only operations prohibiting it procedurally and in principle can enable the high option. One would wonder whether (26) holds for low-applicative languages in general. But I will take (26) as is and focus only on how it helps subsume the English and Chinese facts in (24) under a unified analysis.

In particular, I treat *-ee* to be the nominal variant of a high applicative with the meaning in (22b). As such, *-ee* satisfies (26) by being itself. It is in the nature of merging *-ee* with a verb (or its root), say *employ*, that the latter no longer projects with its theme object. Thus, the very merger of *-ee* is in itself an operation that ruins the default setup for the low applicative, namely the latter's reliance on the theme argument, as Pylkkänen makes clear. In sum, combining *-ee* with *employ* is a self-licensing process in accordance with (26). Once the high applicative strategy is put to work, whatever is UG's reason to position such an ApplP outside the lexical VP (see discussion below) is automatically respected, leading to *-ee* staying structurally external to V and thus heading the V-*ee* cluster and making it denote individuals as defined by *-ee*.

In Pylkkänen's theory, unaccusative verbs are compatible with the low applicative due to the presence of the theme argument. In reality, the prediction is borne out in Finnish but not clearly so in English (see her section 2.1.3.4). What matters here is that English opts to default to the low applicative. Under (26), it takes some operation such as the *-ee* merger to destroy this general setting of the English grammar. It is from this perspective that *stand-ee* can be understood. There is independent evidence that verbs like *stand* and *sit* have a non-agentive use:

27. tai-shang lai-le/ *shuo-zhe/zhan-zhe   yige xuesheng. (Chinese)
    stage-on come-ASP/talk-ASP/stand-ASP   a   student
    'There came/*talked/stood a student on the stage.'

Locative-inversion in Chinese corresponds to the *there*-expletive construction in English, both requiring unaccusative or stative verbs. Since *stand* and its Chinese counterpart can occur in (27), we are given the option of not attributing agentivity to the single party of a standing event. Whether this thematic variant is theme or not, merging *stand* with *-ee* will in principle remove the condition for the low applicative and thereby satisfy (26), leaving *-ee* to be interpreted in the same way as in *employ-ee*.[3]

Moving on to the NCAs in Chinese, there is another fact about this phenomenon that has been occasionally observed (e.g. Zhang 2004) but not analyzed in the UG framework except by Sun and Li (2020), namely, NCAs are allowed only when the verb is monosyllabic. The examples below are from Sun and Li:

28. a. xie/*shuxie   maobi
       write/write   calligraphy.brush
       'write with a calligraphy brush'
    b. kan/*guankan   wangyuanjing
       look/look   telescope
       'look with a telescope'
    c. zhong/*zhongzhi   yangtai
       plant/plant   balcony
       'plant (flowers) on the balcony'
    d. kai/*jiashi   gaosulu
       drive/drive   highway
       'drive on the highway'
    e. fei/feixiang   renzi
       fly   letter.V
       '(for wild ducks to) fly in V-formation'

The pattern is consistent and begs an integral explanation with NCAs.[4]

It is common knowledge that Classical Chinese has mostly monosyllabic words while Modern Chinese words are predominantly multisyllabic. A major means to implement this transition is by combining monosyllabic words into disyllabic ones, often based on the same morphemes – in (28), four of the five disyllabic verbs contain their monosyllabic counterparts. Since this transition is system-wide, Sun and Li suggest that Chinese implements it with a rule. A revision of their proposal is given in (29) with r standing for a lexical root:

29. a. $V = r + sh$, sh being a light verb shell which
     i. provides the categorial specification, and
     ii. singles out the theme argument – if there is one – among all the conceptual factors of the event denoted by r.
   b. Optionally separate the shell from r if r is phonologically monosyllabic.

The shell in (29a) can be thought of as a variant of Hale and Keyser's (1993) l-syntactic light verbs structurally on top of a root. As stated, (29a-i) is consistent with Void$_F$2 in Chapter 3 because, by this design, r is always accompanied by the category-specifying sh so that it is ready to project in syntax. (29a-ii) corresponds to Hale and Keyser's (1993) attribution of the ultimate source of θ-roles to their light verbs. Lastly, (29b) is borrowed from Lin (2001) on NCAs but viewed as a rule in the diachronic context of Chinese.

According to Sun and Li, the logic behind (29) proceeds as follows. In Classical Chinese, a monosyllabic verb composed of $r + sh$ behaves like verbs in all other languages. As part of the mono-to-multi-syllabic transition, monosyllabic verbs (and other categories which are irrelevant to the present concern) were stripped of their shells by (29b) to become bare roots ready for root-level merger in order to form disyllabic words. Since there is no evidence that the transition has completed, (29b) is still available in Modern Chinese, letting a monosyllabic r enter syntax directly. With no shell to single out the theme argument, a syntactically licensed DP, i.e. the subject or object, can be interpreted as any factor bearing on the event denoted by r, subject only to the context and other relevant semantic restrictions identified in Sun (2010). Hence the NCAs.

Before adapting this analysis to the high applicative theory assumed here, I make a clarification regarding (29a-ii). For Hale and Keyser, there are two light verbs that correspond to the shell in our definition, one meaning 'enter into' that results in the final verb having the theme argument, and one meaning 'bring about' that implicates an agent. (29a-ii) borrows the idea of their theme-introducing light verb but discards the rest. In particular, the shell sh does NOT implicate agentivity out of considerations of fact and redundancy.

Recall Marantz' (1997) *destruction* vs. *growth* contrast repeated in (7–8) above. The essence of his analysis is that the agentivity content is part of the semantics of √DESTROY but not of √GROW. For the sake of discussion, let us call this content [ext], mnemonic for "external factor." In the nominal context, the possessor *John's* acquires the agent interpretation only when the root has [ext], which explains why only (7b) is good. But in the clausal context, v provides the agent argument independently of the root and thus licenses (7a) and (8a).

As we noted earlier, however, there are verbs like *die* and *arrive* that are unaccusative in behavior and thus similar to the intransitive *grow* but have no transitive use at all. And there might be something deeper about this contrast. Classical Chinese is well known for (superficial) zero-form causativization (e.g. *sheng* 'alive, live' → *sheng siren* 'make.alive dead.person = resurrect the dead') but an informal corpus search found no case with *si* 'dead, die' used causatively.[5] Minimally, then, a three-way contrast must be made with respect to [ext]: [−ext] for roots like √DIE, [+ext] for roots like √DESTROY, and totally unspecified for √GROW. The agent-introducing v is expected to fail with roots of the [−ext] type, presumably through feature-agreement. The model in (29) is obviously different from Marantz' theory, a subject matter to return to in 4.2.2. But I share Marantz' intuition that the value of the [ext] feature is ultimately dependent on the semantics of the root. E.g. it must be in the core of our conceptualization that an event of destruction necessarily implicates an external force. In brief, (29a) lets the light verb shell *sh* single out the theme party of the event while leaving the pairing between V and the agent-introducing v to the inherent meaning of the root r. [+ext] aside, this result is literally identical to Kratzer's semantics of V in (10a).

Back to the NCAs, the application of (29b) is an operation satisfying (26) because by de-shelling a monosyllabic verb such as *chi* 'eat' (see (4)–(6)), the resulting root r no longer has any grammatically encoded thematic quality in the form of a thematic argument and thus removes the very foundation for the low applicative which critically presumes the verb to have a theme argument. The high applicative strategy is activated now. This much is similar to *-ee* in English. What is different is that the NCAs happen in the clausal context. Let us look at the process step by step.

Since r has no categorial specification, it cannot project in syntax under Void$_F$2 and must parasite to some [+V, −N] head h to form a clause at all. In essence, this is identical to *and* in Chapter 3: r is taken as a cluster of features merged into h. Furthermore, it is most plausible that h is not T. The category-less r, encoding merely a concept, is likely to lack the event role for T to bind (Higginbotham 1985), with the event role presumably brought into existence when r is "grammaticalized" with the verbal category. So h must provide an event role for T but not T in itself. It follows that h can only be v or the high applicative Appl in the limited inventory of UG's clause-building materials, meaning that the NCA construction contains at least T and h. Two interwoven predictions follow. (i) Since T and v/Appl each license a syntactic argument (e.g. via Case), the NCA construction acquires the potential to be "transitive" with both a subject and an object. (ii) In the absence of VP, three structural options are logically available which can help support r and its "arguments": TP with vP alone, with ApplP alone, and with both:

30. a. [__ T [$_{vP}$ Arg$_E$ v+r __]]
     b. [__ T [$_{AppP}$ Arg$_{appl}$ Appl+r __]]
     c. [__ T [$_{vP}$ Arg$_E$ v [$_{ApplP}$ Arg$_{appl}$ Appl+r __]]]

(30a) is the most straightforward scenario (and yields by far the most common form of NCAs), with the subject of the clause being the agent from v and licensed by movement to the Spec of TP. v has its own Case to license the second DP in the complement position "__" of v (via Chomsky's (2000, 2001a, b) probe-goal, for instance). Semantically, this DP can express any event-related factor that is contextually sensible and semantically legitimate by other independent requirements: instrument, manner, location, purpose, or even cases with simultaneously multiple pragmatically appropriate roles (see Huang et al. 2009, Chapter 2). Furthermore, the motivation for activating the *sh*-removing rule in (29b) is almost certainly to introduce an NCA – otherwise one could simply use the default *sh*+r to obtain the theme argument. It follows that there must be two arguments, the agent from v and the NCA semantically affiliated with the bare r. The prediction proves categorically true. As demonstrated in Huang et al. (2009), even typical unergative verbs like *ku* 'cry', *xiao* 'laugh' and *zou* 'walk' all occur with a DP "object" in NCAs (e.g. *ku changcheng* 'cry Great.Wall' → 'cry at/because of the Great Wall').

(30b) makes use of the high applicative, with its argument starting in the Spec of ApplP. In terms of syntactic licensing, this scenario is identical to (30a): Arg$_{appl}$ moves to the Spec of TP while the Appl head Case-licenses an NCA DP in its own complement position in the same way v does in (30a). Semantically, Appl is as unrestricted as the applicative -*i* suffix in Kichaga (see (23)), which can be literally represented by (22a), namely it is just an extra argument whose semantic relation with the lexical predicate is contextually determined. On the surface, this Appl has the same thematic effect as the bare root r with an NCA. But the mechanism and motivation behind the two are fundamentally different. The sole purpose of r is to bring in an NCA, made possible by (29b), whereas the high Appl is used merely to structurally anchor r when v is not around. That another NCA-like argument is enabled by Appl is but an obligatory by-product. This is why (30b) must be equally transitive: The argument that Appl brings in results from an independently available means of UG and thus does not substitute for the initial reason behind the use of the highly language-specific r. Like -*ee* in *employee*, Appl allows Arg$_{appl}$ to acquire what feels to be the "theme" interpretation, yielding examples like (5a). Meanwhile, the NCA following r can be given any contextually appropriate reading, including theme, because, after all, theme is one of the factors of the *r*-denoted event. This explains (5b). Collectively, (5a-b) give the impression that non-agent arguments of the lexical verb are swappable. The possibility for the object to be understood as theme exists for (30a) too, but the result is the agent subject and theme object, non-distinct from not depriving *r* of its light verb shell.

(30c) seems to make a wrong prediction: With three DP-licensers present, namely T, *v* and Appl, one would counterfactually expect NCAs to permit a double-object pattern. To understand why (30c) does not happen, recall that de-shelling in (29b) is a language-specific and clearly marked operation whose utilization is motivated by introducing an NCA. Within the overall cost-sensitive model of syntax, (29b) is the kind of rule more costly than the default "θ-assignment" type. Along the same line of reasoning, the high applicative strategy is another marked and more costly apparatus in Chinese. Since *r* is category-less and UG has Void$_F$2, the high Appl serves as an alternative to *v* for hosting *r* and thus providing the structural environment for *r*'s noncanonical argument. When the clausal structure has only Appl, as in (30b), whether Appl is marked or not is meaningless for there is no less marked *r*-supporting means in the clause to compare with. When both Appl and *v* are put side by side in (30c) for the same purpose, however, the less marked *v* always wins the competition, eliminating Appl's chance to even show up. In this sense, Appl parallels with *do*-support in English: A language-specific and thus more costly operation is performed when and only when some features need a proper host not available in the given context (i.e. negation and T-to-C movement in the absence of auxiliary verbs; see Chomsky 1995).

This brings us back to the initial question about (24): how to reconcile the apparently self-contradicting status of *-ee* in the context of our iconic explanation for *-er*: *-ee* and *-er* both being structurally external to V vs. *-ee* and NCAs being all applicatives and siding with the theme argument. The answer lies again in (29b). What look like monosyllabic verbs in this Chinese construction can be *r* only and thus without any regular thematic specifications. And what look like the arguments of *r* come from three sources: (i) the agent from the UG-standard *v*P, (ii) the non-agent subject from the marked generic high ApplP under (26), and (iii) the object being contextually interpreted with respect to its semantic relation with *r*. (i–ii) are straightforward, but (iii) needs further explication.

If the semantic relation between *r* and the object DP is restricted only by context, it may not be self-evident why the agent reading is completely unavailable to the object, especially when both *v* and Appl are structurally external to VP in the default clausal structure. Crucial here is what separates the agent argument and an applied argument, namely their relations with the lexical verb V, now taken to be *r*+*sh*.

The agent is simply external to the events denoted by V, its structural expression being a consequence of UG's indeterminacy in (18) plus the FICH-USM. The applied arguments have a different reason for staying outside the projection of V: The light verb shell *sh* in (29a) only picks the theme to be the thematic argument of V, and by doing so, essentially closes the grammatical window for other factors of the event, be they location, instrument or purpose, to be manifested as a direct argument of V. The Appl head is one of UG's solutions[6] to express any of these deprived factors in compliance with X'-theory (or whatever forces the binary-branching phrase structure; see Chomsky 2013, 2015), proper thematic saturation and Davidsonian semantics which all collaborate to place ApplP outside VP. To the extent that the applicative strategy is employed, this UG-dictated structural setup must be respected, keeping ApplP and *-ee* outside the projections of V. The only exception to all this is when the *r*-wrapping shell is gone and thus every factor of the event enjoys an equal chance for semantic interpretation with the root. This is also when one sees how Arg_E differs fundamentally from the applied arguments.

In sum, the NCAs and the theme are all elements of the event, distinguished linguistically only by the light verb shell that singles theme out and turns *r* into V and whose removal triggers the high applicative strategy and effectively makes all elements of the event equal. Arg_E is an entirely different animal destined to be external to the event whether *r* is accompanied by the shell or not. Hence the apparent puzzle in (24). Put differently, the apparently free swappability of the Chinese NCAs between the subject and object positions, vs. the agent argument being necessarily the subject, provides a unique piece of evidence that the grammatical status of Arg_E is rooted in a mechanism separate from the standard operations of UG, a mechanism which I argued to be the iconicity of independence implemented through the USM under the FICH. Another significant conclusion from this analysis, in full compliance with $Void_F 2$ of Chapter 2, is that English verbs are *not* bare roots in syntax as claimed by some theories (see 3.1, Chapter 3) but categorially specified verbs because they do not support NCAs.

To wrap up the discussion on how applicatives are involved in that portion of language which results from the UG–iconicity interface, recall the Chinese example (98) in 2.5.5 of Chapter 2 with a ditransitive V1 in an SVC and the applicative-based structure in (102), both repeated below.

31. a. Ping'er ganggang   gei-le   Jia Lian yikuar   yuebing   chi.
       Ping'er a.moment.ago give-ASP JL   a.piece   mooncake   eat
       'Ping'er just gave JL a piece of moon cake to eat.'
    b. ... [$_{vP}$ Ping'er *v* [$_{ApplP}$ JL Appl [$_{VP}$ give a-piece-of-mooncake$_i$ ... eat e_i]]]

For ApplP to be above VP provides the structural basis for V2 (*chi* 'eat') to regard the applied argument of V1, *JL*, as its agent subject due to [+ext] in *eat* (cf. the agent possessor in (7–8)). Furthermore, Chinese differs parametrically from Kwa languages by allowing pragmatics to participate in securing the coindexation of *e*, the object of V2, with the object of V1 (*a piece of mooncake* in (31)). This latter part of the process is critically contingent on the understanding that when *Ping'er* gave the mooncake to *JL*, *JL* owned the cake.

But this reading is precisely what characterizes the low applicative for Pylkkänen, i.e. there exists an inherent relation 'to-the-possession' (2008: 18)) between the low applied argument and the theme of V. Meanwhile, a low applicative is, by her definition, located underneath VP with the semantics in (32b):

32. a.

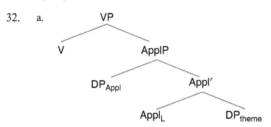

b. $[\![Appl_L]\!] = \lambda x \lambda y \lambda f_{<e, \ st>} \lambda e.f(e, x) \wedge \textbf{theme}(e, x) \wedge \textbf{to-the-possession}(x, y)$

The Appl head merges first with the theme and applied arguments to implement the 'to-the-possession' relation between them, and then takes in V to ensure that the theme argument belongs to V. Meanwhile, (32a) contradicts (31b) in terms of where the low applicative is structurally located.

As it turns out, the SVC examples like (31a) can be easily accommodated by (32) as well: simply adjoin VP2, i.e. [V2 *e*], directly to Appl′ in (32a). There is no semantic complication here because (i) Appl will eventually share its unsaturated event variable, *e* in (32b), with V1 and (ii) it is up to R_T to connect Appl′ and VP2 so that the semantics of each of them is processed separately. When V1 changes from *give* to *steal* (see (103) of Chapter 2), the understood subject of V2 also shifts from the applied argument *JL* of V1 to the agent argument *Ping'er* out of pragmatic considerations. This transition can be viewed as lifting the point of VP2's adjunction from Appl′ to some unexpressed V′ in (32a) so that the two lexical verbs structurally share the agent argument introduced by *v*P. What matters is that in both options, the understood Arg_E of V2 *chi* 'eat' remains structurally external to VP2 and thus complies with the iconic demand explicated earlier.

That an SVC with a ditransitive V1 is friendly with either of the structures in (32) and (31b) is confirmed by another fact:[7]

33. a. Ping'er gei-le/tou-le   Jia Lian henduo dagao   chi.
         Ping'er give-ASP/steal-ASP JL   a.lot.of mooncake eat
         'Ping'er gave JL a lot of mooncakes to eat.' or
         'Ping'er stole a lot of mooncakes from JL to eat.'

b. Ping'er   *gei/tou   Jia Lian   henduo   dagao   chi-le   ge   bao.
   Ping'er   give/steal   JL   a.lot.of   mooncake   eat-ASP   CL   full
   Intended: 'Ping'er let JL eat to his fill by giving him a lot of mooncakes.' or
             'Ping'er stole a lot of mooncakes from JL and ate to her fill.'

It was shown in Chapter 2 that with the instrumental SVC, V2 is the default
main verb in compliance with the syntax of Chinese while V1 becomes the
main verb only when an aspect marker is added (see (33) and (42) therein). In
the consecutive SVC in (33) here, and with V1 being ditransitive, the perfective
aspect marker -le can always occur on V1, shown in (33a), but feels acceptable
on V2 only when V1 is *steal* (33b).

The contrast follows from (32a). When VP1 is headed by *give*, pragmatics
forces VP2 to adjoin to the Appl' of the low applicative (of *give*) as explicated
above, mandatorily making V1 the main verb. To the extent that aspectual
markers, at least in these SVCs, are correlated with the main verb, (33a) is
expected to be acceptable while (33b) is not. On the other hand, when V1 is
steal, VP2 is above the low ApplP ($Appl_L$) in order to share the agent. This
otherwise minor structural difference immediately sets us back to the familiar
scenario: in principle, Chinese syntax allows either V1 or V2 to be the main
verb. That is, VP2 may adjoin to V1', or VP1 may adjoin to V2', depending on
other factors in the language. Hence, (33a-b) are both acceptable with *steal*.
Note, however, that (33) does not rely on Pylkkänen's particular treatment of
$Appl_L$ for explanation. VP2 can equally adjoin to Appl' in (31b) in order to be
lower than the applied argument *JL*, which makes V1 be *give* and necessarily
the main verb. Or with V1 being *steal*, VP2 will stay closer to the agent *Ping'er*.
Then ApplP has the option of adjoining to V2' and turning V2 into the main
verb:

34. ... [$_{vP}$ Ping'er v [$_{VP2}$ [$_{ApplP}$ JL Appl [$_{VP}$ steal a-lot-of-mooncake$_i$]] [$_{V2'}$ ... eat e_i]]]

The analysis of SVCs in this book relies on there being a subject S shared
by V1 and V2 so that S is non-heterologous to e, the object of V2. When V2
is [+ext] as defined above, this makes sense since V2 contains the ultimate
source of agentivity. But what if V2 is based on a root like √GROW that has
[ext] unspecified (see (8) above)? Logically, the agent argument from V1 will
be heterologous to V2 for lack of any semantic connection, and now more
than one argument of V1 would qualify for antecedent to O2, failing the
isomorphic mapping from R_T to R_S under the USM. Remarkably, though,
this undesirable scenario never arises in natural language. Verbs like *grow*
belong to the ergative class, characteristically alternating between the
intransitive inchoative/stative and the transitive causative. In general, the
agent argument from v for these verbs is essentially the external causer that
brings about the change of state described by the intransitive form. When

such a verb is used as V2 in SVCs, its basic semantics immediately subjects the SVC to the resultative interpretation. In turn, O2 can rely on the causal-role algorithm in (105) of Chapter 2 to build the O1–O2 dependency with no need for subject-sharing any longer. Hence, even though such a V2 does not keep O2 and the agent of V1 non-heterologous, the USM is still satisfied. Call it a happy coincidence if you want to. What counts is that the UG-I theory formulated in this work ends up producing all and only good examples for the SVCs.

4.2.2   More on $V = $ r $+$ sh

The account of the NCAs in Chinese paints a picture of bare roots which are not only category-less but also without the typical thematic specifications found in verbs of most other languages. The first trait is well investigated and made use of in the literature (see 3.1 of Chapter 3). The second one, on the other hand, never goes beyond a limited number of works on Chinese initiated by Lin (2001). The theoretical implication of this imbalance gets highlighted if we reverse the logic. To the extent that the bare root account of the NCAs in 4.2.1 is tenable, all works making use of bare roots for other languages are in fact *not* dealing with real bare roots because none of these languages allows NCAs.

The current literature within the general model of UG offers multiple possibilities to implement this conclusion. Out of three considerations, however, I adopt the one already encoded in (29a) which, in turn, is a variant of the long tradition since Generative Semantics to decompose a lexical verb into a concept-encoding root – the bare root in the sense of Chinese NCAs – and some generic light verbs more or less meaning DO, CAUSE, BECOME, etc. In this model, both categorial and thematic specifi-cations result from adding such light verbs to the bare root. To borrow Hale and Keyser's (1993) l-syntactic terms, the light V they paraphrase as 'enter into' not only turns the root √CLEAR into a verb but also brings out its theme argument. Being deprived of such light verbs makes the root lose both category and "θ-roles" in one fell swoop.

Two of three considerations behind this choice are provided by Borer (2014, 2015) and recounted earlier: There is data against associating syntactic argu-ments directly with certain roots (see (12) of Chapter 3), and letting category-less roots participate in syntax fails to capture the interaction patterns involving overt and purported zero-formed category-changing affixes ((6–8) of Chapter 3 and (41) below). The third consideration is due to a pattern of Semitic causa-tivization. The Arabic examples, analytic and morphological respectively, are given below (Y. Li 2005: 13):

35. a. jaʕal-a   l-mudrris-uun$_i$ t-tulaab-a$_j$ yajlis-uun biʒaanib-i
         made-AGR   the-teachers-NOM   the-students-ACC   sit-AGR   next-GEN
         baʕdihum   l-baʕd-i$_{*i/j}$.
         each   the-other-GEN
         'The teachers made the students sit next to each other.'
     b. ʔajlas-a   ʔal-mudrris-uun$_i$ t-tulaab-a$_j$ biʒaanib-i baʕdihum
         made.sit-AGR   the-teachers-NOM   the-students-ACC   next-GEN   each
         l-baʕd-i$_{*i/j}$.
         the-other-GEN
         Same as (35a).
     c. ʔasqat-a   ʔal-mudrris-uun$_i$ t-tulaab-a$_j$ ʕalaa   baʕdihum
         made.fall-AGR   the-teachers-NOM   the-students-ACC   on   each
         l-baʕd-i$_{*i/j}$.
         other
         'The teachers made the students fall on each other.'

36. a. ʔan-nisaaʔ-u$_i$ jaʕl-an   l-banaat-i$_j$ maɣmuumat-in min
         the-women-NOM   made-AGR   the-girls-ACC   upset-ACC   from
         baʕdinin   l-baʕd-i$_{*i/j}$.
         each   the-other-GEN
         'The women made the girls upset with each other.'
     b. jaʕal-a   ʕalii-un$_i$ hasan-an$_j$ nasruur-an min   nafsi-h$_{*i/j}$.
         made-AGR   Ali-NOM   Hassan-ACC   happy-ACC   from   self-him
         'Ali made Hassan happy about himself.'
     c. ʔan-nisaaʔ-u$_i$ ʔaɣmam-na   l-banaat-i$_j$ min   baʕdinin
         the-women-NOM   made.upset-AGR   the-girls-ACC   from   each
         l-baʕd-i$_{i/*j}$.
         the-other-GEN
         'The women made the girls upset with them (the women).'
     d. sarr-a   ʕalii-un$_i$ hasan-an$_j$ min   nafsi-h$_{i/*j}$.
         made.happy.AGR   Ali-NOM   Hassan-ACC   from   self-him
         'Ali made Hassan happy about him.'

In (35a), the causative verb and the embedded verb are expressed separately. As expected from Binding Condition A, the reciprocal anaphor *baʕdihum l-baʕd* 'each other', being part of the embedded clause, must be bound by the local subject *t-tulaab* 'the students'. (35b) is the morphological counterpart of (35a) in which the lexical root for sitting, *j ... l ... s*, is causativized with the corresponding vowels. The same anaphor has the same binder, a well-known fact since Baker's (1988) underlyingly bi-clausal account of morphological "verb-incorporation" in Bantu languages. (35c) illustrates morphological causativization on the root *s ... q ... t*, understood as an unaccusative. The anaphor is again bound only by *t-tulaab* 'the students', the thematic argument of the root.

(36a-b) are analytic causatives paralleling (35a), differing in that in (35a), the embedded predicate is a verb, shown by the agreement marker *-uun*, while the embedded predicates in (36a-b), meaning 'upset' and 'happy', are not verbal and thus are marked with the accusative case markers -*in* and -*an*. For the sake of easy reference, these embedded predicates will be called adjectives. As will become clear later on, what matters here is not the exact category of these words but the fact that they have a non-verbal one. Category aside, the anaphors in the analytic causatives behave as expected: bound only by the embedded subject of each sentence in accordance with Binding Condition A. But the pattern breaks down when the roots of the embedded predicates, y ... m ... m and s ... r ... r, are morphologically causativized. The anaphor in semantic connection with the roots must now take the subject of the entire sentence as the antecedent, skipping what corresponds to the embedded subject of the analytic versions (i.e. *the girls* in (36c) and *Hassan* in (36d)).

(37) summarizes this contrast between (35) and (36):

37. a. If a root *r* has a simple verbal form, both analytic and morphological causatives in Arabic act as a bi-clausal construction for the purpose of anaphor-binding;
     b. If *r* only has a simple adjectival form, the analytic causative still behaves bi-clausally as expected but the morphological variant is clearly mono-clausal.

That the disparity is category-sensitive can be best seen by putting (36c-d) side by side with (35c). Thematically, none of the roots in them, *happy* and *upset* in the former and *fall* in the latter, supports an agent argument in their intended semantics. This fact eliminates the possibility that the argument structure of a given root is the culprit for the binding-related difference at hand, as erroneously suggested by Ackema (2006: 209–210). The only grammatical factor separating the roots for *happy* and *upset* from the roots for *fall* and *sit* is that these two groups differ in the basic lexical categories that they are associated with. Somehow, a root incapable of a simple verbal use results in a mono-clausal structure even after morphological causativization.

The category-based contrast in (37) is not limited to Arabic. (38) illustrates the same pattern in Hebrew. See Y. Li (2005: 84–85) for more examples:

38. a. Hem$_i$ hisnii   'et   Moshe   al   'acmam$_i$.
         they   made.hateful ACC   Moshe   P   themselves
         'They made Moshe full of hate to them.'
     b. Hem$_i$ hixtivu   la-yeladimi$_j$ sipur   al   'acmam$_{*i/j}$.
         they   made.write   to-the.boys   a.story about themselves
         'They made the boys write a story about themselves (the boys).'

With (38a) containing an adjectival root and (38b) a verbal one, how the anaphor *'acmam* 'themselves' picks its antecedent is identical to their Arabic counterparts. But why so?

Suppose a category-less root *r* participates in syntactic structure-building (contra Void$_F$2). No problem arises with analytic causatives. Simply place *r* in a verbal context (e.g. in the complement position of *v*) or an adjectival context (e.g. created with *a*), followed by moving *r* to *v*/*a*, and we derive (35a) and (36a-b) where *r*+*v* and *r*+*a* take the simple verbal and adjectival forms. The bi-clausal structure determines binding as expected. Turning to morphological causativization, let r_v stand for the type of roots that have simple verbal manifestations (to derive verbs meaning 'sit' and 'fall' in Arabic and 'write' in Hebrew) and r_a for the type of roots with only simple adjectival manifest-ations (for adjectives meaning 'upset' and 'happy' in Arabic and 'hateful' in Hebrew).

First suppose such roots to occur in exactly the same structural environ-ment as the analytic version, namely as the structural complement of *v* and *a*:

39. ... *caus* [$_{xP}$ ... *x* [$_Y$ ... *r* ...]]

If $r = r_v$, $x = v$. Head-movement creates $v+r_v$ first and then moves the cluster further to the matrix *caus* to yield the morphological causative. Irrelevant details aside, this is the standard Baker-style verb-incorporation in which *x*P serves as the binding domain for any anaphor located within Y provided that the " ... " preceding *x* is occupied by the syntactic subject of *x*P. Hence the bi-clausal coindexation pattern in (35b-c) and (38b). Now let $r = r_a$ and thus $x = a$. Moving r_a to *a* must be grammatical because r_a can manifest as an adjective. But there must be something wrong with further moving $a+r_a$ to *caus* since, should this be legitimate, the resulting morphological causa-tive would be structurally indistinguishable from when $r = r_v$. Then one would wrongly predict *x*P in (39) to be the binding domain for an anaphor in Y regardless of categories, contra (36c-d) and (38a). In conclusion, at least for the purpose of the derivation at hand, moving the adjectival $a+r_a$ to the verbal *caus* must be prohibited for some fundamental reason R. Because of R, morphological causativization does not get wrongly derived from the underlyingly bi-clausal structure (39) when a root only has a simple adjectival manifestation.

But R does not explain how r_a can be morphologically causativized in the first place. With (39) out of the picture, the only logical alternative is (40) given the working assumptions that *r* participates in syntactic operations and that word formation is syntactic in nature:

40. ... *caus* [$_Y$ ... *r* ...]

That is, *r* moves directly to *caus* to form *sarr* 'made.happy' for instance and thereby bypasses R. Furthermore, since (40) is (39) minus the extra layer of structure labeled as *x*P, one may plausibly reason that the *caus*+r_a thus formed with (40) resides in an effectively mono-clausal context for an anaphor inside

Y. The problem with this analysis is that if head-movement could happen in (40) when $r = r_a$, it ought to happen just as legitimately when $r = r_v$. Then whatever logic makes $caus+r_a$ act mono-clausally for anaphor-binding would predict $caus+r_v$ to act the same way, contrary to the mandatory bi-clausal behavior in this latter case. In conclusion, neither (39) nor (40) is the correct structural source for morphological causativization as long as a uniform account is being sought. (39) is wrong either for letting both r_v and r_a generate bi-clausal anaphor-binding if without R or for failing to even permit r_a to be causativized when R is around. (40) may be exempt from R by definition, but it erroneously predicts r_a and r_v to equally have mono-clausal behavior for binding.

Since (39–40) together exhaust the ways a category-less root is used in syntax for morphological causativization[8] and neither of them is capable of accounting for the data pattern in (37), I conclude that Semitic causativization favors not letting category-less roots be part of syntactic structure-building. Logically, this entails that roots enter Semitic syntax already equipped with a category. On one hand, this is consistent with the analysis of the Chinese NCAs based on $V = r + sh$ and fully complies with $Void_F2$. On the other hand, it differs from some popular practices such as Distributed Morphology. Plus, its tenability is contingent on giving a coherent explanation for the Semitic data and on accommodating the key data from those theories which make critical use of the bare root. The rest of this subsection aims to address these two concerns.

As a practical approach to the second task, I will re-examine the core facts from Marantz (1997) and Borer (2015), both mentioned in Chapter 3. Marantz' analysis is based on the grammaticality of an agent-denoting DP varying with the roots $\sqrt{\text{DESTROY}}$ and $\sqrt{\text{GROW}}$ in their verbal and nominal uses. Taking the feature [+ext] to be only in $\sqrt{\text{DESTROY}}$, suppose that the roots merge with the light verb, aka the shell in (29), to form *destroy* and *grow* independently of syntactic head-movement. In the clausal context, v provides the actual agent argument so that *destroy* is used transitively. In comparison, the root $\sqrt{\text{DIE}}$ has [−ext], making its verbal form *die* incompatible with the agent-introducing v and forcing the verb to be unaccusative only (recall from (29a-ii) that the shell *sh* only singles out theme from r). *Grow* is unspecified for [ext], readily accepting either v with the agent or no v for the unaccusative use. For the current purpose, whether *destruction* and *growth* are formed by merging the roots directly with some light noun shell or result from morphologically nominalizing the verbs *destroy* and *grow* makes no difference. *Destruction* still carries [+ext] and *growth* still does not. As long as the DP context contains no syntactic element, be it D or n, that introduces agent, only the possessor for *destruction* can be associated with [+ext] and interpreted accordingly. In other words, Marantz' insight remains valid whether r enters syntax by itself or already acquires categorial specification defined in (29). I return to the redundancy issue in theorization shortly.

Borer's (2015) key fact is (6–8) of Chapter 3, partially repeated below:

41. a. the form   to form
    b. an arrival   *to arrival
      *a fatten   to fatten
    c. wallpaper   to wallpaper
      math teacher   *to math teacher

A derivationally simple form as in (41a) may alternate between V and N but an overtly derived form cannot (41b). Furthermore, the same contrast holds with compounds in (41c) so that "simple compounds" pattern with (41a) and "derived compounds" pattern with (41b). Recall that for Borer, these examples motivate two kinds of X-equivalent categorial complement space (CCS): {Ex(X)} in syntax and $C_{Y[X]}$ in derivational morphology. When a word W can be used as either V or N without any derivational clue, as in (41a), it is because the root of W is directly placed in the corresponding syntactic CCS. See section 3.1 of Chapter 3 for details.

Of the two sources that provide categories for bare roots in this exoskeletal model (XSM), the morphological CCS is fully consistent with (29a). *Fatten*, for instance, enters syntax as a verb and is capable of projecting VP regardless of its internal structure. Regarding the syntactic CCS and contra Lexical Phonology and Morphology (LPM),[9] Borer (2015: 113) notes that letting derivationally simple words like *form* in (41a) be a verb independently of syntax, as is assumed by LPM, contains a theoretical redundancy: T selects a verbal complement, and *form* is separately labeled as a verb. In contrast, XSM only needs the first requirement because the root of *form* is directly placed in the V-equivalent CCP of T. The same redundancy exists with (29a).

One should be aware, though, that one of the sources of this redundancy is unavoidable in XSM too. Consider *form* and *formal*, of which only *form* can be either V or N. The XSM analysis attributes *form* to the syntactic CCS (= the complement of T or D) and *formal* to the morphological CCS (= the stem of *-al*). Since words from the second CCS also participate in syntax, it must be guaranteed in XSM that the syntactic context for adjectives, say [BE *formal*], is good while *[T *formal*] is not. In XSM parlance, the copula or whatever licenses the use of adjectives defines an A-equivalent CCS and *formal*, being A due to *-al* = $C_{A[N]}$, fits into the space. In contrast, T defines a V-equivalent CCS incompatible with the already adjectival *formal*. It is this categorial mismatch that rules out, say, the infinitive *to formal* or the tense-inflected *formaled*. In sum, when the rest of UG is taken into consideration, even XSM must require the CCS-defining head, D or T or whatever else, to perform a categorial check on a complement which already has its own lexical category.

With category-checking inevitable no matter what, it is not clear that XSM has a meta-theoretical advantage over LPM or (29a) in terms of redundancy. The decisive factor boils down to whether there is compelling empirical evidence for bare roots to play critical roles in syntax or not. The aforementioned observation by Borer (see (12) of Chapter 3) that *verbalize* cannot possibly have its thematic arguments from the root $\sqrt{\text{VERB}}$, already proves that at least some roots "have no syntactic properties" (= no projection or θ-role assignment), much as in our analysis of the Chinese NCAs.[10] Semitic causativization presents further evidence that allowing bare roots to participate in syntactic head-movement for the purpose of morphological word formation fails the facts. The same reasoning holds with (some implementations of) Distributed Morphology, which Borer's case of *verbalize* is explicitly aimed to refute. Overall, a blanket ban of bare roots from doing anything in syntax, namely $Void_F2$, would seem to be the theoretically simplest as long as it is capable of explaining various cross-linguistic facts in a uniform manner.

4.2.3   Mapping Morphology to Syntax

One such fact is anaphors in Semitic causativization summarized in (37). Given the proof that no syntactic head-movement of a bare root allows a unified account in this case, consider the Structural Mapping Hypothesis (SMH), a slightly revised version of Y. Li's (2005) proposal on mapping word-internal structure to syntax:

42. a. Every morphologically complex word W is formed with Merge in syntax whose input and output are both heads.
    b. For a constituent consisting of components X and Y with a semantic relation R, R maps to phrasal structure iff the mapping is legitimate according to UG.

Prosodic words such as *I'd've* that are not based on structural constituency are not included in (42a). By definition, phrases treated as words, as in *the old the-dog-ate-my-homework excuse*, extensively investigated by Bruening (2018: 7), are compatible with but not the concern of (42) given his argumentation that "the output of the phrasal system feeds word formation" (ibid.: 2). Specifically, (29) and (42) together dictate this design: When a lexical item L1 is used for Merge, it may serve as a head or a phrasal projection for the purely structural purpose (see Chomsky 1995); if the second party of this Merge is also a lexical item (L2) and both of them are regarded as heads, then the outcome is a new head. A bare root *r* can be one such head but is regulated by $Void_F2$. In effect, then, the L1-L2 cluster is but a syntactically formed new "lexical item" (call it

L3) via Merge that is ready to serve as the head of a phrase in syntax. This L1+L2=L3 process defined by (42a) corresponds to what Bruening, with a long linguistic tradition, refers to as "word formation." His statement above simply further allows a phrase to be reanalyzed as – literally squeezed into – a new head, a possibility that will not concern us here.

Though appearing to restate the lexicalist model of word formation, (42a) is in fact derivable from the most restrictive implementation of Merge, presumably the only operation for structure-building in UG (see Chomsky 2013, 2015 for recent thoughts on this). By definition, Merge concatenates two constituents – aka terms – that are either lexical items or constituents already undergoing Merge to form a new constituent. Thus, Merge (A, B) yields $\{A, B\} = C$. Consider External Merge (EM) first. Two scenarios of EM are frequently talked about: $\{X, YP\}$ and $\{XP, YP\}$. The first one projects X to XP with YP being the complement. The second one is the typical structure for adjuncts and specifiers.[11] Logically, however, there is a third scenario, $\{X, Y\}$, where both elements are lexical items and neither one qualifies for a maximal projection (e.g. due to UG principles such as thematic saturation and $Void_F2$). The result is a newly generated head H available for the next round of EM. The basic idea is that EM may produce either a phrase or a head, depending on other factors in UG. After all, if merging two phrasal constituents yields a new phrase, why can't merging two heads yield a new head?

For $\{X, Y\}$ to participate in EM as a head includes a large portion of (42a). It covers all the products of Borer's morphological CCS and compounds in general (independently of their components being bare forms or derived); it accommodates the $V = r + sh$ cases in (29a) if we think of Hale and Keyser's l-syntactic light verbs to be among the lexical items ready for EM; it also resolves a puzzle in Harley (2005). Observing that the lexical root of a denominal verb such as *hammer* (e.g. *hammer the metal for/in five minutes* (ibid.: 60)) is semantically an instrument to the event and "has no effect on the potential telicity of the vP", Harley makes this remark (p. 61):

> How can an element conflate with v from an adjunct position? While I do not pretend to understand how this can happen, since it runs counter to the assumption that incorporation of Roots in l-syntax is governed by the same principles that restrict head-movement in the overt syntax, it seems clear that some mechanism must be proposed which has exactly this effect.

The answer is that the task is indeed impossible if Merge only happens in phrasal contexts – $\{XP, YP\}$ in Harley's case, but $EM(\sqrt{HAMMER}, v)$ simply yields a "root-enriched" v when Merge exercises in the most general way: The outcome can be either a head or a phrase, determined by other parts of UG. The bare root $\sqrt{HAMMER}$ cannot project under $Void_F2$ and v cannot project for missing a complement. If one desires, this can be easily thought of as

UG-imposed head-level modification just as *with a hammer* modifies a verbal projection at the phrasal level. And just as Merge constructs a PP and then merges the cluster with the existing VP (V′ in X′-theory), so does Merge construct the √HAMMER-*v* head and then merge it with whatever complement *v* expects.

Moving to Internal Merge (IM), aka movement, (42a) clearly deviates from the popular practice of moving a head to the closest c-commanding head (Travis 1984) to form a morphologically complex word. However, it deserves noting that explaining morphological phenomena with head-movement is at the cost of a sloppy (bottom-up) Merge and a complicated c-command with questionable empirical implications. (43) is the structure for moving X to Y, both heads:

43.

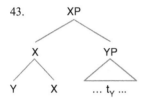

Prior to moving Y, the standalone constituent/term is XP, not X. Strictly speaking, then, (43) should not even happen because Y is not merged with another term but rather with a term of a term. And there is no compelling evidence that Merge of this kind exists at the phrasal level. To illustrate, Rudin (1988) regards parentheticals as evidence that in Bulgarian and similar Slavic languages, all fronted *wh*-expressions form an inseparable constituent resulting from first putting one *wh* in the Spec of CP position and then adjoining the other *wh* to it, a phrasal counterpart of what happens to Y and X in (43):

44. a. Koj   kakvo   ti   e   kazal?   (Rudin 1988 (28a))
         who   what   2s   has   told
         'Who told you what?'
     b. ?*Koj, spored   tebe, kakvo e   kazal? (Rudin 1988 (46a))
         who   according.to 2s   what   has   said
         'Who, according to you, said what?'

But as Bošković (2002: footnote 15) points out: "This is true under the adjunction-to-Spec, CP analysis, but not under the multiple-specifiers analysis. Under this analysis [(44b)] can be ruled out owing to a feature clash: a [−*wh*, −*focus*] element is located in a [+*wh*, +focus] CP." Overall, clear cases of phrasal movement characteristically avoid the phrasal counterpart of (43), a welcome generalization since IM in particular and Merge in general will be kept simpler and cleaner.

A direct consequence of allowing (43) is to force c-command to be sensitive to segments so that Y can still license its trace by ignoring the top segment of X. And this is not merely a theoretical complication. With Chomsky's (1995) bare phrase structure increasingly adopted, there is no structural distinction between a segment such as the higher X in (43) and what used to be called XP immediately dominating the Spec position, both being projections of X. If Y can c-command its own trace by ignoring the X segment above it, so should the possessor DP of the subject c-command the object. Clearly, this is not the case: *Whose friends admire *himself/him/the bastard*. In conclusion, a syntactic theory adopting the simplest form of IM will prevent (43), simplify c-command consequently, and maximally unify the structural behavior of heads and phrases while promising to fare better with facts. As a matter of fact, if (43) is never generatable in UG so that (42a) is the only means to merge morphemes into syntactic heads, we not only eliminate one more non-trivial difference between EM and IM (see Chomsky 2013), but are also enabled to explain the Semitic data pattern in (37), to which we turn now.

Given (42a) and (29a), the morphologically causativized *ʔajlas* 'made.sit' in (35b), labeled V given our intuition (though nothing critical hangs on it), literally results from multiple times of head-level Merge (tense ignored):

45. $[_{v_1} [caus [_{v_2} [sh j \ldots l \ldots s]]]] = \textit{ʔajlas} = V$

The demonstration of how the morphological complex in (45) behaves in syntax follows left-to-right sentence-generation in Chapter 3 and section 4.3 later.

At Step *n*, the structure is (46):

46. $\ldots$ T $[_{vP1}$ subj1 $[_{v'}$ V $[_{VP1}$ V$_{copy}]]]$

Subj1 is from v_1 inside V. The semantic relation R between $v1$ and the rest of (45), i.e. what starts with *caus*, falls under (42b) and must be represented in syntax iff it can. Assuming Kratzer's theory of agentivity, this R is event-identification and maps to v_1 with a VP complement in UG. Given the standard assumptions about IM, the head of this VP complement would place the overt copy at the v_1 location and keep the *in situ* copy phonologically empty, marked in (46) with V$_{copy}$. Other than the direction of structure-generation, the standard head-movement differs from the current analysis only in that a lexical verb/root and v start in different spots and the verb/root is moved up to build (43), which I already rejected. Consequently, what the so-called head-movement involves is *always* a separately formed head word with all the intended morphemes inside it through Merge, namely V in (45). Coupled with left-to-right gener-ation, V in the v_1 position of (46) is the whole *ʔajlas* 'made.sit', so is V$_{copy}$ heading VP1. Critically, because (46) is a legitimate structural representation of the semantic relation R between v_1 and the rest of V in (45), it must be so represented in accordance with (42b).

The next few steps of derivation follow exactly the same reasoning. The semantic relation between *caus* and $[v_2 [sh j \ldots l \ldots s]]$ in (45) is obviously one of thematic object, which also maps to the head–complement relation in syntax, further expanding VP1 in (46). At Step $n+i$, (46) becomes (47):

47. ... T $[_{vP1}$ subj1 $[_{v1'}$ V $[_{VP1}$ V$_{copy}$ $[_{vP2}$ subj2 $[_{v2'}$ V$_{copy}$ $[_{VP2}$ V$_{copy}$ $(\ldots)]]]]]]$

At this point, the only two components in V of (45) whose semantic relation is not syntactically reflected are the verbal shell *sh* and the bare root. I admit to being uncertain what kind of semantic relation holds between them, but this uncertainty does not matter because, given Void$_F$2, the bare root $j \ldots l \ldots s$ has no categorial specification and thus does not project in syntax anyway. In other words, whatever R is between *sh* and the root, its syntactic representation is not doable by UG and thus $sh+j \ldots l \ldots s$ must act as a non-decomposable single unit in syntax. Applied to (47), this means no further structural expansion from the internal semantics of the morphological causative *ʔajlas* 'made.sit'. The more familiar counterpart of this situation would be for the V$_{copy}$ inside VP2 to be (the trace of) the simple verbal form of the root, namely the intransitive use of *sit* (see (35a)).

The "(...)" in (47) stands for any constituent affiliated with the *sh+r* part of (45). If there is an anaphor in " ... ", its binding domain must be *v*P2, making subj2 the only legitimate binder, already seen in (35) and (38b) and summarized in (37a). If the root is part of an unaccusative verb (e.g. (35c)), *sh+r* will have a theme argument also in " ... ". But other requirements from UG such as Case and/or the Extended Projection Principle will make it subj2 so that the complement of V1 remains the binding domain for any anaphor still in "(...)". In brief, even though the frequently assumed (43) is replaced by (42a), (42b) still explains why morphological causativization, aka verb-incorporation, behaves like a bi-clausal structure for binding as Baker (1988) demonstrated. This is so because (42b) forces the syntactically formed and compositionally complex head, V in (45), to map to the structure (47).

The morphological causatives in (36), say *ʔaɣmam* 'made.upset', are created via Merge in the same way:

48. $[v [caus [a [sh_A \gamma \ldots m \ldots m]]]] = ʔaɣmam = $ V

(48) differs from (45) only in the shell being adjectival as demanded by the root. Whereas *v* is responsible for providing the agent argument, exactly how the semantic subject of adjective is related to a separate head such as *a* is less certain (see Bowers 1993, Baker 2002, Y. Li 2005 on relevant discussions). As will become clear shortly, however, whether there is the small *a* in (48) does not

matter as long as syntax has a way to have the subject of the adjective expressed in the clausal context so as to satisfy the θ-criterion.

At Step n, the syntactic structure generated from left to right under (42b) is (49), no different from (46) at this point of derivation:

49. ... T [$_{vP}$ subj [$_v$ V] [$_{VP}$ V$_{copy}$]]

Step $n+1$ is to (try to) map the semantic relation between *caus* and [a [sh_A y ... m ... m]] in (48) to syntax as dictated by (42b). Whether or not a is present in this case, the second portion of the morphological causative is adjectival in category. The semantic relation R at hand is again one of thematic object (cf. *make [someone upset]*). If this R is mapped to syntax, the structure would be (50):

50. ... T [$_{vP}$ subj1 [$_v$ V] [$_{VP}$ V$_{copy}$ [$_{aP/AP}$ subj2 a/A ...]]]

Unlike (46) earlier, though, (50) cannot even be generated if UG employs Merge.

Recall that V$_{copy}$ = *ʔaymam* 'made.upset' = V ≠ A. In order to expand the structure of VP in (49–50) to reflect R between *caus* and the rest, the only means is to have another V$_{copy}$ so as to head the complement of *caus*. But V$_{copy}$ only projects to VP/vP and not the desired AP/aP. In sum, the semantic relation between *caus* and the adjectival component in (48) has no legitimate representation in syntax. By (42b), if this relation is not syntactically representable, it is not represented at all. It follows that the syntactic structure for (48) stops expanding at (49), intuitively corresponding to *caus+A* necessarily functioning as a non-decomposable unit. As (49) is but a mono-clausal structure, the thematic argument of the adjectival component, be it from a or the shell, must act as the object of the *caus+A* head inside the one and only VP. If there is another VP-internal constituent introducing an anaphor, as in (36) and (38a), the binding domain for it must be the entire clause. Other parts of Semitic grammar qualify the subject from v to be the only antecedent in (49).[12]

At this point, three clarifications are called for. First, while the analysis is presented with left-to-right sentence-generation, the outcome with respect to Semitic causativization remains the same in the reversed bottom-up model. As long as (42a) is adopted, the head-level Merge necessarily creates a verb out of an adjectival root. And a verb, by nature, does not project an AP/aP, thereby preventing the semantic relation between *caus* and A/a from any phrase-level expression. Second, the foregoing analysis assumes that what we perceive to be a causativized verb is always formed under (42a) and consists of the root, the default shell and the agent-introducing embedded v, among other components. With these contents, the verb and its copies are capable of projecting VP and vP. In contrast, a similar verb with an adjectival component cannot project AP or *a*P. I take this contrast to result from the values of the categorial features: *v* and V share [+V, −N], so a verbal head containing *v* qualifies to act as head of either *v*P or VP. A and *a* are categorially [+V, +N] and no AP/*a*P can be projected from a verbal head with [+V, −N]. The analysis also assumes that a proper part of the product of head-level Merge can participate in the phrasal mapping but is unable to form a copy of its own in this mapping. E.g. the *a*+A cluster in (48) cannot be singled out from the entire morpheme string and used as a standalone head to generate (50). I return to this restriction later.

Lastly, while (42b) plays a critical role in regulating the mapping between the inter-morphemic relations inside a word and their syntactic representations, it expectedly has zero effect on components involving phrases. Let Merge generate {A, B} = C with at least one of A and B being phrasal. By definition, whatever is the semantic relation R between A and B is already represented at the phrasal level. If R were not legitimately represented, C could not be formed in the first place. Thus (42b) is met automatically. Its effects become visible for head-level merging precisely because a cluster of morphemes treated as a single head H has two options: If some R in H has a UG-sanctioned phrasal expression, the latter will become reality under (42b); if this mapping fails, H is not ruled out but instead simply stays as a non-decomposable head. It is this second choice that is not only underneath the Semitic adjective-rooted causatives but also the very mechanism for many kinds of compounds. For instance, *house-dog* encodes a semantic relation of modification R_M.[13] Mapping R_M to phrasal structure would yield an adjunct structure which blocks movement (recall Harley's puzzle above). Hence R_M has no legitimate phrase-level representation. But all is not lost because we have the option of falling back to treating *house-dog* simply as a non-decomposable N for syntactic purposes.

I end the exploration of (42) by looking at noun-incorporation, of which the representative fact is given in (11). The relevant fact is the subject–object asymmetry: In the incorporated N-V form, N must be interpreted as the semantic object of V and never the subject. Hence the contrast between (11b-c) which Baker (1988) derives from syntax:

51.

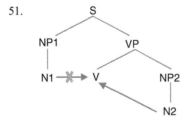

Moving N2 to V is grammatical because NP2 is not an island and the movement targets a c-commanding position. Neither condition is met if N1 moves to V, resulting in the observed asymmetry.

The success in explaining this morphological phenomenon with independently motivated syntactic apparatuses constitutes one of two major arguments from Baker – the other being the bi-clausal behavior of verb-incorporation – for the head-movement approach to word formation. But like verb-incorporation, the head-movement in (51) results in N2 adjoining to V, the same pattern as (43) which I replaced with (42a). More significantly, there is now an alternative way to account for the subject–object asymmetry in noun-incorporation. Let Merge form a head-level $\{N, V\}$ with these two logical options (linear order irrelevant):

52. a. $[_N \text{ N V}]$
     b. $[_V \text{ N V}]$

If N is meant to be for Arg_E, the fact that its semantic relation with V is neither thematic nor modificational leaves UG unable to choose between (52a, b) as the R_S for N and V, a head-level counterpart of the phrasal dilemma in (18). Hence the USM interferes by mapping the external nature of Arg_E to being structurally external to any projection of V under the iconicity of independence. Consequently, (52a) is chosen, which, as discussed extensively earlier, takes the form of -er in English and the large set of individual-denoting nominal morphemes in Chinese (see (12)). Meanwhile, since (52b) is banned by the USM, it is never possible to have an agent-denoting N in noun-incorporation. See Y. Li (2005) for accounting for other aspects of the phenomenon.

This alternative analysis of noun-incorporation immediately creates a redundancy: In the mainstream theory of UG, both the structural representation of Arg_E and head-movement (with head-adjunction in (43) permitted) can derive the subject–object asymmetry in (11). Initially, the head-movement approach is favorable because syntax shows the promise to subsume morphology (and word formation in general; see Hale and Keyser 1993, 2002) in a principled manner. Letting syntax do word formation is the position of this work as well. The difference lies in whether adjunction to another head via movement is the right way to go. (53) summarizes the theoretical and empirical disadvantages of (43):

53. a. Keeping Merge from its simplest form of always targeting the outer edge;
     b. Complicating c-command with segments;
     c. Unclear how to account for Semitic morphological causativization;
     d. Unable to form many kinds of words (cf. Harley's (2005) puzzle);
     e. Creating a redundancy in noun-incorporation.

Especially worth attention is (53d). If many compounds (e.g. *house-dog* and *whiteboard*) and derived words (e.g. *hammer* as V) rely on directly merging morphemes, then (42a) is a must-have in UG, which in turn argues for resolving (53e) by forbidding UG from adjoining a head to another via movement. That taking this step also helps simplify other parts of UG in (53a-b) is a theoretical plus. A unified explanation of morphological causativization based on cross-linguistic data proves that (42) can do what (43) can, but not vice versa. Last but not least, the SMH in (42) endorses head-movement – the instances of V_{copy} in (47) are all "traces" of the causativized verbal root ending up in the matrix v_I if one adopts the bottom-up order of clause-generation. What the SMH replaces is the particular implementation of head-movement with all the issues in (53).

4.3   Linearizing Arg_E and Its Cohorts

At this point, four cases of iconicity interacting with UG have been looked into. Of these, three involve linear iconicity and one, iconicity of independence that maps the expression of Arg_E to a hierarchical structural design (e.g. *v*P above VP). Of interest to us is that even Arg_E exhibits a striking property in linearization, namely there is an extremely strong tendency – with almost 97 percent of the languages of the world – for the subject to precede the object. This section is dedicated to understanding this side of Arg_E.

Within the tradition of UG, linearization has been taken as a parameterized function of the hierarchical structure, what we describe with the R_S-to-R_L mapping throughout this book (except when iconicity takes over the task). As it turns out, there are two compelling reasons for articulating a theory of linearization for the UG-I interface which must be different from what are found in the literature.

First, the multi-plane model of coordination in Chapter 3 rests critically on generating sentences from the structurally highest constituent downward so that the first conjunct, for instance, acquires the needed superiority in grammatical behavior. Thus, a theory of linearization is needed to guarantee that this direction of structure-building is at the core of the F_{HL} in the way of a non-negotiable law. Not every specific implementation of UG has this property. Chomsky's (1995) Minimalist Program even explicitly assumes the exactly opposite bottom-up generation. The only explicit systematic attempt at tying word order with structural hierarchy is Kayne's (1994) antisymmetric syntax. As will be shown later, however, his theory has both insights to be kept and fundamental weaknesses sufficient to call for an alternative. Such an alternative will be formulated in 4.3.4 so that top-down sentence-production is enforced.

Second, recall from Chapter 2 that the linear arrangement of the verbs in SVCs is not decided by UG but by iconicity. Underneath this analysis lies the logical necessity that the product of iconicity is at least compatible with what is permitted by UG. The same expectation is already stated in (5b) of Chapter 1, that any iconicity-induced R_S would have to be "UG-compliant" since the corresponding constituent structure is still within the scrutiny of UG and any deviation would be trashed. The R_S-to-R_L mapping is no different. As a concrete example, suppose the linearization algorithm used by languages were Kayne's Linear Correspondence Axiom (LCA) which pairs linear precedence obligatorily with asymmetric c-command. It would follow that VP2 could not even be a right-adjoined adjunct for V1, contra the fact from Sranan (see (117) of Chapter 2 and the discussion thereabout). The same problem arises from the multi-plane theory of coordination. With all conjuncts inevitably linearized, a parallel structure is downright impossible for the LCA, as made clear by Kayne's own adoption (and adaptation) of &P. In brief, the right theory of linearization for F_{HL} must be flexible enough to accommodate the multiple structural options for the SVCs and the symmetric relation among conjuncts. For sure, a more "conventional" model of linearization which does not advocate a 1-to-1 correspondence between hierarchy and linearization is indeed flexible for these purposes. As will be shown, however, it would be too flexible to explain the linear location of Arg_E (and other clause-initial constituents). Again, a theory of linearization which incorporates the strengths of these existing ones while accommodating the word-order issues in this book is an unavoidable portion of the UG-I theory.

Equally worth keeping in mind is the general goal of this work: to identify, explore and eventually understand the boundaries of UG, namely how many interfaces there are beyond the familiar ones (e.g. sensorimotor, conceptual–intentional). It turns out that the alternative theory of linearization articulated later in this chapter indeed explores a new area of interaction between UG and an extra-linguistic factor.

4.3.1   The Locations of Arg_E and the Theoretical Challenge

(54) reports the word order typology survey by Dryer (2013) on the linear distribution of the subject (S), verb (V) and object (O). The parenthesized numbers discount those languages "lacking a dominant word order" (ibid.); the percentages are calculated by me with this discount (see below for the mixed group):[14]

54.	SOV	SVO	VSO	VOS	OVS	OSV	Mixed	Total
	564	488	95	25	11	4	189(0)	1376(1187)
	>47.5%	>41.1%	>8%	>2%	<1%	>0.3%		100%

Since Emonds (1980), robust evidence has been accumulated that VSO is derived from the same underlying structure as SVO plus verb-raising over the subject (see Roberts 2001 for a literature review). Together, SVO and VSO count for slightly more than 49.1 percent of the total languages in the survey and highlight three patterns:

55. a. SOV + (SVO + VSO) > 96.6%
    b. These three popular word orders are correlated with S before O.
    c. SOV (>47.5%) and SVO+VSO (>49.1%) essentially evenly divide (55a).

Also see Tomlin (1986) for a 402-language survey with a similar result.

(55a-b) suggest an overwhelmingly strong factor favoring S before O. If we equate S to Arg_E[15] (but ignore the subject of unaccusative verbs which we will see later to pose no problem with our analysis), the strong tendency maps to the Spec of vP or TP predominantly preceding the complement. In fact, not only does the 3.3 percent of the other three types make one wonder whether they are only apparent exceptions, especially considering that none of these languages are, to my knowledge, as carefully and extensively studied as, say, Chinese, English and Hebrew, but there also exists a promising perspective in which the rare word orders can be subsumed under the prevalent ones. In Arabic, both SVO and VSO are popular. For one thing, this fact supports the conclusion that VSO is a variant of SVO – it is simply a matter of inter- or intra-linguistic variation. For another, this realization opens a door to understanding the rare types. For instance, Dryer finds that OVS only coexists with SOV in a single language. It becomes plausible, then, that what appears to be OVS should be grouped into SOV. I return to more details later.

Out of these considerations, we will assume for now that the Spec of TP always linearly precedes the complement. In fact, Kayne's LCA, informally stated below, generalizes this word order to all phrases in all languages (with structural height defined in terms of asymmetric c-command):

56. Structurally higher iff linearly earlier.

Part of the LCA is empirically substantiated: The subject, topic and *wh*-phrase all move to higher structural positions and all cross-linguistically occur earlier than the rest of the clause. In this sense, there exists a truly universal generalization:

57. The perceived production of a clause is always from top downward.

The question is why.

It must be noted that the LCA is not in itself the answer to the question but rather a precise statement of (part of; see below) the fact, there being no self-evident reason for the correlation in (56) to be true but its reversal to be false. Aware of this fact, Kayne (1994) offers "a possible explanation" (p. 36) which consists of three parts:

58. a. Since there is a root node that dominates every node except itself in any given structure but there is no comparable "root node" for c-command, a parallel "abstract node A" is proposed that "asymmetrically c-commands every other node ... [by] being adjoined to the root node" (ibid.).

   b. Assuming A to dominate "an abstract terminal *a*," *a* should precede all other terminals (vs. following them) if sentence-production keeps track of the total substring of terminals at that point (e.g. *ab*, *abc*, *abcd*) and if *a* is expected to be present in each substring (a string-final *a* would occur only in the final substring: *b*, *bc*, *bcd*, *bcda*) (p. 37).

   c. With *a* preceding all other terminals, the mapping function *D* from any pair of nodes <X, Y>, where X asymmetrically c-commands Y, to the pair of terminals <*x*, *y*> with a linear relation R must have R to be precedent because inputting <A, Y> to *D* yields <*a*, *y*> and *a* precedes *y* due to (58b) (ibid.).

Hence the LCA in (56).

The stipulative nature of (58a) is obvious since there is no *a priori* reason for asymmetric c-command to parallel dominance. In fact, the very effort to make them similar draws the two apart. First, the root node for dominance is not "abstract" the way A is. Second, dominance is a pure hierarchical relation independent of time, but the hierarchical relation of asymmetric c-command is not as pure for being tied to time via (58b). Third, does dominance hold for full nodes only just as asymmetric c-command does under the LCA? If it does so that the two relations are truly parallel, then the full root node does not dominate the abstract node A since A is adjoined to the root node R and thus is outside a segment of R. So R does not dominate all terminals, in particular not *a*, after all. If dominance applies to all nodes including segments, the top segment of R indeed dominates A, but this will distinguish dominance fundamentally from asymmetric c-command since the latter only holds for full nodes. All in all, the very nature of dominance and asymmetric c-command prevents them from being fully parallel. Then why should partial similarity matter at all and in this particular manner so as to result in the LCA?

(58b) is intuitively appealing if we keep a track of how much of a clause has been generated at any point of derivation. But it already assumes asymmetric c-command to play a role in a particular manner. In fact, with the bottom-up repetitive application of Merge in the Minimalist Program, it would seem totally natural that a clause be incrementally produced along the way. Let Merge start with X and Y. The particular language determines parametrically to set one of them as (dominating) the all-preceding terminal, say *y*. From this point onward, each application of Merge will yield a substring, *yx*, *yxz*, *yxzw*, . . ., till the completion of the sentence. So *y* precedes all other terminals in each substring, just as (58b) does with the abstract terminal *a*, but it differs from *a* in not needing to be hypothesized because *y* is simply a real lexical item that the language picks to start Merge with. It follows that the core idea in (58b) could easily lead to the opposite direction of sentence-generation plus the flexibility of allowing head-initial and head-final structures, a desirable property I return to shortly.[16]

(58c) not only presumes (58a-b) for explication but also risks circularity. The critical element of the LCA is a consistent mapping between asymmetric c-command and a constant linear order, a claim which is plausible and even attractive but not automatically true. The mapping function D encodes this element, so logically, D cannot participate in an independent justification of the LCA. Imagine D to allow any inter- or intra-linguistic parametric variation and thus to not necessarily be a uniform mapping function. Adopting a as assumed in (58a,b) certainly has D map <A, Y> to <a, y> so that a precedes y, which could be argued to hold universally. But this outcome says nothing automatically about "non-abstract" terminals that are assembled, say, in a head-final pattern. In other words, the uniform mapping of the LCA cannot be "explained" by assuming a uniform mapping.

In conclusion, the LCA in (56) is a stipulation with no explanation. Given what has been learned in the past decades of syntactic research, its empirical validity is confirmed only with respect to the higher portion of the clause, namely (57). Below, I will go through a few reasons why (57) is a more accurate generalization than (56).

First, whereas (56) holds with the upper portion of a clause – hence (57), it is not clear that it is empirically or even theoretically validated with the rest of the clause. A direct consequence of (56) is that the head H must precede the complement XP because H asymmetrically c-commands everything inside XP. It follows that all human languages should be head-initial while, factually, there is an even division between head-initial and head-final languages, shown in (55c). Kayne's solution is to hypothesize the complement to parametrically raise to some local Spec position (1994: Section 5.1) but no motivation is given for such a raising operation. So why do half of human languages opt for moving all of their complements up while the other half choose to keep them *in situ*?

This question is better appreciated from a meta-theoretical perspective. Letting the LCA regulate the linearization of all human languages seems to simplify UG. In reality, it is a partial shift of labor. As Uriagereka (1998) notes, not all behaviors of a biological system need to be genetically programmed. The leopard must have a built-in mechanism (muscle contractions and nervous activities) to leap into the air, but the rest of the leap is taken care of by the laws of physics. Similarly, once UG sets up the head–complement relation, a language only needs to make a cross-categorial generalization, aka parameterization, from the two choices provided by probability. With the LCA, none of these factors and decisions are eliminated – one simply shifts the probability-governed options in pure linearization to the language-specific but statistically randomized decision to keep the complement *in situ* or not. In addition, an extra operation of movement is needed for half of the languages. I take it that a theory of linearization relying on probability alone is a better one than one relying on probability plus movement, provided that (57) can be derived from some general principle, as will be shown below.

The LCA is equally challenged on empirical grounds. A substantial portion of its linearizing power rests on ignoring segments. A purely linguistic complication without any mathematical meaning, the distinction between full nodes and segments makes a number of wrong predictions about how language behaves in syntax. Some of these were already mentioned previously. With (31) of Chapter 3, we recounted that Kayne analyzes *We know whose article those are* by letting the *wh*-possessor c-command the [+*wh*] C beyond the DP *whose article*. That a *wh*-expression inside a DP is indeed in the Spec of DP is confirmed by expressions like *I wonder* [[*how good an idea*] *he can produce.*] where the *wh*-AP occurs left of the determiner *an*. Then the LCA wrongly predicts the *wh*-possessor to c-command the rest of the clause for binding (see (32) of Chapter 3). At the beginning of section 4.3 earlier, the LCA's problems with the various structural options of SVCs were also emphasized. In sum, if segment-blindness makes the LCA overly powerful, the syntactic properties of the SVCs prove it to be not permissive enough. In comparison, since (57) is concerned only with the upper portion of the clausal structure, enough room is left for different variations in the VP-internal structure, which is exactly what is needed to accommodate SVCs. (57) is but a generalization. The precise formulation of the alternative theory of linearization with the effect of (57) will be such that parametric head-locations and the parallel structure of coordination are naturally permitted as well.

Li et al. (2012) present a different kind of fact against the LCA-induced structure of syntax. Adverbs are known to fall into different semantically identifiable classes with corresponding syntactic positions (their (82), (84) and (86b, d), respectively):

59. a. John regularly noisily drinks his soup.
    b. *John noisily regularly drinks his soup.

60. a. *John drinks his soup regularly noisily.
    b. John drinks his soup noisily regularly.

61. a. Regularly, John drinks his soup noisily.
    b. Noisily, John drinks his soup (*regularly).

Frequency adverbs (Fr) such as *regularly* are known to be higher than manner adverbs (Ma) like *noisily* (Cinque 1999). When preverbal, this structural hierarchy maps to linear precedence by left adjunction, shown in (59) and in compliance with the LCA. The complication arises when both classes occur postverbally in (60), where acceptability correlates with the mirror images of

(59), namely Fr must follow Ma to be good. The contrast in (61) confirms that even when postverbal, *regularly* is still structurally higher than *noisily* so as to prevent the latter from being fronted.

The pattern in (59–61) is easily accounted for with the non-LCA theory of adjunct linearization: Each class adjoins on either side to the responding verbal projection (Bowers 1993); since the adjunction spot for Fr must be higher than that for Ma (V′), the mirror images follow automatically and (61b) results from moving *noisily* across the higher *regularly*, a typical minimality effect (Rizzi 1990). But this analysis becomes unavailable to the LCA because, again, right-adjunction (i.e. $[_{X'}\ [_{X'}\ V\ DP]\ AdvP]$) is disallowed for being higher than the head and complement but linearly later, directly contradicting (56). In order for the postverbal *regularly* to stay structurally higher than *noisily*, [*drink his soup*] must move across the adverbs so as to strand them behind. As Li et al. (2012) point out, there are two derivational routes to this end (p. 249):

62. a.   ... [__ [$_{FP1}$ *regularly* F1 [$_X$ [$_{VP}$ *drink his soup*] [$_{FP2}$ *noisily* F2 t$_{VP}$]]]]
    b-i. ... [[$_X$ [$_{VP}$ *drink his soup*] [$_{FP2}$ *noisily* F2 t$_{VP}$]] [$_{FP1}$ *regularly* F1 t$_X$]]
    b-ii. ... [[$_{VP}$ *drink his soup*] [$_{FP1}$ *regularly* F1 [$_X$ t$_{VP}$ [$_{FP2}$ *noisily* F2 t$_{VP}$]]]]

(62a) is the shared step, with the VP in a Spec position before FP2, the phrase that supports *noisily* as demanded by the LCA. (62b) gives the options from this point onward. In (62b-i), the entire X in (62a) moves to the "__" position of the same kind as the first landing site of VP. This derivation yields the desired word order in (60b). Since *noisily* is inside the raised X, which in turn must be in a Spec position, it can be plausibly prevented from further movement if the Spec is a subject island. This explains (61b). But short of ad hoc stipulations, UG equally permits (62b-ii) where VP moves successive-cyclically from the pre-FP2 position to the pre-FP1 position, under the logically inevitable assumption that either position can accept VP (cf. [*drink his soup* [$_{FP1}$ *regularly* t$_{VP}$]]). But this route generates the unacceptably ordered (60a), highlighting the empirical disadvantage of the structure proliferation necessitated by the LCA.

Even some claimed empirical supports for the LCA lose their force or end up being problematic for it. Its initial motivations, the set of X′-theoretic properties, no longer need the LCA for an explanation. Binary-branching, unique-headedness, etc. are now the natural outcome of Merge. The unique Spec is never a clearly universal fact given the well-known multiple *wh* in Slavic languages (see the discussion of (44) above) and the multiple nominatives in East Asian languages. A correlation was observed by Kayne, "that agglutinative YX (where Y originates below X) will primarily be found in strongly head-final languages" (Kayne 1994: 53). Given the LCA which only allows head-initial XPs, a head-final language like Korean must implement the (aforementioned) system-wide raising of complements to Spec positions:

63.

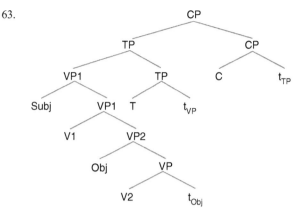

Assuming the lexical verb to stay at V2, (63) creates a linear adjacency for the three heads V2, T and C which are spelled out in a row but do not form a constituent all by themselves. For Kayne, this explains why strong head-final languages are correlated with morphological agglutination, namely each morpheme has a single grammatical or semantic function. Now consider the much simpler alternative structure in which being head-final results from the probability-based parametric choice of the language:

64.

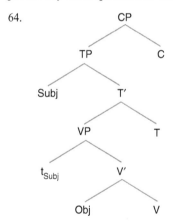

V, T and C are still linearly adjacent. As long as there are independent principles against moving V to T and T to C, and there are indeed (see below), (64) is clearly preferred over (63) with a simpler structure and fewer – not to mention obscurely motivated – operations.

Consider another correlation bearing on (63): "that interrogative *wh*-movement is generally absent from SOV (i.e. from consistently head-final) languages" (Kayne 1994: 54). Attributing this fact to Bach (1971), Kayne reasons that *wh*-movement is blocked because the Spec of CP, the destined landing site for *wh*, is now occupied by the raised TP in (63). But this analysis is refuted by Kayne's own account of the examples in (65) (1994: 24, examples (21–22); my (31) of Chapter 3), with the structures added to help explication:

65. a. We know [$_{CP}$ [$_{DP}$ whose [$_{DP}$ D articles]] C$_{[+wh]}$ [$_{TP}$ those are]].
     b. *We know [$_{CP}$ [$_{DP}$ articles by who(m)] C [$_{TP}$ those are]].

With *whose* in the Spec position of *whose articles* plus c-command blind to segments (= the outer DP segment in (65a)), *whose* asymmetrically c-commands the [+wh] C and thereby licenses the embedded *wh*-clause. In contrast, *who* in (65b) is inside the full DP node and cannot c-command C outside DP, leading to ungrammaticality. Logically, then, the Spec of the Spec of the Spec, indefinitely down the tree, is still able to c-command outward because each Spec is separated from the outside only by a segment of the node it is the Spec of. It follows that (63) cannot block *wh*-movement after all: Even though TP fills the Spec of CP and VP fills the Spec of TP, there must exist some Spec along the leftmost branches of the tree, e.g. the subject in VP1, that does not have a Spec of its own. And this Spec c-commands the rest of the clause. Moving a *wh*-phrase to this position would be both allowed for movement and permit the *wh*-phrase to c-command C asymmetrically. In sum, while Bach's observation deserves an explanation, the LCA-based theory of syntax is not up to the task.

Overall, the inclusion of the LCA in UG is at the cost of increased structures and extra operations (compare (63) and (64)), complicated definitions and analyses (like c-command, segments and insufficiently motivated operations), obscure empirical advantages (e.g. the facts correlated with agglutination) and even contra-fact predictions (see (59–61) and *wh*-possessors unable to bind beyond the DP containing them). Meanwhile, the LCA has the insight into the upper part of clauses (including Arg$_E$ but not limited to it), as summarized in (57). Ideally, what UG needs is a theory of linearization that derives (57) while giving just the right amount of flexibility for the rest of the clause.

4.3.2   Deriving (57): The Theory

If the LCA is set aside, one naturally wonders why (57), the desirable part of the LCA, is universally true. An apparently viable road to pursue is information structure. One could imagine that structurally higher (i.e. symmetrically c-commanding) constituents represent old information and that some hardwired human cognitive trait favors laying out old information before introducing new information. The study of cartographic syntax (see Cinque and Rizzi

2010) has made explicit how information structure is represented in syntax. Consider the Italian example below (Rizzi 1997: 290):

66. A Gianni, QUESTO, domani, gli dovrete dire.
    to Gianni this tomorrow 3s you.should tell
    'To Gianni, THIS, tomorrow, you should tell him.'

In a clause, there can be multiple topics (*a Gianni* and *domani* 'tomorrow' in (66)) but no more than one focus (*questo* 'this'). Rizzi's explanation is that a Focus head introduces new information through the constituent in its Spec position (= *questo* 'this') and takes its complement to be the presupposition; since presuppositions are by definition infelicitous with new information, no FocusP may recursively exist inside the complement of the Focus head. Topics, themselves expressing old information, merely take what follows as comments and nothing prevents a topic-comment expression from serving as the comment of another topic (or the presupposition for focus). Significant to our concern is that (i) QUESTO 'THIS' expresses new information but still occurs earlier and higher than the rest of the clause which (ii) includes *domani* 'tomorrow' being the second topic with old information as well as the subject, the Arg$_E$ whose linear order has initiated the current discussion. In a word, the distribution of QUESTO complies with (57) but information structure is at least insufficient for explaining its structural position.[17]

Another possible line of reasoning to pursue for (57), which I believe is more or less on the right track, is the direction of binding. We know for certain that movement always happens from a structurally lower domain to a structurally higher domain. Suppose that there exists an advantage in letting the moved constituent linearly "antecede" its trace. The result would lead to the antecedent in a higher spot preceding the origin of the movement inside a lower domain. But one needs to be careful about utilizing this logic. For one thing, other coindexed dependencies are not as strict on the antecedent being linearly earlier:

67. a. Her$_i$ relatives all adore Sarah$_i$.
    b. The rumors about each other$_k$ have made Jack and Jill$_k$ very amused.

For another, certain *in situ* constituents, e.g. quantifiers and *wh*-phrases, are well known for projecting their scopes to higher functional regions of a clause. Since scopes are represented through operators, an *in situ* scopal element relies on a dependency relation structurally indistinguishable from a movement chain – in fact, many scholars have argued, at least since May (1977), that the two are from the same operation. It can be concluded, then, that UG allows either end of a dependency to be phonologically spelled out. If so, what prevents a language from choosing an incremental bottom-up spell-out of sentences? For sure, this option would have the structurally lower trace produced earlier than the moved and overt binder. But that would simply have the temporally latter end of the dependency assume the overt form. Other than reversing the direction of sentence-production, the process would be the direct counterpart of keeping a *wh*-phrase *in situ*.

Given these considerations, I propose that (57) is the outcome of UG's sensitivity to operational cost under the 2nd law of thermodynamics,[18] starting with a brief introduction of the latter for readers unfamiliar with this subject matter.

Thermodynamics has the 2nd law stated in multiple ways. In this section, we take the definition that "[n]atural processes are accompanied by an increase in the entropy of the universe" (Atkins 1994: 32), where entropy is a measurement of chaos, namely the degree of dispersal of initially localized energy. The particular equation – $S = k \log W$ – from Ludwig Boltzmann is carved at the top of his gravestone (Figure 4.1): In the equation, S is the entropy of an isolated thermodynamic system T_S, k is Boltzmann's constant which, for the purpose of the current discussion, may be taken as the multiplicative identity (i.e. 1), log is natural logarithm and W is the number of possible arrangements

Figure 4.1 Boltzmann's entropy equation and tombstone
Photograph by Thomas Schneider, 2002, http://users.fred.net/tds/lab/boltz mann.html, with owner's permission

Figure 4.2 T$_S$ with 10 gray on-particles and 40 white off-particles

of the energetically "on-particles" in T$_S$ while the total number of on-particles in T$_S$ remains the same.

To illustrate how entropy S measures chaos, consider a T$_S$ with 50 particles of which 10 are energetically on-particles and 40 are off-particles. Furthermore, suppose T$_S$ starts with all the on-particles stacked together (Figure 4.2): For convenience' sake, one could imagine a freezingly cold room with a red-hot iron cube of a 10-particle size at one corner. In this state, there are 6 × 4 = 24 ways to arrange the on-particles as a whole. Hence, W = 24, S = ln 24 = 3.178.

But nature determines that adjacent particles will bump into one another and thereby pass (kinetic) energy from an on-particle to an off-particle. Intuitively, this spreading of on-ness, aka energy dissipation, is why, over time, the hot iron cube becomes cooler and the rest of the room becomes warmer, ending with everything "at room temperature." In terms of entropy, this intuition is expressed as follows. Assuming the room in Figure 4.2 to be an energetically isolated system so that no energy goes out nor in, the random spreading of the on-particles produces a total of 50!/(10!*(50–10)! = (50*49* ... *41)/10! = 10,272,278,170 ways (= number of microstates = W) to arrange the on-particles throughout the 50-particle space.[19] The entropy S of the room due to this natural dissipation is 23.053, a huge logarithmic increase from 3.178. What matters for us is that the entropic increase reflects the natural tendency for energy to dissipate as dictated by probability: Of the over 10 billion ways to arrange the on-particles, only 24 are when all 10 of them are stacked together. Thus, short of the initial state in Figure 4.2, the chance of this happening is minuscule even in a tiny thermodynamic system of only 50 particles.

Back to syntax, I take it for granted that any syntactic operation depends on energetically activating a population of neural computational units (*cu*s) of some kind. Against this background, consider Yang's (2013) comparison between early child language and the linguistic performance of Nim Chimpsky, a chimpanzee taught to use American Sign Language. According to Yang, the former case "is consistent with a productive grammar" while the latter case "does not show the expected productivity of a rule-based grammar" (p. 6324). This outcome has two implications bearing on the consensus in the field of syntax on the lexical-functional distinction of words/morphemes. First, as Yang points out (personal communication), "if one regards productivity as a prerequisite for functional words, then chimps clearly don't have it." I agree. In other words, functional categories are likely to be a later development in evolution. Second, there has always been a debate regarding "to what degree ontogeny really does recapitulate phylogeny" (Jackendoff 2002: 237). To use more recent works as an example, Gleason and Ratner's (2017: 85, Table 4.1) vocabulary of younger-than-20-months children contains only lexical words, mostly nouns, if we put aside sound-effect words such as *moo* and negation. This seems to suggest functional words to develop later than lexical words. On the other hand, Dye et al. (2019) argue for functional categories playing critical roles in early-stage language acquisition. What Yang's discovery means is that "[t]he continuity between the ontogeny and phylogeny of language ... is not supported by the empirical data" (Yang 2013: 6326–6327), that the debate on the presence or absence of functional categories in early child language is not automatically correlated with the validity of our first point. Consequently, I will take it to be plausible that neurological operations involving lexical elements would be more basic to our species. Specifically, I hypothesize that processing lexical elements consumes less computational resources than processing functional ones:

68. Computational Unit Disparity Hypothesis (CUDH)
    It takes a concentration of more energetically activated *cus* to represent
    a constituent *c* inside a functional environment than to represent *c* inside a lexical
    environment.

The CUDH will be shown to play a vital role in deriving the cross-linguistic fact of word orders in (57).

There is independent evidence that, at least in head-initial languages, either the verb or the subject or both must move overtly into a functional phrase such as TP. Apparently, it is impossible for all constituents inside VP to stay *in situ* (Julien 2000). Whatever is the linguistic reason for this phenomenon (Pollock 1989, Baker 2002, Y. Li 2005; also see Alexiadou and Anagnostopolou (2001) and Chomsky (2013) with different concerns but the same effect), the outcome is that some constituent A must be evaluated in a functional context FP while leaving a copy (Chomsky 1995) in the original lexical domain LP. The schematic representation is given as follows, presumably for all languages:

69. $[_{FP} \ldots A \ldots [_{LP} \ldots A_{copy} \ldots]]$

Now let N_1 be the size of the cluster of *cus* for processing A inside FP at time t_1 and N_2 be the one for processing A_{copy} inside LP at time t_2. Hence we have

(70). N_1 is larger than N_2 due to the CUDH in (68), and there must be a difference between t_1 and t_2, of which either one is allowed to mark the beginning time for processing [A, A$_{copy}$], corresponding to a direction of sentence-production.

70. a. $N_1 > N_2$
    b. $|t_1 - t_2| = \Delta t > 0$

In this setup, the cluster of *cus* activated for processing a syntactic element is viewed as a thermodynamic system. Next consider generating a sentence of the structure (69) either from top downward (also conveniently referred to as from left to right) or from bottom up (= from right to left).

Let us start with the essence of the idea, at the cost of over-simplification for the moment. Because $N_1 > N_2$ according to the CUDH, suppose for the sake of explication that even the inevitable energy dissipation affecting N_1 still leaves enough activated *cus* to handle N_2. Consequently, the total amount of *cus* to be activated for the movement chain [A, A$_{copy}$] is just N_1 if A is processed prior to A$_{copy}$. Now let's reverse the direction and start with A$_{copy}$. The total amount of *cus* to be energetically activated for processing first A$_{copy}$ and then A, is the sum of these three portions:

71. a. The initial N_2
    b. The difference between N_1 and N_2
    c. The lost amount of *cus* due to natural energy dissipation

(71a) is straightforward. So is (71b) since N_1 is needed to process A. But the 2nd law determines that the initial N_2 will decrease between t_2 and t_1. This is (71c). (71a) plus (71b) is identical to N_1. (71c) is the additional amount of *cus* that must be activated in order to make up for the energetic loss and to successfully generate [A, A$_{copy}$] from right to left. In brief, the left-to-right process only needs N_1 (= (71a)+(71b)) but the right-to-left option needs N_1 +(71c). If sentence-generation is sensitive to computational cost, the left-to-right direction is always the less costly option and therefore is always the winner.

Now the formal proof.

(70) is given. I assume that the rate of entropic energy dissipation per Δt is reflected in a positive value *val*, be its calculation based on a percentage, a constant or some more sophisticated formula. Intuitively, *val* is such that a larger population of activated *cus* will take a longer time to fully "die down" from dissipation than from a smaller population.

72. $f(N, \Delta t) = N\text{-}val$
    $\therefore N > f(N, \Delta t)$

That is, the amount N of energetically activated *cus* after Δt decreases by *val* (e.g. 30 per Δt or 30% of N per Δt). First consider generating the structure (69) from left to right. One of the three cases below must be true:

73. a. $f(N_1, \Delta t) > N_2$
     b. $f(N_1, \Delta t) = N_2$
     c. $f(N_1, \Delta t) < N_2$

For the purpose of processing A and A_{copy}, (73a) and (73b) are no different because a single group of energetically activated *cus* of the size N_1 is enough for both copies of A within Δt, collectively stated in (74):

74. $N1 > f(N_1, \Delta t) \geq N_2$

Now suppose (69) is processed from right to left, starting with the structurally lower A_{copy}. The initial amount of *cus* to be activated is N_2. (75a) is necessarily true. So the total amount of *cus* needed to complete the A ... A_{copy} chain is (75b), as explained in (71):

75. a. $N_2 > f(N_2, \Delta t)$
         $\therefore N_2 - f(N_2, \Delta t) > 0$
     b. $N_2 + (N_1 - N_2) + (N_2 - f(N_2, \Delta t)) = N_1 + (N_2 - f(N_2, \Delta t)) > N_1$

In (75b), the first addend N_2 is for A_{copy}, the second addend $(N_1 - N_2)$ is the difference between the two amounts, and the third addend $(N_2 - f(N_2, \Delta t))$ calculates what is left of N_2 after Δt because of energy dissipation. The sum of all three is what is needed to process A_{copy} and then A. Because of (75a), this sum must be larger than N_1 alone. That is, in the scenarios of (73a, b), starting from A inside the functional domain to A_{copy} in the lexical domain is guaranteed to cost less energy than the opposite direction due to the 2nd law. If operational cost is how the human language faculty selects among alternative derivations as the Minimalist Program assumes and as adopted in this work (e.g. our analysis of coordination in Chapter 3), then the left-to-right production of the generic (71) is the only direction of sentence-generation.

Next consider (73c), namely what is left of N_1 after Δt is less than N_2. Clearly, more *cus* must be activated to make up for the difference. The total amount of *cus* for processing A first is calculated in (76):

76. $N_1 + (N_2 - f(N_1, \Delta t))$

with the second addend being the extra activated *cus* for processing A_{copy}. Reversing the order of processing still needs the total amount in (75b), *viz.* $N_1 + (N_2 - f(N_2, \Delta t))$. Critical here is to compare this result with (76):

77. $\therefore f(N_1, \Delta t) > f(N_2, \Delta t)$
     $\therefore (N_2 - f(N_1, \Delta t)) < (N_2 - f(N_2, \Delta t))$
     $\therefore (N_1 + (N_2 - f(N_2, \Delta t))) > (N_1 + (N_2 - f(N_1, \Delta t)))$, namely (75b) > (76)

The starting premise in (77) is taken for granted: Since N_1 is larger than N_2, more activated *cu*s will be left from a larger population after Δt than from a smaller population after the same lapse of time. To illustrate with concrete numbers, suppose N_1 to be 90, *val* in *f* to be either 30 or 30% of 90 (see (72)), and N_2 to be 80 (assuming (73c)). $f(N_1, \Delta t)$ is either $90 - 30 = 60$ or $90 - 90*30\% = 63$, both numbers smaller than 80 ($= N_2$). $f(N_2, \Delta t)$ is $80 - 30 = 50$ or $80 - 80*30\% = 56$, smaller than 60 and 63, respectively. This is the first line of (77). Subtracting either of these numbers from the same N_2, the larger the subtrahend, the smaller the difference. E.g. $(80 - 63) < (80 - 56)$, illustrating the second line of (77). Remember that this line compares the numbers of additionally activated *cu*s to make up for the loss from energy dissipation in (73c) in different directions of structure-generation. Finally, the left-to-right needs the smaller addition $(80 + (80 - 63) = 97$ in total) to process [A, A$_{copy}$] according to (76) while the right-to-left needs the larger addition $(80 + (80 - 56) = 104)$. Again, left-to-right costs less energy than right-to-left.

In conclusion, (73) exhausts all possible scenarios for energy consumption in the structure (69), and in all of them, we have proven the left-to-right (or top-down) process is less costly than the opposite direction. If the human brain is indeed sensitive to computational cost (ultimately to energy consumption) in syntactic operations and always opts for the less costly route of derivation, then top-down sentence-generation becomes the only route to go. Logically, another scenario is for the dissipation rate function *f* to yield 0, namely at the end of the time interval Δt, there is no longer any (usable) activated *cu*s left and the speaker must fire up a completely new set of *cu*s to process the latter member of the movement chain. Whether this scenario happens to other types of dependencies, I surmise that it will not be for local movement chains. That is, the very nature of a local copy such as A$_{copy}$ in (69) lies in making use of at least a subset of the original *cu*s; otherwise, the natural language would not make multiple copies of the same constituent in the first place. Put differently, I propose that the very existence of movement in natural language results from the same initially fired *cu*s as the basis for handling multiple copies of a constituent. Because *cu*-activations necessarily accompany the creation of a constituent and its copy in some structural context, the top-down sequence of sentence-generation must be how a sentence is generated by the brain, there being no possibility in this theory to *first* create a sentence from bottom up and *then* verbalize it from top down. Not only would the first half of such a split model run counter to the least-cost principle, but the split itself would also double the amount of energy consumed for a single string of words.

With left-to-right sentence-generation enforced in this theory of linearization, the implementation of Merge is restated accordingly (see Chapter 5 for related discussion):

78. Merge targets A and merges B to it, with A the linearly last constituent which Merge affected.

The "last constituent" condition in (78) capitalizes on the fact that any linearization theory inevitably involves the time factor either tacitly or explicitly (e.g. Kayne's LCA and my use of Δt above). Since targeting A is part of Merge affecting it, (78) allows the initial selection of any simple constituent, say a morpheme, to qualify as A ready for Merge, giving [$_C$ A B]. At this point, B qualifies for the "linearly last constituent" affected by Merge while A does not since it is arranged earlier than B in the left-to-right process. Furthermore, if B is affected by Merge, C containing B is also affected by Merge, and C as a whole counts as the linearly last constituent. Hence, a new constituent D has the option of being merged either with B or with C. The former case yields [$_C$ A [$_E$ B D]], corresponding to, for instance, structurally expanding V (= B) into a VP (= E, with D being the object of V). The latter option has [$_E$ [$_C$ A B] D], which may be exemplified by a sentential subject (= C) merging with T (= D). The exact choice is determined by other principles of UG, as is expected whether Merge operates in a top-down or bottom-up process of sentence-generation. Lastly, Epstein's (1999) insight on the nature of c-command remains intact: C-command is simply a derivative relation at the point of Merge.

4.3.3   On Word Order Typology

The universal generalization (57) is now understood as follows: The upper portion of the clausal structure is composed of functional phrases which serve as the destinations of independently necessitated movements; the 2nd law and the preference for less costly syntactic operations jointly determine that processing the moved copy inside a functional domain first is always the favored direction of derivation. This understanding obviously holds with all forms of constituent-fronting, including *wh*-movement, topicalization, focus, neutral-preposing, subject-raising, passivization, etc. Also note that this result is fully consistent with the left-to-right generation of sentences adopted in Chapter 3 for coordination and with other parts of our account of Arg$_E$ and syntactic "word formation" in section 4.2. At the same time, if obligatory linear precedence is now attributed to movement into a functional domain, it also makes clear predications on the linearization of constituents that do not move. In this subsection, we focus on the word order typology with respect to S, V and O from this new perspective.

Recall from (54) that SVO and SOV languages represent more than 88.6 percent (41.1 + 47.5 percent) of languages in Dryer's (2013) survey. That SVO moves at least S to the Spec of TP is well established (see Julien 2000), so is V to T in some languages (see e.g. Pollock 1989 and the references therein).

With some details put aside for now, both movements start from a lexical domain, the traditional VP, to the functional domain of TP and therefore are captured by the schematic structure in (69). Direct evidence regarding SOV is less easy to come by because moving S to the Spec of TP is string-vacuous. Still, there is enough theoretical reason, such as the Extended Projection Principle (also see Alexiadou and Anagnostopolou 2001), for assuming this movement to be the default operation. Note, however, that the 2nd-law-based account of (57) forbids V from moving to T in the head-final context because T is functional and V in T would cost more energy to process than V staying inside VP according to the CUDH in (68). It follows that V in T must be processed earlier than the *in situ* V-copy and not later, contra the head-final premise. This restriction is welcome because it allows the simplest head-final structure in (64) to explain why strong head-final languages are morphologic-ally agglutinative: While V, T and C are linearly adjacent and subject to forming a PF word, we now have an entirely separate reason to forbid V-to-T (see below for T-to-C) movement, effectively keeping each head *in situ* and simply manifesting its own grammatical/semantic content.

What appears like a complication is the 8 percent of VSO languages. On one hand, V moving to T before S is expected since, again, V in T must be processed first due to the CUDH. On the other hand, the existing analyses of VSO rely crucially on S staying *in situ*. Without movement, why does S still precede O? A truly satisfactory answer would clearly depend on substantially investigating more languages of this type. For now, I will offer a typological perspective based on the surface values[20] of the statistics from Dryer (and similar works such as Tomlin 1986) plus the assumption – drawing on Julien (2000) – that the default word order of language results from independently motivated move-ments of V-to-T and/or subject-to-SpecTP.

If V moves to T while S is *in situ*, then S can either precede the constituent of the V-copy and O in [S [t$_V$ O]] or follow it in [[t$_V$ O] S] in my CUDH-based theory of linearization. The latter appears as VOS, the most popular (over 2 percent of the total sample) of the minority group in which S follows O. At least, then, the linear position of the *in situ* S does not resemble the moved constituents (*wh*, topic, focus, etc.) which absolutely respect the higher-equals-earlier generalization in (57). In fact, another set of numbers from Dryer (2013) indicates the postposed *in situ* S to be even slightly more common:

79. **Languages with "two primary alternating orders"**

SOV/SVO	VSO/VOS	SVO/VSO	SVO/VOS	SOV/OVS	Total
29	14	13	8	2	66

(79) is a portion of the 189 languages without a dominating word order in (54). Since the different word orders in a single language are taken to be inherently

connected (e.g. the SVO–VSO alternations in Arabic), the chart in (79) is a window to understanding the nature of word-order patterns better.

The SOV/SVO alternation will be set aside for involving the two most popular orders. I merely note that without substantial studies, Modern Chinese could easily fall into this group because the default postverbal object is frequently fronted in discourse. See Mei (1980) for references and discussions. SVO/VSO is a well-understood alternation and behind the consensus that both orders are underlyingly head-initial. Remarkably, two alternation types show VOS. VSO/VOS, the second largest group in (79), can be taken as V-to-T movement plus the freedom to prepose or postpose the *in situ* S as our CUDH-based theory predicts. The SVO/VOS alternation is of potential significance for two closely interlaced reasons. First, it may reflect a language that implements the default V-to-T movement plus the postposed *in situ* S but has the option of moving S to the Spec of TP. Without the second movement, such a language would be the postposed-S counterpart of Irish; with the second movement, it would correspond to French. Second, to the extent that this analysis is plausible, there may well be some SVO languages that are simply movement-concealed VOS languages.

By the foregoing logic, the least popular alternation in (79), SOV/OVS, suggests that the rare OVS shares the same underlying structure as the most popular SOV, both being head-final. If some constituent originating in the lexical domain must move into a functional domain, as assumed here, SOV results from the obvious choice of moving S to the Spec of TP, while OVS results from fronting either the entire head-final VP or O alone, as Alexiadou and Anagnostopolou (2001) suggested within the Minimalist Program. In the latter case, S would again be *in situ* and postposed. All these put together, there may well be more languages with an *in situ* S after [V O], consistent with the CUDH.

Notably missing in (79) is the rarest OSV, with 0.3 percent in (54). In the 402-language survey by Tomlin (1986), this order was not found at all. Lack of an alternating order leaves no direct clue to its relation with other word orders. But the very separation of V and O suggests that some movement must be involved. Since the clause-final V cannot move to T in our theory, I can only surmise as follows. OSV is derived from the underlying head-final structure of SOV plus raising O into some functional domain. Given UG as we know it, this is clearly a questionable way to construct a default clause: The raising of O into TP across the *in situ* S violates minimality, so perhaps some extra-UG motivation is "grammaticalized" to focus-front O as new information (see 4.3.2 above), a clearly atypical operation for default clausal order. Its low status improves slightly for OVS, the next rarest type with the same head-final structure as I suggested earlier. The atypical object-fronting competes in this case with an equally marked VP-fronting (= moving OV to a higher position across the *in situ* S) for basic clause-construction. Somehow, a similarly unpopular companion boosts one's chance of survival.

4.3.4   The CUDH Theorem

The CUDH-based theory of linearization limits Kayne's higher-equals-earlier insight to the upper portion of a clause where movement lands in functional domains, with the desirable result of explaining why Arg_E predominantly precedes the object. At the same time, constituents staying inside the lexical domains and/or without movement, not being subject to the CUDH, are predicted to enjoy freedom in linearization. Multiple desirable consequences follow. First, the evenly divided head-initial and head-final word order clearly seen through (54–55) can be simply attributed to probability at work given that the CUDH has nothing to say about V and O inside the lexical VP. Second, for the same lack of restriction in this portion of a clause, SVCs are able to give V1 and V2 different structural relations, one of the distinctive properties of the phenomenon. Third, since conjuncts are "base-generated" in nature and the conjunction never projects to its own phrase anyway, coordination is another case exempt from the CUDH. As we have learned from Chapter 3, the linearization of conjuncts has to be totally separate from hierarchical structure because conjuncts are not hierarchically connected in the first place. Of these three consequences, the last two link the CUDH directly to the central concern of this work, i.e. defending a UG-I theory that provides a coherent explanation for some recalcitrant facts for UG alone. By providing the word-order restriction in (57) and the flexibility elsewhere in the clause, the CUDH-based theory of linearization becomes an integral part of the overall model of the UG–iconicity interface and thus substantiates the general justification at the start of section 4.3 of our UG-I theory needing a matching theory of linearization.

Because of the important role that the CUDH plays in this work plus the fact that it is an entirely new idea in linguistics, I will, indeed am obliged to, explore one of its inevitable implications. Given that the CUDH is based on the different energetic costs of processing constituents in the lexical and functional domains, there are logically four possible scenarios with movement linking X and Y:

80. a. $[_{FP} \ldots X_i \ldots [_{LP} \ldots Y_i \ldots]]$
     b. $[_{FP} \ldots X_i \ldots [_{FP} \ldots Y_i \ldots]]$
     c. $[_{LP} \ldots X_i \ldots [_{LP} \ldots Y_i \ldots]]$
     d. $[_{LP} \ldots X_i \ldots [_{FP} \ldots Y_i \ldots]]$

(80a) is (69), the proven good case. (80d) is practically prohibited by the current formulation of UG: Movement is triggered by grammatical features characteristically carried by functional heads while the probe-goal model of syntactic dependencies effectively eliminates the need for raising to the matrix object position.[21] When UG rules out (80d), the 2nd law does not even have a chance to assess the directionality of its generation.

Before diving into (80b-c), it should be made clear what the CUDH theory of linearization predicts. When both ends of a movement are located in the same kind of domain for the purpose of energy cost, there is no way to determine which direction to generate the structure in, and hence linearization becomes impossible. I will call this the CUDH theorem:

81. No movement exists in language which starts and ends in the domains of the same X-kind, with X being lexical or functional.

Intriguingly, (81) bans (80b-c) even though both scenarios are abundantly found in the syntactic literature.

A prime representative of (80b) is successive-cyclic *wh*-movement from one Spec of CP to the next up the tree. Since both ends of the movement are inside functional domains, it runs squarely against (81). But there is a plausible solution inspired by successive cyclicity. (82) is the first approximation:

82. The linguistic processing of each event starts a new round of energy-cost calculation.

Equating each clause to the expression of an event for now, the copies of *wh* in the two Specs of CP belong to different rounds of entropic processes and are exempt from the cost-based assessment. The complete structure of *wh*-movement is schematically shown in (83), with certain details to be added shortly:

83. $[_{CP1} \, wh \ldots [_{CP2} \, wh_{copy} \ldots [_{LP} \ldots wh_{copy} \ldots]]]$

With Merge, the process of generating (83) must be either from the highest *wh* or from the lowest *wh*$_{copy}$. The second choice can never happen given the CUDH, leaving only top-down generation as the route to go. The two *wh* copies in the Specs of CP1 and CP2 are evaluated separately according to (82), which leaves the highest *wh* with no "trace" to compare the energetic cost with. In essence, this is no different from a higher-class adverb base-generated inside a functional domain. As we already know from multiple cases so far and from the literature, even a more costly operation is legitimate when no comparison is around, provided that it satisfies UG otherwise.[22]

(83) is not the only case bearing on the status of (80b). Raising from one Spec of TP to another is of the same nature as (83) and is analyzed in the same way, with the head and tail of the movement in different clauses. Three constructions that confirm the ungrammaticality prediction will be looked into in separate subsections. For now, consider what looks like a direct counterexample: the

West Germanic verb-second phenomenon. The standard analysis since den Besten (1983) has T move to C, both in functional domains and thus in opposition to the CUDH theorem. However, there obviously exists an inherent agreement between C and T, seen in the fact that the [-*wh*] complementizers *that* and *for* are necessarily paired with the finite and infinitive TPs, respectively. Based on both such facts and general theoretical considerations such as Case probes in phases, Chomsky (2001b: 15) reasons that "C-T are really functioning as a unit inducing agreement" (also see the references therein on other languages and motivations). The idea fits in (80b) well: T-to-C movement is prohibited as predicted, but C is allowed to carry all the grammatically relevant content of T via the probe-goal apparatus of agreement with T. What has been treated as T-to-C movement simply reflects the parametric decision by some languages to spell out this agreement on C under the restriction of the CUDH. After all, for C to conditionally manifest T is not observed in every language. The same logic extends to the "inflected C" investigated in the literature (e.g. Shlonsky 1997, Hofherr 2003).

Moving to (80c), Kayne's raising of the complement of V or P to the local Spec is ruled out by the CUDH theorem since it involves movement completely within a lexical domain (see VP2 of (63) for head-final languages and our critique of it thereabout). Baker's (1988) syntactic analysis of verb-incorporation is another case of L-to-L movement, which takes the form of (47) under the SMH in (42). It is easy to see that this is the head-movement counterpart of long-distance *wh*-movement or raising, with the embedded V and matrix V expressing different events and thus free from cost-assessment according to (82). At the same time, verb movement elsewhere also demands that (82) be theoretically fine-tuned.

Recall the VSO order in 4.3.3 above, which is believed to have V moved to T. The structure in our left-to-right clause-generation is given below, but the same logic holds equally with head-movement plus head-adjunction:

84. $[_{\text{TP}}\ V\ [_{vP}\ \text{subj}\ [_{v'}\ V_{\text{copy}}\ [_{VP}\ V_{\text{copy}}\ \text{obj}]]]]$

where V is formed by merging morphemes into a head with the internal structure of $[_T$ tense-affix $[_v\ V]]$ if we ignore the syntactically unrepresentable light verb shell *sh* and the bare root (see 4.2.2). Given Grimshaw's (2000) extended projections, v should be functional, which also matches the semantic characterization of v adopted throughout this book. Other than agentivity, which is easily thought of as a grammatical feature, v contains no other semantic content found with roots or lexical verbs. But the problem with (84) exists independently of whether v is functional or lexical. Either way, (84) has the V_{copy} in v' paired to V on the left and to another V_{copy} on the right. If $v = F$, the first pair belongs to (80b); if $v = L$, the second pair belongs to (80c). Because

(84) is mono-clausal and expresses a single event, the middle V_{copy} causes trouble no matter what.

The solution provides a unique argument for the existence of phases (Chomsky 2001a). Let (82) be revised as follows, in which "event-related phases" refer to CP and vP:

85. The linguistic processing of each event-related phase starts a new round of energy-cost calculation.

With two phases in (84), V in TP is comparable to the wh-phrase in the matrix CP in (83) for lacking any relevant copy in the CP phase for energy-cost assessment. Continual merger brings the derivation to the two V copies inside vP, the next phase, and the one in the functional domain of vP must be processed earlier than the one inside the lexical VP.

The last case to consider on head-movement is the high and low applicatives. For this discussion, I will assume Appl to be lexical in the intuitive sense that it helps define the overall encompassment of the event denoted by V. Also recall that the NCAs in Chinese act on a par with the theme argument rather than with the agent, proving their relations with the root to be internal in contrast with the clearly external nature of agent. (86) gives the heads produced by Merge with the low and high applicatives in accordance with Pylkkänen's (2008) theory:

86. a. $[_v \, v \, [_V \, V \, Appl_L]]$
     b. $[_v \, v \, [_{Appl} \, Appl_H \, V]]$

While the semantic relation between v and the rest in each string can and must be legitimately mapped to a syntactic representation, as seen in (84), the structural "expansion" of the relation between V and Appl deserves a closer look. (86b) is straightforward. Both ApplP and VP are lexical domains in the same phrase (= vP) and the copies of the verbal cluster inside them would create the impossible (80c). It follows from (42b) of the SMH that $Appl_H$ V must act like a structurally non-decomposable verbal head much like the causativized adjectival root in Semitic languages. Depending on whether V is ergative or transitive in itself, the resulting morpheme cluster, call it V merely for easier reference, acts either as a transitive or ditransitive which projects to (87) under the SMH:

87. $[_{vP} \, V \, [_{ApplP} \, DP_{Appl} \, [_{Appl'} \, V_{copy} \, (DP_{theme})]]]$

With V in a functional domain and V_{copy} in a lexical one, (87) can be properly linearized.

The complex head in (86a) might be expected to act just the same way since both V and $Appl_L$ are lexical and not subject to phrasal expansion. So its syntactic performance would be indistinguishable from (87). The complication arises with the co-occurrence of Appl$_L$ with the depictive small clause (Pylkkänen 2008: 21):

88. a. I gave Mary the meat raw.
     b. *I gave Mary the meat hungry.

The depictive (Dep) is good with the theme argument but not with the applied argument. Assigning to Dep the semantic type <e, <s, t>>, Pylkkänen explains (88) with (89), the same as (34) plus her semantic representation of V:

89. a.

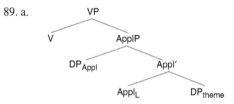

   b. $[\![Appl_L]\!] = \lambda x \lambda y \lambda f_{<e, \; st>} \lambda e.f(e, x) \wedge \textbf{theme}(e, x) \wedge \textbf{to-the-possession}(x, y)$
   c. $[\![V]\!] = \lambda x \lambda e.\textbf{V}(e) \wedge \textbf{theme}(e, x)$

In (89a), the only node with the same <e, <s, t>> type is the bare transitive V. This identical semantic type allows Dep and V to merge before other constituents through predicate modification, which in turn guarantees the depictive to be predicated of the theme argument of V, yielding (roughly) 'give (x) & raw (x)' as part of the semantics of (88a). Since the goal-introducing ApplP is yet to be added at this point of derivation, Dep (e.g. *hungry* in (88b)) cannot be semantically connected with the goal *Mary* (cf. Pylkkänen 2008: 28).

This account crucially relies on representing V and (the projection of) Appl$_L$ separately in syntax so that Dep can target V only. If the V–Appl$_L$ cluster could not be structurally expanded into (89a) due to the SMH, we would lose the syntactic means to make only V available to Dep and thus become unable to explain (88).

It turns out that this is not the only challenge that Appl$_L$ presents for syntactic theorizing. First, (89a-b) together contradict our understanding of UG: Semantically, Appl$_L$ treats V as an argument through λf in (89b) but syntactically, what gets projected is the argument, namely V to VP in (89a), when the two merge. In no part of UG would this be expected.[23] Second, it is rather counterintuitive and clumsy that the theme argument of V is doubly introduced by another head which leads to a semantic repetition. The relevant part of (88a) has the semantics below, with the repetition underscored. No semantic inconsistency arises for sure, but typical (and ideal) expressions of compositional semantics do not produce this kind of redundancy:

90. ⟦give Mary the meat⟧
$= \lambda f_{<e,\ st>}\lambda e(f(e,\ \text{the-meat}) \wedge \textbf{theme(e, the-meat)}$
$\qquad\qquad \wedge \textbf{to-the-possession(the-meat, Mary)})(\lambda x \lambda e.\text{give}(e) \wedge \textbf{theme}(e, x))$
$= \lambda e.\textbf{give}(e) \wedge \textbf{theme(e, the-meat)} \wedge \textbf{theme(e, the-meat)}$
$\qquad \wedge \textbf{to-the-possession(the-meat, Mary)}$

Still another puzzle has to do with the linear position of Appl_L in Bantu verbal morphology, of which the generic pattern is (91) (see Pacchiarotti 2017: 226–227):

91. AGR_{subj}-T-AGR_{obj}-root-APPL/CAUS-PASS-ASP/FV

As Y. Li (2005) points out, the verbal root r serves as the divider: The farther away a morpheme m is from r on either side, the higher in location m represents. In particular, all the derivational heads – vs. inflectional ones – that help build the (extended) projections of r occur right of r and are clearly aligned from low to high given the current understanding of the clausal structure. In this sequence, it would seem significant that the immediately postverbal position is for the high and low applicatives alike in all Bantu languages. At least on the surface, this ordering is consistent with placing Appl_H above VP but raises doubts about positioning Appl_L below VP as given in (89a). Also note that this consideration echoes the syntax–semantics mismatch earlier: If Appl_L indeed takes V as a semantic argument, then Appl_L should take V (or some projection of it) as complement and not the other way around.

Lastly, consider the paradigm for the English verb *tell*:

92. a. I told (Sam) a story about the book.
　　b. I told a story about the book to Sam.

93. a. I told *(Sam) that I have the book.
　　b. *I told that I have the book to Sam.

(92) indicates that *tell* has both the simple transitive use or the double-object use, the latter typically attributed to the applicative strategy in the approach represented by Pylkkänen (2008). Furthermore, because *Sam* in (92) ends up knowing the story, s/he acquires the latter's "ownship," which results by definition from Appl_L. (93a) with the same applicative *Sam* is still good, leading to the wrong prediction that *tell* has the option of taking a single CP complement (cf. (89c)).

Given these complications, it is fairly clear that we are yet to fully understand the low applicative. I will leave it for future investigation, noting merely that the precise location and treatment of Appl_L has been shown to be neutral to other contents of this book.

Back to the CUDH theorem in (81), recall that the movement pattern in (80b) is predicted to be unacceptable for lack of proper linearization when (85) does not apply. The rest of this chapter examines three cases of *wh*-movement, each departing in behavior from the typical *wh*-movement and some with no existing explanation at all. Interestingly, all of them can be attributed to the CUDH theorem:

94. a. *Wh*-possessors must pied-pipe.
    b. The English *wh*-subject does not trigger *do*-support.
    c. Structurally higher adverbs have no *wh*-form.

Furthermore, despite the different looks of these three cases, there exists a coherent explanation from UG for why they differ from one another in these particular ways.

4.3.5   On the Wh-*adverbs and* Wh-*subject*

We start with (94c). Frequency (Fr) and manner (Ma) adverbs can undergo *wh*-movement whereas evaluative (Ev) and epistemic (Ep) adverbs cannot. The examples below are from Y. Li et al. (2012: 220) (henceforth LSL).

95. a. How regularly/consistently/frequently did John send his children money?
    b. How skillfully/clumsily/cautiously did John mow his lawn?

96. a. *How luckily/regrettably/surprisingly did John send his children money?
    b. *How probably/likely/presumably did John mow his lawn?

There is no clear semantic reason why the division exists because most of the adjectival stems of the Ev and Ep classes have legitimate *wh*-forms:

97. a. How lucky/regrettable/surprising is it that John sent his children money?
    b. How probable/possible/likely would that be?

Other anti-*wh*-adverb classes examined in LSL display the same mystery:

98. a. *How frankly/honestly is it going to be a nightmare?   (LSL's (91a))
    b. How frank/honest are you to say that it is going to be a nightmare?
    c. *How wisely/stupidly/clumsily did he buy some flowers?   (LSL's (91c))
    d. How wise/stupid/clumsy of him is it to buy some flowers?

The unacceptable (98a,c) illustrate the speech act (Sa) and the subject-oriented (So) classes. Just like the Ev and Ep classes, their adjectival counterparts are generally susceptible to *wh*-movement with the intended interpretations, shown in (98b,d), respectively. Worth bearing in mind is that the So class typically can also be used as Ma, an ambiguity both in meaning and in syntactic behavior, as highlighted in LSL.

The acceptability pattern of *wh*-movement of these adverb classes is predicted by the CUDH theorem given a long-held distinction of adverbs. The Fr and Ma classes, capable of *wh*-movement, have been traditionally called VP adverbs, meaning that their default positions are inside what used to be regarded as VP and is now widely accepted as *v*P. If V moves to *v* by default, the fact that Fr and Ma can occur preverbally places them as adjuncts inside *v*P.[24] In contrast, sentence adverbs are all located in structurally higher positions outside *v*P, as reflected by them linearly preceding Fr and Ma and by (99) with causative verbs like *make* and *let* (see Y. Li 1990b for relevant discussion):

99. I made/let Chris (*wisely/*foolishly) answer those trick questions.

The mandatory absence of the infinitive *to* indicates the verbal complement of such verbs to be a bare *v*P. The fact that even So, the lowest class of all sentence adverbs (Cinque 1999, Y. Li et al. 2012; again the reader is reminded that some So adverbs also have the Ma readings), is rejected in its embedded use is evidence that sentence adverbs are true to this name tag, located necessarily in the TP-CP portion of a clause:

100.   a. [$_{CP}$ ... [$_{TP}$ ... [$_{vP}$ Fr/Ma [*v* VP]]]]
       b. [$_{CP}$ ... [$_{TP}$ ... Sa/Ev/Ep/So ... *v*P]]

Given (85), the *wh*-form of Fr and Ma in (100a) can move to the Spec of CP because the two ends of this movement belong to different phases. But there is no legitimate movement for the *wh*-form of the adverb classes in (100b). Being outside *v*P means that these adverbs are inside some functional domain or another which shares the same phase as CP. No *wh*-form of such an adverb is allowed, as predicted by the pattern in (80b). This is the fundamental reason why sentence adverbs are unfriendly to *wh*-movement. A complete explanation of (100) will await the other two *wh*-oddities being treated.

The examples below illustrate (94b):

101.   a. Who did you dance with?
       b. Who danced with you?
       c. *Who did dance with you?

In the absence of a modal or auxiliary verb, *do*-support is obligatory in a root question, shown in (101a). The standard analysis, paralleling the West Germanic verb-second phenomenon, is for the *wh*-phrase to move to the Spec of CP accompanied by whatever occupies T raising to C (or by manifesting the content of T in C via agreement motivated by the filled Spec of CP; see the relevant discussion below (83)). Since English verbs stay inside VP/*v*P (Emonds 1978, Pollock 1989), there is no lexical item in T to move and the semantically empty *do* must be inserted. The question is why *do* is prohibited when and only when the subject is a *wh*-word (101b–c).

This exception is also expected by the CUDH theorem. With both CP and TP being functional, moving the *wh*-subject to the Spec of CP would leave a copy in the Spec of TP and thereby create a local structure that cannot be linearized, another instance of (80b). The solution is for *who* to be kept *in situ*, in the Spec of TP. Without *wh*-movement to fill up the Spec of CP, there is no longer motivation for *do*-support. C still needs [+*wh*] for interpreting the CP as an interrogative, a task otherwise accomplished with a *wh*-phrase in the Spec of CP. But with the *in situ* *wh*-subject, it is done via the aforementioned C-T agreement (Chomsky 2001b). But unlike *yes-no* questions that need an overt C to mark the interrogative status, the *wh*-subject is enough for the job, removing the motivation for spelling C out. Note also that this *in situ* analysis of (101b) would be problematic with the government-binding model of *wh*-islands, where the blockage results from the Spec of CP, an "escape hatch," being filled by a *wh*-expression to prevent any other *wh*-phrase from escaping the clause. But this logic no longer matters with the probe-goal model of syntactic dependencies. Even if the *wh*-subject stays in the Spec of TP, it is still structurally higher than other constituents in the same clause. Therefore, it still counts as the closest with [+*wh*] for C in the next higher clause. The same reasoning applies to superiority, only in the local context.

That the *wh*-subject is *in situ* in (101b) receives an interesting support from English topicalization investigated by Lasnik and Saito (1992: 110f):

102.　a.　*John thinks that Mary likes himself.
　　　b.　John thinks that himself, Mary likes.
　　　c.　*John thinks that Mary said that himself, Susan likes.
　　　d.　*John thinks that himself likes Mary.

(102a) is unacceptable because *himself* has no binder in the embedded clause, a stereotypical Binding Condition A violation. Apparently, topicalization allows the binding domain to be recalculated so as to become the next higher clause, shown in (102b). (102c) proves that a topicalized anaphor still acts as expected in its new binding domain, including that it cannot skip the now-local *Mary* to reach the faraway *John*. Collectively, (102a–c) should predict (102d) to be good. The embedded anaphoric subject has no binder in the local clause, but it ought to be able to salvage itself through local topicalization, just as the anaphoric object does in (102b). With the recalculated binding domain, *himself* would be locally bound by *John* in (102b) and (102d) alike. Lasnik and Saito resolved this problem with the standard assumption at the time that a trace must be properly governed by a head (p. 109, (17)) and that topicalization does not create such a head. Since government is removed from the theory of UG (correctly; see Chapter 5), a separate explanation is needed for the subject–object asymmetry in (102).

The asymmetry follows directly from the CUDH theorem. The topicalized object originates inside VP and can be moved into a functional domain (presumably above TP). But both TP containing the origin of the intended subject topicalization and whatever is to host the topic, presumably TopP (see (66) above), are functional domains in the same phase. Hence topicalization is no solution for *himself* to meet Binding Condition A. The same logic also explains another reported phenomenon with the subject. The Vata examples below are from Rizzi (1990):

103. a. àló   *(ò) le   saká   la?
          who   he   eat rice   Q
          'Who ate rice?'
      b. Yi   Kòfí le   (*mí) la?
          what Kofi eat it   Q
          'What did Kofi eat?'

Descriptively, the *wh*-subject in Vata must be accompanied with an *in situ* resumptive pronoun like *ò* 'he' while the *wh*-object rejects the resumptive strategy. Rizzi attributes the asymmetry to lack of proper government through parametric Spec-head agreement on C. In the absence of government, the contrast is readily attributed to the CUDH theorem. Since the *wh*-subject in the Spec of TP cannot move to the Spec of CP, English opts to keep it *in situ*, whereas Vata base-generates the *wh*-form in the Spec of CP and places a resumptive pronoun in the Spec of TP to avoid the problem of proper linearization. It is worth noting that a resumptive pronoun is not a copy of the *wh*-phrase in the Spec of CP. The latter case has two identical copies which, in our entropic theory, are processed on the basis of the same population of *cu*s. A resumptive pronoun is still a pronoun, composed of the φ-features and used through co-referentiality. It is an entirely different DP from the *wh*-subject in (103a) and with no base for energy-cost comparison.

So far, we have seen two strategies for dealing with the immovable subject: English opts for no movement whatsoever, be it a *wh*-form or a topic, while Vata appeals to the resumptive strategy. The third scenario is long-distance *wh*-movement, accompanied by the so-called *that*-t effect:

104. Who do you think [$_{XP}$ (*that) __ danced with you]?

With the CUDH theorem, (104) follows from the Phase Impenetrability Condition (PIC; Chomsky 2001b), informally stated below:

105. Operations access a phase only through its edge (Spec, head).

By the PIC, moving *who* out of the embedded clause in (104) requires going through the edge of the complement CP, namely its Spec. Since *who* is the subject, it cannot move to this edge because of the CUDH. The solution in English is not to have CP so that the embedded clause is a bare TP. Given the inherent C-T relation, TP serves as the phase so that (i) *who* in the Spec of this TP is at the edge of a phase and satisfies (105) and (ii) this TP starts a new round of entropic process.[25] Together, (i) and (ii) allow *who* to move into the matrix clause in (104). Meanwhile, the absence of CP leads to the necessary absence of the complementizer *that*.

In this context, French acts more like Vata (with *t* for the original position of movement; the examples below are from Haegeman 1991: 425–426):

106. a. l'homme [que je pense [que Maigret a   arrêté   *t*]]
        the.man   that I think that Maigret has arrested
        'the man that I think that Maigret arrested'
     b. l'homme [que je pense [qui   a   été   arrêté]]
        the.man   that I think   QUI has been arrested
        'the man that I think was arrested'

Where English forces *that* to be absent (see the translation of (106b)), French requires *qui* rather than the default *que*. In our theory, *qui* is the *wh*-form of a resumptive pronoun in the Spec of TP. No movement also means no need for deleting C, so *qui* is likely the phonological merger of the resumptive pronoun and the immediately preceding complementizer *que*.

This line of reasoning also predicts, correctly it seems, that the subject may move to the local Spec of CP in VSO languages. VSO is taken to result from the subject staying in the original Spec of *v*P position (see 4.3.3 earlier). It follows that moving the *wh*-subject directly to the local Spec of CP spans two different phases and thus is immune from the energy-cost comparison. Irish offers a way to verify this prediction (Carnie 2002: 284):

107. Cé a^L bhí sa   seomra?
     who C   was in-the room
     'Who was in the room?'

The language is known to have overt complementizers like *a^L* even in a *wh*-question. The fact that *cé* 'who' is left of C is good indication for local *wh*-movement. But *cé* is also the subject originating inside the lower phase rather than in the Spec of TP. Hence its movement into the Spec of CP both complies with UG and is exempt from the CUDH theorem.

4.3.6   On the Wh-*possessor*

Moving to (94a), that a *wh*-possessor must pied-pipe in English is not readily derivable from any well-established UG principle:

108. a. [$_{CP}$ [$_{DP}$ Whose books] do you read t]?
      b. *[$_{CP}$ Whose do you read [$_{DP}$ t' D [$_{NP}$ t books]]]?

If a possessor can move from the Spec of NP to the Spec of DP for the genitive Case, why can't its *wh*-form move from the Spec of DP to the otherwise equally legitimate Spec of CP? The contrast in (108) is echoed by (109):

109. a. [$_{CP}$ [$_{DP}$ How good a pilot] is she t]?
      b. *[$_{CP}$ How good is she [$_{DP}$ t' a [$_{NP}$ t pilot]]]?

(109a) confirms that inside a DP, a *wh*-phrase must move locally to the left of D (= *a*). Again, pied-piping always wins over an otherwise "leaner" extraction of just *how good*. The contrast becomes even more mysterious given the fact that a *wh*-phrase in the Spec of a complement CP has no problem with further movement.

(108–109) are predicted by the CUDH theorem. The DP-internal *wh*-movement starts in the NP, a lexical domain, and ends inside DP, a functional one. But further extracting *whose* or *how good* to the Spec of CP (or first to the edge of *v*P) creates copies that are both in functional domains, another instance of the impossible (80b). It is also worth pointing out that the syntactic cycles for the entropic processes under consideration, as defined in (85), are apparently only those phases related to grammatically event-denoting, namely *v*P and CP. Whether DP is a syntactic phase or not (e.g. Svenonius 2004), it does not denote events and thus, unlike *v*P and CP, is unable to start a new entropic process for movement, at least not the kind that the CUDH theorem cares about.

This account of (108–109) is as straightforward as the *wh*-unfriendly sentence adverbs and the lack of *do*-support with a *wh*-subject. But there is an extra layer of complication with possessors, i.e. their apparent separation from the possessum in the form of possessor raising (PR) and movement to a functional domain such as CP.

The literature on PR is immense. See Deal (2013, 2017) for representative references and a review. The examples below are Deal's (2013: (391–392)), with "μ" in (110b) standing for an Appl-like morpheme associated with the "raised" possessor:

110. a. German
          Tim hat   der   Nachbarin   das   Auto   gewaschen.
          Tim has   the   neighbor.DAT.FEM the   car   washed
          'Tim washed the neighbor's car.'
      b. Nez Perce (Sahaptian)
          Haama-pim hi-nees-wewkuny-e'ny-∅-e   ha-haacwal-na lawtiwaa.
          man-ERG   3SUBJ-O.PL-meet-μ-P-REM.PAST   PL-boy-OBJ   friend.NOM
          'The man met the boys' friend.'

In both languages, the semantically understood possessor (Poss hereafter) of the theme object can or must act as an argument of the verb, bearing the dative (110a) or object case and even triggers object agreement (-*na* and -*nees* in (110b)). If this lifted grammatical status results from moving Poss from the Spec of DP into the clausal structure, PR would argue against the CUDH theorem and (85).

Two major approaches exist for analyzing PR: movement vs. a base-generated Poss binding a possessive *pro* inside the theme DP. Delving into this topic would carry us too far from the central concern of the UG–iconicity interface. Instead, I will try to sort out a few elements that bear directly on the CUDH theorem.

Deal notes that "[s]everal decades of research into external possession constructions have uncovered numerous examples of languages where external possession behaves like control, and extraordinarily few clear cases where it behaves like raising." (2013: 393) One fact in favor of base-generating PR is what Deal calls "a requirement of possessor affectedness," that the German example in (110a) "is infelicitous, even morbid, if the neighbor is dead" (ibid.). This extra semantics has been frequently analyzed as the clause housing an affected argument that binds the possessive *pro* inside the theme DP (see Deal 2013 for references). To the extent that Deal's assessment is valid, the treatment of PR *sans* movement is obviously in favor of our theory of linearization: Since Poss in the Spec of DP cannot move out due to (85), languages turn to base-generation plus binding instead.

Following the same logic, lack of any semantic addition from PR becomes evidence for the "extraordinarily few" cases of PR derived with movement. And this is how Deal analyzes Nez Perce PR by way of two assumptions: that the PR-accompanying morpheme *e'ni*, glossed as μ, is an "object shifter ... merged below *v* that forces A-movement" (pp. 408–409) and that using genitive case on the DP-internal Poss is "a kind of last resort PF repair" (pp. 411–412). Leaving the reader to refer to the original work for details, I will merely make three points.

First, PR in Nez Perce displays what Deal refers to as "relative locality," namely the minimality effect in (111a) (Deal's (31); the bracket structure is my adaptation of Deal's tree (33)):

111. a. *pro* 'ew-'nii-yey'-se-0   Angel-ne   pike   taaqmaai
         pro 3OBJ-give-μ-IMPERF-PRES   Angel-OBJ   mother.NOM   hat.NOM
         i. 'I'm giving Angel's mother a hat.'
         ii. '*I'm giving a/the mother Angel's hat.'
      b. [... *give* [$_{\mu P}$ Angel μ [$_{VP}$ [$_{DPgoal}$ e_1 mother] [$_{V'}$ t$_V$ [$_{DPtheme}$ e_2 hat]]]]]

For Deal, the contrast in (111a-i, ii) follows from moving the raised possessor *Angel* out of either the goal DP or the theme DP. In the latter case, the raising from the e_2 position must cross the c-commanding goal argument, in violation of minimality. But the same pattern is equally expected from base-generating *Angel*. Let e_2 be *pro* defined in (93) of Chapter 2; its content-recovery relies on the closest heterologous DP. The goal *mother* qualifies for this purpose whether by c-command or not (note that e_2 is semantically associated with *hat*, not with the verb *give*), contradicting the grammatically encoded possessive relation with *Angel*. In other words, (111a) is compatible with the movement analysis of PR in Nez Perce, but not compelling.

Second, a genitive-marked *wh*-possessor must pied-pipe (Deal's (21); also see her (70)):

112.   a.   'isii-nm   'iniit-pe   'ee   wee-s-0?
            who-GEN   house-LOC   you   be-P-PRES
            'Whose house are you at?'
       b.   *'isii-nm   'ee   wee-s-∅   'iniit-pe?
            who-GEN   you   be-P-PRES   house-LOC

Note first that (112) is exactly like English, which solidifies the cross-linguistic basis of the pied-piping pattern of *wh*-possessors and that of the CUDH theorem. At first sight, the contrast follows equally from Deal's movement account: Due to *wh*-movement of the entire object DP, the Spec of µP right above VP no longer c-commands the possessor *who*; so *who* can only stay *in situ* and get the last-resort genitive case. By this logic, however, it is actually *not* clear why *who* cannot be extracted by itself in (112b). After all, a possessor is allowed to move out of DP in Deal's theory. Being *wh* makes it move to the edge of *v*P by the PIC in (105) and then to the Spec of CP, each step leaving *who* not c-commanded by the Spec of µP. This *who* gets no Case from µ just as *who* in pied-piping does not, but that is exactly what the genitive case is for by hypothesis. Crucially, the problem cannot be solved by forcing *who* to target the Spec of µP for Case prior to *wh*-movement since the same demand would apply to (112a), leaving unexplained why (112a) is even possible.

Third and lastly, it is theoretically possible that (85) be parameterized to restrict the entropic calculation of movement to event-related phases or all phases if so motivated empirically. At least for PR, all clear data, from English and Nez Perce alike, not only favor the event-only definition but also constitute the absolute majority of the relevant facts according to Deal. There must be some reason why this is so. For now, I am still waiting to see truly persuasive evidence for parameterizing (85).

The other set of facts complicating the CUDH treatment of possessor movement is the linear discontinuity between the perceived Poss and the possessum. In this respect, a significant line of research started with works by Szabolcsi (1983, 1992, 1994) on Hungarian possessors, taken to move from the Spec of DP into some functional domain away from the possessum. This

analysis, referred to by Kiss as the "'standard' theory of the Hungarian possessive construction" (2002: 160), has been extended to other languages.
Gavruseva (2000), for instance, postulates a parametric account of possessor
behaviors between the Germanic languages (including English) on one hand
and Hungarian, Tzotzil and Chamorro on the other, with the latter group
representing possessor extraction. And a key element in Gavruseva's theory
is for the possessor to use the Spec of DP as the "escape hatch" for further
movement. Like PR but in a more direct manner, the facts at issue bear on the
validity of subsuming possessor pied-piping under the CUDH theorem.

Once again, the simplest solution is to parameterize (85) so that some
languages calculate the energetic cost of all phases. What matters, however,
is that each case quoted by Gavruseva, for instance, includes extra facts that
bring in yet-to-be-understood complications.

Gavruseva's Tzotzil data and their analysis come from Aissen (1996):

113. a. I-k-il-be   s-tot   li   Xun-e.   (ibid. (31a))
         ASP-1-see-IO 3-father the Xun-CLITIC
         'I saw Xun's father.'
      b. Buch'u   s-tot   av-il-be?   (ibid. (34))
         who   3-father   2-see-IO
         'Whose father did you see?'
      c. *S-tot   buch'u   av-il-be?   (ibid. (36))
         3-father   who   2-see-IO
         Intended reading: Same as (113b).
      d. Buch'u   av-il-be   s-tot?   (ibid. (31b))
         who   2-see-IO   3-father
         'Whose father did you see?'

(113a) illustrates the default word order inside a DP, with the possessor
following the possessum noun. A *wh*-possessor must occur to the left
(113b–c), which is taken as evidence that it must first raise to the Spec of DP.
(113d) shows the *wh*-possessor separated from the possessum, presumably by
movement from inside DP to the Spec of CP.

But Aissen makes a footnote on these examples. In the quotation below,
"(31a)" is our (113a) and "(31b)" is (113d).

It is not obvious that (31b) involves genitive extraction from a direct object. The source,
(31a), is analyzed in Aissen (1987) as an example of Possessor ascension (PA), signaled
by the suffix -*be* on the verb. Under the PA analysis, the possessor functions as clausal
indirect object, and (31b) could then be an example of indirect object extraction, rather
than genitive extraction. (Aissen (1996): footnote 7)

It appears, then, that (113) boils down to figuring out the precise nature of
possessor raising (Aissen's PA) in Tzotzil, with all the considerations

mentioned earlier. As long as agreement marker -*be* seems obligatory, all (113) demonstrates is just *wh*-movement of the indirect object.

The core fact about Chamorro possessor extraction is from Chung (1991):

114. a. Ti   man-mäguf   i   famagon-na   si   Jose.   (ibid. (35c))
          Not   T.PL-happy   the   children-AGR   Jose
          'Jose's children are unhappy.'
      b. Hayi   ti   man-mäguf   (*i)   famagon-na?   (ibid. (36c, 40a))
          who   not   T.PL-happy   the   children-AGR
          'Whose children are unhappy?'
      c. *Hayi   asagua-na   na'a'nao-mu?   (ibid. (65))
          who   spouse-AGR   afraid-2s
          'Whose wife are you afraid of?'

As in Tzotzil, the default position of the possessor is after the possessum noun (114a) and the *wh*-possessor can occur in the Spec of CP alone (114b). But, unlike Tzotzil in (113b), Chamorro does not allow (even superficial) pied-piping (Chung 1991: 128), shown in (114c). In addition, possessor extraction clearly happens to the object of a transitive verb and the single argument of an unaccusative or passivized verb. A relevant fact is the use of the definite determiner *i* 'the'. It occurs in the DP argument headed by the possessum noun only if possessor extraction does not happen, demonstrated with a comparison of (114a and b). Independently, the subject of an unergative or transitive verb must have *i*, making it impossible to determine whether possessor extraction out of the subject is allowed or not (p. 110).

Collectively, these facts in Chamorro lend themselves to multiple plausible analyses, from complex predicates (e.g. Baker and Harvey 2010) to possessor raising, none of them contingent on Gavruseva's extraction route from the Spec of DP to the Spec of CP. But I will explore one with the simplest implementation of the CUDH theorem. Given the facts that the subject is in effect never involved and that possessor extraction in the language is necessarily accompanied by the absence of the definite determiner *i*, (114b-c) readily fit into Massam's (2001) "pseudo-noun-incorporation." The essence of the theory is for a verbal head to take a bare NP complement, i.e. [V NP]. Assigning such a structure to (114b) immediately explains the missing *i*: The bare NP complement simply has no place to host D. Since the possessum is a bare NP, the *wh*-possessor may well originate inside this NP and move into the edge of *v*P with a lexical-to-functional step that satisfies (85), and then further on to the Spec of CP in a different event-related phase.

Lastly, we consider Hungarian, where richer data are documented and the analyses vary greatly. (115) represents the most frequently referenced fact:

115. a. Jánosnak   a   könyv-e   ((12) from Kiss 2002: Chapter 7)
          John-DAT   the   book-POSS
          'John's book'
     b. Jánosnak   ellopták   a   könyv-ét.
          John-DAT stole-they the   book-POSS-ACC
          'They stole John's book.'

116. a. (a)   János   könyv-e   (13)
          the   John   book-POSS
          'John's book'
     b. *János   ellopták   a   könyv-ét.
          John   stole-they the   book-POSS-ACC
          Intended reading: Same as (115b).

As possessor, *János* may occur on either side of the determiner *a* 'the', but the left-side occurrence is associated with *-nak*, the dative case marker elsewhere in Hungarian. Since the extracted possessor also has *-nak*, it is taken by researchers such as Szabolcsi and Gavruseva as evidence that the movement is out of the Spec of DP to the left of D.

But there are other related facts that have led to different analyses.

117. a. ?*Csak (én)nekem   a   könyv-em   veszett el.   (15)
          Only   1-DAT   the   book-POSS-1SG lost   VM
          'Only my book got lost.'
     b. az   õ   diák-ja-i-k   (46b)
          the   he   student-POSS-PL-3PL
          'their students'

118. A   fiúknak   ellopták   a   labdá-já-t/j-uk-at.   (48)
      the   boys-DAT   stole-they the   ball-POSS-ACC/POSS-3PL-ACC
      'The boys' ball was stolen.'

119. a. *Nekik   elopták   a   labdá-já-t.   (49)
          they-DAT stole-they the   ball-POSS-ACC
          'Their ball was stolen.'
     b. Nekik   elopták   a   labdá-j-uk-at.
          they-DAT stole-they the   ball-POSS-3PL-ACC
          Same as (119a).

As the possessor internal to the possessum DP, a pronoun is good to the right of D and without taking the dative form, shown in (117b). According to Kiss (2002: 158), "[m]ost speakers reject a pronominal possessor in pattern [(117a)]." Furthermore, pronominal possessors always trigger agreement on N whether extracted (119) or not (117b), whereas agreement becomes optional when the possessor is non-pronominal and extracted (cf. (117a) and (118)).

Theory-neutrally, (117a) already raises a question. If a dative pronominal possessor is not acceptable when pre-D, how likely is it to derive an extracted pronominal possessor as in (119b) from inside the possessum DP?[26] And to

explain the contrast in (118–119), den Dikken (1999) argues for two derivational routes for possessor extraction, given his assumption that only pronouns
trigger agreement. *A fiúknak* 'the boys-DAT' moves from inside the possessum
DP to the Spec of CP in (118a) and no agreement on *labdá* 'ball' is expected.
The optional agreement *-uk* '3PL' results from a "null resumptive pronoun"
(see Kiss 2002: 172). When the possessor is a pronoun in itself in (119),
agreement is triggered whether the possessor moves out or relies on
a resumptive pronoun.

Critically, the resumptive pronoun (*pro*$_{res}$) strategy suggests that the dative
Case of the extracted possessor has other sources than from inside the possessum DP. And indeed there are. Quoting Szabolcsi, Kiss (2002: 161) notes that
the *-nak* suffix is also seen with left-dislocated modifiers such as *Boldog-nak
boldog vagyok* 'Happy I am'. Later on in section 9.4 of her book, Kiss presents
data where the infinitive complement to an impersonal main predicate has its
DP subject marked with *-nak*. All these factors put together, a plausible
approach is to take all extracted possessors in Hungarian to be base-
generated outside DP while allowing the resumptive *pro*$_{res}$ it is coindexed
with to have the option of carrying [person], a plausible assumption since the
antecedent of *pro*$_{res}$ varies in [person] value. (118) follows from *pro*$_{res}$ choosing
to have this φ-feature or not. With the feature, agreement is expected; without
it, no agreement is observed, comparable to the East Asian *pro* that exists
totally independently of verbal agreement (Huang 1982). The non-pronominal
possessor imposes no effect on this choice given Kiss's (2002: 168) idea that
non-pronominals in Hungarian do not have [person] at all. When the extracted
possessor is a pronoun in (119), its coindexation with *pro*$_{res}$ necessarily passes
[person] to the latter, resulting in obligatory agreement.

In sum, possessor extraction in Hungarian is correlated with a large collection of other facts yet to receive a unified analysis, and some of these facts, such
as (117–119), suggest other reasons than movement for the phenomenon. In
fact, the dative-possessor seems to be a rare fact in itself. As Nikolaeva (2002)
notes, "no similar constructions are attested in other Uralic languages, all
researchers agree that it has appeared as a result of internal Hungarian development" (p. 1 in online source). Minimally, then, it remains unclear whether
Hungarian is a counterexample to *wh*-possessors in need of pied-piping.
Overall, the reported exceptions are all accompanied by related facts suggest-
ive of alternative analyses that are more friendly to pied-piping.

4.3.7   The Functional Domain Island

It is one thing to demonstrate that the CUDH theorem explains the three
deviations in (94) from regular *wh*-movement. It is a quite different question
why the three cases result from the same cause but appear very differently:

A *wh*-possessor pied-pipes, a *wh*-subject stays *in situ*, and sentence adverbs simply do not have any *wh*-form at all. Why isn't it, for instance, that we had a *wh*-evaluative adverb *in situ* while a possessor was prohibited from having a *wh*-form? As it turns out, these different behaviors of the same CUDH "violation" are not accidental. They are exactly how things should be in UG.

While a *wh*-possessor in the Spec of DP cannot move out, it turns D into [+wh] via Spec-head agreement. This is why *Whose article did you read?* is grammatically good even though the locus of the question is not the article but the author. In other words, pied-piping of (94a) happens because a handy UG mechanism, Spec-head agreement, guarantees a legitimate *wh*-movement when the possessor cannot move by itself. The same solution is not available to a *wh*-subject whether the C–T connection is at work or not. If the *wh*-subject agrees with T/C on [+wh], the whole clause is the question and a question itself does not move. Without agreement on [+wh], the clause is not a question in the first place and irrelevant to *wh*-movement. In other words, no [+wh] constituent containing the *wh*-subject and relevant to *wh*-movement can be created in UG in this context, leaving pied-piping with no phrase to apply to. When *wh*-movement is impossible for principled reasons, *wh-in situ* of (94b) (or a resumptive pronoun in Vata) is UG's alternative for forming *wh*-questions.

The curiosity about the anti-*wh*-adverb classes of (94a) is why, if unable to move out or pied-pipe, they cannot be *wh-in situ* just like the subject. Noticeably, the situation is reminiscent of a well-known argument-adjunct asymmetry:

120.   When inside a syntactic island, only a *wh*-argument may have the wide-scope interpretation outside the island and a *wh*-adjunct may not.

A functional domain has been shown to prevent a *wh*-expression from moving out due to the CUDH theorem. For any *wh*-expression E_{wh} inside a functional phrase FP, FP is an island for E_{wh}. It is natural, then, that the asymmetry in (120) holds for this "functional domain island" (FD island) as well. I admit to being uncertain how energy-cost calculation extends to LF movement. However, Reinhart's (1998; also see Reinhart 2006) account of *wh-in situ* with choice functions fits perfectly in this context.

Defending the theoretical and empirical need for a non-LF-movement treatment of wide-scope existential quantification, Reinhart appeals to Karttunen's semantics of questions so that a *wh*-question "denotes the set of propositions which are true answers to it" (Reinhart 1998: 36). Combining this with choice functions CH(f) which "[apply] to a non-empty set and [yield] an individual member of the set" (ibid.: 39), she associates them with *in situ wh*-phrases. In her theory, the *in situ wh*-subject in (101b) has this semantics (setting aside the irrelevant detail of expressing agentivity in 4.1 above):

121.   a.   Who danced with you?   (= (101b))
       b.   {P|∃f.CH(f) ∧ P = ^(f(**person**) **dance-with-you**) ∧ true(P)}

That is, the question in (121a) is a set of true assertions about individuals dancing with you and there is a choice function f (hence the perceived wh-scope from (121b)) selecting each such individual from the person set. Since wh-adverbs range over higher-order entities and not individuals – recall our discussion in Chapter 2 on θ-roles defining first-order entities, "they cannot be interpreted via choice functions selecting an individual from a set" (Reinhart 1998: 45). In sum, being *in situ* is not even an option for wh-adverbs inside the functional domain island because no choice function can be constructed for its intended scope over the entire clause.

What is left to be answered is why a wh-adverb in this unfriendly context cannot be saved by movement into the next higher phase. After all, *how evidently* is impossible whether it modifies the main clause or an embedded one (e.g. **How evidently do you think [$_{CP}$ that Sam t dislikes scorpions]?*). Consider the two structural contexts for such a movement to take place. If the embedded CP is present, CP is the phase and the PIC would require *how evidently* to move through the edge of the phase, i.e. the Spec of CP. But this is prohibited by the CUDH theorem. The only possibility left is for the wh-adverb to be simultaneously *in situ* and at the edge of a phase, much like the moved wh-subject in the Spec of TP plus CP-deletion (see the discussion below (104) on *that*-trace). However, there must exist fundamental reasons for separating the subject in the Spec of TP from the sentence adverbs in their original positions, be it the Extended Projection Principle or something else. While the subject can capitalize on the C–T connection so that a CP-deletion places the subject at the edge of the provisional TP phase, an *in situ* wh-adverb is incapable of benefiting from the same convenience. In a word, the wh-form of a sentence adverb cannot move to the local Spec of CP due to the CUDH theorem; it does not have an *in situ* interpretation because it lacks a proper choice function; and it can neither move out of the local CP under the PIC nor take advantage of a CP-deletion. The wh-form is truly stuck. This is why sentence adverbs do not have wh-forms even though their adjectival roots do. The situation also forms an enlightening contrast with VP adverbs, of which at least some (e.g. Fr) are most likely located inside vP, another functional domain. But Fr may well adjoin to vP and thus is already at the edge of this phase. So its wh-form can move directly out of vP into another event-related phase while still respecting the PIC.

Now we have this picture on the three odd cases of wh-movement in (94). Since wh-movement starting and ending both in functional domains is disallowed for lack of thermodynamic asymmetry, UG copes with it in three increasingly "receding" ways: (i) when a wh-expression cannot move, try pied-piping (= (94a)); (ii) when pied-piping is not available, try *wh-in situ* (= (94b)) or the resumptive pronoun strategy; if even *wh-in situ* is no good, the expression and its class are denied a *wh*-form (94c).

This particular analysis of *wh*-adverbs has implications of which I briefly consider two. First, sentence adverbs can be fronted for topicalization, focalization and/or neutral-preposing (Rizzi 2004, Y. Li et al. 2012) and thus appear to contradict our CUDH-based explanation of their *wh*-unfriendliness. I do not claim to have a full solution but will sketch a direction of investigation similar to the idea independently explored by Bošković and Takahashi (1998) on scrambling: Differing from *wh*-movement, other forms of fronting at least have the option of base-generating adjuncts in higher positions (e.g. inside FocusP or TopP).

Underneath this possibility are three considerations. (i) There is a fundamental difference between *wh*-movement and the rest. Whereas *wh*-movement participates in turning the entire CP into a question, the same cannot be said about the other fronting constructions. Focalization, for instance, only puts focus on the fronted constituent itself; it does not turn the rest of the clause inside FocusP into a focus. (ii) Adverbials are by nature "peripheral" in the overall semantics of a clause, not encoded in the meanings of V or *v*, for instance. Ultimately, this is also why Davidsonian semantics works with adverbs and what prompts the discussion of Pair-Merge (Chomsky 2000, 2004b) at the structural level. (iii) At least in Chinese, some form of long-distance modification is inevitable anyway (section 3.4 of Chapter 3). Now suppose a focalized adverb Adv is base-generated inside FocusP to literally modify the Focus head for local semantic satisfaction, therefore distinguishing itself fundamentally from what happens between a *wh*-phrase and C. See Ernst (2002) for the same distinction. Being so modified, Focus inherits Adv's semantic expectation for the corresponding head H, which enables probing for H down the tree. Meanwhile, base-generating Adv exempts it from the movement dilemma.

Second, interpreting (certain) *wh*-expressions *in situ* without even covert movement, as Reinhart argues for, bears on the analysis of bound variables discussed in the foregoing chapters. Recall from Chapters 2 and 3 that c-command in overt syntax is not a necessary condition for bound variables, suggesting a local QR at LF so that the QP object of PP, for instance, could adjoin to PP and license the bound variable across a c-command-invisible segment of PP. With this stipulated property of segments dispensed with in the overall theory of UG-I (see Chapter 3), Reinhart's choice function approach is exactly what is needed. The QP inside PP simply stays *in situ* and projects its quantificational force over the entire PP via a choice function. Let this operation associate the [+quantificational] feature of the *in situ* *wh*-argument to the entire PP so as to license a bound-variable pronoun down the tree. Since QP does not move up at all, a bound-variable epithet can choose to literally target the non-c-commanding QP to satisfy Binding Condition C at least for those speakers who share the judgment of (95) in 3.3.4. See my discussion thereabout.

4.4   Conclusion

This chapter concerns three separate aspects of the external argument Arg_E: (i) its structural relation with the lexical verb, (ii) its comparison with the various realizations of the applicatives (*-ee*, Chinese NCAs, Bantu applicatives and the internal structure of double-object verbs), and (iii) its linearization pattern viewed together with other constituents in the upper portion of a clause.

Aspect (i) is within the central theme of the UG-I interface, exploring how the iconicity of independence is underneath the structural setup between a lexical verb and its Arg_E, a relation recognized but not explained up till now. Unlike the phenomena of SVCs and connectors where UG interacts with iconicity in rather intricate manners invoked by $Void_F1$–2, Arg_E embodies a simple solution: If a factor is external to events, it stays external in linguistic representation. Nevertheless, even a simple case of UG–iconicity synchronization like this one may need non-trivial proof that an extra-UG "third-factor principle" is indeed at work.

The particular analysis given for Arg_E compels a comparison between *-er* and *-ee* because both yield individual-denoting words after combining with event-denoting verbs. Had this chapter not included section 4.2 where a highly detailed applicative-based analysis of cross-linguistic facts was articulated and accompanied by a theory of the morphology–syntax relationship culminating in the SMH, it is almost a certainty that such obvious data as *-ee* would propel a reader to question the validity or tenability of the iconic treatment of Arg_E. Likewise, though $Void_F2$, taking UG to reject structural projections of bare roots, was shown to help explain the miscellaneous traits of connectors in Chapter 3, the active role of bare roots in current syntactic and morphosyntactic research might make one wonder how $Void_F2$ would fare in this part of language. All these issues make (ii) an indispensable addition to the theory of UG-I in this work. The fact that all of them received a coherent and unified account from $Void_F2$ plus the SMH in 4.2.3 becomes the indicator that the implications of our UG-I theory extend far beyond exclusively iconicity-related portions of the human language faculty, all made possible once we gain finer understandings of the UG–iconicity interactions (e.g. the structural nature of Arg_E).

Seen in isolation, (iii) is an entirely different subject matter from iconicity. As stated at the onset of section 4.3, however, my theory of UG-I not only would lose much persuasive power if left-to-right sentence-generation is not only a less popular option in the UG model of language, but also actually jars with an algorithm of linearization which, for all the perceived meta-theoretical advantage, applies to every part of a clause uniformly and leaves "parametric" variations to additional operations of movement. An ideal fit for the proposed UG-I interface should have these properties regarding word order:

122.   a. making left-to-right sentence-generation the only way to construct sentences;
        b. allowing enough structural flexibility inside lexical phrases or where no movement is involved;
        c. having the potential to accommodate known and new facts;
        d. being derivable from more general principles rather than by pure stipulation.

(122a) is both needed to explain coordination and retains the valid portion (= the upper part of a clause) of Kayne's (1994) insightful observation. (122b) underlies the different structural relations between verbs in SVCs and the multi-plane structure among conjuncts. Furthermore, if a head is not involved in movement, it is not subject to thermodynamic assessment by the CUDH; this explains why there are many head-final languages whether a head is lexical or functional. (122c) is illustrated with the adoption of left-to-right generation on a wide range of linguistic facts throughout the book as well as on the first-observed "functional domain island" in 4.3.5–4.3.7. The CUDH-based theory of linearization possesses all these qualities as well as (122d), namely it enforces (122a) by the collaboration of cost-sensitivity and the 2nd law of thermodynamics while leaving (122b) to probability paired with the unavoidable language-specific decision on favoring a cross-categorial linearization pattern.

Overall, section 4.3 helps build the foundation on which my theory of UG-I operates. In addition, it reduces a large portion of word order to physics, thus further shrinking what must be included in UG. To wit, if the CUDH proves to be on the right track, the 2nd law of thermodynamics will be another "third-factor principle" interfacing with UG through phases and copies to create language. And at least in principle, claims made regarding this interface ought to be more readily testable as technologies evolve.

5   Meta-Theoretical Reflections

This book subscribes to the claim that language is not completely reducible to other cognitive functions. Debating on whether this claim is true is too daunting a task to undertake at the moment – to my knowledge, there is yet to be a systematic effort to account for all linguistic facts accumulated in the past few decades, some highly intricate, exclusively with non-linguistic laws. Meanwhile, it is much more manageable to investigate how much of what we perceive to be language is unique to language proper and what is not. To this end, two approaches have been explored. One is represented by Chomsky's Minimalist Program, especially in his recent works of the 2010s. In this approach, the boundary of UG is determined *a priori* in the sense that it is pre-set by the guiding hypothesis of "virtual conceptual necessity" (Chomsky 1995). The other approach is embodied by many research works on the various old and new interfaces, this book included, which look into the minute details of certain linguistic facts with the hope of identifying those derivable with independently motivated UG mechanisms versus those that must be attributed to extra-UG apparatuses. At this level of investigation, rigorous argumentations are a must so as to come up with testable – and hopefully correct – claims on where a specific section of the UG boundary lies. This is why the algorithm in (5) of Chapter 1 has been carefully followed throughout these chapters.

The two approaches to finding the boundaries of UG come from the opposite ends of the intellectual pursuit of knowledge. My own view, certainly nowhere near being novel, is that both are needed and that they complement each other, especially if we look beyond the specific wordings and keep their essences.[1] I take it for granted that ultimately the delimitation of UG must be determined by all and only relevant linguistic facts. Interestingly, this not only is the obvious justification for the second and "empirical" approach but also highlights the motivation for the *a priori* one. At the current stage of linguistics, language is such a complex phenomenon to us – with so many superficial variations to sort out, so much data to account for, so many possible factors collaborating in yet unclear ways and who knows how many unknown facts still out there – that the field is simply far from being certain what "all and only relevant linguistic facts" are with respect to the exact boundaries of UG. When facts appear miscellaneous, theories are necessarily partial and overlapping analyses are plenty, it is only natural for theoreticians to appeal to more general guidelines such as Occam's razor. Minimally, a conscious and continual effort to keep the theory of UG lean and clean, even at the risk of overdoing it, will play the role of helping to prevent it from becoming overly powerful and/or unfalsifiable.

It is unclear how many researchers would disagree on the general "synthetic" position described above. I find it reminiscent of a remark by Mayr (1997: 158) on the history of biology:

> That the ultimate answer in a long-lasting controversy combines elements of the two opposing camps is typical in biology. Opponents are like the proverbial blind men touching the different parts of an elephant. They have part of the truth, but they make erroneous extrapolations from these partial truths. The final answer is achieved by eliminating the errors and combining the valid portions of the various opposing theories.

The particular part of biology that prompted this remark is the two-century-long debate between the epigenesist and preformationist theories in developmental biology, eventually resolved by genetics proving that both sides have captured some truth and erred in other ways. Mayr's words bear on the study of UG in two respects: the synthesis of different or even seemingly opposing views, and the nature of biology given the biolinguistic take on UG. I will use this last chapter of the book to share my own thoughts on these two topics, which, at least for me, also drive the theory of the UG-I interface.

5.1 When Theories Differ

The human effort to understand a natural phenomenon P rests on an assumption and a fact. The assumption is that there exists an ultimate explanation for P which we call the truth. The fact is that, to the extent that P is worth looking into, the road to the truth behind it is paved with different hypotheses, some right, some wrong and many somewhere in between. Trying to figure out the amount of truth contained in each hypothesis gives rise to the intellectual debates familiar to every researcher. Though Mayr only described biology, there is no evidence that linguistics is different (see Boeckx and Piattelli-Palmarini 2005 for relevant thoughts). Syntacticians were no less confident and eloquent about transformational rules and government-binding than they are about the Minimalist principles partly because one simply has to deal with what one has at any point of time. What Mayr emphasizes in the quotation above, however, suggests a research strategy when a theoretical disagreement proves hard to resolve. Assuming both sides of the debate to be fundamentally rational, the very fact that neither side can successfully annex the entire empirical basis of the other, which is why the debate arises and lasts in the first place, might be an indicator that each side has "part of the truth" while making "erroneous extrapolations from these partial truths." And this is when attempting a synthesis becomes a plausible alternative to resolve the debate. The challenge lies in identifying "the valid portions of the various opposing theories," and there is no guarantee that the effort will pay off well. But it is worth trying because a similar path to the truth has proven to be "typical" in biology, to which different theoretical models in linguistics have analogized themselves independently of the biolinguistic name tag.

This line of logic plays a significant role in the research reported in this book. UG and iconicity are the key elements from the so-called formal and functional theories, respectively. As the brief literature review in Chapter 1 indicates, these theories differ in perspectives, premises, basic concepts and specific focuses, there being little constructive interaction in between. What has been done in the current book is to find where their strengths can be proven to meet and jointly explain certain recalcitrant facts in languages, all via a highly specific theory of the UG–iconicity interface.

Another case of the same nature is the SMH in Chapter 4. The debate on which component(s) of UG form words has been ongoing for decades. While the syntactic approach has been the popular one most of the time, from Generative Semantics all the way to Distributed Morphology, there are nonetheless facts that point at the inadequacy of doing everything in phrasal syntax. Harley's puzzle in Chapter 4 arises from a subtype of denominal verbs, but it extends directly to a large portion of morphologically complex words, either superficially or in an abstract sense, whose components are connected through modification. This is where the head-movement-style syntactic approach gets stuck, as Harley realizes, but is what the lexicalist word-formation model handles like a piece of cake. Semitic morphological causativization offers more evidence for direct morpheme concatenation independent of phrasal syntax, even when one of the morphemes (= the root) indeed holds a thematic relation with the other (= the causative affix). My synthetic solution consists of four parts: (i) recognize the empirically substantiated need for morpheme concatenation without syntactic head-movement, namely the essence of the lexicalist theory; (ii) recognize the equally robust conclusion that a superficial word may have to be paired with an underlying multi-phrase syntactic structure, as is typical of the syntactic model of word formation; (iii) capitalize on the inevitable quality of Merge that two heads together may still yield a head (otherwise syntax would be incapable of forming words to begin with); (iv) map head-internal semantic relations to phrasal structure under UG principles. Parts (i) and (ii) are the proven strengths of the two competing theories. (iii) is actually a shared assumption by both sides because even syntactic head-movement must allow a head to adjoin to another head to still result in a head. Forming words in syntax with either head-movement or direct morpheme merger lets the theory over-generate and contain redundancy. Such negative effects of (iii) are offset by (iv), the core of Y. Li's (2005) idea behind the SMH that connects the lexicalist and syntactic insights. The resulting theory not only covers the empirical bases of both theories but also simplifies the definition of c-command to its minimum.

The very fact that a synthesis can indeed be done on competing theories and with empirical gains is encouraging. How my specific attempts will fare awaits further assessments through more linguistic data. In order to substantiate the view that Mayr's observation holds equally well with linguistics, I will consider a case in which time has given the verdict in favor of synthesizing key ideas from different theories so as to formulate a better one.

In the government-binding theory of the 1980s, UG was conceptualized as a set of submodules, each responsible for a sector of syntax and all regulated by government (except the X'-module which provides the structure for defining government). It was pointed out by Y. Li (1987), however, that there was a logical flaw in the theory: An argument must receive a θ-role due to the θ-criterion; θ-assignment relies on a Case to make the argument "visible"; Cases are assigned under government; PRO must not be governed due to the PRO-theorem derived from the binding submodule; but PRO must receive a θ-role to satisfy the θ-criterion! In addition, Li also asked what it meant for Case to make an argument "visible" for θ-assignment.

Assuming the key status of Case, Li's solution was to redefine this notion with the semantic types from Montague grammar, triggered by Richard Larson's observation (in a lecture) that the compositional representation of semantic types encodes θ-roles:

1. Case assignment is the process of semantic type-matching between an argument and the θ-role it is supposed to receive.

Borrowing Montague's treatment of nominal arguments (NPs) to be of type $\ll e, t\gg, t>$ and VP to be $<e, t>$, the theme argument of a transitive verb V_t receives a Case under (1) merely because the object θ-role of V_t is also of type $\ll e, t\gg, t>$. E.g.

2. a. *fly*: $\lll e, t>, t>, <e, t\gg$
   b. *an airplane*: $\ll e, t>, t>$
   c. *fly an airplane*: $\lll e,t>,t>, <e,t\gg \ll e,t>,t> \rightarrow <e, t>$

That is, when an argument and the θ-role of V_t at hand match in semantic type, the standard algebraic operation during the concatenation of V_t and NP "cancels" them out against each other. This matching is what is called Case assignment, which necessarily accompanies "θ-assignment," namely the successful representational cancellation of what V_t expects (= an argument of the type <<e, t>, t>) and the NP argument itself (= <<e, t>, t>).

In this reformulation of Case, T (called Infl at the time) and PRO are defined in (3):

3. a. T_{finite}: <<e, t>, <<<e, t>, t>, t>>
    b. T_{inf}: <<e, t>, <e, t>>
    c. PRO: e

Since a functional category such as T is given a semantic type, it was tacitly assumed that T not only takes in a VP for proper interpretation but also inherits and/or shifts the semantic type of the agent θ-role of VP (= e in <e, t>).[2] Departing from the Montaguean tradition (see Partee 1986), however, pronouns were taken to be always <<e, t>, t>, leaving the type <e> for PRO only, which Li assumed to be the type never overtly spelled out. In this model, [*to* VP] is of type <e, t> after *to* concatenates with VP (see (3b)) and inherits the subject θ-role of the <e> type from VP. So PRO receives this θ-role and has a Case as well, according to (1), with government playing no role at all in these operations. Passivization is the operation of type-shifting the theme θ-role from <<e, t>, t> to <e> (plus suppressing the subject θ-role as was commonly assumed then):

4. *flown*: <e, t>   (vs. (2a))

The <e> type of the theme role does not match the <<e, t>, t> type of the NP argument. There can be neither Case nor θ-assigned, forcing the NP object to move up to the Spec of the finite TP because T_{finite} shifts <e> back to <<e, t>, t> (see (3a)). The same analysis applies to unaccusative verbs. Similarly, grammatical Case-assigners like *of* all perform two intertwined tasks: inheriting a θ-role from some lexical item and type-shifting it to <<e, t>, t> for the NP argument.

The analysis presented in Y. Li (1987) focused only on resolving the immediate logical flaw of the government-binding theory explicated above, and its wider implications were not explored. For instance, there is evidence that reconstruction does not happen with A-movement (Chomsky 1993):

5. a. Which claim that John was asleep was he willing to discuss *t*?
    b. The claim that John was asleep seems to him [*t* to be correct]?

The r-expression *John* and the pronoun *he/him* can co-refer only in (5b), suggesting reconstruction to be a must in A′-movement (and thus subject to Binding Condition C) but not in A-movement. Since reconstruction is now subsumed under the copy theory of movement, the contrast in (5) amounts to A′-movement necessarily interpreting the trace as a copy of the moved constituent while A-movement has the option for the trace not to be a copy. This difference can be made to follow from (2a) vs. (4). If the NP argument in A-movement such as passivization and raising cannot receive a θ-role *in situ* due to the hypothesized type-mismatch, it is plausible that UG at least has the choice not to interpret the original site as a full copy of the moved NP, since a copy in that position has no interpretation by itself for being unable to "receive" a θ-role. Another potential of (1–3) is to solve the puzzle about *wanna*-contraction, first noticed by Pesetsky (1982): If the trace of *wh*-movement blocks the contraction for being between *want* and the infinitive *to*, why doesn't PRO do the same? Now given (3), PRO has <e>, so does the subject θ-role of VP. Logically, PRO could simply receive this θ-role and get a Case directly from VP without moving to the Spec of the infinitive TP. As such, PRO at least has the option of being physically absent between *want* and *to* and truly leaving the two adjacent for the contraction.

Taking the nominal argument and the corresponding Case-friendly θ-roles to be of type <<e, t>, t> is obviously inconsistent with what is assumed in this book: that θ-roles are sets of first-order entities. Still, we can look at this alternative Case theory of 30-plus years ago from a general perspective. First, Case and θ-assignment are carried out independently of government. In fact, recall that the requirement for government was the origin of the logical flaw that (1) was designed to get rid of so that PRO, presumably not governed, still has a Case and thus is "visible" for receiving a θ-role. In other words, within the theory of UG throughout the 1980s in which government was given the axiomatic status, (1) severed at least two submodules of UG – θ-theory and Case theory – from government. Second, with Case defined by semantic types, it is no longer a linguistic "entity" to be given out and received. Rather, it is a process of (i) matching a certain (ii) shared property p of two constituents (e.g. NP and the θ-role of T) at the point of concatenation by (iii) removing p from the representation (iv) so that both can be properly interpreted, and (v) this process may drive movement as well (e.g. passivization).

Pertinent to my linguistic take on Mayr's statement is that several years later, the two general theoretical claims in Y. Li (1987) became the core elements of the Minimalist Program. Government was totally removed from the current model of UG. And all the technical details of (i) through (v) in implementing Li's definition of Case found their direct counterparts in feature-agreement for proper interpretation as the trigger for syntactic operations. In fact, there is a meta-theoretical sense to favor reducing Case to semantics if doable. While morphological cases have the clear function of facilitating communication – there is the general observation that case-rich languages tend strongly to enjoy freer word orders, the more abstract Case as a "licensing" requirement remains mysterious to this day. If Case can eventually be reduced to semantics, the Minimalist model will be further minimalized. This consideration aside, the effort to fix a logical flaw in the government-binding theory of UG by synthesizing the core elements of two very different approaches to language led to the ideas that have turned out to be more likely on the right track. Had these ideas on a specific portion of UG had the opportunity to be explored along their natural paths, the theory of syntax might have spent fewer years on the later-abandoned axiomatic notion of government and the complications it incurred.

To end this section, it cannot be emphasized enough that a fruitful application of the synthesis method rests on a condition: Neither one of the competing theories can subsume the other despite continual efforts, a scenario typically found in a long-lasting debate. Only then can one be reasonably certain that each side is likely to "have part of the truth" so that there is a ground for theoretical synthesis. UG and iconicity, the lexicalist and syntactic theories of word formation, the government-binding theory and Montague grammar, all satisfy this condition. The epigenesist vs. preformationist debate mentioned by Mayr ended with genetics during the progress of our biological knowledge, but the very fact that neither side persuaded the other for two centuries is sufficient evidence that the same condition above was met. In brief, when a theoretical debate resists a solution over a period of time, it might pay off to step out of one's theoretical comfort zone and try to be a synthesizer.

5.2   The Role Models for Linguistics

The two mature fields of natural science that linguists look to most frequently as role models are biology and physics (in fact, biolinguistics links linguistics directly to biology; see Chomsky 2004a, Wexler 2017). Though both fields are grounded in facts while offering explanations with theoretical apparatuses abstracted away from the superficial data, one should be equally aware that the two fields are different enough to give rise to this remark, again from Mayr (1997: 36–37):

Perhaps the greatest failing of the philosophy of science, until only a few years ago, was that it took physics as the exemplar of science. . . . This has changed. . . . . . . the rejection of strict determinism and of reliance on universal laws, the acceptance of merely probabilistic predication and of historical narratives . . . and many other aspects of biological thought have affected the philosophy of science fundamentally.

Whatever one's response is to these words, the situation they describe has been underscored by the existence of the bi-monthly journal of *Biology & Philosophy* since 1986. At the least, then, when a linguist draws on natural sciences for support of their particular approach to language, awareness becomes necessary that there may well exist more than one model for reference.

5.2.1   How Complex Is UG?

I do not have an answer to this question, and neither does anyone else at the moment. One view is expressed with these words by Berwick and Chomsky (2016: 71):

[T]he principles of language are determined by efficient computation, and language keeps to the simplest recursive operation designed to satisfy interface conditions ... Optimally, recursion can be reduced to Merge.

This way, the burden on the account of language evolution would be reduced to its minimum since all it would have taken was a genetic mutation to bring in Merge, presumably a desirable outcome (ibid., especially Chapter 3). Meanwhile, the syntactic literature within the UG framework is represented by characteristically complex and intricate analyses "in order to capture the empirical phenomena of language and their apparent variety" (ibid.: 93). To my knowledge, there is no published work, whether singularly or collectively, to prove that even the core set of facts accumulated in the past few decades can be derived merely by Merge plus independently established interface conditions. This does not mean, of course, that the proof will never be possible. Still, one would be hard pressed not to notice that the complexity and intricacy of the UG-based analyses are compatible with a neo-Darwinian model of language evolution that permits incremental accumulation of traits (Pinker and Bloom 1990). Or as Progovac (2016: 995) puts it (mostly still needing substantial proof), "one can decompose the attested complexities of syntax into evolutionary stages/primitives."

In the same spirit as section 5.1 above, I believe that both approaches are worthwhile endeavors, especially if UG is thought of as being biological in nature.

Since the recursive and hierarchical structure is an unavoidable trait of language, there is a conceptual advantage in maximizing its responsibilities as long as the effort is empirically substantiated and theoretically natural and coherent.[3] At the same time, it is dubious that recursion/Merge is adequate for linguistic facts even when accompanied by some unified form of minimality. Consider the locality behaviors of PRO and anaphors:

6. a. Chris told Sam [PRO to leave].
    b. Chris told Sam [a rumor about himself].

In (6a), PRO must be bound by *Sam*, the closest c-commanding DP; in (6b), however, *himself* can be bound by *Chris* for every native speaker of English and by *Sam* for some.[4] It is unclear how this contrast can follow from Merge plus a simple notion of minimality. Furthermore, even if the fact is attributed to the conceptual–intentional interface, it is not obvious what would be gained. Surely UG could be simple, but the whole burden of subtly separating PRO and *himself* plus the different locality behaviors is shifted now to the interface IF. Whether this is more plausible or not, should we imagine such a functionally sophisticated IF to have evolved through a simple genetic mutation? Is there proof/evidence that IF is not language-specific? And ultimately, why would such a burden-shift be easier on evolution than letting the genetic mutation simply shape what we call UG?

Similar points can be made easily in biology too. How neurons communicate is well understood: Neuronal activities change the membrane's electrical potential at the cell's synapse, the junction with another neuron; how the potential is changed determines whether the presynaptic neuron releases positive or negative ions, aka neurotransmitters, into the postsynaptic neuron via the latter's receptors; which starts the subsequent round of neuronal activities, and so on. The mechanism is obviously very basic – just electrical and chemical. And no one would question whether this knowledge is not worth obtaining. Facial recognition is a cognitive function based on neuronal activities, and it has been found that multiple parts of the brain participate in the perception (Rossion et al. 2012) in such a way that some of them recognize different parts of the face while others do a holistic job. Still, the precise mechanism underlying this cognitive capability remains unclear and is thus an area of active research. This example offers a rather clear message. A cognitive function or biological system may well be complex enough so that multiple layers of "realities" and their descriptions are needed for a full understanding. It is practical to start solving the puzzle at one layer, and there is no *a priori* starting point. Some might lend to the initial attempt their fundamental side and others, their directly observable side. It just seems that language offers more than one window to look into.

Lastly, as long as linguistics compares itself with biology, LeDoux's (1996) findings on fear (see section 2.6 of Chapter 2) are worth keeping in mind. If this seemingly simple cognitive function involves two neurological routes, presumably from different stages of evolution, why can't the much more sophisticated linguistic function be the result of multiple evolutionary accumulations?

5.2.2   Let Things Be Gradient

The biological world is full of facts spread over a spectrum (vs. a binary black-and-white distribution).[5] In general, two types of macro-spectrum are easy to see: intermediate existence between the good and the bad, and a set of well-formed inherently related entities differing gradually by some standard. The first type is shown by interspecies hybrids such as mules. Reproductivity is a definitive trait of life. A healthy interspecies individual lacks this capacity in its nature but has all other biological traits intact (e.g. kinetic, digestive, etc.) and thus is not fully "well formed" by the biological standard. Darwin's finches illustrate the second type with their different beak sizes and shapes (Figure 5.1). Both types of spectrum find counterparts in language.

Comparable to interspecies hybrids are the marginal examples richly documented in the syntactic literature. What demands attention, if one takes the

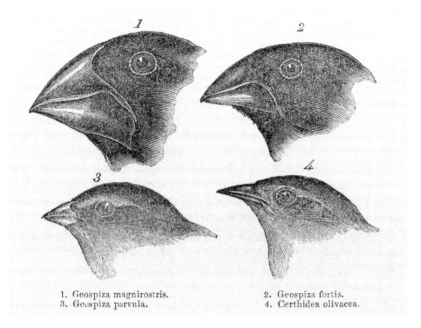

1. Geospiza magnirostris.   2. Geospiza fortis.
3. Geospiza parvula.   4. Certhidea olivacea.

Figure 5.1 Darwin's finches
This image is from Wellcome Images, a site of historical images operated by
the Wellcome Trust, United Kingdom.

biological nature of language seriously, is that the hybrid's incapacity to
reproduce is explained by the theory of biology, while little attention has
been given to finding answers to the marginal status of linguistic data.
Chomsky (1986) suggested n-Subjacency, which correlates the severity of
marginality of a given example E to the number of barriers to be crossed by
a moved constituent in E, but few subsequent works (Frampton 1990, Tellier
1991) pursued this line of reasoning in non-trivial ways. Still, marginality in
language is a fact and its explanation ought to be part of the theory of linguistics. Whether the source of a particular form of marginality is from UG or not is
an empirical question. What matters is that the field as a whole should not
ignore this phenomenon. If the explanation for the different degrees of marginality with non-constituent conjuncts in Chapter 3 proves tenable, at least some
such cases are the result of UG.

The linguistic versions of both the sterile mule and Darwin's finches are
dubbed "squishes" by Ross (1972). For the latter type, one of his examples is
The gas station is nearer the supermarket than the bank. For *near* to be suffixed
with *-er* would suggest its being adjectival, but the DP object assures the

prepositional nature of *nearer*. For Ross, *nearer* is between A and N. Y. Li (2014) gives a close examination of the second verbal morpheme of the resultative compounds in Chinese. It is observed that in this position, verbs may deviate along three axes: semantic, phonological and morphological. On the semantic axis, for instance, a verb may retain its full meaning, drop one of the semantic features, keep only one semantic feature, or get totally bleached so as to act out the purely grammatical role of this second position, namely to mark the termination of the event denoted by the first verb. A detailed recount aside, it is a fact that language, like the world of biology, displays certain facts on a spectrum. As a field, we should not and ultimately cannot brush them aside, and not just because they are part of the subject matter. Mixed traits of hybrid peas formed the empirical base of Mendel's laws of inheritance; the gradation of beak sizes and shapes of Darwin's finches underlaid the theory of evolution. If linguistics seriously regards biology as a role model or even thinks of itself as biological in nature, it is certainly possible that some linguistic spectrums might reveal part of UG more clearly than only black-and-white facts.

5.2.3   Observable Facts vs. Galilean Idealization

The quotation below comes from an interview of Chomsky by Jay Keyser in 2009.

If you want to understand phenomena there's only two ways, one is brute force which would be some weak correlations, the rest just abstract away from them and study ideal cases. And that's called the Galilean style, attribute more reality to the ideal case even in a nonexistent system like a frictionless plane, than we do to the phenomena that are just too complicated because there's too many variables and too many interacting sort of things. And that's quite important for the study of language. In fact it's a live battle in the study of language. Should we just study the massive phenomena and use brute force methods to try to model them somehow. Or should we abstract away from the complex phenomenon, and try to find ideal cases that we'll be able to investigate and maybe find some principles. (https://mitpress.podbean.com/e/noam-chomsky-and-samuel-jay-keyser/. The transcript was from www.mitpressjournals.org/userimages/ContentEditor/1256764313049/Keyser_Chomsky_Podcast_Transcript.pdf, which is no longer available.)

At any stage prior to finding the truth, a researcher almost certainly must sacrifice some possibly relevant facts in order to theorize. Even one who is only after "weak correlations" has to accept, tacitly or not, that there may exist some yet unnoticed/unknown phenomena that might alter the patterns, namely that the facts one has at the moment are "ideal" for the conclusion one draws from them.

Meanwhile, it is no less important to note that physics and biology always aim to maximally match theoretical abstraction from data idealization with the observable fact. Boltzmann's equation in Chapter 4, S = k log W, is a highly abstract description of the highly abstract concept of entropy, but S is meant to capture our direct experience that a heater in a cold room will gradually warm up the whole space, rather than a warm room naturally getting colder and colder while one of its corners becomes increasingly hot. Though acceleration, defined as the rate of change of velocity and calculated mathematically with the derivative of the latter with respect to time t, is an abstract concept (represented as dv/dt), it is grounded on the common observation that the higher an object falls from, the faster it goes. And the notions of both entropy and acceleration need idealizations for their formulation: an energetically isolated thermodynamic system for the former and lack of friction/resistance when the latter is used in computing, say, the distance traveled. But even these idealizations are consistent with our direct experience.

In the first case, a thermally better-insulated room is easier to become heated and stay that way. While 100 percent insulation is impossible in our common sense, it is neither difficult nor against our experience to imagine such a thermally perfect room so that the heat brought into it stays there. More than once in the interview mentioned earlier, Chomsky brings up the frictionless context for the formulation of classical mechanics. Indeed, Newton's classical mechanical laws led the initial theory of friction of Amontons by twelve years (1687 vs. 1699). Nevertheless, everyone with the experience of icy winters knows that different materials and surface roughness, etc. affect friction dramatically (e.g. coarse-surfaced wood on rubber vs. smooth-surfaced steel on ice). Like thermodynamics, the early period of physics could conveniently draw on observable facts to be inspired about where to seek idealization for theorizing and why a frictionless system is not empirically absurd.

The point being made here is that Galilean idealization in the pursuit of the truth is typically motivated by observable facts and not by a totally subjective decision (which does not exclude occasional insights of a genius surpassing all human experience). Furthermore and no less significantly, even the facts set aside by idealization are eventually brought back into the overall theory of the field. Friction, for instance, turns out to be mechanics plus various other factors, a major one being the coefficient of friction, μ, an empirical property of the materials in contact which incorporates our common knowledge into the picture:

7. Coulomb friction law: $F_f \leq \mu F_n$

F_f is the force of friction and F_n is the force that each surface in contact exerts on the other. When μ is very small (e.g. between steel and ice), F_f decreases accordingly, exactly what our experience tells us. To the extent that linguistics refers to physics for guidance, it pays to keep such actual cases of physics in mind when we construct UG by idealizing, say, different degrees of marginality or well-formed squishes out of the data set.

As my last example, Berwick and Chomsky (2016: 71) refer to snowflakes in this remark:

> language is something like a snowflake, assuming its particular form by virtue of laws of nature – in this case principles of computational efficiency – once the basic mode of construction is available, and satisfying whatever conditions are imposed at the interfaces.

As a matter of fact, snowflakes are more informative to linguistics than offering this general theory design. The molecular structure of water (H_2O) gives rise to weak polarities of the two hydrogen atoms and one oxygen atom, making them attracted to other polar molecules (and ions), including other water molecules. When temperature drops, this polar attraction extends the initial ice crystal with more water molecules and determines the hexagonal shape. This much corresponds to Chomsky's implementation of Merge (plus whatever factors, if there are any, affect what to merge with and how to project).

What is not mentioned in this analogy is the temporal direction of events. When a snowflake grows bigger from molecular merger, we observe a positive correlation between the passing time and the physical growth of the snowflake. This is where theory and fact coincide perfectly. Merge applied to language by Chomsky yields exactly the opposite. On one hand, Merge is based on constituency, a robust fact in linguistics. On the other hand, the default repetitive applications of Merge from an initial pair of lexical items to an increasingly larger constituent, paralleling the polar attraction of more water molecules to the existing snowflake, implements a bottom-up sequence of clause-generation, exactly opposite of human experience, creating a negative correlation between the time passed and the claimed incremental process of structure-building. If we take physics as a serious role model, this contrast is no small matter. Some critical factor must be at work. In this sense, the thermodynamic theory of linearization in Chapter 4 is an attempt at removing the negative correlation.

To analogize sentence-generation with the formation of snowflakes more closely, three components can be singled out. (i) a constituent is a linguistic molecule; (ii) its internal structural design, sequence of generation and "valency" with other constituents are all determined by general laws of linguistics and nature (e.g. the 2nd law of thermodynamics); it is also feasible that (iii) Merge as given in Chapter 4 be restored to its simplest rendition: merely a name for the combinatorial process without any other inherent property. But (ii) must include a general linguistic principle either directly imposing a linear adjacency condition on Merge – perhaps as part of the definition for linguistic valency – or preventing a structural constituent from becoming discontinuously expressed. How exactly such a condition is built into F_{HL} is yet to be decided. What matters for the immediate concern of this book is that the positive correlation thus produced between time and the sequence of the events of Merge fares well with both the role model of physics and the theory of the UG-I interface articulated on these pages.

5.3   Final Words

The work reported in this book formulates a UG-I theory by arguing for two functional voids of UG, $Void_F$ 1 and 2, and for the requirement that the mapping from R_C to R_S must be deterministic in all circumstances of clause-construction and that computational cost is an omnipresent requirement in the human language faculty. From these follow the rest of the iconicity-related analyses in the book and their natural implications and extensions to a much broader range of linguistic facts. A new theory of linearization is formulated which (i) handles all word-order issues that arise in the book and (ii) retains the insights of the existing models of linearization, another linguistic implementation of theory-synthesis which Mayr finds "typical" of biology. This book is the first systematic attempt to articulate a theory of UG-I with enough technical and empirical details to be theoretically falsifiable. I end the book with a quotation from Progovac (2016: 996). "Simply making claims about things and hoping to be right is not nearly as useful as generating specific and testable hypotheses, even if they turn out to be wrong." Seemingly paradoxically, the last clause of this quote actually expresses a researcher's confidence that we are doing something in the right direction.

Notes

Chapter 1

1. We leave Pirahã aside because (i) it is an extremely rare case unable to represent many other languages under examination and (ii) having a toolbox available is logically different from making use of all the tools in it.
2. A clarification of the term "sentence" is in order. We take a sentence to be simply a main clause. As a result, sentence-generation and clause-generation are synonyms for the purposes of this book, indicating the same applicational domain that UG is known for.
3. For a different view on the building blocks of sentences, see Distributed Morphology (DM), first articulated in Halle and Marantz (1993), which operates on features in syntactic environments instead of "whole" words/morphemes. The difference does not matter for the current concern, however, because concepts must be encoded with some syntactic or lexical means and that would be sufficient for the primary purpose of this book. I return in Chapters 2 and 4 to discussions bearing on DM.
4. The removal of D-structure in the Minimalist Program does not affect Newmeyer's reasoning. One only needs to say that the initial point of Merge for any constituent iconically reflects the predicate–argument relation.
5. From what I can see, the same problem exists with the functionalist literature, albeit from the opposite side. Thus, while this work looks at the subject matter primarily from the "formalist" angle, the essence of its central theme, that a more constructive and less partisan approach to the UG–iconicity relationship is called for, constitutes advice for the general field of linguistics and not just for any particular school of thought.

Chapter 2

1. There are apparent exceptions which are due to the previously mentioned lack of precise identification of the conditions for iconicity, as will become clear in the course of this chapter.
2. A reviewer notes the existence of "quite a literature pointing out how 'unminimalist' [parameters] are." I am certainly all for the continual effort to formulate the simplest theory of language possible. Meanwhile, one should also bear in mind the old issue of whether a simpler theory ends up shifting part of the burden elsewhere and, if this happens, in a more desirable manner. As an example, Kayne's (1994) antisymmetric syntax apparently removes the head-initial vs. head-final parameter, with the Linear Correspondence Axiom forcing all languages to have the head-initial structure. In place of this parameter,

however, half of the languages in the world must implement all-around movements so as to appear head-final. Two questions arise. First, no independently established motivations are given for why such movements happen in, for instance, Japanese VP but not in Chinese VP. Second, even if a motivation is articulated, it is in nature parametric for its being not at work in head-initial languages. Minimally, one would need to prove this new parameter to be overall more advantageous to the old one where the ordering between a head and its complement is simply the system-wide grammaticalization of probability-determined options. See Section 4.3 of Chapter 4 for relevant discussions.

3. Part of the content of this section is published as Y. Li and Ting (2013).
4. This remark came from a journal reviewer on an earlier draft of Li and Ting's (2013) paper and was endorsed by the assistant editor of the journal at the time.
5. Within the principles-and-parameters model, this observation is usually attributed to Muysken (1988). Newmeyer's (2004) doubt about this kind of iconicity is addressed below.
6. Also see Newmeyer (1992, 1998) for similar views on linear iconicity.
7. We take *wul*, translated by Foley and Olson as 'afraid', to be a verb. Foley (1991, section 3.3) discusses evidence to distinguish verbs from adjectival verbs. If *wul* is adjectival, then example (9b) may not even be relevant for the discussion of the SVC. See 2.4.1 and 2.5.2 of this chapter for how word orders are sensitive to categories in the context of the SVC.
8. See Collins (1997) for independent evidence that there is at least the option that the instrumental NP is the shared object of both verbs.
9. A reviewer brings up *a decrepit old red barn* in English as a possible case of "serial adjectives." The theoretical question here is whether the three adjectives all share a multiple-headed single AP; see Cinque and Rizzi (2010) for how adjectival adjuncts are structurally represented. On the factual side, since serial verbs are used as predicates, it is also worth noting that *This barn is decrepit old red.* is unacceptable.
10. Also see Tang (1990) for relevant discussions conceptually similar to ours. Several authors have assumed/argued for *pro* inside the SVC structure (Byrne 1985, Larson 1991, Law and Veenstra 1992, Collins 1997, Carstens 2002, Baker and Stewart 2002) while some evidence for *pro* is also questioned (Y. Li 2005: 196). But the current discussion is independent of such technical details.
11. One may question, as a reader of a previous draft of this chapter did, the statement here that part of the UG literature has a uniform treatment of SVCs, given that none of the references reviewed in this chapter, e.g. Baker (1989), explicitly claims to cover the SVCs in all languages. Such an objection is true only in the superficial sense. For anyone working within the UG model, making a theoretical claim about a few languages automatically implies that *unless otherwise stated*, the proposal is intended to be part of UG, whether in the form of a principle or a parameter. The clearest evidence for this is Baker (2001), where his multiple-headed VP option is clearly taken to be one of the major parameters to classify languages (p. 141). More evidence is seen in the current UG literature on the SVC – see our references throughout this chapter – where the projection of one verbal element is always placed in the complement position of the other. If this structural setup for the SVC

were not viewed as being universal, why would different authors assume it for different languages with hardly any case-by-case justifications?

12. *Random House Webster's College Dictionary*, for instance, defines *orderly* as "arranged or disposed in a neat, tidy manner or in a regular sequence."

13. Ultimately, this is one of the reasons for the current work to formulate a separate theory of linearization from Kayne's (1994) antisymmetry model. See Chapter 4.

14. *Gei* 'give' in this case is the true V1 of an SVC since it can accept an aspectual marker. Compare it with the preverbal and aspect-rejecting *gei* in 2.1.4 above, which is likely to be a preposition.

15. A journal editor (p.c.) dismissed the theoretical significance of these Chinese examples due to their marginal status, with which I disagree. The sole value of (48–51) lies in the stable degree of acceptability inside each pair of examples, of which one is demonstrably without a c-commanding binder for the pronoun. Provided that the weak marginality does not change, the conclusion can be drawn that c-command in overt syntax does not matter to the bound-variable interpretation. This reasoning is as straightforward and valid as any that are based on marginal data (which form part of the core in the UG literature).

16. *Nali* 'there' in (50a-b) is a localizer required by prepositions like *cong* 'from' whose complement must refer to a location. In other words, while *from every candidate* is well-formed in English, one must say something like *from every candidate's place* in Chinese, which embeds the QP even more deeply than the object of P and makes our objection to Carstens even stronger.

17. The first *mai* carries the 3rd tone and means 'to buy'; the second *mai* has the 4th tone and means 'to sell'.

18. A reviewer ponders on (i-ii) in English and observes that "we never have two transitive verbs":

    i. Go find the hammer.
    ii. Come look at the rainbow.

    Interestingly, native speakers of English find it hard to let this construction occur in a finite declarative sentence:

    iii. *Sam went find the hammer.
    iv. *Chris came visit me.

    No such contrast is ever observed with SVCs.

19. Which might be a reason for the SVC data to be misinterpreted, including some cases reviewed earlier in this chapter.

20. Japanese is often said to have adjectives taking tense (Nishiyama 1999: 183):

    i. miti-ga   hiroi/hirokatta.
       road-NOM   wide.pres/wide.past
       'The road is/was wide.'

    But as Nishiyama (ibid.: 192) argues on the basis of historical data and the Japanese inflectional paradigms, what is taken to be an adjective is actually composed of the adjectival root, a predicate morpheme and a copula which takes the zero form in present tense.

21. Note that V1 in (86a) is of type <s, t> and thus matches the semantic type of *P* in (86b). That is, purely in terms of semantic types, V1 can actually serve as semantic

argument of R_T-V2. However, this "argument" is not thematically saturated and thus is illegitimate for UG. See relevant discussions above.

22. Recall from 2.4.2 how SVCs contrast with causative verbs like *make*, which may indeed take a vP/VP complement. Verbs that take bare vP/VP objects may appear to contradict the text where we suggest that an argument must be thematically saturated because vP/VP, in itself, has an event role to saturate. But the theory of UG already has more than one proposed mechanisms to handle the apparent problem. Williams (1981) argues that the θ-role of a noun such as *book*, which he calls the R-role to imply its referential function, is automatically saturated at the moment the NP receives a θ-role from a verb through θ-role coindexation. Simply put, it is in the grammatical capacity of V to make sure that its argument is thematically saturated. Note that this idea cannot be extended to the R_T-V case because, critically, each V must stay as denoting a set of sub-events, having its event role unsaturated, so that the entire serial verb VP still denotes a set of composite events. Another idea is from Diesing (1992), placing a default existential quantifier at the edge of vP/VP which indiscriminately binds (and thus saturates; see Higginbotham 1985) the thematic position(s) in the object. In this model, the embedded verbal complement of *make* will have its event role bound by the existential closure at the edge of the matrix vP/VP, just like all other indefinite NP objects, and thus make the embedded vP complement saturated. But the event role of a verb manifesting a sub-event in E must not be treated this way. It must be interpreted as a segment of E which in turn is bound by T like the event role of any main predicate.

23. Apparently, movement is no sufficient motivation for Chinese to turn V1 into the main verb. In an intuitive sense, this is no surprise. After all, the bi-clausal risk at hand is simply a potentially complicating factor without in itself violating UG. So it is up to a specific language to decide to what extent to avoid it.

24. See Miyagawa et al. (2013, 2014) for an evolutionary account for how human languages end up having TP and CP above VP.

25. It must be emphasized at this point that both the USM and its isomorphic manifestation is from R_C to R_S in the current theory of UG-I. Lexicalization may be viewed as UG's way to meet this requirement, so that 'theme of' is always lexicalized into a θ-role. Structural ambiguity (e.g. *break the cup in the kitchen*), sometimes used as evidence for lack of isomorphism between meaning and form, is irrelevant to how the concept is used in this book. Structural ambiguity results from the linear R_L being unable to distinguish differences at the level of R_S, while our concern is between R_C and R_S.

26. Pylkkänen (2008) actually distinguishes two kinds of applicatives. See Chapter 4 for details and their pros and cons.

27. Given Y. Li (1999), the causal role algorithm in (105) applies both clause-internally and to separate sentences, the latter outside the territory of UG. Hence, I regard it as part of F_{HL} for the current content. It may well be more general than linguistic. Keep in mind, however, that at least inside a clause, (105) has the effect of readjusting the standard thematic hierarchy and thus appears directly involved in UG operations. See my discussion bearing on this last issue in Chapter 2 of Huang et al. (2009).

28. Chen and Li (2021) offers unequivocal evidence that the lexical root of an ergative verb does not have to have the agent argument represented in syntax provided that the absence of vP satisfies the rest of the grammar in a particular language. Hence, an unergative V1 in the hypothetical Japanese compound in (106b) is not automatically bad because there is no argument in the example expressing its agentivity.

29. What matters here is that (107) satisfies the USM so that V1 is given the unequivocal headhood for causal interpretation. Japanese syntax also treats V2 as the head of the compound due to the language being head-final. But that is a separate operation and there is no logical necessity for the USM to look beyond its own immediate satisfaction, especially in the overall minimalist design of the language faculty.

Chapter 3

1. It should be noted that Marantz' (1997) theory, as is presented, cannot explain why √GROW and √BREAK have the causative uses while √DIE does not. See 4.2.1 of Chapter 4 later for our solution.

2. I share with a reviewer that (16c) does not sound great, but interpret Zwart's English examples as the closest counterparts of the various coordination forms in other languages.

3. See Mithun (1988) and Zwart (2005) for reasons against treating the summary and comitative elements as conjunctions.

4. 3.2.2 and 3.2.3 benefit sigificantly from Progovac (2003).

5. Unless a reference is given, the judgments of the English examples in this book are all from Rebecca Shields, to whom this author is immensely grateful.

6. A reviewer notes the attempt in the government-and-binding period (GB) of syntax "to predict the degree of unacceptability based on the nature of Subjacency and ECP violations," which shares with the depth-based account of NCCs the goal of accounting for "relative acceptability." An even closer comparison is Chomsky's (1986) practically transient n-Subjacency. While I obviously hold the view that marginality deserves due attention because it is part of our linguistic reality, it is not clear to me how the ECP-Subjacency approach to bad vs. marginal examples is more than simple stipulation: no logic, either in its general sense or internal to the GB model, would explain why one UG principle leads to a more severe outcome than another, especially when both were presumably based on government. See relevant discussions on government and n-Subjacency in Chapter 5.

7. See Hornstein and Weinberg (1981) for an analysis of English preposition stranding and its conditions. Presumably, reanalysis happens to English which allows P to be treated as part of a "compound verb" and thus exempted from normal restrictions. Note that this compound verb approach obviously will not help improve P-deletion. Also keep in mind that verbs are indeed subject to gapping: *Jack ordered a beer and Sam, just a cup of tea.*

8. Unless one forms a constituent conjunct c, does necessary deletions and only then calculates what is left of c on the surface. But such a reassessment would be very strange given that the structure itself remains valid throughout.

9. Conceptually though not technically, this account of the CSC is comparable to Sag's (2000) proposal that a displaced conjunct leaves no trace and thus what stays *in situ* has no constituent to conjoin to. In (82b), no trace is possible for a conjunct because the latter simply cannot move in the first place.

10. These properties do not describe the conjunction *but*, on which the literature seems scarce and uncertain. Barwise and Cooper (2002: 107) "assume that the interpretation of *but* is the same as that of *and* for the purpose of truth conditional semantics" but with important differences. E.g. unlike *and*, *but* rejects iteration at the syntactic level, which "might be related" to its unique semantic requirement/ preference for mixed increasing and decreasing quantifiers. Pragmatics is also associated with the analysis of *but* (e.g. Peterson 1986/2008). I see no intrinsic incompatibility between the essence of the theory presented here and *but*, but feel obliged to leave this word aside until a reasonably robust understanding of it can be reached.

11. Also note that even if we adopt the DM/XSM approach to allowing bare roots in the functional context, UG is never known to have functional heads capable of providing extended projections of *and* in the same way that v or D projects √FORM.

12. Zoerner (1995) and Progovac (2003) discuss "sub-group coordination" and its correlation with the use of *'n* (e.g. *Tom and [Mary 'n Jim]*), taking this to be evidence for recursive &Ps. In my view, this is likely to be iconicity at work, mapping an intended "tighter" semantic connection to a bound PF form by skipping R_S as seen with SVCs.

13. So can Korean, according to two TAs from the East Asian Department of University of Wisconsin-Madison.

14. To my knowledge, this observation was first made by McCawley (1982).

15. A couple of details in (92b) are not accurate by the APT due to limited space, but they do not matter for discussing the island effect.

16. A reviewer finds (95a) unacceptable, which I believe reflects a dilemma such examples inevitably face: The bound variable reading of the epithet requires c-command, while as an r-expression, the epithet must not be bound. See the analysis below this example and in Chapter 4.

17. Also worth noting is a further generalization over (98) and the O1 . . . *e* dependency for SVCs. There seems to exist an independent and cross-linguistic rule on the linear direction of such coreferential dependencies so that **e . . . O2* is just as impossible as reversing the linear sequence of an r-expression and a coindexed pronoun in (98).

18. A reviewer points out that this example "is fine in informal English." Apparently, "informal English" has essentially abandoned the language-specific agreement strategy between T and the postverbal NP and, instead, makes T agree directly with the expletive *there*, comparable to the *Il y a* . . . construction in French. This "dialect" of English, then, simply provides no data for the agreement phenomenon under discussion.

19. It is worth noting that these examples are unlikely to be accounted for with a deletion theory. For such a theory to apply here, it is minimum to assign each conjunct with an underlying VP for (107), *announced that he intended to retire and announced his year-end report on the stock market* for (107b), for instance. The

expression may sound a bit repetitive, but such an underlying structure certainly would not explain why (107b) is detectably worse.

The types of example in (107) display variation in acceptability. Zoerner (1995), for instance, takes the example in (i) below to be good. To the three informants consulted for this work, however, it forms a sharp contrast with (ii):

i. ??/*Robin realized that the sky was falling and the gravity of the situation.
ii. Robin realized the gravity of the situation and that she must act right away.

Our analysis in the text is based on this difference in acceptability. For anyone finding (i–ii) and (106a–b) to be equally good, the simplest explanation is that lexical category is the only factor checked on the main plane, leaving Case to whichever plane hosting the "DP material".

20. To remove what I perceive to be redundancies, the summary in (110) is mine based on Bošković's work but does not exactly reflect the way he sorts out the agreement pattern. Also, Bošković only discusses how the first conjunct with a semantically interpretable feminine gender affects LCA in section 3.3. Whether a non-first conjunct of that gender affects FCA is not mentioned (cf. (111b, c-ii)).

21. As an example, Zoerner (1995) makes the generalization that with Case derivation, all conjuncts except the last one will share the same Case, as shown in (123d). At first sight, this appears to comply with placing all the non-final conjuncts in the Spec positions of &P, thereby making them behave alike in syntax (cf. Bošković's analysis of tri-conjunct coordination). But it is not a direct derivative of the current theory of UG that the non-final conjuncts get the nominative Case when &P is the object, nor is it clear to what extent the factual generalization itself holds, as (123c) shows. A reviewer notes the possible relevance of Emonds (1986) where *them and us* is argued to be more natural for UG than *we and they*.

22. Unless stated otherwise, the analysis and core facts in this subsection are all based on Chen (in press), though the specific examples may be adjusted to facilitate my discussions.

23. The contrast reported here in (140) and its comparison with (139) are based on consistent judgments by four native speakers, all with graduate-level linguistic training.

24. This logic excludes the case of A being part of a compound since -*de* embodies *syntactic* modification.

25. I adopt the idea from Diesing (1992) that the predicate phrase, YP in (147) has an existential closure by default, which in this case saturates the event position of V. Also see Enç (1986) and Schwarz (2012) for arguing that situation variables inside arguments may be bound internally.

26. Compared with -*que* in Latin (see (87) of Chapter 3)), -*de* is purely prosodically dependent with no reference to morphological structure. Thus, its linearization cannot be resolved through morphology as -*que* is and must appeal to iconicity.

27. There is another layer of complication on this topic: whether Chinese syntax can be properly captured with a uniform head-initial phrase structure given the fact that Chinese DPs appear to be strictly head-final like the neighboring Altaic languages. See Cheng and Sybesma (1999, 2005), A. Li (1999), Zhang (2010), X. Li (2013), Y. Li (2015), Her (2017), Her and Tsai (2020), Tan and Li (2020) either on or related to the debate.

28. This possibility was brought up by an anonymous reviewer of a paper that reported an earlier stage of the analysis of -*de* in this chapter.

29. Another implication of this analysis is that the small clause SC in the V-*de* construction (144a) should still be a projection of A (AP or *a*P) so as to justify the unique semantics of -*de*.

30. I thank Zhe Chen for an informal survey of eleven Cantonese speakers with these sentences and their judgments. The original examples have tones which are irrelevant and thus are not shown here.

Chapter 4

1. Baker does not gloss the prefixes and suffixes that are characteristic of Mohawk morphology, so I simply avoid giving the noun root here. This level of detail is irrelevant to the current concern.

2. Note that being in the complement position does not entail being the theme argument of V. There is enough evidence (see Rizzi 1990, Levin and Rappaport-Hovav 1995, Ting and Li 1997, Huang et al. 2009, among others) that resultative (small) clauses occupy the complement position. Also see our analysis of the Chinese postverbal adjective in Section 3.4 of Chapter 3.

3. *Escapee, retiree* and *attendee* may all be treated parallel to *standee*, with -*ee* being in the states denoted by the verbal roots. Also note the Chinese example (i) that parallels (27):

    i. jianyu-li   zuijin   tao-le   haojige   fanren.
       prison-in   lately   escape-ASP   several   inmate
       ?'There have escaped from the prison several inmates lately.'

    The inversion between *tao* 'escape' and *escape* suggests minimally that the single argument of this verb does not have to be an agent.

4. See Sun and Li (2020) for tests that screen out apparent counterexamples where the verb is disyllabic. They also demonstrated the same pattern in several Southeast Asian languages. Zhang (2018) presents an analysis of the Chinese NCAs based on Ramchand's (2008) syntactic structure of event decomposition and, in essence, treats an NCA as "the complement of an unergative" (p. 1410). In addition to the fact that Zhang's analysis does not – and probably cannot as far as I can see – accommodate the monosyllabic requirement on V and the noncanonical subject, there are too many disagreements between her core data and our judgment (by this author and the multiple informants consulted), of which only one is given here for illustration:
    According to Zhang and as part of her evidence for the unergative analysis, a noncanonical object "is not allowed to be a pronoun, and is not allowed to be classifier-initial, either" (p. 1398). But (i–ii) are perfect:

    i. guoqu   sannian   ni   zhiyi   zai   chi   fumu.   Xianzai   ni
       past   three.year   2s   always   ASP   eat   parents   now   2s
       dasuan   chi   women   ma?
       intend   eat   1PL   Q

'You've been eating (= living) on your parents in the past three years. Now are you planning to eat (= live) on us?'

ii. shitang   de   fan   bu   haochi.   Wo   xiang   chi   (yi)   jia
    cafeteria   DE   food   not   tasty   1s   want   eat   a   CL
    canguang,   huanhuan   kouwei.
    restaurant   have.a.change.of   flavor
    'The cafeteria food doesn't taste good. I wanna eat in a restaurant and try a different flavor.'

The pronoun *women* 'us' has the malfactive reading after *eat* in (i) and the numeral *yi* 'a' is totally optional to produce a "classifier-initial" NCA in (ii). More disagreements on data will be presented in a separate work.

5. I am grateful to Dr. Jingshu Hu for doing the survey.

6. Another solution is to use pre-/post-positions, as reflected in the well-known dative alternations: *send a gift to X* vs. *send X a gift*. PPs presumably can be inside VP.

7. The pattern in (33) is only preliminary because of the well-known fact that there are two *-le*s in Mandarin Chinese. One suffixes to V for perfective aspect and the other at the end of a sentence, presumably to mark a "change of state" (Lü 1984: 314). The semantic overlap is further muddled by the fact that only one *-le* may occur when no other constituent follows V. This is why *ge bao* 'CL full' is added in (33b) – so as to make sure that the *-le* after V2 is the same as the one after V1 in (33a). Given such interferences, precise minimal pairs are not always easy to come by. In (33a), for instance, *ge bao* 'CL full' is not possible for reasons I do not understand.

8. There is a third possible structure for morphological causativization: that *caus* takes a full clausal complement (Pylkkänen 2008). But this option is obviously irrelevant for the current concern because for anaphor-binding, CP and *v*P yield identical outcomes. Also, because the category-sensitivity summarized in (39) happens within the same language, hypothesizing different types of *caus* depending on the category of the root it pairs with is not the solution but just another way of stating the problem at issue.

9. Borer points out two empirical problems with LPM which treats the null verbalizer $\emptyset_V$ in [$_N$ form]-$\emptyset_V$ as Level II and the null nominalizer $\emptyset_N$ as Level I. As such, derived nouns of the same Level II are wrongly predicted to be used directly as verbs (e.g. *to ability-$\emptyset_V$); also, since compounding is a Level II process as well, the different behaviors of the compounds in (41c) cannot be distinguished. What is apparently missed in this critique of LPM is that allowing a bare root to directly occur in a syntactic CCP so as to act as V or N for (41a), is functionally equivalent to re-ranking the LPM system by treating the null verbalizing $\emptyset_V$ to be a Level I affix too. In this sense, XSM is not empirically advantageous to the revised LPM provided that no other data is sacrificed.

10. A reviewer points out that there are many "zero-derivation nouns that allow full argument structure (e.g. *my constant change of mentors from 1992–1997*), which may appear as problematic data for Borer's conclusion from *verbalize* that bare roots do not take arguments." My response is two-fold. First, the reviewer's examples help explain why this book does not simply adopt a theory like XSM. In contrast, both *verbalize* and the nominal use of *change* fit well in my own view of word-formation under Void$_F$2. As no root participates in syntax directly anyway, both words at issue enter phrasal syntax already with their categories, with or without overt derivational morphemes which enable them to take arguments.

Second, despite the noted problem with data, Borer's reasoning based on *verbalize* remains valid: contra Harley, the *do so*-test is not reliable evidence that there must exist a syntactic constituent consisting of a bare root and its semantic object.

11. The issue of Pair-Merge (Chomsky 2000) is not considered here.

12. Apparently, whether a c-commanding object qualifies as a binder varies not only inter-linguistically but also intra-linguistically. See (6) and note 4 in Chapter 5.

13. Note that R_M is clearly not reducible to Higginbotham's (1985) θ-identification. For one thing, *house-dog* does not define the intersection of the house-set and the dog-set. For another, event identification happens both between an adverb and V and between *v* and V, but the two pairs have fundamentally different structures. Thus we need something more for the relation of modification, a welcome conclusion that also unites my analysis of linkers in Chapter 3.

14. All the information I use from this survey is based on the online source provided in the reference. The same atlas is also accessible through the library system, but this particular chapter from the latter source contains less information than the online version.

15. Ultimately, there is also an important issue of defining Arg_E. E.g. in *The forest surrounds the village*, is the subject an agent? See Dowty (1991) for defining proto-agent with multiple semantic features; also see Chen and Li (2021) for applying Dowty's idea to agentivity in Chinese.

16. Depending on how the starting terminal is chosen in this bottom-up model, one could even enforce all human languages to have the underlying head-final structure, exactly opposite of Kayne's LCA outcome. See Fukui and Takano (1998) and Li (2005) for phrase structure models with this result.

17. Hawkins (1990) tries to explain the word-order possibilities by efficiency of parsing. However, nothing is said about the linear location of the subject. Also, it is not clear to me at all how his theory even allows *wh-in-situ*. While overt *wh*-movement certainly helps recognize and construct an interrogative CP instantly in the left-to-right parsing, an *in-situ wh* in the object position effectively delays the recognition (e.g. [+*wh*] in C in modern terminology) till much later in the sentence. Shouldn't this be avoided at all costs?

18. This content is a revised version of Y. Li (2017) which benefited from comments by two medical physicists (Drs. Qince Li and John Wakai) and an anonymous reviewer specializing in thermodynamics.

19. The number is calculated with the combination formula (rather than the permutation formula) because merely swapping two on-particles in the same two room cells makes no difference for the overall energy-spreading pattern in the room (i.e. the way heat "distributes" in the room feels exactly the same).

20. Dryer treats German as a language alternating between SVO and SOV, but the SVO option is but one of many superficial word orders of West Germanic main clauses and all of them receive a uniform account based on the SOV structure. Unfortunately, we do not have a similarly in-depth understanding of most other languages.

21. Also see Anderson (1992: 18) on Kʷakʷ'ala morphology in which the determiner of the object attaches to V, appearing like D-to-V movement, but there is clear evidence that the functional morphemes in this language are simply structure-blind enclitics.

22. If one adopts the proposal that *wh*-movement goes through the edge of *v*P before reaching the Spec of CP, the *wh* will form a two-member chain with the trace in the matrix *v*P. This detail has no effect on the logic in the text. The role of the *v*P phase is addressed below.

23. Even in the initial formation of Montague grammar, where NP literally takes VP as its argument, the syntactic structure is a clause and not a further projection of V. Also worth pointing out is that 'λf' in (89b) runs counter to Void$_F$1 since f stands for non-first order predicates. So Pylkkänen's particular semantic definition of Appl$_L$ cannot be adopted in this work anyway.

24. But see Bowers (1993) and Alexiadou (1997) for associating VP-adverbs to the VP structure. Also see (89a) where, contra Larson (1988), even a double-object verb does not need to move V to v to yield *give Jill a gift*. Treating So as a sentential adverb is inconsistent with Chen and Li's (2021) placing it inside *v*P. Still, the key point being made there remains legitimate: There exists a verbal projection of some kind which allows a So adverb but not a subject depictive and which is correlated with the absence of the agent argument.

25. The same analysis is independently explored by Chomsky (2015: 11): "phrasehood is inherited by T ... along with all other inflectional/functional properties of C (φ-features, tense, Q), and is activated on T when C is deleted."

26. An analysis of (117a) is provided by Kiss (2002) with the assumption that KP (K for Case) is not acceptable in the Spec position of any nominal functional head (pp. 168–169).

Chapter 5

1. See a response to virtual conceptual necessity by Postal (2003). Like one of the reviewers of this book, I admit to not understanding how exactly to determine what counts as "virtual conceptual necessity" so as to guarantee its general application in a meaningful manner. But this part of Chomsky's wording does not prevent us from evaluating his more specific ideas on language.

2. The tacit assumption here prompted one of the questions raised by Chomsky (personal communication): How does the subject get a Case? Presumably, his logic was that T has no θ-role and thus is unable to satisfy (1) at all.

3. My own view, however, is that the recent efforts to make the projection fully predictable from Merge (Chomsky 2013, 2015) begin to acquire the flavor of the continuous but failed effort to make government axiomatic in UG. Some contents of the current book rely on Merge as the combinatorial mechanism but critically do not adopt this part of Chomsky's theorizing, as seen clearly in Chapters 3–4.

4. This data is based on over 1,000 American students in my introduction-to-syntax course.

5. This subsection is based on Y. Li and Chen (2018).

References

Aboh, Enoch Olade. 2009. Clause structure and verb series. *Linguistic Inquiry* 40: 1–33.

Ackema, Peter. 2006. *Review of Yafei Li*, X°: A theory of the morphological-syntax interface. *Journal of Linguistics* 42: 205–211.

Ahlner, Felix and Jordan Zlatev. 2010. Cross-modal iconicity: A cognitive semiotic approach to sound symbolism. *Sign Systems Studies* 38: 298–348.

Aikhenvald, Alexandra. 2006. Serial verb constructions in typological perspective. In Aikhenvald and Dixon, 1–68.

Aikhenvald, Alexandra and R. M. W. Dixon (eds.). 2006. *Serial verb constructions: A cross-linguistic typology*. Oxford: Oxford University Press.

Aissen, Judith. 1987. *Tzotzil clause structure*. Dordrecht: D. Reidel.

Aissen, Judith. 1996. Pied-piping, abstract agreement, and functional projections in Tzotzil. *Natural Language and Linguistic Theory* 14: 447–491.

Aissen, Judith. 2003. Differential object marking: Iconicity vs. economy. *Natural Language and Linguistic Theory* 21: 435–483.

Alexiadou, Artemis. 1997. *Adverb placement: A case study in antisymmetric syntax*. Amsterdam: John Benjamins.

Alexiadou, Artemis and E. Anagnostopolou. 2001. The subject-in-situ generalization and the role of case in driving computations. *Linguistic Inquiry* 32: 193–231.

Alsina, Alex. 1992. On the argument structure of causatives. *Linguistic Inquiry* 23: 517–556.

Anderson, Stephen. 1992. *A-morphous morphology*. Cambridge: Cambridge University Press.

Anderson, Stephen. 1999. A formalist's reading of some functionalist work in syntax. In Darnell et al., vol. 1, 111–136.

Atkins, P. W. 1994. *The 2nd Law: Energy, chaos, and form*. New York: Scientific American Books.

Babyonyshev, Maria. 1997. Covert feature checking and conjunction agreement in Russian. Paper presented at 1997 Formal Approaches to Slavic Linguistics (FASL), University of Connecticut, Storrs.

Bach, Emmon. 1964. *An introduction to transformational grammars*. New York: Holt, Rinehart & Winston.

Bach, Emmon. 1971. Questions. *Linguistic Inquiry* 2: 153–166.

Bach, Emmon. 1986. The algebra of events. *Linguistics and Philosophy* 9: 5–16.

Bachrach, Asaf and Roni Katzir. 2009. Right-node raising and delayed spellout. In Kleanthes K. Grohmann (ed.) *Interphases: Phase-theoretic investigations of linguistic interfaces*. Oxford: Oxford University Press.

Baker, Brett and Mark Harvey. 2010. Complex predicate formation. In M. Amberber, B. Baker and M. Harvey (eds.) *Complex predicates: Cross-linguistic perspectives on event structure*, 13–47. Cambridge: Cambridge University Press.

Baker, Mark. 1988. *Incorporation: A theory of grammatical function changing*. Chicago, IL: Chicago University Press.

Baker, Mark. 1989. Object sharing and projection in serial verbal construction. *Linguistic Inquiry* 20: 13–33.

Baker, Mark. 1996. *The polysynthesis parameter*. New York: Oxford University Press.

Baker, Mark. 2001. *The atoms of language: The mind's hidden rules of grammar*. New York: Basic Books.

Baker, Mark. 2002. Building and merging, not checking. *Linguistic Inquiry* 33: 321–328.

Baker, Mark and Osamyimen Stewart. 2002. *A serial verb construction without construction*. Ms. Rutgers University, New Jersey.

Barwise, Jon and Robin Cooper. 2002. Generalized quantifiers and natural language. In Paul Portner and Barbara Partee (eds.) *Form semantics: The essential readings*, 75–126. Oxford: Blackwell.

Bautista, Calixto Agüero. 2014. Weak crossover and the syntax–phonology interface. *Berkeley Linguistics Society* 40.

Belletti, Adriana. 2004. (ed.) *Structures and beyond: The cartography of syntactic structures*. Oxford: Oxford University Press.

Benmamoun, Elabbas. 1992. *Functional and inflectional morphology: Problems of projection, representation and derivation*. Ph.D. dissertation, University of Southern California.

Berwick, Robert and Noam Chomsky. 2016. *Why only us? Language and evolution*. Cambridge, MA: MIT Press.

Bickerton, Derek. 1990. *Language and species*. Chicago, IL: University of Chicago Press.

Blevins, James. 1990. *Syntactic complexity: Evidence for discontinuity and multidomination*. Ph.D. dissertation, University of Massachusetts.

Bloomfield, Leonard. 1933. *Language*. New York: Henry Holt.

Bobaljik, Jonathan David. 2015. *Distributed morphology*. Ms. University of Connecticut, Storrs.

Boeckx, Cedric and Massimo Piattelli-Palmarini. 2005. Language as a natural object, linguistics as a natural science. *Linguistic Review* 22: 447–466.

Bolinger, Dwight. 1977. *The form of language*. London: Longman.

Bolinger, Dwight. 1982. Intonation and its parts. *Language* 58: 505–533.

Borer, Hagit. 2005. *The normal course of events*. Oxford: Oxford University Press.

Borer, Hagit. 2014. Wherefore roots? *Theoretical Linguistics* 40.3/4: 343–359.

Borer, Hagit. 2015. The category of roots. In A. Alexiadou, H. Borer and F. Schafer (eds.) *The syntax of roots and the roots of syntax*, 112–148. Oxford: Oxford University Press.

Bošković, Željko. 2002. On multiple *wh*-fronting. *Linguistic Inquiry* 38: 351–383.

Bošković, Željko. 2009. Unifying first and last conjunct agreement. *Natural Language and Linguistic Theory* 27: 455–496.

Bošković, Željko and Daiko Takahashi. 1998. Scrambling and last resort. *Linguistic Inquiry* 29: 347–366.

Bowden, J. 2001. *Taba: Description of a South Halmahera language*. Canberra: Pacific Linguistics.

Bowers, John. 1993. The syntax of predication. *Linguistic Inquiry* 24: 591–656.

Bresnan, Joan and Lioba Moshi. 1993. Object asymmetries in comparative Bantu syntax. In Sam A. Mchombo (ed.) *Theoretical aspects of Bantu grammar*, 47–91. Stanford, CA: CSLI Publications.

Bruening, Benjamin. 2018. The lexicalist hypothesis: Both wrong and superfluous. *Language* 94: 1–42.

Byrne, Francis. 1985. Pro$_{prox}$ in Saramaccan. *Linguistic Inquiry* 16: 313–320.

Carnie, Andrew. 2002. *Syntax: A generative introduction*. Malden, MA: Blackwell.

Carrier, Jill and Janet Randall. 1992. The argument structure and syntactic structure of resultatives. *Linguistic Inquiry* 23: 173–134.

Carstens, Vicki. 2002. Antisymmetry and word order in serial constructions. *Language* 78: 3–50.

Chao, Yuen-Ren. 1968. *A grammar of spoken Chinese*. Berkeley, CA: University of California Press.

Chaves, Rui. 2012. On the grammar of extraction and coordination. *Natural Language and Linguistic Theory* 30: 465–512.

Chen, Zhe. 2017. *The classification of Chinese adverbials, interrupted scopes and the nature of minimality in non-movement dependencies*. Ph.D. dissertation, University of Wisconsin, Madison.

Chen, Zhe. in press. Probed by a modifier at the bottom of a clause. *Journal of Chinese Linguistics*.

Chen, Zhe and Yafei Li. 2016. Looking at *v*P from the Chinese perspective. *Foreign Language Teaching and Research* 4: 483–497.

Chen, Zhe and Yafei Li. 2021. Bipartite agentivity expression in Chinese passives. *Syntax* 24: 123–141.

Cheng, Lisa and Rint Sybesma. 1999. Bare and not-so-bare nouns and the structure of NP. *Linguistic Inquiry* 30: 509–542.

Cheng, Lisa and Rint Sybesma. 2005. Classifiers in four varieties of Chinese. In Guglielmo Cinque and Richard Kayne (eds.) *Handbook of comparative syntax*, 259–292. Oxford: Oxford University Press.

Chomsky, Noam. 1957. *Syntactic structures*. The Hague: Mouton.

Chomsky, Noam. 1970. Remarks on nominalization. In R. Jacobs and P. Rosenbaum (eds.) *Readings in English transformational grammar*, 184–221. Waltham, MA: Ginn.

Chomsky, Noam. 1981. *Lectures on government and binding*. Dordrecht: Foris.

Chomsky, Noam. 1982. *Some concepts and consequences of the government-binding theory*. Cambridge, MA: MIT Press.

Chomsky, Noam. 1986. *Knowledge of language: Its nature, origin and use*. New York: Praeger.

Chomsky, Noam. 1995. *The minimalist program*. Cambridge, MA: MIT Press.

Chomsky, Noam. 2000. Minimalist inquiries: The framework. In Roger Martin, David Michaels and Juan Uriagereka (eds.) *Step by step: Essays on minimalist syntax in honor of Howard Lasnik*, 89–155. Cambridge, MA: MIT Press.

Chomsky, Noam. 2001a. Derivation by phase. In Michael Kenstowicz (ed.) *Ken Hale: A life in language*, 1–52. Cambridge, MA: MIT Press.

Chomsky, Noam. 2001b. Beyond explanatory adequacy. *MIT Occasional Papers in Linguistics* 20.
Chomsky, Noam. 2004a. *Biolinguistics and the human capacity.* Lecture at MTA, Budapest.
Chomsky, Noam. 2004b. Beyond explanatory adequacy. In Belletti, 104–131.
Chomsky, Noam. 2007. Approaching UG from below. In Uli Sauerland and Hans-Martin Gärtner (eds.) *Interfaces + Recursion = Language? Chomsky's Minimalism and the View from Syntax-Semantics*, 1–29. Berlin: Mouton de Gruyter.
Chomsky, Noam. 2012. *The science of language: Interviews with James McGilvrary.* Cambridge: Cambridge University Press.
Chomsky, Noam. 2013. Problems of projection. *Lingua* 130: 33–49.
Chomsky, Noam. 2015. Problems of projection: Extensions. In Elisa Di Domenico, Cornelia Hamann and Simona Matteini (eds.) *Structures, strategies and beyond: Studies in honour of Adriana Belletti*, 3–16. Amsterdam: John Benjamins.
Chomsky, Noam and Howard Lasnik. 1993. The theory of principles and parameters. In Joachim Jacobs, Arnim von Stechow, Wolfgang Sternefeld and Theo Vennemann (eds.) *Syntax: An international handbook of contemporary research*, 506–569. Berlin: Walter de Gruyter.
Christensen, Peer, Riccardo Fusaroli and Kristian Tylén. 2016. Environmental constraints shaping constituent order in emerging communication systems: Structural iconicity, interactive alignment and conventionalization. *Cognition* 146: 67–80.
Chung, Dae-Ho. 2004. Multiple dominance analysis of right node raising constructions. *Language Research* 40: 791–812.
Chung, Sandra. 1991. Functional heads and proper government in Chamorro. *Lingua* 85: 85–134.
Chung, Sandra and William Ladusaw. 2004. *Restriction and saturation.* Cambridge, MA: MIT Press.
Cinque, Guglielmo. 1999. *Adverbs and functional heads.* Oxford: Oxford University Press.
Cinque, Guglielmo and Luigi Rizzi. 2010. The cartography of syntactic structures. In Bernd Heine and Keiko Narrog (eds.) *The Oxford handbook of linguistic analysis*, 51–65. Oxford: Oxford University Press.
Citko, Barbara. 2005. On the nature of merge: External merge, internal merge, and parallel merge. *Linguistic Inquiry* 36: 475–496.
Collins, Chris. 1997. Argument sharing in serial verb constructions. *Linguistic Inquiry* 28: 461–497.
Couvee, Sascha and Roland Pfau. 2018. Structure and grammaticalization of serial verb constructions in Sign Language of the Netherlands: A corpus-based study. *Frontiers in Psychology* 9: 993.
Creissels, Denis. 2016. Transitivity, valency and voice. Ms., European Summer School in Linguistic Typology, Porquerolles. www.deniscreissels.fr/public/Creissels-ESSLT.pdf.
Croft, William. 1990. *Typology and universals.* Cambridge: Cambridge University Press.
Croft, William. 1991. *Syntactic categories and grammatical relations.* Chicago, IL: University of Chicago Press.
Croft, William. 1995. Autonomy and functionalist linguistics. *Language* 71: 490–532.

Croft, William. 1999. What (some) functionalists can learn from (some) formalists. In Darnell et al., vol 1, 87–110.

Croft, William. 2003. *Typology and universals*. Cambridge: Cambridge University Press.

Culicover, Peter and Ray Jackendoff. 2005. *Simpler syntax*. Oxford: Oxford University Press.

Darnell, Michael, Edith Moravcsik, Michael Noonan, Frederick Newmeyer and Kathleen Wheatley (eds.) 1999. *Functionalism and formalism in linguistics*, vols. 1–2. Amsterdam: John Benjamins.

Deal, Amy Rose. 2013. Possessor raising. *Linguistic Inquiry* 44: 391–432.

Deal, Amy Rose. 2017. External possession and possessor raising. *The Wiley Blackwell companion to syntax*, 2nd edition. Wiley Online Library: https://doi.org/10.1002/9781118358733.wbsyncom047.

Déchaine, Rose-Marie. 1993. Serial verb constructions. In Joachim Jacobs, Arnim von Stechow, Wolfgang Sternefeld and Theo Vennemann (eds.) *Syntax: An international handbook of contemporary research*, 799–825. Berlin: Walter de Gruyter.

de Vries, Mark. 2009. On multidominance and linearization. *Biolinguistics* 3.4: 344–403.

den Besten, Hans. 1983. On the interaction of root transformations and lexical deletive rules. In Werner Abrahams (ed.) *On the formal syntax of the Westgermania*, 47–131. Amsterdam: John Benjamins.

den Dikken, Marcel. 1999. On the structural representation of possession and agreement: The case of (anti-)agreement in Hungarian possessed Nominal Phrases. In István Kenesei (ed.) *Crossing boundaries: Theoretical Advances in Central and Eastern European Languages*, 137–178. Amsterdam: John Benjamins.

den Dikken, Marcel. 2006. *Relators and linkers*. Cambridge, MA: MIT Press.

Deng, Dun. 2013. *The syntax and semantics of event quantifiers in Mandarin Chinese*. Ph.D. dissertation, University of Wisconsin, Madison.

Di Sciullo, Anna Maria and Edwin Williams. 1987. *On the definition of word*. Cambridge, MA: MIT Press.

Diesing, Molly. 1992. *Indefinites*. Cambridge, MA: MIT Press.

Diessel, Holger. 2008. Iconicity of sequence: A corpus-based analysis of the positioning of temporal adverbial clauses in English. *Cognitive Linguistics* 19: 465–490.

Dik, Simon. 1968. *Coordination: Its implications for the theory of general linguistics*. Amsterdam: North-Holland.

Dik, Simon. 1989. *The theory of functional grammar, part 1: The structure of the clause*. Dordrecht: Foris.

Dingemanse, Mark, Damian E. Blasi, Gary Lupyan, Morten H. Christensen and Padraic Monaghan. 2015. Arbitrariness, iconicity, and systematicity in language. *Trends in Cognitive Sciences* 19: 603–615.

Dowty, David. 1991. Thematic proto-roles and argument selection. *Language* 67: 547–619.

Dryer, Matthew S. 2013. Order of Subject, Object and Verb. In Matthew S. Dryer and Martin Haspelmath (eds.) *The World Atlas of Language Structures Online*. Leipzig: Max Planck Institute for Evolutionary Anthropology. Available online at http://wals.info/chapter/81.

Dye, Christina, Yarden Kedar and Barbara Lust. 2019. From lexical to functional categories: New foundations for the study of language development. *First Language* 39: 9–32.

Eckardt, Regina. 1995. Does information flow in event structures? In Geroen Groenendijk (ed.) *Ellipsis, underspecification, events and more in dynamic semantics*, dyana-2 deliverable r2.2.c, 49–72. ILLC/Department of Philosophy, University of Amsterdam.

Embick, David and Rolf Noyer. 2001. Movement operations after syntax. *Linguistic Inquiry* 32: 555–595.

Emonds, Joseph. 1978. The verb complex V′-V in French. *Linguistic Inquiry* 9: 151–175.

Emonds, Joseph. 1980. Word order in generative grammar. *Journal of Linguistic Research* 1: 33–54.

Emonds, Joseph. 1986. Grammatically deviant prestige constructions. In M. Brame, H. Contreras and Frederick Newmeyer (eds.) *A Festschrift for Sol Saporta*, 93–131. Seattle, WA: Noit Amrofer.

Enç, Mürvet. 1986. Toward a referential analysis of temporal expressions. *Linguistics and Philosophy* 9: 405–426.

Epstein, Samuel David. 1999. Un-principled syntax and the derivation of syntactic relations. In Samuel David Epstein and Norbert Hornstein (eds.) *Working minimalism*, 317–345. Cambridge, MA: MIT Press.

Ernst, Thomas. 2002. *The syntax of adjuncts*. Cambridge: Cambridge University Press.

Ernst, Thomas. 2014. The syntax of adverbs. In Andrew Carnie, Yosuke Sato and Daniel Saddiqi (eds.) *The Routledge handbook of syntax*, 108–130. London: Routledge.

Feng, Shengli. 1995. GB theory and passive sentences in Chinese. *Studies in Chinese Linguistics* 1: 1–28.

Feng, Shengli. 2000. *Prosodic syntax in Chinese*. Shanghai: Shanghai Education Press.

Fischer, O. C. M. 2006. Grammaticalization and iconicity: Two interacting processes. In H. Grabes and W. Viereck (eds.) *The wider scope of English: Papers in English language and literature from the Bamberg Conference of the International Association of University Professors of English*, 17-42. Bamberger Beiträge zur englischen Sprachwissenschaft; No. 51.

Fitch, W. Tecumseh, Marc D. Hauser and Noam Chomsky. 2005. The evolution of the language faculty: Clarifications and implications. *Cognition* 97: 179–210.

Foley, Williams. 1991. *The Yimas languages and New Guinea*. Stanford, CA: Stanford University Press.

Foley, Williams and Mike Olson. 1985. Clausehood and verb serialization. In J. Nichols and A. Woodbury (eds.) *Grammar inside and outside the clause: Some approaches to theory from the field*, 17–60. Cambridge: Cambridge University Press.

Fortescue, Michael. 2014. The iconicity of lengthening and reduplicating suffixes in Nuuchahnulth. *International Journal of American Linguistics* 80: 533–552.

Frampton, John. 1990. Parasitic gaps and the theory of wh-chains. *Linguistic Inquiry* 21: 49–77.

Fu, Jingqi. 1994. *On deriving Chinese derived nominals: Evidence for V-to-N raising*. Ph.D. dissertation, University of Massachusetts, Amherst.

Fukui, Naoki and Yuji Takano. 1998. Symmetry in syntax: Merge and Demerge. *Journal of East Asian Linguistics* 7: 27–86.

Gärtner, Hans-Martin. 2003. On object-shift in Icelandic and partial iconicity. *Lingua* 114: 1235–1252.

Gavruseva, Elena. 2000. On the syntax of possessor extraction. *Lingua* 110: 743–772.

Gazdar, Gerald, Geoffrey K. Pullum, Ivan A. Sag and Thomas Wasow. 1982. Coordination and transformational grammar. *Linguistic Inquiry* 13.4: 663–676.

Gazdar, Gerald, Ewan H. Klein, Geoffrey K. Pullum and Ivan A. Sag. 1985. *Generalized phrase structure grammar*. Cambridge, MA: Harvard University Press.

Giannakidou, Anastasia. 2000. Negative . . . concord? *Natural Language and Linguistic Theory* 18: 457–523.

Givón, Talmy. 1990. *Syntax: A functional-typological introduction*. Amsterdam: John Benjamins.

Gleason, Jean B. and Nan B. Ratner. 2017. *The development of language*. Boston, MA: Pearson.

Goldberg, Adele and Ray Jackendoff. 2004. The English resultative as a family of constructions. *Language* 80: 532–568.

Goodall, Grant. 1987. *Parallel structures in syntax: Coordination, causatives and restructuring*. Cambridge: Cambridge University Press.

Grano, Thomas. 2012. Mandarin *hen* and universal markedness in gradable adjectives. *Natural Language and Linguistic Theory* 30: 513–565.

Greenberg, Joseph. 1963. Some universals of grammar with particular reference to the order of meaningful elements. In Joseph Greenberg (ed.) *Universals of language*, 73–113. Cambridge, MA: MIT Press.

Grimshaw, Jane. 1990. *Argument structure*. Cambridge, MA: MIT Press.

Grimshaw, Jane. 2000. Locality and extended projection. In Peter Coopmans, Martin Everaert and Jane Grimshaw (eds.) *Lexical specification and insertion*, 115–134. Amsterdam: John Benjamins.

Guo, Jimao. 1999. Pondering the object of intransitive verbs. *Chinese Language Studies* 270: 337–346.

Haegeman, Liliane. 1991. *Introduction to government and binding theory*. Oxford: Blackwell.

Haiman, John. 1980. The iconicity of grammar: Isomorphism and motivation. *Language* 56: 515–540.

Haiman, John. 1983. Iconic and economic motivation. *Language* 59: 781–819.

Haiman, John. 1985. *Natural syntax: Iconicity and erosion*. Cambridge: Cambridge University Press.

Haiman, John. 2008. In defense of iconicity. *Cognitive Linguistics* 19: 35–48.

Hajek, John. 2006. Serial verbs in Tetun Dili. In Aikhenvald and Dixon, 239–253.

Hale, Kenneth. 1991. Misumalpan verb sequencing constructions. In Lefebvre, 1–36. http://lingphil.mit.edu/papers/hale/papers/hale041.pdf.

Hale, Kenneth and Samuel Jay Keyser. 1993. On argument structure and the lexical expression of syntactic relations. In K. Hale and S. J. Keyser (eds.) *The view from Building 20*, 53–109. Cambridge, MA: MIT Press.

Hale, Kenneth and Samuel Jay Keyser. 2002. *Prolegomenon to a theory of argument structure*. Cambridge, MA: MIT Press.

Halle, Morris and Alec Marantz. 1993. Distributed morphology and the pieces of inflection. In Kenneth Hale and Samuel J. Keyser (eds.) *The view from Building 20*, 111–176. Cambridge, MA: MIT Press.

Harley, Heidi. 2005. How do verbs get their names? Denominal verbs, manner incorporation and the ontology of verb roots in English. In Nomi Erteschik-Shir and Tova Rapoport (eds.) *The syntax of aspect*, 42–64. Oxford: Oxford University Press.

Haspelmath, Martin. 2003. *Against iconicity and markedness*. Talk given at Stanford University.

Haspelmath, Martin. 2008. Frequency vs. iconicity in explaining grammatical asymmetries. *Cognitive Linguistics* 19: 1–33.

Haspelmath, Martin. 2016. The serial verb construction: Comparative concepts and cross- linguistic generalizations. *Language and Linguistics* 17: 291–319.

Hauser, Marc D., Noam Chomsky and W. Tecumseh Fitch. 2002. The language faculty: What is it, who has it, and how did it evolve? *Science* 298: 1569–1579.

Hawkins, John. 1990. A parsing theory of word order universals. *Language* 21.2: 223–261.

He, Chuansheng and Dandan Tan. 2019. On the constituency of the numeral-classifier cluster in Chinese. *Language and Linguistics* 20: 335–360.

Henderson, Brent. 2007. Matching and raising unified. *Lingua* 117: 202–220.

Her, One-Soon. 2017. Structure of numerals and classifiers in Chinese: Historical and typological perspectives and cross-linguistic implications. *Language and Linguistics*. 18.1: 26–71.

Her, One-Soon and Hui-Chin Tsai. 2020. Left is right, right is not: On the constituency of the classifier phrase in Chinese. *Language and Linguistics* 21: 1–32.

Heycock, Caroline. 1993. Syntactic predication in Japanese. *Journal of East Asian Linguistics* 2: 167–211.

Higginbotham, James. 1985. On semantics. *Linguistic Inquiry* 16: 547–593.

Hiraiwa, Ken and Adams Bodomo. 2008. Object-sharing as symmetric sharing: Predicate clefting and serial verbs in Dagaare. *Natural Language and Linguistic Theory* 26: 795–832.

Hofherr, Patricia Cabredo. 2003. Inflected complementizers and the licensing of non-referential pro-drop. In W. E. Griffin (ed.) *The role of agreement in natural language: TLS 5 proceedings*, 47–58. Texas Linguistics Forum.

Hornstein, Norbert and Amy Weinberg. 1981. Case theory and preposition stranding. *Linguistic Inquiry* 12: 55–91.

Hornstein, Norbert and Amy Weinberg. 1990. The necessity of LF. *The Linguistic Review* 7: 129–167.

Huang, James. 1982. *Logical relations in Chinese and the theory of grammar*. Ph.D. dissertation, MIT.

Huang, James. 1989. Pro-drop in Chinese: A generalized control theory. In Osvaldo Jaeggli and Kenneth Safir (eds.) *The null subject parameter*, 185–214. Dordrecht: Kluwer.

Huang, James, Audrey Li and Yafei Li. 2009. *The syntax of Chinese*. Cambridge: Cambridge University Press.

Huang, Shuping and Lily I-wen Su. 2005. Iconicity as evidence in Saisiyat linguistic coding of causative events. *Oceanic Linguistics* 44: 341–356.

Husband, E. Matthew. 2010. *On the compositional nature of stativity*. Ph.D. dissertation, Michigan State University.

Jackendoff, Ray. 1972. *Semantic interpretation in generative grammar*. Cambridge, MA: MIT Press.

Jackendoff, Ray. 1990. *Semantic structure*. Cambridge, MA: MIT Press.

Jackendoff, Ray. 2002. *Foundations of language*. Oxford: Oxford University Press.

Jackendoff, Ray and Steven Pinker. 2005. The nature of language faculty and its implications for evolution of language. *Cognition* 97: 211–225.

Jansen, Bert, Hilda Koopman and Pieter Muysken. 1978. Serial verbs in the creole languages. *Amsterdam Creole Studies* 2: 125–159.

Johannessen, Janne. 1998. *Coordination*. Oxford: Oxford University Press.

Julien, Marit. 2000. *Syntactic heads and word formation*. Ph.D dissertation, University of Tromsø.

Kaiser, Lizanne. 1999. Representing the structure-discourse iconicity of the Japanese post-verbal construction. In Michael Darnell et al. (eds.) *Functionalism and formalism in linguistics*. Amsterdam: John Benjamins.

Kandybowicz, Jason. 2006. *Conditions on multiple copy spell-out and the syntax phonology interface*. Ph.D. dissertation, University of California, Los Angeles.

Kayne, Richard. 1984. *Connectedness and binary branching*. Dordrecht: Foris.

Kayne, Richard. 1994. *The antisymmetry of syntax*. Cambridge, MA: MIT Press.

Kiss, Katalin É. 2002. *The syntax of Hungarian*. Cambridge: Cambridge University Press.

Koopman, Hilda. 1984. *The syntax of verbs: From verb movement rules in the Kru languages to Universal Grammar*. Dordrecht: Foris.

Koopman, Hilda and Dominique Sportiche. 1982. Variables and the bijection principle. In J. Kaye, H. Koopman and D. Sportiche (eds.) *Projet sur les langues kru: Premier rapport*, 176–202. Montreal: University du Quebec at Montreal.

Kratzer, Angelika. 1996. Severing the external argument from the verb. In Johan Rooryck and Laurie Zaring (eds.) *Phrase structure and the lexicon*, 109–137. Dordrecht: Kluwer.

Kratzer, Angelika. 2002. *The event argument and the semantics of verbs*. Berkeley, CA: Bepress.

Kratzer, Angelika. 2004. Building resultatives. Ms., University of Massachusetts, Amherst. http://semanticsarchive.net/Archive/GY4ZThjZ/Building%20Resultatives .pdf.

Kuno, Susumu. 1987. *Functional syntax: Anaphora, discourse and empathy*. Chicago, IL: Chicago University Press.

Lakoff, George. 1986. Frame semantic control of the coordinate structure constraint. In Anne M. Farley, Peter T. Farley and Karl-Erik McCullough (eds.) *Papers from the Chicago Linguistic Society* 22, Part 2, 152–167.

Landsberg, Marge E. (ed.) 1995. *Syntactic iconicity and linguistic freezes: The human dimension*. Berlin: Mouton de Gruyter.

Larson, Richard. 1988. On the double object construction. *Linguistic Inquiry* 19: 335–392.

Larson, Richard. 1991. Some issues in verb serialization. In Lefebvre 1991a, 185–210.

Larson, Richard. 2014. *On shell structure*. London: Routledge.

Larson, Richard. 2018. AP-*de* adverbs in Mandarin. *Studies in Chinese Linguistics* 39.1: 1–28.

Lasnik, Howard and Mamoru Saito. 1992. *Move α: Conditions on its application and output?* Cambridge, MA: MIT Press.

Law, Paul and Tonjes Veenstra. 1992. On the structure of serial verb constructions. *Linguistic Analysis* 22: 185–217.

Le Bruyn, Bert and Henriëtte de Swart. 2014. Bare coordination: The semantic shift. *Natural Language and Linguistic Theory* 32: 1205–1246.

LeDoux, Joseph. 1996. *The emotional brain: The mysterious underpinnings of emotional life*. New York: Simon and Schuster.

Lefebvre, Claire (ed.). 1991a. *Serial verbs: Grammatical, comparative and cognitive approaches*. Amsterdam: John Benjamins.

Lefebvre, Claire. 1991b. Take serial verbs in Fon. In Lefebvre, 37–78.

Levin, Beth and Malka Rappaport-Hovav. 1995. *Unaccusativity* 1991a. Cambridge, MA: MIT Press.

Li, Audrey Y.-H. 1990. *Order and constituency in Mandarin Chinese*. Dordrecht: Kluwer.

Li, Audrey. Y.-H. 1999. Plurality in a classifier language. *Journal of East Asian Linguistics* 8: 75–99.

Li, Charles and Sandra Thompson. 1981. *Mandarin Chinese: A functional reference grammar*. Berkeley, CA: University of California Press.

Li, Xu Ping. 2013. *Numeral classifiers in Chinese: The syntax–semantics interface*. Berlin: Walter de Gruyter.

Li, Yafei. 1987. Case in categorial terms. General exam paper, MIT.

Li, Yafei. 1990a. *Conditions on $X°$-movement*. Ph.D. dissertation, MIT.

Li, Yafei. 1990b. $X°$-binding and verb incorporation. *Linguistic Inquiry* 21: 399–426.

Li, Yafei. 1990c. On V-V compounds in Chinese. *Natural Language and Linguistic Theory* 8: 177–207.

Li, Yafei. 1991. On deriving serial verb constructions. In Lefebvre 1991a, 103–136.

Li, Yafei. 1993. Structural head and aspectuality. *Language* 69: 480–504.

Li, Yafei. 1995. The thematic hierarchy and causativity. *Natural Language and Linguistic Theory* 13: 255–282.

Li, Yafei. 1997. An optimized UG and biological redundancies. *Linguistic Inquiry* 28: 170–178.

Li, Yafei. 1999. Cross-componential causativity. *Natural Language and Linguistic Theory* 17: 445–497.

Li, Yafei. 2005. *$X°$: A theory of the morphology–syntax interface*. Cambridge, MA: MIT Press.

Li, Yafei. 2009. The syntactic structure of coordination and the significance of marginal data. *Contemporary Linguistics* 11: 289–298.

Li, Yafei. 2014. Placing Chinese morphemes in a coordinate system: Reflecting on the scientific nature of linguistic theorization. *Language and Linguistics* 15: 89–113.

Li, Yafei. 2015. Revisiting the internal structure of Chinese noun phrases. *Chinese Language Studies* 365: 99–104.

Li, Yafei. 2017. Universal direction of sentence-generation and three odd cases of *wh*-movement: An entropic perspective. *Contemporary Linguistics* 19: 159–180.

Li, Yafei and Zhe Chen. 2018. What can biolinguistics learn from biology? *Foreign Language Teaching and Research* 50: 323–341.

Li, Yafei and Jen Ting. 2013. Is UG like a chunk of Swiss cheese? Evidence for a "third-factor principle". *Language and Linguistics* 14: 737–754.

Li, Yafei, Rebecca Shields and Vivian Lin. 2012. Adverb classes and the nature of minimality. *Natural Language and Linguistic Theory* 30: 217–260.

Lin, T.-H. Jonah. 2001. *Light verb syntax and the theory of phrase structure*. Ph.D. dissertation, University of California, Irvine.

Link, Godehard. 1998. Algebraic semantics in language and philosophy. *CSLI Lecture Notes*, vol. 74.

Liu, Chen Sheng. 2013. Reduplication of adjectives in Chinese: A default state. *Journal of East Asian Linguistics* 22: 101–132.

Lord, Carol. 1974. Causative constructions in Yorùbá. *Studies in African Linguistics, Supplement* 5: 195–204.

Lü, Shuxiang. 1984. *Xiandai hanyu babai ci*. Beijing: Commercial Press.

Marantz, Alec. 1984. *On the nature of grammatical relations*. Cambridge, MA: MIT Press.

Marantz, Alec. 1989. Clitics and phrase structure. In Mark Baltin and Anthony Kroch (eds.) *Alternative conceptions of phrase structure*, 99–116. Chicago, IL: The University of Chicago Press.

Marantz, Alec. 1993. Implications of asymmetries in double object constructions. In Sam A. Mchombo (ed.) *Theoretical aspects of Bantu grammar*, 113–150. Stanford, CA: CSLI Publications.

Marantz, Alec. 1997. No escape from syntax: Don't try morphological analysis in the privacy of your own lexicon. *UPenn Working Papers in Linguistics* 4.2: 201–225.

Massam, Diane. 2001. Pseudo noun incorporation in Niuean. *Natural Language and Linguistic Theory* 19: 153–197.

May, Robert. 1977. *The grammar of quantification*. Ph.D. dissertation, MIT.

Mayr, Ernst. 1997. *This is biology*. Cambridge, MA: Harvard University Press.

McCawley, James. 1982. Parentheticals and discontinuous constituent structure. *Linguistic Inquiry* 13: 91–106.

McCloskey, James. 1996. Subjects and subject position in Irish. In R. Borsley and Ian Roberts (eds.) *The syntax of the Celtic languages*, 241–283. Cambridge: Cambridge University Press.

Mei, Kuang. 1980. Is Modern Chinese really a SOV language? *Cahiers de Linguistique Asie Orientale* 7: 23–45.

Meir, Irit, Carol Padden, Mark Aronoff and Wendy Sandler. 2013. Competing iconicities in the structure of languages. *Cognitive Linguistics* 24: 309–343.

Mithun, Marianne. 1988. The grammaticalization of coordination. In J. Haiman and S. A. Thompson (eds.) *Clause combining in grammar and discourse*, 331–359. Amsterdam: John Benjamins.

Miyagawa, Shigeru, Robert Berwick and Kazuo Okanoya. 2013. The emergence of hierarchical structure in human language. *Frontiers in Psychology* 4: 71–77.

Miyagawa, Shigeru, Shiro Ojima, Robert Berwick and Kazuo Okanoya. 2014. The integration hypothesis of human language evolution and the nature of contemporary languages. *Frontiers in Psychology* 5: 564–570.

Moltmann, Friederike. 1992. *Coordination and comparatives*. Ph.D. dissertation, MIT.

Müller, Stefan. 2013. Unifying everything: Some remarks on simpler syntax, construction grammar, minimalism and HPSG. *Language* 89: 920–950.

Munn, Alan. 1993. *Topics in the syntax and semantics of coordinate structures*. Ph.D. dissertation, University of Maryland, College Park.

Murane, Elizabeth. 1974. Daga grammar: From morpheme to discourse. *Summer Institute of Linguistics Publications in Linguistics and related Fields 43*. Norman, OK: Summer Institute of Linguistics.

Muysken, Pieter. 1988. Parameters for serial verbs. In Victor Manfredi (ed.) *Niger-Congo syntax and semantics*, vol. I, 65–75. Boston, MA: Boston University African Studies Center.

Newmeyer, Frederick. 1992. Iconicity and generative grammar. *Language* 68: 756–796.

Newmeyer, Frederick. 1998. *Language form and language function*. Cambridge, MA: MIT Press.
Newmeyer, Frederick. 2004. *Some thoughts on the serial verb construction*. Paris: Fédération TUL. www.typologie.cnrs.fr/fr/gabarits/06a_ates-colloques.php.
Newmeyer, Frederick. 2017. Form and function in the evolution of grammar. *Cognitive Science* 41: 259–276.
Nida, Eugene. 1949. *Morphology: The descriptive analysis of words*. Ann Arbor, MI: University of Michigan Press.
Nikolaeva, Irina. 2002. The Hungarian external possessor in a European perspective. In C. Hasselblatt and R. Blokland (eds.) *Finno-Ugrians and Indo-Europeans: Linguistic contacts*. Maastricht: Shaker. http://citeseerx.ist.psu.edu/viewdoc/download?doi=10.1.1.452.3412&rep=rep1&type=pdf.
Nishiyama, Kunio. 1998. V-V compounds as serialization. *Journal of East Asian Linguistics* 7: 175–217.
Nishiyama, Kunio. 1999. Adjectives and the copulas in Japanese. *Journal of East Asian Linguistics* 8: 183–222.
Nunes, Jairo. 2001. Sideward movement. *Linguistic Inquiry* 31: 303–344.
Nunes, Jairo. 2004. *Linearization of chains and sideward movement*. Cambridge, MA: MIT Press.
Oomen, Marloes. 2017. Iconicity in argument structure: Psych-verbs in Sign Language of the Netherlands. *Sign Language & Linguistics* 20: 55–108.
Pacchiarotti, Sara. 2017. *Bantu applicative construction types involving *-id: Form, functions and diachrony*. Ph.D. dissertation, University of Oregon.
Partee, Barbara. 1986. Noun phrase interpretation and type-shifting principles. In J. Groenendijk, D. de Jong and M. Stokhof (eds.) *Studies in discourse representation theories and the theory of generalized quantifiers*, 115–144. Dordrecht: Foris.
Peirce, Charles Sanders. 1867/1931. On a new list of categories. *Proceedings of the American Academy of Arts and Sciences* 7: 287–98. Reprinted in Charles Hartshorne and Paul Weiss (eds.) *Collected papers of Charles Sanders Peirce*, vol. 1: Principles of philosophy, 287–305. Cambridge, MA: Harvard University Press.
Peirce, Charles Sanders. 1902/1932. The icon, index, and symbol. In Charles Hartshorne and Paul Weiss (eds.) *Collected papers of Charles Sanders Peirce*, vol. 2: Elements of logic, 156–73. Cambridge, MA: Harvard University Press.
Perniss, Pamela and Gabriella Vigliocco. 2014. The bridge of iconicity: From a world of experience to the experience of language. *Philosophical Transactions of the Royal Society B* 369: 1–13.
Perniss, Pamela, Robin L. Thompson and Gabriella Vigliocco. 2010. Iconicity as a general property of language: Evidence from spoken and signed languages. *Frontiers in Psychology* 1: 1–15.
Perry, Lynne K., Marcus Perlman and Gary Lupyan. 2015. Iconicity in English and Spanish and its relation to lexical category and age of acquisition. *PLoS One* 10(9): e0137147.
Pesetsky, David. 1982. *Paths and categories*. Ph.D. dissertation, MIT, Cambridge.
Pesetsky, David and Esther Torrego. 2007. The syntax of valuation and the interpretability of features. In Simin Karimi, Vida Samiian and Wendy Wilkins (eds.) *Phrasal and clausal architecture*, 262–294. Amsterdam: John Benjamins.

Peterson, Carole. 1986/2008. Semantic and pragmatic uses of "but". *Journal of Chinese Language* 13.3: 583–590. (Published online by Cambridge University Press in 2008.)

Phillips, Collin. 2003. Linear order and constituency. *Linguistic Inquiry* 34: 37–90.

Pinker, Steven and Paul Bloom. 1990. Natural language and natural selection. *Behavioral and Brain Sciences* 13: 707–784.

Pinker, Steven and Ray Jackendoff. 2005. The faculty of language: What's special about it? *Cognition* 95: 201–236.

Pollock, Jean-Yves. 1989. Verb movement, Universal Grammar, and the structure of IP. *Linguistic Inquiry* 20: 365–424.

Postal, Paul. 1998. *Three investigations of extraction.* Cambridge, MA: MIT Press.

Postal, Paul. 2003. (Virtual) conceptual necessity. *Journal of Linguistics* 39: 599–620.

Progovac, Ljiljana. 1998. Structure for coordination. *Glot International* 3.7-8: 3–9.

Progovac, Ljiljana. 2000. Coordination, c-command and "logophoric" n-words. In Laurence Horn and Yasuhiko Kato (eds.) *Studies in negation and polarity*, 88–114. Oxford: Oxford University Press.

Progovac, Ljiljana. 2003. Structure for coordination. In Lisa Cheng and Rint Sybesma (eds.) *The second GLOT international state-of-the-article book: The latest in linguistics*, 241–288. The Hague: de Gruyter.

Progovac, Ljiljana. 2016. Review of *Why only us? Language* 92: 992–996.

Pustejovky, James. 1995. *The generative lexicon.* Cambridge, MA: MIT Press.

Pylkkänen, Liina. 2008. *Introducing arguments.* Cambridge, MA: MIT Press.

Ramchand, Gillian. 2008. *Verb meaning and the lexicon: A first phase syntax.* Cambridge: Cambridge University Press.

Reinhart, Tanya. 1998. *Wh-in situ* in the framework of the minimalist program. *Natural Language Semantics* 6: 29–56.

Reinhart, Tanya. 2006. *Interface strategies: Optional and costly computations.* Cambridge, MA: MIT Press.

Rizzi, Luigi. 1990. *Relativized minimality.* Cambridge, MA: MIT Press.

Rizzi, Luigi. 1997. The fine structure of the left periphery. In Lillian Haegeman (ed.) *Elements of grammar*, 281–337. Amsterdam: Kluwer.

Rizzi, Luigi. 2004. Locality and left periphery. In Belletti, 223–251.

Roberts, Ian. 2001. Head movement. In Mark Baltin and Chris Collins (eds.) *The handbook of contemporary syntactic theory*, 114–147. Malden, MA: Blackwell.

Rosen, Sara. 1989. Two types of noun-incorporation: A lexical analysis. *Language* 65: 294–317.

Ross, John R. 1967. *Constraints on variables in syntax.* Ph.D. dissertation, MIT.

Ross, John R. 1972. The category squish: Endstation hauptwort. *Chicago Linguistic Society* 8: 316–328.

Rossion, Bruno, Bernard Hanseeuw and Laurence Dricot. 2012. Defining face perception areas in the human brain: A large scale factorial fMRI face localizer analysis. *Brain and Cognition* 79: 138–157.

Rothstein, Susan. 1999. Fine-grained structure in the eventuality domain: The semantics of predicative adjective phrases and *be. Natural Language Semantics* 7: 347–420.

Rudin, Catherine. 1988. On multiple questions and multiple *wh* fronting. *Natural Language and Linguistic Theory* 6: 445–501.

Sadock, Jerrold M. 1985. Autolexical syntax: A proposal for the treatment of noun incorporation and similar phenomena. *Natural Language and Linguistic Theory* 3: 379–439.

Sag, Ivan. 2000. Another argument against wh-trace. In Sandy Chung, Jim McCloskey and Nathan Sanders (eds.) *Jorge Hankamer Webfest*. https://babel.ucsc.edu/jorgewebfest/sag.html.

Schwartz, Bonnie. 1985. Case and conjunction. *Southern California Occasional Papers in Linguistics* 10: 161–186.

Schwarz, Florian. 2012. Situation pronouns in determiner phrases. *Natural Language Semantics* 20: 431–475.

Sebba, Mark. 1987. *Syntax of serial verbs: An investigation into serialization in Sranan and other languages*. Amsterdam: John Benjamins.

Shlonsky, Ur. 1997. *Clause structure and word order in Hebrew and Arabic*. Oxford: Oxford University Press.

Simpson, Andrew. 2002. On the status of "modifying" DE and the structure of the Chinese DP. In Sze-Wing Tang and Chen-Sheng Luther Liu (eds.) *On the formal way to Chinese languages*, 74–101. Stanford, CA: CSLI Publications.

Sober, Elliott. 2015. *Ockham's razor: A user's manual*. Cambridge: Cambridge University Press.

Song, Hongkyu. 2005. *Causatives and resultatives in Korean*. Ph.D. dissertation, University of Wisconsin, Madison.

Sproat, Richard. 1985. Welsh syntax and VSO structure. *Natural Language and Linguistic Theory* 3: 173–216.

Stahlke, Herbert. 1970. Serial verbs. *Studies in African Linguistics* 1: 60–99.

Stewart, John. 1963. Some restrictions on objects in Twi. *Journal of African Languages* 1: 145–149.

Stowell, Tim. 1981. *Elements of phrase structure*. Ph.D. dissertation, MIT.

Sun, Tianqi. 2010. *A study on the licensing pattern and mechanism of non-core arguments in Mandarin Chinese*. Ph.D. dissertation, Peking University, Beijing.

Sun, Tianqi and Yafei Li. 2010. Licensing non-core arguments in Chinese. *Chinese Language Studies* 334: 21–33.

Sun, Tianqi and Yafei Li. 2020. An analysis on the mechanism of oblique object constructions in Chinese: The monosyllabic constraint and the "bare root" theory. *Contemporary Linguistics* 22.2: 199–216.

Svenonius, Peter. 2004. On the edge. In David Adger, Cécile de Cat and George Tsoulas (eds.) *Peripheries*, 259–287. Dordrecht: Kluwer.

Szabolcsi, Anna. 1983. The possessor that ran away from home. *The Linguistic Review* 3: 89–102.

Szabolcsi, Anna. 1992. Subject suppression or lexical PRO? The case of derived nominals in Hungarian. *Lingua* 86: 149–176.

Szabolcsi, Anna. 1994. The noun phrase. In Ferenc Kiefer and Katalan É. Kiss (eds.) *The syntactic structure of Hungarian: Syntax and semantics* 27, 179–274. San Diego, CA: Academic Press.

Tai, James. 1985. Temporal sequence and Chinese word order. In John Haiman (ed.) *Iconicity in syntax*, 49–72. Amsterdam: John Benjamins.

Tan, Dandan and Yafei Li. 2020. *What don't tell us (much) about the structure of classifiers as one would hope?* Ms., Hunan University and the University of Wisconsin, Madison.

Tang, Jane C.-C. 1990. *Chinese phrase structure and the extended X'-theory.* Ph.D. dissertation, Cornell University.

Tellier, Christine. 1991 *Licensing theory and French parasitic gaps.* Dordrecht: Kluwer.

Thomas, James. 1993. Thinking about genetic redundancy. *Trends in Genetics* 9: 396–399.

Ting, Jen. 1995. *A non-uniform analysis of the passive construction in Mandarin Chinese.* Ph.D. dissertation, University of Rochester, New York.

Ting, Jen and Yafei Li. 1997. Manner *de* and resultative *de.* Paper presented at the Conference of the International Association of Chinese Linguistics, University of Leiden.

Tomioka, Naoko. 2003. The lexicalization patterns of verbs and V-V compounds. In *The proceedings of TROSS 03.* Trondheim: Norges teknisk naturvitenskapelige universitet.

Tomlin, Russell. 1986. *Basic word order: Functional principles.* London: Croom Helm.

Travis, Lisa. 1984. *Parameters and effects of word order variation.* Ph.D. dissertation, MIT.

Uriagereka, Juan. 1998. *Rhyme and reason.* Cambridge, MA: MIT Press.

van Langendonck, Willy. 2010. Iconicity. In Dirk Geeraerts and Hubert Cuyckens (eds.) *The Oxford handbook of cognitive linguistics.* (Online publication) Oxford: Oxford University Press.

van Leynseele, Hélène. 1975. Restrictions on serial verb constructions in Anyi. *Journal of West African Languages* 10: 189–217.

van Riemsdijk, Henk. 2006. Free relatives. In Martin Everaert and Henk van Riemsdijk (eds.) *The Blackwell companion to syntax,* vol. II, 338–382. Oxford: Blackwell.

Veenstra, Tonjes. 1996. *Serial verbs in Saramaccan: Predication and creole genesis.* The Hague: Holland Academic Graphics.

Webelhuth, Gert. 1992. *Principles and parameters of syntactic saturation.* New York: Oxford University Press.

Wellwood, Alexis. 2016. States and events for S-level gradable adjectives. *Proceedings of SALT* 26: 166–184.

Wexler, Kenneth. 2017. A program for the genetics of grammar. *Biolinguistics* 11: 295–323.

Wexler, Kenneth and Peter Culicover. 1980. *Formal principles of language acquisition.* Cambridge, MA: MIT Press.

Wilder, Chris. 2008. Shared constituents and linearization. In Kyle Johnson (ed.) *Topics in ellipsis,* 229–258. Cambridge: Cambridge University Press.

Williams, Edwin. 1978. Across-the-board rule application. *Linguistic Inquiry* 19: 31–43.

Williams, Edwin. 1980. Predication. *Linguistic Inquiry* 11: 203–238.

Williams, Edwin. 1981. Argument structure and morphology. *Linguistic Review* 1: 81–114.

Williamson, Kay. 1965. *A grammar of the Kolokuma dialect of Ijo.* Cambridge: Cambridge University Press.

Winter, Bodo, Marcus Perlman, Lynn Perry and Gary Lupyan. 2017. Which words are most iconic? Iconicity in English sensory words. *Interaction Studies* 18: 433–454.

Wurmbrand, Susi. 2011. *On agree and merge.* Course notes. University of Connecticut.

Xing, Fuyi. 1991. On the phenomenon of object-replacement in Chinese. *Chinese Teaching in the World* 2: 76–84.

Yang, Charles. 2013. Ontogeny and phylogeny of language. *Proceedings of the Natural Academy of Sciences* 110.16: 6324–6327.

Yang, Yongzhong. 2007. The syntax of NP in V+NP. *Language Studies* 2: 58–65.

Yngve, Victor. 1960. A model and a hypothesis for language structure. *Proceedings of the American Philosophical Society* 104: 444–466.

Zhang, Niina. 2010. *Coordination in syntax*. Cambridge: Cambridge University Press.

Zhang, Niina. 2018. Non-canonical objects as event kind-classifying element. *Natural Language and Linguistic Theory* 36: 1395–1437.

Zhang, Yunqiu. 2004. *A study on patient object sentences in Chinese*. Shanghai: Xuelin Press.

Zoerner, Ed. 1995. *Coordination: The syntax of &P*. Ph.D. dissertation, University of California, Irvine.

Zwart, Jan-Wouter. 2005. Some notes on coordination in head-final languages. *Linguistics in the Netherlands 2005*: 231–242.

Index

For EU product safety concerns, contact us at Calle de José Abascal, 56–1°,
28003 Madrid, Spain or eugpsr@cambridge.org.